Hooks and Ladders

Hooks and Ladders

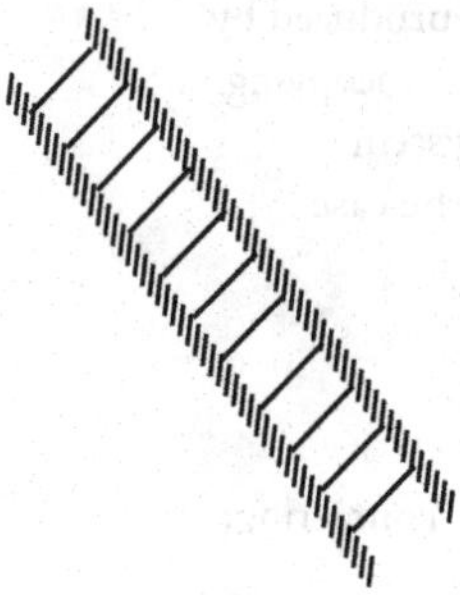

A Journey on a Bridge to Nowhere with American Evangelical Christians

Billy Wheaton
with **Joy Fuller**

iUniverse, Inc.
New York Bloomington

Hooks and Ladders
A Journey on a Bridge to Nowhere with American Evangelical Christians

iUniverse books may be ordered through booksellers or by contacting:

iUniverse
1663 Liberty Drive
Bloomington, IN 47403
www.iuniverse.com
1-800-Authors (1-800-288-4677)

ISBN: 978-1-4401-0738-2 (sc)
ISBN: 978-1-4401-6307-4 (dj)
ISBN: 978-1-4401-0739-9 (ebk)

Library of Congress Control Number: 2009930726

Printed in the United States of America

iUniverse rev. date: 07/15/2009

Contents

Foreword by Joy Fuller

MY NAME IS JOY FULLER, and I am an ex-Evangelical Christian. I've only recently come to accept this title, although I've enjoyed the status for years. Like most people who move on from Evangelicalism, I called myself after my destination. Most people say, "I am an atheist now," "I became a Buddhist," or, defensively, "I'm still a Christian." They blend in with their new crowd and become indistinguishable from any other atheist, Buddhist, or non-Evangelical Christian. I don't think that's a bad thing. Moving on should mean really moving on. But I've come to see the value of reflecting on my origins.

You've heard of a cradle Catholic? I was as close as you can come to a cradle Evangelical. My Evangelical parents came from Evangelical families. Almost all of my parents' friends came from the Evangelical community. My mother led me to Christ as we sat on the sofa in our Florida living room when I was five. I spent my childhood at Good News clubs, Fellowship halls, early services, youth groups, and Bible studies. On my own, I read the Bible and tried to pray without ceasing. I witnessed—I even became a missionary for a summer. I didn't smoke. I didn't dance. I believed in the Trinity, in original sin, in the virgin birth, in the life of the world to come. I believed Methuselah lived for nine hundred years. I believed Noah built the ark. I believed the sun stood still and the walls of Jericho came tumbling down.

And yet ... there were troubling signs that I was not on as straight a path to the celestial city as my appearance might have suggested. I was a smart girl with a strong sense of self—not the best collection of traits for living *la vida* Evangelical. The Bible said that in Christ there is neither male nor female, but in Evangelicalism there certainly was; our very own separate but (not really) equal. My Christian mentors taught that God gave us intelligence so that we could use it to his greater glory, but I saw that often they treated intelligence with derision. They told me what things I shouldn't think and what things I shouldn't question or ask. By high school, I realized that Evangelicals expected me to say things that didn't make sense and that I knew were probably untrue. I spoke honestly about my doubts, assuming that other Evangelicals shared my desire to know the truth. They did not. Many called me a "doubting Christian."

Of course I ended up at Wheaton College, the eighth member of my family to attend the school. *Here's my chance,* I thought. *With so many of the smartest Evangelicals on the same campus, I will surely find answers here.* And I really tried. I learned ancient languages so I could read for myself what the Bible had to say. I church-shopped, looking for a place I could be at home. But after all my efforts, I realized I didn't believe in hell. I didn't believe in Satan. I didn't believe in salvation. I learned the Bible had errors, and I knew I could no longer mimic my mentors and claim the Bible held literal truth.

I met Billy while at Wheaton. Like me, he didn't avoid the hard questions. Like me, he considered achieving certainty through faith a form of cheating, especially when the truth was less certain. Billy was ready to leave Evangelical Christianity even then (and he assures me now that I wasn't nearly as understanding of this as I remember). I, on the other hand, wasn't ready.

When my break with the Evangelical community came a few years later, it was sudden and sharp but hardly clean. Breaking with the community meant breaking with most of my friends and family as well, and it was undeniably painful. Afterward, it was as though I had smashed through a windshield; my head may have cleared and my face may have healed, but years later, pieces of glass still worked their way to the surface, unpleasant reminders of the impact.

So when Billy wrote me out of the blue, twenty years after we graduated from Wheaton, and asked me to read a book he'd written about Evangelical Christianity, I almost said no. I was as done with Evangelical Christianity as it was done with me. But when I read the book, it was as if we were still on the dorm stairs, having a late-night conversation about why, why, why most of our fellow students were the way they were. How could they simply accept what they were told because a church leader had said it? How could they tell who was a "real Christian," and why was it so important? How could they be sure that God was speaking to them and that they weren't just hearing the whispers of their own feelings and desires? And what made some people different?

Billy's book was written to and for Evangelicals as a how-to book. He described how he was inspired to write it by his wife, Brooke, and by other smart, hard-working Evangelicals whose talents and energies were wasted playing Hooks and Ladders. He thought he could show them a better way.

So I pointed out to him what I thought was the sad truth: the Evangelicals he wanted to reach would never read his book. *Come on, Billy,* I wrote, *Can you really see this book sitting in the Christian bookstore next to* Evidence That Demands a Verdict? *You compare Paul—St. Paul!—to a person with a serious mental illness and tell Evangelicals that they don't know how to think. It's not exactly something that Zondervan or Tyndale will be fighting to publish.* But I had another idea for him.

Since leaving the Evangelical community, I had realized that very few outside of the faith had a good understanding of what it meant to be an Evangelical. Some people thought Evangelicals were a bunch of toothless, evolution-denying, red-state hypocrites, perhaps a little too eager to usher in the Apocalypse but basically harmless. Others saw the Evangelical community as a sinister conspiracy, orchestrating the ascent of an American theocracy in which copies of Richard Dawkins' books would be confiscated, public Bible readings would be mandatory, and all dissenters would be water-boarded. I told Billy he should rewrite the book and direct it at non-Evangelicals who wanted to understand how Evangelicals think and why arguing with them was such an infuriating experience.

At first, I merely told Billy what I thought he needed to do, and then I just barged in and did it. Don't get me wrong. We have written Billy's story based on Billy's ideas and his work. If you see anything of me in the book, it is only in the margins, the interstices, and the occasional metaphor. I am a "with" author rather than a "by" author, and I don't want to claim credit (or take the blame!) unfairly.

But I share Billy's goals for the book. For all you non-Evangelicals out there, especially those of you who couldn't find the book of Nahum with a GPS device and a trail of breadcrumbs, I challenge you: if you think Evangelical Christians are a blight on the body politic and a threat to our shared democratic values of equality and freedom, what are you doing about it? I've seen some well-meaning non-Evangelicals attempt to engage believers, only to end up shouting at them to abandon their ignorance and come to the light. Unsurprisingly, that has about the same effect on Evangelicals that a lengthy sermon studded with Bible verses most likely has on non-Evangelicals; it serves only to confirm the sad belief that there are plenty of deluded people in the world.

Effectively discussing Christianity with Evangelicals is hard work, calling for the unglamorous qualities of patience and kindness in addition to intellect. Without an understanding of the Evangelical mindset and of the Evangelical concepts of sin, salvation, death, life, self, God, and what Billy describes as "Evangelical autism," your conversations will be an exercise in frustration. Without an understanding of the Evangelical milieu, the power of church authority, and the importance of community, even the most elegantly logical argument is doomed to fail.

Billy writes that he dreams of getting together with his old Evangelical friends and working with purpose toward a greater good. I dream of the same, but I know that as long as Hooks and Ladders has its grip on the church, it will never happen. My contribution to this book is also my contribution toward making those reunions a reality.

Joy Fuller
November 30, 2008

1. Introducing Hooks and Ladders

Sin and God's Will

SUPPOSE I SET MY ALARM CLOCK FIVE MINUTES AHEAD. I plan to trick myself so I make it to school on time. Am I lying to myself and sinning? My older brother Mike and I debated this question for almost two hours in the car while heading to an Evangelical retreat at Lake Okoboji in Iowa. Mom drove most of the way. Mike asked Mom what she thought about turning a clock five minutes fast. This prompted Tom, my younger brother, to speak up. He said, "Mom's too busy breaking the law speeding by going sixty-five miles per hour on a fifty-five-miles-per-hour interstate right now."

Mom replied, "Thomas, on these treacherous roads I need to concentrate. You act like I thumb my nose at the law if I go a little over the speed limit."

Tom said, "In the middle of the summer on a sunny day, I see how you can find the roads treacherous, especially on the interstate through Iowa farmland."

Mike had just finished his first year at the Evangelical Wheaton College. Mike, then eighteen, and Tom and I, at fifteen and sixteen, had already spent years arguing and competing in almost everything. For us, *normal* included discussing things like the sin I might have committed by setting my clock ahead on purpose. Mike and I had discussed whether *bearing false witness* only applied to *neighbors* and not to self-deception, and we thought we had cleverly found a loophole.

When we arrived at Okoboji, Mike still felt psyched about exploring the sinfulness of setting a clock ahead. He tried to drum up interest with our pastors and the men from our church. He got nowhere. They could not have cared less. One of our pastors even expressed disapproval. He told Mike, "You need to consider that a weaker brother in the Lord may take what you say to heart. If he, unlike your brother, struggles with his faith, you may cause him to get discouraged and stumble."

Reluctantly, Mike dropped the subject. I never did. It seemed clear then—anything I did against "God's will" made me a sinner. God had no need to bend the rules about lying so that I could get to school on time. It became increasingly clear to me over the next few years, however, that Evangelicals consider anything outside God's will wrong. Anything someone's personal god wants becomes God's will, right, and acceptable. This fuels the relentless pursuit of Evangelicals to find God's intentions for them. For most Evangelicals, God places no value on whether they wear a blue shirt or a white shirt, for example. But for many Evangelicals, God places tremendous value on whether they vote for Hillary Clinton, Barack Obama, Mike Huckabee, or anyone else. God cannot support all of them. For many Evangelicals, he obviously does not support Hillary (even though he loves her). Thus, for these Evangelicals, a vote for Hillary goes against God's will. Thus, I am a sinner if I vote for Hillary, and the wages of sin is death. Simply put, for most Evangelicals, God will tolerate me setting my clock five minutes ahead in order to arrive on time to vote or campaign against Hillary.

Ex-Evangelical

In recent years, Evangelicals have had significant public exposure. As a result I have found many people, including Evangelicals, who have serious concerns about the potential harm of Evangelical Christianity.

At this point, you may want to understand just what I know about any of this. At age eleven, in the mid 1970s, I became a born-again Christian. After being raised Catholic, the message of Jesus and salvation taught to me by Evangelicals made more sense. Aside from my father, the rest of my family had converted as well. We became quite involved in the church. We usually went to church multiple times a week, and my mother kept our radio on and tuned to a Christian radio station all day long. I heard people like James Dobson, who hosts *Focus on the Family,* and Chuck Swindoll, who hosts *Insight for Living,* virtually every day. My family and I attended programs like Bill Gothard's Institute in Basic Youth Conflicts and even the occasional good, old-fashioned revival.

After high school, following in my brother's footsteps I enrolled in and later graduated from Wheaton College. Wheaton is an Evangelical Christian liberal arts college that some have called, "the Harvard of Evangelical Christian Colleges." Wheaton, Illinois, a suburb of about forty thousand just west of Chicago, hosts the college along with many Evangelical missions, organizations, and publishers. It is also home to the influential publisher of *Christianity Today.*[1] Wheaton College has educated too many Evangelical leaders to list, although Billy Graham remains the most influential and well-known Wheaton graduate. Many regard Wheaton as the Evangelical capital of the world.

I think I can claim as thorough a familiarity with Evangelical Christianity as almost anyone. I have lived it along with my entire family. I have studied it at Wheaton, at church, and on my own. I have discussed it with Christians and non-Christians, with janitors and astrophysicists. I hope my experiences will improve understanding and communication between Evangelicals and nonbelievers, although the truth about Evangelicals may be hard for some to take.

But first, an aside. In my discussions with Evangelicals, I have found a tendency to play "Pin the Flawed Worldview on the Infidel" with anyone who disagrees with them, assigning the supposed apostate a particular *ism* in order to dismiss his or her views. For those readers who may be inclined to do this, I implore you to allow me to explain my position in this book, and please resist the urge to dismiss it as another representation of this or that *ism*.

I should make my position clear. Although I discuss only Evangelical Christianity, this is not a back-door endorsement of another religion. I do not endorse any religion. Nor do I represent any *ism* (liberalism, atheism, secular humanism, postmodernism, or any other set of beliefs). I have unofficially joined, however, a rather small group of people—ex-Evangelical Christians.

As well, I should make it clear that in this book I discuss only the dominant Evangelical culture in the United States. Thus, when I refer to Evangelicals, I am referring to Evangelicals living in America who are predominantly from white northern European Protestant backgrounds and who attend churches where the majority of churchgoers share this background. I have intentionally omitted other Evangelical groups from my discussions because I have not had significant exposure to these other Evangelical cultures, either at Wheaton College or while participating in other Evangelical institutions, and therefore I am unable to comment about them with confidence. By leaving these groups out, I did not mean, and did not mean to imply, that the analysis or the conclusions that I have drawn have any relevance to other Evangelical cultures. Nor did I mean to imply that other Evangelical churches could not legitimately call themselves Evangelical if they did not share the views or the culture of the white Evangelicals I have described in this book.

Hooks and Ladders

How did I become an ex-Evangelical? When I accepted Jesus at age eleven, it seemed to be the right thing to do. I wanted to be good. I wanted to live like Jesus. Of course, I also wanted to go to heaven. Therefore, I prayed the "Sinner's Prayer":

> Dear Lord,
>
> I know that I, Billy, have sinned against you, and I am incapable of paying the penalty for those sins and incapable of living without sin. Because of my sin, I am deserving of eternal damnation; for the Bible tells us, "The wages of sin is death."[2]
>
> I pray that through your Son Jesus, you will forgive me of my sins. Your word tells us, "If we confess our sins, he is faithful and just to forgive us our sins, and to cleanse us from all unrighteousness."[3]
>
> Your word says that whosoever believes in your Son Jesus will have eternal life. I know I do not deserve salvation. I am a hopeless sinner. Please come into my heart and take over control of my life, as the Lord of my life. I accept Jesus as my Lord and Savior. I thank you, Lord, for your free gift of salvation.
>
> I pray these things in Jesus' name, Amen.

After accepting Christ into my heart, I went to the fellowship center, where I had confidence that my new born-again Christian role models would help me learn to live like Jesus. It took me a few years to realize that Evangelical Christianity had a well-established culture that had almost nothing to do with living like Jesus. I did not realize how much energy and resources Evangelical culture spent on fighting the ongoing battle between believers and nonbelievers—a battle they believed the whole world participated in on one side or the other. Although I did not know it then, I had unwittingly stepped into a complex and toxic Evangelical Christian mind game that I now call Hooks and Ladders. Like the child's board game Chutes and Ladders, in Hooks and Ladders you move up and down status levels in the Evangelical world. Sometimes, if you make the wrong move, a hook will grab you and send you down a level or two. Losing Hooks and Ladders has far more serious consequences than losing the child's board game does. Quitting, losing, or getting pushed off the board will result in falling into a gruesome, fiery pit—for all eternity. In this regard, Hooks and Ladders has much in common with fighting a four-alarm fire. Unlike the hooks and ladders that a company of fire-fighters use, in Hooks and Ladders the hooks hold nothing and the ladders lead to nowhere.

Many believers never figure out that the Evangelical Christian world operates under a completely different set of rules· than the rest of the world, possessing its own language and cultural norms. Failure to see the differences seems understandable. After all, a healthy percentage of Evangelical Christians grew up with Evangelical parents and never knew anything else. But still, many, who like me entered from the outside, do not seem to realize the extent to which they have stepped into a different universe. In the universe of Hooks and Ladders, however, the ordinary principles of cause and effect and right and wrong simply do not apply.

Because many believers never see their own involvement in the game, they never find a problem with the rules of Hooks and Ladders and consequently barely know they play by its rules. Nevertheless, every Evangelical church, school, and community enforces the rules of Hooks and Ladders. The rules of Evangelical communities have remarkable consistency despite having virtually nothing to say about living like Jesus.

RULE 1: EVANGELICAL CHRISTIANS ALWAYS WIN HOOKS AND LADDERS. Every Evangelical Christian group has a set of rules that you can usually find in a document called the Statement of Faith. Evangelical Christian groups with the fewest rules tend to call themselves non-denominational, which helps give the impression of open-mindedness and tolerance.

The basic premise of Evangelical Christianity—that a person *can know for sure* he or she will someday live with God in heaven—makes the dysfunctional rules of Hooks and Ladders predictable. Evangelicals teach that a person can wind up in hell despite living more like Jesus did than most Christians do. Alternately, a person whose life may have had little in common with Jesus' can gain eternal life from accepting Jesus as Lord and Savior. Indeed, the cornerstone of Evangelical Christianity rests on salvation coming from God as based on faith and not works. Virtually every Evangelical Christian, when asked about their salvation, will recite Ephesians 2:8–9:

> For by grace are ye saved through faith; and that not of yourselves: it is the gift of God: Not of works, lest any man should boast (KJV).

For Evangelical Christians, complete certainty equals great faith. Conversely, a person who says, "I do not know" or "I am not sure," has weak faith. Furthermore, Evangelicals often consider those with weak faith unstable, and they justify this belief with quotes from the Bible. For example:

> If any of you lacks wisdom, he should ask God, who gives generously to all without finding fault, and it will be given to him. But when he asks, he must believe and not doubt, because he who doubts is like a wave of the sea, blown and tossed by the wind. That man should not think he will receive anything from the Lord; he is a double-minded man, unstable in all he does (James 1:5–8 NIV).

Thus, it seems predictable that a system that praises and rewards certainty over behavior would eventually have rules that reflect this preference. Rule 1 in Hooks and Ladders reflects this certainty.

Simply put, if you accept Jesus as Savior, then you win. If you do not accept Jesus as Savior, then you lose. Most Christians never consider how many assumptions they will have to make based on this premise. After all, why would anybody who had "heard the good news of Jesus" fail to accept him as Savior? Evangelical Christians must reconcile why others did not feel compelled to give their life to Christ. Given that Evangelicals equate certainty with great faith, they do not accept other people's claims that the Bible did not convince them of Evangelical claims. Therefore, a person who does not believe in the claims of the Bible must have willingly rejected the obvious truths of the Bible.

This profoundly disturbing rationalization almost eerily makes sense. After all, how else can Evangelical Christians believe that they have a loving God if he sends honest people to hell? To force this square peg into their round hole, they must believe that rejection of Evangelical claims stems from an underlying flaw that "blinded them to the truth." Evangelicals usually surmise the person's sinful arrogance or "love of sin" makes him or her reject the truth.

Evangelical Christian communities virtually always emphasize their support of Rule 1. For example, Wheaton College's Statement of Faith includes:

> WE BELIEVE that the Lord Jesus Christ died for our sins, according to the Scriptures, as a representative and substitutionary sacrifice, triumphing over all evil; and that all who believe in Him are justified by His shed blood and forgiven of all their sins.
>
> WE BELIEVE in the bodily resurrection of the just and unjust, the everlasting punishment of the lost, and the everlasting blessedness of the saved.[4]

Most people who accepted Jesus as their savior probably had no idea that they would have to consider many people liars in order to make sense of their beliefs. Most people did not try to figure out the implications of applying their beliefs to common situations. Nevertheless, when a person becomes a born-again Christian and joins an Evangelical community, he or she has committed to the rules of Hooks and Ladders. Evangelical Christians must suspend reason and ignore evidence in order to maintain standing in their communities.

RULE 2: EVANGELICAL CHRISTIANS ARE ALWAYS CORRECT.

Rule 2 explains how Evangelical Christians win Hooks and Ladders: they win because *they are always correct.* It is easiest to explain this with an example. Wheaton has a sentence in its Statement of Faith, as did my church, which falls under Rule 2:

> WE BELIEVE that Jesus Christ was conceived by the Holy Spirit, born of the Virgin Mary, was *true God* and *true man* [my emphasis], existing in one person and without sin; and we believe in the resurrection of the crucified body of our Lord, in His ascension into heaven, and in His present life there for us as Lord of all, High Priest, and Advocate.[5]

An Evangelical Christian is not free to question whether Jesus Christ was "true God and true man." Whether or not it makes sense does not matter. To maintain status as a True Christian, I would have to claim I believed in this *truth* of God's Word. No mechanism exists to question or contest this belief without repercussion. Believers must believe Jesus was true God and true man because Evangelical Christianity is always right.

Many have suggested to me that tenets like, "Jesus Christ was true God and true man" represent the collective wisdom of two thousand years of great men of God. They contend that concerns such as mine have gone through the paces of evaluation and investigation from students and scholars of the Bible. Therefore, they ask, "How could you presume to think you can better two thousand years of finely tuned collective wisdom?" After all, they argue, God chose the church as the vehicle to reveal himself to the community of believers. As well, many have enumerated the changes in their community over the years as evidence that God continues to work through his church. They consider this a reasonable rebuttal to Rule 2—*Evangelical Christians are always correct.*

The fair-minded historian, however, will find extensive evidence supporting my contention that Evangelicals believe they are always correct. In my lifetime, many Evangelicals have radically changed their views about the age of the earth, evolutionary biology, and the inherent demonic nature of rock 'n' roll music. Yet, on any given day and at any given time, Evangelicals claim to have possession of the truth, *now*. They do not accept, and likely will not accept, responsibility for past erroneous beliefs. Nor will they accept that their Evangelical thinking may have led them to erroneous conclusions.

For example, many Evangelical Christians will not acknowledge that non-Christian scientists provided overwhelming evidence for the age of the earth and evolution. They will not admit that many Evangelicals have felt compelled to change their position as the avalanche of evidence against their previous positions forced their hands. They will not acknowledge that their teachings led to widespread acceptance of erroneous beliefs. Rather, they will say a discerning believer readily recognizes the advanced age of the earth as true. They will say the Bible clearly alludes to an advanced age of the earth, even though thirty to forty years ago Evangelicals argued precisely the opposite. They contend others may have merely misinterpreted or overlooked these clear truths in the Scriptures. Some will even contend that they do not fault those other believers. They will say that others do not always have the level of spiritual maturity that they do. Some will pass off their dismissal of past Evangelical failures as a gesture of tolerance and compassion.

But at one time—and that time was not so long ago—Evangelical Christians contended that others could not credibly challenge them, that they alone were in possession of truth, and that *anyone who disagreed* must have lived in the thrall of Satan and *could be safely ignored.* Although Evangelicals readily admit that past Evangelicals erred, they never acknowledge the possibility that their current beliefs may have flaws.

Because Evangelicals are always right, those who disagree with the current version of Evangelical doctrine are not merely wrong—they are damned. It requires profoundly delusional thinking to believe that every student of the Bible who disagrees with the current version of Evangelical Christian doctrine must have done something worthy of eternal damnation. Adding to the problem, Evangelical communities do not attempt to rein in delusional judgments from members of their group. Any member can boldly claim that anyone else is, "an agent of Satan," "a person who hates and rejects truth," "weak and led astray by liberal professors who must have infiltrated Wheaton," "a person who never truly committed his life to Christ," "too proud to recognize that he needs

God," or "a good example of what can happen if you're not ready to answer the false teachings of the (fill-in-the-blank)*ists* who seduce weak minds with their evil teaching of (fill-in-the-blank)ism." In most Evangelical communities, an Evangelical can make one, or all, of the above claims with no regard for providing evidence.

These types of claims fall under Rule 2, and Evangelicals consider them truth. Therefore, a person violates Rule 2 if they say, "Billy claims that he thoroughly and honestly investigated the claims of Christianity and I have no good reason to doubt him." In the game of Hooks and Ladders, accepting the testimony of an admitted non-Christian will send the player down three floors. Most likely, this gullible believer will have to show evidence of intolerance in order to advance in the future or else the believer will run afoul of Rule 3. After receiving a label like "not a True Christian," he or she will be thrown out of the community by the winners in their mind game.

RULE 3: ONLY EVANGELICAL CHRISTIANS HAVE THE PRIVILEGE TO DETERMINE TRUTH.

How do you know whether someone deserves trust and a voice as a representative of Evangelical Christians? See Rules 1 and 2. Do they agree with you and the rest of the Evangelical Christian community? Are they winning Hooks and Ladders? They have the perfect loop. Rule 3 derives from Rule 2, yet due to the precarious nature of Evangelical beliefs, Evangelicals need a specific and strictly enforced rule to ensure members do not figure out that Rule 2 has no basis in reality. Thus, Rule 3: *only Evangelical Christians have the privilege to determine truth.* Evangelicals must consider only other Evangelical Christians as honest, intellectually capable, and worthy of having a voice in matters of truth.

Hooks and Ladders Rule 3 requires Evangelicals to accept claims of truth only from other Evangelicals regarding subjects that relate to their faith. They must disregard everything a non-Evangelical claims, no matter how credible. The implementation of this rule clearly comes into play during Sunday-morning church services. Only Evangelicals can speak, pray, sing, or even read a Bible passage. The community remains a captive audience that Evangelicals diligently ensure will not have corrupting influences.

Of course, most Evangelical groups state this rule in their Statement of Faith. Most make it clear that only Evangelicals have the special abilities necessary to ascertain the truths of the Bible. For example, Wheaton College's Statement of Faith includes:

> WE BELIEVE that the Holy Spirit indwells and gives life to believers, enables them to understand the Scriptures, empowers them for godly living, and equips them for service and witness.[6]

Some Evangelical Christians may recognize the absurdity of this rule. Most who remain Evangelicals, however, never seem to accept that this rule stems from the flawed reasoning inherent to their faith. For example, a youth pastor who never scored higher than a "C" in a science class may end up teaching a Sunday-school class about evolutionary theory. Based on the delusional belief that the pastor has a spirit that enables him to understand the Scriptures, Evangelicals will consider this youth pastor a superior teacher and of greater intellect than the most highly regarded evolutionary biologists.

Many bright Christians seem conflicted about the abuses they witness in the name of Rule 3. For example, they may recognize that many Christians do not have the background to honestly claim understanding of many of the issues of evolutionary biology. They rarely, however, seem to identify that this problem stems from an integral aspect of their faith. They fail to grasp that their belief that something magical happens to them when they accept Jesus naturally leads to this consequence. Perhaps the most common excuse bright Evangelicals give for the bad behavior of Evangelicals addresses Rule 3. For instance, a non-Christian may have decided that following Christian teachings put people at risk of succumbing to the harmful behaviors that have plagued Christianity. In support of this position, a non-Christian might point to an Evangelical like Pastor Ted Haggard as a recent example of the way in which Christian attitudes toward sexual matters leads to hypocrisy and deceit. Haggard secretly engaged the services of a male prostitute while serving as the leader of a large Evangelical organization.

However, the Evangelical will not accept that the behaviors of an Evangelical Christian like Haggard resulted as a consequence of Evangelical beliefs. Instead, the bright Evangelical may say that a person who rejects God based on the poor conduct and behavior of many people who call themselves Christians make a mistake. For example, Francis S. Collins, a renowned geneticist, a Christian, and the author of *The Language of God,* wrote, "All of us as human beings have fallen ... The church is made up of fallen people. The pure, clean water of spiritual truth is placed in rusty containers, and the subsequent failings of the church down through the centuries should not be projected onto the faith."[7]

My Story Continued

Why could I see that my born-again beliefs had trapped me in a mind game while many others, including many other smart people, could not? I still do not know for sure, but finding the answer to this question motivated me to write this book. However, I can describe how it happened even though I cannot say for certain why it happened. It occurred to me early on, when I began to question the meaning of Jesus living as fully human and fully God, and why Evangelical Christians thought this made sense.

I had noticed a small bump on my chin. I had to go look in the bathroom mirror and make sure I did not have a pimple. I had spent years doing this, fearing that every bump heralded the beginning of acne, which my brother Mike had dealt with for many years. I did not know if I had the courage to deal with the problem the way Mike had. Simply put, I knew that I would have to deal with uncertainties, including the prospect of acne, for the rest of my life. If Jesus had lived in a human body while remaining fully God, I surmised, who cares what Jesus would do? Jesus would have never had to deal with uncertainty. I reasoned that if Jesus lived as God then he did not meet the criteria necessary to considering him fully human.

I asked my youth group leaders for an explanation of how Jesus could be fully man if he were God at the same time. Bad move on my part. First, I did not get an answer to my question at all but instead replies like this: "If you pray and ask God to give you the wisdom that only comes through the Holy Spirit, you will understand some day," one college-aged chaperone explained. Others asked me questions: "Do you like public schools?" "You have to remain vigilant, Billy, of the socialist agenda of the NEA. Do you know they target vulnerable teens like you? Have you prayed about this?" One older youth pastor even asked, "Billy, do you spend much time listening to rock music?" He explained, "It must make your heart ache having your parents separated. Even though it seems like God has not treated you fairly, Billy, at times like this it helps to find strength in God's Word."

Even worse, I found that upon asking this question, a phantom hook had reached out and lowered me down a few floors in the game. I would have to work hard to regain my status of true believer. I would have the label "doubting Christian" until I slowly climbed my way back to full acceptance, and I would no longer have the same trust from the godly members of the church. For example, they would not allow me to teach a third-grade Sunday school class because they could not rely on me to teach the truths of the Bible.

Whether or not I could make sense of Jesus as true God and true man did not matter. To shed my new label of "doubting Christian," I would have to follow the rules and claim I believed in this *truth* from God's Word. If I stubbornly insisted that I could not honestly claim that this belief made sense, then I would ultimately lose Hooks and Ladders. Other Evangelicals would essentially kick me out of the game. If I readily shared my views—or even my questions—on this topic, I would not have the privileges that come with playing Hooks and Ladders. I could not preach, teach, or participate as a fellow believer in most Evangelical Christian communities.

Worse yet, I found that whenever I questioned any of the church's teachings, my Evangelical Christian brothers and sisters regarded me as a liar. When I began to examine my faith in the light of reason, I fully expected to find validations of my Evangelical beliefs. But I did not. Despite starting with a bias as a believer, I found that Evangelical teachings employed faulty methods and reasoning and led to dubious conclusions.

I conducted my exploration honestly, seriously, and thoroughly. Consequently, I know with certainty that I did not "willingly reject truths of the Bible," "succumb to false teachers," "decide to live in sin," "decide I did not need God," or any other typical Evangelical rationalization. Yet, no one would know this if he or she asked an Evangelical Christian. Thus, I know firsthand that Evangelical Christians have a strong commitment to immoral principles. One may have good reasons for not accepting my conclusions, but nobody, however—not even an Evangelical—has any reason or morally sound justification for doubting my honesty and motives. Yet they did and still do.

When I accepted Jesus as my personal savior, I did not know this made me a participant in the game. Perhaps time, reflection, and for me, at eleven, education and maturity, would have allowed me to realize how silly I had been. To be sure, I do not consider silly my desire to live a wholesome life and have wisdom like Jesus in the Bible. Naively thinking something magical happens by reciting the "Sinner's Prayer," however, deserves the label! Nonetheless, wanting to live like Jesus and even accept him as savior still seems to me like a sensible decision. Just like me, most born-again Christians probably had pure intentions for becoming born-again. Jesus, a man that even most non-Christians admire, provides Evangelicals with the hook to launch them into the mind game, Hooks and Ladders.

Many of the Evangelicals I know make an honest effort to adhere to principles that serve them and their communities well. Thus, I used to feel skittish about confronting them. Nonetheless, I never felt skittish about answering Evangelicals who confronted me. And almost every year I've had Evangelicals try to convince me that they had fresh insights about Christianity that would convince me I had made a mistake—*if I kept my heart and mind open to the Lord.* Some attempts ended quickly, as it became clear that I knew far more about the Bible and Evangelical Christianity than they had anticipated. But even these brief encounters invariably (and I do mean invariably) ended with an appeal that I seek out one of their Christian mentors—usually their pastor—who could "answer my questions" better than they could.

Most of the discussions I had with the Evangelicals who confronted me, however, went further. I spoke with Evangelicals from many parts of the country, and yet every encounter had an eerie similarity. The conversations began with the Evangelical treating me as if I knew next to nothing about Evangelical Christianity. Invariably (and once again I do mean invariably), I was directed to books written by Evangelical authors that Evangelicals believe make a credible, scholarly case for the merits of Evangelical Christianity. I took the Evangelical's advice and read the recommended books. I either marked up these books almost cover to cover, detailing the seemingly endless number of flaws, or else I wrote detailed notes about the books and gave my comments back to the person who suggested I read them. I never had anyone respond to my criticisms of their books.

After years of such encounters, I grew frustrated with this process. Then my future wife Brooke wrote me a letter explaining her angst with me because, as she wrote, "You have turned your back on God." Along with the letter, Brooke sent a number of books that she felt might help convince me that I had made a mistake. Brooke had become an important part of my life, so I knew I had to answer her letter. Since I had put so much work into responses in the past, and because I felt a little guilty for not cataloguing my concerns about Evangelical Christianity sooner, I decided I would respond to Brooke in a way that I could use to respond to others later. I knew I had more than enough material to write a book, and since the concerns I had with Evangelical Christianity went far beyond the weaknesses I found in books by Josh McDowell, I decided to focus on the issues that Evangelicals do not usually address. Evangelicals have many resources that give them detailed instructions about how to *answer the skeptics*. However, you will not find the concerns I outline in this book addressed in those resources—at least not yet.

Because I wrote this book to respond to Brooke and to the many Evangelicals who had engaged me in conversation over the years, I initially intended for this book to address Evangelicals directly.* Joy Fuller then persuaded me that Evangelicals would not read the book as it was written. She also helped convince me that non-Evangelicals had too few resources to help them understand Evangelical Christianity, and those non-Evangelicals would likely provide a better audience and allow the book to have a greater impact.

Beyond mere restructuring, I have completely reworked the tone and contents. For example, when I originally addressed Evangelicals, I felt the most important thing to establish was that I understood their language and culture. I wanted to reach out to them in their terms. In addressing non-Evangelicals, my concerns were nearly the opposite. I had to *translate* the world of Hooks and Ladders into terms that non-Evangelicals could understand. I could not avoid doing this because the Evangelical community has become far more exclusive and isolated than most people recognize. As a result, one of my chief aims is to emphasize that Evangelicals *speak a different language*, even if it appears they look and sound like everybody else.

Addressing the Evangelical Community

Individual Evangelicals have little control over the behavior and message that comes out of the Evangelical community. The behavior and message predictably results from implementing the rules of Hooks and Ladders. Much to the dismay of Evangelicals who are dissatisfied with the behavior of their communities, they have no ability to fix the problem. As soon as they mention a problem, they become a doubting Christian and slip further down the game board.

---

* Ironically, writing this book has taken too much time away from the time I can spend with my wife and family. Yet, my wife has tolerated the distraction from family life. Some days, though, she gets frustrated and says, "I wish I never sent you that letter."

These rules logically result from a community where the vast majority of people believe they have a special communication pathway for understanding God's messages. Most believe they became a winner of Hooks and Ladders the day they said a prayer that entered their name in *The Book of Life.* The rules clearly support the belief that believers have magical powers to interpret the Bible and the world around them that nonbelievers lack. Every believer willingly signed up to participate in Hooks and Ladders. Unwittingly or not, believers agree with the beliefs that provide the rules for Hooks and Ladders. Their beliefs bolster a system that promotes immoral behavior, and Evangelicals cannot separate this logical outcome from the core tenets of their faith. They cannot credibly attribute this solely to bad people. To look past the bad behavior of flawed Christians, as many suggest, requires poor reasoning and judgment.

I hope to provide an understanding and framework for discussing Evangelical Christianity with those disillusioned by the conduct of Evangelicals. I hope to highlight how the well-intentioned Evangelical may maintain the shallow thinking that started when they became born-again. I hope to show how the average Evangelical's personal god requires different behaviors from them than their community usually requires. Despite these differences, I intend to show how Evangelicals have no way of separating their personal god's mandates from their community's rules. As well, I detail how both individual and community beliefs have no basis in reality.

Although at times it may not seem true while you read this, my dream is that we can do away with the rules of Hooks and Ladders and with the most toxic aspects of the Evangelical community, such as the reliance on untrustworthy authorities, living and dead, and with the vain quest for certainty that isn't there. I dream of getting together with my old friends—smart, hard-working, Jesus-like people—who had a passion for life and a reason to get up in the morning. It is exhilarating to be around people excited about working together with others to make the world a better, more loving, and happier place.

2. The Rules, Paul, and Paranoid Schizophrenia

MANY PEOPLE MIX EVANGELICALS in with other brands of Christianity and consider their beliefs similar. This is a false assumption. To understand Evangelical Christian values and the rules of Hooks and Ladders, familiarity with the life of Jesus, the Bible, and the history of Christianity will not help much.

Evangelicals give the impression that Jesus and the Bible matter to them. However, they actually do not, or at least not in the way you might think. Consider, for example, someone who believes all of these things—things that seem important to being a Christian, even an Evangelical Christian:

- Jesus, his Father, and the Holy Spirit make up one God called the Trinity.
- Jesus' death and resurrection paid the penalty for everyone's sins.
- The Bible constitutes the Word of God.
- Eternal damnation is a just punishment for unrepentant sins.
- Humans did not evolve from other life forms.
- Jesus is your Lord and Savior.

Evangelicals believe all these things; you could not be an Evangelical if you didn't. Does every person holding these beliefs qualify for entry into heaven according to Evangelicals? Nope! After all, many liberals and Catholics believe these same things, and yet they have not received the gift of salvation and the indwelling power of the Holy Spirit.

How does this work? The Internet and computers provides an easy way of discussing the difference between Evangelicals and other believers. For example, many people believe God, or a god, exists and hears their prayers. For these people, prayers are like e-mail. Just like e-mails, we might send to anybody, however, we have a difficult time proving our prayers went where we sent them. Even if the e-mail shows up in the right inbox, we have even more difficulty proving the recipient cared about it or even read it. We may say the same about God's inbox. We hope God receives our e-mails. We hope he cares about them and reads them. Let's call this process *uploading* and people that believe a god receives prayers but does not respond personally to them *upload believers.*

For Evangelicals, however, believers need a special plug-in called "HOLYSPIRIT" to upload and download messages from God. To operate effectively in any capacity the believer has had to install the special HOLYSPIRIT plug-in. Furthermore, people without the HOLYSPIRIT plug-in, like a computer program running uncontrolled, may corrupt the system much like a computer virus. A person without the plug-in cannot reliably do anything. For example, if a defective person reads the Bible, unless he opens his heart (files) to the HOLYSPIRIT plug-in he will not understand God's message. God's messages remain inaccessible. Evangelical Christianity has little to do with the Bible, Jesus, or "Christian values" and everything to do with downloaded messages from God. These downloaded messages are clearly seen and understood by Evangelical Christians, who are often puzzled at or even angered by non-Evangelicals' insistence that they do not see the same thing.

With this in mind, it is easy to see where Rule 3 comes from. Because only Evangelicals can decipher the downloaded messages properly, only Evangelical Christians have the privilege to determine truth. Rule 2—Evangelical Christians are always correct—comes from the same place. If God himself, through the HOLYSPIRIT plug-in, communicates to believers, of course they can know they have the truth. God does not make mistakes.

How do Evangelical Christians end up this way? Let's look at what happens when nonbelievers become Evangelicals and accept Jesus into their hearts.

Becoming an Evangelical Christian

Earlier, I described my conversion at the age of eleven as praying the "Sinner's Prayer." Praying consisted of me repeating the phrases aloud as the minister read them. Within Evangelical Christianity, many have had almost an identical conversion experience.

Here is another prayer, known as the "Salvation Prayer."[1]

HERE'S A SUGGESTED PRAYER:

"Lord Jesus Christ, I know I am sinner and do not deserve eternal life. But, I believe you died and rose from the grave to purchase a place in heaven for me. Lord Jesus, come into my life; take control of my life; forgive my sins and save me. I repent my sins and now place my trust in You for my salvation. I accept the free gift of eternal life."

If this prayer is the desire of your heart, look at what Jesus Promises to those who believe in Him:

"Verily, Verily I say unto you, he that believeth on Me hath everlasting life" (John 6:47).

This prayer comes from Evangelism Explosion (of which I am a not-so-proud graduate), an Evangelical Christian program that trains Christians to "witness" to others and convince them to become Evangelical Christians.

This prayer, a condensed version of the "Sinner's Prayer," provides all the important steps to conversion. Here are the steps:

1. Confession of sins: admit and take responsibility for your sins
2. Ask for forgiveness
3. Ask Jesus to come into your life and take control

After praying this prayer—but only if you really mean it!—you are a "born-again Christian." We will examine the prayer in detail later. However, for now, let us discuss the soon-to-be Evangelical Christian's state of mind at the time of conversion.

Both conversion prayers I have quoted require the people praying to state that they are not worthy of the very things for which they are asking: forgiveness and a new life in Christ. Both prayers also require the would-be converts to abdicate their own identity and allow God to control their lives. By earnestly saying one of these prayers, the new believer has installed the HOLYSPIRIT plug-in. Both prayers promise the new Evangelical access to a different world. The believer exchanges his or her old, worthless identity for a new one. With the new self, the believer receives and understands messages from the Creator and can clearly see truths that others cannot or will not. The believer has assurance that he or she will live forever.

Ordinarily when we meet people who say that they receive *secret messages* from an otherworldly being that only they can discern and that this being has given them special powers of insight and knowledge, we begin backing slowly away. Many consider this crazy. Suppose a group of "normal" people, like most Evangelicals, does not back away from someone who talks about visions and secret messages. Suppose the group considers the person "talking crazy" to be an oracle from God and consider his words to be the Word of God. With regard to the Apostle Paul, Evangelicals have done just that. Put in these terms, Evangelical Christian thinking might have certain things in common with the thought processes of persons we might classify as mentally ill. For this reason, to understand Evangelical Christians it is more helpful to be familiar with paranoid schizophrenia than with the story of Jesus in the Bible.

Do not close the book! I know very well that this is the point at which I might lose many people. They might feel, as others have, that I have gone beyond the pale in comparing Evangelical Christians with people who have serious mental illnesses, and it is about to get worse. Nevertheless, please bear with me.

Understanding the Apostle Paul

Before we discuss anything further about Evangelical Christians or delusional thinking, it is necessary to take a detour through the writings of the Apostle Paul—in particular, his letters to newly formed first-century churches in Rome, Corinth, Ephesus, Galatia, Philippi, Colossae, and Thessalonica. Evangelicals emphasize the teachings of Paul more often than they do Jesus' teachings. More importantly, Evangelicals derive their beliefs about what it means to be a True Christian almost entirely from the Apostle Paul. Consequently, we can learn far more about Evangelicals from studying Paul than we can from studying Jesus. We should probably call them "Evangelical Paulians," since they revere Paul and adopt his thinking. In a sense, however, all Christians pay homage to Paul by using Paul's term, "Christ," instead of the name "Jesus" to establish their identity. We will review later how little Paul's Christ and the man from the gospels named Jesus have in common.

The underpinnings of Evangelical Christianity come from Paul's descriptions of sin and salvation. Evangelical Christians developed the

"Sinner's Prayer" from Paul's writings, which tell Evangelicals that new converts must simultaneously proclaim their worthlessness and shed their former personal identity by giving control of their lives to God. Paul promises Evangelical Christians a new life through the person he calls "Christ." Through Paul, Evangelicals understand that they can have the Holy Spirit dwell inside them. The Holy Spirit, Paul's letters explain, will enable the believer to understand messages from the Creator properly.

I want to make it clear what I am saying. I am not saying that Paul was a paranoid schizophrenic. I do not know that, and neither does anyone else. I am also not saying that Evangelical Christians are paranoid schizophrenics. I am saying that Paul's writings suggest his thinking has many characteristics in common with paranoid schizophrenic thinking. Too, Paul gives his readers insight into how he viewed himself. His self-description, although not typical of the average Evangelical, has fundamental elements in common with people at high risk for paranoid schizophrenia. Consequently, Evangelicals who place considerable emphasis on Paul's doctrinal views seem to adopt Paul's beliefs and style of reasoning. I intend to show that many core elements of Evangelical thought and behavior stem from their adoption of Paul's thoughts and ideas. In particular, they stem from Paul's concept of human worthlessness and toxic, sinful nature, and his perception that God controlled him.

Paul the Abortion

In his letters, Paul repeatedly writes about his lack of identity, his toxic nature, and his self-hatred—in short, his utter worthlessness and inability to do anything on his own.[2] Paul believes himself to be so worthless and toxic that he refers to himself as an "abortion" (1 Cor 15:8 NIV). The word "ἐκτρωμα" literally translates as "miscarriage" or "abortion." The meaning has confounded translators for years and usually is translated as "untimely born." Paul calls his toxic essence "sin nature." He literally believed that sin inhabited his body and controlled his actions. For example, he writes, "Now if I do what I do not want to do, it is no longer I who do it, but it is sin living in me that does it" (Rom 7:20 NIV). Another example: "Therefore do not let sin reign in your mortal body so that you obey its evil desires" (Rom 6:12 NIV). As sin's slave, Paul did not have the power to control his own actions.[3] Evangelicals, like Paul, believe sin to be something with a unique existence. They think of it in much the same way that people think of a virus, for example. Sin, much like a virus, can live, die, inhabit, invade, overwhelm, destroy, and reveal. Other people can remove, forgive, forget, and inherit sin.

Paul's writing about commandments qualifies as one of the oddest manifestations of lack of a sense of identity. For example, Paul wrote:

> What shall we say, then? Is the law sin? Certainly not! Indeed I would not have known what sin was except through the law. For I would not have known what coveting really was if the law had not said, "Do not covet." But sin, seizing the opportunity afforded by the commandment, produced in me every kind of covetous desire. For apart from law, sin is dead. Once I was alive apart from law; but when the commandment came, sin sprang to life and I died. I found that the very commandment that was intended to bring life actually brought death.
>
> For sin, seizing the opportunity afforded by the commandment, deceived me, and through the commandment put me to death. So then, the law is holy, and the commandment is holy, righteous and good. Did that which is good, then, become death to me? By no means! But in order that sin might be recognized as sin, it produced death in me through what was good, so that through the commandment sin might become utterly sinful (Rom 7:7–13 NIV).

Attempting to decipher meaning from someone who has such a lacking sense of identity can prove difficult. Indeed, the phrase, "through the commandment sin might become utterly sinful," lacks any coherence. Still, Paul presented his thoughts fairly clearly.

Paul believed the commandments made him *know* sin, which caused him to sin. He believed he would have had no idea that coveting meant "sin" if the commandments did not tell him. Without knowing, he would not have coveted. He believed this *knowledge* of sin was "intended to bring life." However, this awareness only made him sin. Paul sinned because the sin living inside him made him sin. His brief life of awareness ended and he died.[4]

Paul did not actually do anything. Commandments made him aware. A controlling power, "seizing the opportunity," made him act out sin. He had good thoughts controlled by God warring against bad thoughts controlled by sin. Paul, essentially dead, experienced his body performing actions and thoughts in the control of outside entities.[5] Paul's only sense of identity seems to have come as a brief awareness that he had a toxic, sinful nature.

For Paul, giving up control of his life, to the extent he even had such control in the first place, probably seemed like a good idea.[6] Evangelical Christians follow this model.

PAUL'S CONCRETE THINKING

Some claim that Paul speaks metaphorically about his worthlessness and his emptiness. They have no grounds for that belief, as there is there is no reason to think that Paul did not literally mean what he said when he wrote it.

We already reviewed how Paul perceived he came into the world as an abortion. This self-assessment must seem incomprehensible to many translators, who, after all, have a sense of personal identity and therefore struggle to find Paul's true meaning. Nevertheless, Paul likely meant abortion when he wrote the word. Perhaps he did not mean it in the sense that he had the same size and shape as a mutilated fetus but in the sense that he uses this word to convey what he thinks of himself—an essentially dead, useless, and rotting piece of flesh. Indeed, calling himself an abortion likely helps convey that he thought of himself as not only worthless but also as a vehicle for bringing sadness and pain into the world. In addition, like an abortion, Paul could not do anything about his wretchedness. He had no way of fixing his toxic nature.

Although most Evangelicals do not believe Paul stopped sinning after giving control of his life to Christ, when Paul said he had no sin and could no longer sin, he likely meant it. Paul wrote repeatedly that once he had his life controlled by Christ, he stopped sinning. Paul said he believed that *before* Christ controlled his life, the Law controlled him and made him sin. As well, he states quite clearly that he could not sin without the Law. In Paul's world, *he simply had the Law abolished,* taken away, and replaced by grace (Rom 6:14 NIV). No Law equaled no sin. For Paul this formula probably made sense.

Paul repeatedly wrote that once someone gives control over to Christ, he or she has no way of sinning.[7] I cannot find a single verse where Paul claimed that he sinned *after* his conversion. Many seem to misinterpret Paul's laments and humility as an indication that he still sinned. This interpretation does not fit Paul's claims, however. Rather, in lamenting his imperfect life, Paul acknowledged that Christ had a lousy piece of equipment to work with when he controlled Paul's body.[8] He seemed amazed that Christ could accomplish so much with his wretched corpse. Paul talked as if he were a reporter describing what Christ did with his corpse. Regardless, Paul reported that he, as a part of Christ and despite his humility and lamenting, had no sin and could not sin.

Paul claimed he "died" repeatedly. In one of many examples, Paul wrote, "I have been crucified with Christ and I no longer live, but Christ lives in me" (Gal 2:20 NIV).[9] Paul told others they must die also. Nothing about this claim has a basis in reality. We know Paul did not die before writing his letters. As well, Christ—the entity that Paul claimed had taken over his corpse—could not have written them. What did Paul mean by this?

Evangelicals take Paul's claims seriously and often claim they have died. In some cases, they will say that they have "died to sin" but are "alive in Christ" (Rom 6:11 NIV). If we make this a metaphor it becomes, "I live *as if* I died to sin as a devoted follower of Jesus' teachings." This translates to, "I am trying to be a good person" or "I am trying to follow the teachings of Jesus." However, Paul clearly did not mean this since he did not believe that he, the abortion, had even the ability to *try* to be a good person. Neither do Evangelicals. Like Paul, they often believe they had a worthless existence controlled by sin. They have worth only after they give control of their lives to Christ.

Paul the Mind-Reader

Paul, who believed God controls his mind and body, had no personal identity. As an amorphous part of God, the omniscient creator of the universe, Paul believed he knew about the thoughts and motivations of others. After all, the controller of his body knew everything about everybody. Certainly, his controller, God, could tell him about others. Paul would have had no way of knowing, like Evangelicals do now, that all his thoughts, feelings, impulses, and behavior came from physical processes that took place in his brain. He would have had no way of knowing that controlling entities like sin, the Law, demons, or Christ did not have access to his brain. Once Paul believed that God controlled him, he tapped into God's mainframe computer. Paul would have had no reason to doubt that God implanted beliefs and thoughts about other people inside him.

The following passage gives an example of Paul's misguided belief that he knew the thoughts and motivations of others. (Please note how he does not think he has control of his body, as he warns against judging immediately after writing very harsh judgments.)

> The wrath of God is being revealed from heaven against all the godlessness and wickedness of men who suppress the truth by their wickedness, since what may be known about God is plain to them, because God has made it plain to them. For since the creation of the world God's invisible qualities—his eternal power and divine nature—have been clearly seen, being understood from what has been made, so that men are without excuse.
>
> For although they knew God, they neither glorified him as God nor gave thanks to him, but their thinking became futile and their foolish hearts were darkened. Although they claimed to be wise, they became fools and exchanged the glory of the immortal God for images made to look like mortal man and birds and animals and reptiles.
>
> Therefore God gave them over in the sinful desires of their hearts to sexual impurity for the degrading of their bodies with one another. They exchanged the truth of God for a lie, and worshiped and served created things rather than the Creator—who is forever praised. Amen.
>
> Because of this, God gave them over to shameful lusts. Even their women exchanged natural relations for unnatural ones. In the same way the men also abandoned natural relations with women and were inflamed with lust for one another. Men committed indecent acts with other men, and received in themselves the due penalty for their perversion.
>
> Furthermore, since they did not think it worthwhile to retain the knowledge of God, he gave them over to a depraved mind, to do what ought not to be done. They have become filled with every kind of wickedness, evil, greed and depravity. They are full of envy, murder, strife, deceit and malice. They are gossips, slanderers, God-haters, insolent, arrogant and boastful; they invent ways of doing evil; they disobey their parents; they are senseless, faithless, heartless, ruthless. Although they know God's righteous decree that those who do such things deserve death, they not only continue to do these very things but also approve of those who practice them.
>
> You, therefore, have no excuse, you who pass judgment on someone else, for at whatever point you judge the other, you are condemning yourself, because you who pass judgment do the same things (Rom 1:18–2:1 NIV).

Paul here claimed to understand what other people saw, what they knew, and what they thought about it. Other people—people with a toxic, sinful nature like Paul's own—clearly saw "God's invisible qualities," plainly knew "everything there was to be known about God," and yet failed to "glorify him as God." How did Paul know that these other people knew the truth about God and rejected it? For that matter, how did Paul know what God thought or felt about those people? It was because he, Paul, knew these things. How did Paul know these things? He knew because God utterly controlled him. Paul never entertained the idea that his knowledge might not be accurate. How could he have made a mistake? God does not make mistakes.

Paul had undergone a transformation from the most miserable abortion, a slave to sin, to living in and through the most powerful being imaginable. Although, as noted below, Paul still saw what he had left of himself as weak and corrupt. He reveled in the triumphant feelings that he attributed to Christ:

> I came to you in weakness and fear, and with much trembling. My message and my preaching were not with wise and persuasive words, but with a demonstration of the Spirit's power, so that your faith might not rest on men's wisdom, but on God's power (1 Cor 2:3–5 NIV).[10]

Evangelical Christians follow this model as well.

Understanding Paranoid Schizophrenia

We've identified some of Paul's unusual and unique ideas. In order to better understand these ideas and the mind-set and reasoning behind them, it is helpful to understand how they are similar to the mind-set and reasoning found in persons with paranoid schizophrenia. Most agree that the reasoning associated with paranoid schizophrenia limits the people who use it significantly. Greater understanding of schizophrenic reasoning, and noting the similarities to Paul's writings, should help us understand Paul and his limitations. Secondarily, it should help identity problems Evangelicals have created by incorporating Paul's reasoning heavily into their most important doctrines.

Ensuring a common understanding may prove difficult since most people have had almost no exposure to paranoid schizophrenics. Paranoid schizophrenia carries a social stigma and many people have misguided or otherwise incorrect opinions about schizophrenia. For example, when most people think of a paranoid schizophrenic, they may think of the disheveled homeless woman they passed on their way to work, wearing a coat in the middle of summer, her wig askew, pushing her possessions around in a cart, and muttering to herself about the CIA. However, this paints an incomplete picture. It does not capture the typical nature of the schizophrenic's mental world.

(1) Lack of Self

Paranoid schizophrenics have a very poor sense of self, lacking an "I" at the core of their identity; in fact, this dismal view practically defines paranoid schizophrenia. Listen to these testimonies from those most familiar with the schizophrenic lack of identity:

> The feeling of "self," which provides unity, consistency, and security is painfully absent ... The question "who am I?" represents the existential core of schizophrenia....
>
> Schizophrenics often lack a sense of self. Typically, patients report that the feeling of being "unreal" has been with them for a long time. In exploring their childhood feelings they are often unable to recall any period of time in which they felt comfortable with their identity. It would seem that, in most cases, this basic insecurity about one's place in the world predates the onset of any florid psychotic symptoms by many years.[11]

This same book provides an example from a man with schizophrenia. This patient described himself:

> I am in no small degree, I find, a sham—a player to the gallery. Possibly this may be felt as you read these analyses.
>
> In my life, in my personality, there is an essence of falseness and insincerity. A thin, fine paper of fraud hangs always over me and dampens and injures some things in me that I value.
>
> It may be that the spirit of falseness is itself a false thing—yet true or false, it is with me always ... This element of falseness is absolutely the very thinnest, the very finest, the rarest of all the things in my many sided character.
>
> It is not the most unimportant.
>
> I have seen visions of myself walking in various pathways. I have seen myself trying one pathway and another. And always it is the same: I see before me in the path, darkening the way and filling me with dread and discouragement, a great black shadow—the shadow of my own element of falseness.
>
> I cannot rid myself of it.
>
> I am an innate liar.[12]

In *Dante's Cure*, Daniel Dorman, a clinical professor of psychiatry at UCLA, described how one of his patients, Catherine, was able to overcome the scourge of schizophrenia. In a subsection of Dorman's book titled, "The Lack of an 'I': the Role of Self Development and Psychosis," Catherine describes her former self:

> I didn't have any sense of me—myself. Do you remember that time we were invited to speak at the UCLA seminar on recovery from schizophrenia? Afterward the instructor got up and said my recovery was unusual because schizophrenics don't usually have the ego strength to involve themselves in a therapeutic relationship. That doctor didn't get it at all. Ego strength? I didn't have an ego ... There was no ego in me for life to stick to ... My life was like sand being blown away little by little until I was left with nothing. The only thing I could do was resort to craziness to have a me.[13]

Dr. Dorman goes on to explain:

> If one looks to the experience of other schizophrenics, this same theme—the lack of an ego, or self—is repeated again and again. Sigmund Freud's famous patient, Shreber, talked about soul-murder. Catherine talked about having "no nucleus, no central self." A schizophrenic man said, "Gradually I can no longer distinguish how much of myself is in me, and how much is already in others. I am a conglomeration, a monstrosity modeled anew each day" ... This lack of self development is central to schizophrenia.[14]

Dr. Dorman reinforces this idea by quoting Julian Jaynes from his book, *The Origin of Consciousness in the Breakdown of the Bicameral Mind*:

> Jaynes also refers to the lack of "I" as responsible for the schizophrenic's inability to get logical answers. There is no "unifying conceptive purpose," he says, since answers to questions must come from a person's mind-space. The schizophrenic tries to tie answers to external circumstances. When the schizophrenic says he is commanded by outside forces, the psychiatrist regards it as a delusion, a falsification of reality, but Jaynes says, "with the loss of the analogous 'I,' its mind-space, and the ability to narrate, behavior is either responding to hallucinated directions, or continues on by habit. The remnant of self feels like a commanded automaton."[15]

As we saw above, Evangelical Christians learn from Paul that they have no inherent worth. They must affirm this worthlessness as a pre-condition to conversion. Evangelical Christians, following Paul, believe that people cannot fix their own worthless, sinful nature. They preach the "good news" that no one can have any useful identity unless God takes control of their lives and they live as "commanded automata."

(2) CONCRETE THINKING

We have seen above Paul's use of *literal* and *concrete* language. Translators and readers struggle at times to make sense out of Paul's use of the term "death," for example, since it is plain that he has not died, and yet he means something beyond a mere comparison, a mere *as if*.

When asked about a common proverb such as, "A rolling stone gathers no moss," a paranoid schizophrenic often seems unable to understand the intent of the saying as a metaphor. In this example, his or her thoughts will focus on a real stone and real moss. Many paranoid schizophrenics seem to ignore the possibility that this saying may intentionally represent a metaphor. They do not recognize the adage as an elegant way of describing the benefits of stability and putting down roots. When a person either cannot or does not consider the abstract meaning of something, we label this *concrete thinking*.

The concrete thinking of most Evangelical Christians seems to confuse many people who have little knowledge of Evangelical culture. I hope to shed light on this issue for readers with little exposure to Evangelicals. Plenty of Evangelicals appear to have normal abstract reasoning ability, and many unknowing observers will interpret remarks as metaphors that the Evangelical means concretely. For example, a very bright Evangelical friend once told me, "I used to resent other Christians that spent so much energy trying to get rich and obtain the material possessions that plague our society. Through prayer and time studying the Bible, however, God has changed my heart. He has washed away the bitterness and instilled a passion in me to help those who have given in to materialism." It may seem difficult to understand that a bright person would think of this concretely. Yet, the vast majority of Evangelicals would and do. They literally mean, "God changed my heart." They literally mean, "God washed away my resentment." They literally mean, "God instilled a passion in me." Even the brightest Evangelicals will often make concrete statements like my friend did.

This feature makes it difficult to use language for its standard purpose of social communication. Conversation depends on its participants being able to supply meaning to the words spoken by each other. If one party in a conversation uses a word in a way that has a private meaning unknown to the others, communication does not necessarily take place. The speaker may believe the conversation is about one thing while her listeners may believe it is about something else.

Evangelical Christians following Paul's examples use words that at least initially seem to be words used in standard exchanges among reasonable, literate adults; words like "confess" and "forgive." As I explain in more detail in the next chapter, when examined closely, these words, as used in the Evangelical community, have a startlingly different meaning than they do in the world at large.

(3) Paranoid Delusional Systems

This is not all that sets the paranoid schizophrenic apart. The schizophrenic has a fairly well-formed, coherent delusional system. By delusions, I mean, "false ideas that are not correctable by reasoning."[16] Paranoid schizophrenic delusions differ from many other kinds of delusions.*

Because his or her delusional system has well-formed and seemingly coherent elements, a paranoid schizophrenic does not necessarily sound too crazy. As the *DSM-IV-TR*, the standard diagnostic text of the mental health profession, notes, a paranoid schizophrenic *does not exhibit the disorganized speech or behavior* of other schizophrenics. This does not mean that their beliefs are less delusional, only that within the bounds of the delusion the system has a certain logic that often appears to hang together well.

Paul shares this trait with schizophrenics. This trait may create a much greater barrier to understanding and communicating with a person absorbed in a delusional world than many outside that world realize.

Again, consider this about Paul: although his letters are ostensibly about Jesus, Paul did not seem to care at all about the actual person. If we tried to describe Jesus using only Paul's letters, we would have next to nothing to go on. Paul's thoughts had a paucity of content—another common feature of paranoid schizophrenia[17]—outside of his otherworldly system.

Before moving on, let us clear up and dispel any notion that most of us will ever fully comprehend what Paul or a paranoid schizophrenic may think based on what they tell us. We need to consider how we may

---

* These ideas are sometimes described as "unfixable" because they cannot be "fixed" through rational discussion or persuasion. We will discuss these "unfixable" ideas later.

overlay our own otherworldly thoughts onto people with a greater capacity to detach their thoughts from our shared world.

For example, imagine that it is your grandfather's birthday, but he died five years ago. Suppose you remember him fondly as a happy old man who made everyone laugh. Even people who do not believe in an afterlife will at times think about loved ones as if they still existed—perhaps in heaven. Most of us would imagine our grandfathers looking and acting just as they did when alive. Though we may imagine a few rough edges smoothed over, grandpa in our imaginations still looks and acts as grandpa did when alive. We may imagine him going up to St. Peter with his mischievous grin, the same one he wore on his birthday ten years ago, and say, "Pull on my finger, St. Peter." Indeed, many of us cannot create a mental picture of grandpa that looks or acts significantly different than he did when alive. Moreover, many of us will resist thinking of someone in a way that runs counter to how we perceived that person in *real* experiences and *real* memories. Most people, by far, will imagine a spiritual world that seamlessly integrates with our physical world. As a result, we may assume incorrectly that we understand people like the Apostle Paul.

The Apostle Paul, who expressed plainly that he had no interest in attaching worldly characteristics to the characters in his spiritual world, may not have had the same limitations a *normal* person has. Yet, because *normal* people have no frame of reference for understanding ideas detached too far from reality, they assume that the expounder of these ideas has an understanding or is part of a social dynamic that may not exist. Simply put, even people that we may consider "way off base" yet still within the wide bounds of *normal* still often have unmistakably hinged their otherworldly ideas to common perceptions. For instance, many people read the book of Revelation as a history book. They read it as a history of the future not the past. Many people, including me, consider this way off base. Nevertheless, we may see a picture these people have made of Jesus' second coming. We might see Jesus mounted on a massive white horse with a regal crest on the chest of his garments and holding a Bible in the air. Despite this triumphant Jesus having little in common with Jesus of the Gospels, more often than not, he has first-century clerical robes, sandals, long hair, and a beard. Perhaps—in graphic renderings of Jesus—we may even find stigmata of Jesus' crucifixion on his forehead, hands, and feet. Despite Jesus' extreme makeover, we still recognize the Jesus of the Gospels. Given that people who we may consider way off base retain characteristics of our shared perceptions in their fantasy worlds, we naturally assume that someone like Paul does this as well.

Have we assumed too much about Paul and his Christ?

Imagine for a moment that one of your friends writes you a twenty-page letter passionately wanting to share her excitement about a new teacher. This letter has only one topic—your friend's new teacher. At the end of her letter, you still do not know one thing about her teacher. Yet, Paul presents the central figure of his theology this way. In fact, Paul kindly tells us he could not care less about Jesus, the man from Galilee, writing:

> So from now on we regard no one from a worldly point of view. Though we once regarded Christ in this way, we do so no longer (2 Cor 5:16 NIV).

For those of us not lost in a world of delusions, it might seem impossible to imagine how Paul could avoid telling one story or parable of—or fail to note one physical trait or personal quality of—Jesus. Nevertheless, Paul's lack of interest in or even curiosity about the life of Jesus fits a characteristic pattern of paranoid delusions. A person consumed with his or her delusions has little energy for thoughts devoted to other subjects. Rational people, having had the transformative encounter with Christ that Paul describes, might enjoy learning everything they could about him. They might want to walk where Jesus walked. They might want to meet Jesus' friends and family. Not Paul—he tells us that he served Christ for seventeen years before seeking out Jesus' disciples in Jerusalem aside from Peter and James, the brother of Jesus.[18] He writes emphatically that he had nothing to learn from them.

Through his delusions, Paul already knew everything he wanted to know about Jesus, a man he never met. Did Paul's Christ have pierced hands? Did he wear a robe and have long hair? Did he resemble a man at all? Did Paul's Christ like to fish? We do not know. Paul never—ever—told us! As well, based on the verses we reviewed, along with Paul's claims that *all Christians make up Christ's body*, Paul did not seem to think of Jesus as a man from Galilee. Indeed, some will recognize Paul's claim to fellow Christians where he wrote, "Now you are the body of Christ, and each one of you is a part of it" (1 Cor 12:27 NIV). We may assume too much if we take for granted that Paul thinks of Jesus in a way that even remotely resembles the man from Galilee.

It is possible for us to contemplate facts about the life of Jesus. For example, many people doubt that Jesus had a virgin mother. Since the details of Jesus' life have a real-world historical context, we can attempt to confirm those details in some way. In fact, many, if not most, Evangelical apologetics are dedicated to sifting through the available historical facts about first-century Palestine and the culture and the habits of persons living in that time and place.

However, we cannot do that with Paul's Jesus. Paul has detached himself so much from the reality of Jesus' earthly life that the object of his delusions, Jesus, takes on a new name—Christ. Paul describes "Christ" in his letters with passion. He describes that he has given Christ complete control of his body to the point where he, Paul, has died. After his death, and after his new life in Christ, he takes on the qualities and powers of Christ. By "Christ," Paul refers to the entity from his delusions that took control of his life.

Every claim in the Gospels about Jesus could prove accurate, but that would not alter one thing about Paul's claims about his Christ. Even if Jesus lived and then died on a cross, we should feel confident that the Apostle Paul had nothing to do with him. Paul's Christ has next to nothing in common with Jesus—except his death on a cross. Paul's claims about Christ do not contain information based in reality, and regardless of whether the Gospel stories truly happened, Paul's letters would still only represent his own musings. This is a good example of a "coherent, well-formed delusional world" with "ideas that are not correctable by reasoning."

(4) Delusions of Grandeur and Magical Thinking

The delusional systems of schizophrenics differ in particulars but share certain characteristics. Such systems "tend to be grandiose, in that the patient believes himself to be special, to be powerful, often to be magical. The other side of the coin is intense mistrust of others—since he is so important; his enemies are trying to harm him."[19] As well, the group labeled paranoid schizophrenics "includes people who consistently believe that they have a different identity from their real one, who believe that they have a function that they do not have, or who believe that other people are plotting to harm them."[20]

The first chapter of Paul's letter to the Roman Church, which I quoted extensively above, provides a good example of this aspect of magical thinking. We have seen that Paul believes that because Christ controls his body he can know the thoughts and feelings of others (Rom

1:18–32). He can know God's thoughts and has taken on the power and authority of God and Christ. Because of this, the enemies of God and Christ became his enemies as well, and they were "given over" to every form of depravity and wickedness. Paul tells his readers in other places that their enemies—who are God's enemies as well—are both evil and strong. As he famously put it:

> For we wrestle not against flesh and blood, but against principalities, against powers, against the rulers of the darkness of this world, against spiritual wickedness in high places (Eph 6:12 KJV).

Paul quite plainly attributes his knowledge of Christ to visions and revelation, not facts. For example, he writes:

> I want you to know, brothers, that the gospel I preached is not something that man made up. I did not receive it from any man, nor was I taught it; rather, I received it by revelation from Jesus Christ …
>
> I did not consult any man, nor did I go up to Jerusalem to see those who were apostles before I was, but I went immediately into Arabia and later returned to Damascus (Gal 1:11–12, 16–17 NIV).

Or again:

> I must go on boasting. Although there is nothing to be gained, I will go on to visions and revelations from the Lord. I know a man in Christ who fourteen years ago was caught up to the third heaven. Whether it was in the body or out of the body I do not know—God knows. And I know that this man—whether in the body or apart from the body I do not know, but God knows—was caught up to paradise. He heard inexpressible things, things that man is not permitted to tell (2 Cor 12:1–4 NIV).

Paul did not distinguish facts from his visions. We have seen before that Paul knew that other people had rejected God because God's invisible qualities were "clearly seen." Paul expected his readers to accept that he had seen Christ in the same way they saw a tree, a fence, or any other object. For Paul, Christ became a clearly visible part of the universe. Even though Evangelicals do not have visions, they follow Paul and accept Christ as a clearly visible part of the universe.

Evangelical Beliefs of Grandeur and Magical Thinking

Let us now turn to beliefs held by modern-day Evangelical Christians that share some of the characteristics outlined previously. We have discussed some of those, such as the belief that human beings are toxic and worthless, and we will revisit that idea in the following chapter. How would we characterize other Evangelical spiritual beliefs?

First, Evangelicals have an elaborate and coherent spiritual world. Evangelicals share a belief in a spiritual society. Led by God, some will end up in the good neighborhood. Lost souls will end up in the bad neighborhood. However, while we live on earth, we cannot go and visit these neighborhoods or even confirm their existence. As we have seen, a well-formed and coherent delusional system defines paranoid schizophrenia. If untreated, paranoid schizophrenics will insist their beliefs have as much basis in reality as anything else. Just as we cannot examine the Evangelical's spiritual neighborhoods, we cannot examine a schizophrenic's delusional neighborhood to see if it really exists.

Next, this vision of the world comes with a special role for Evangelical Christians. They often believe, as Paul did, that God chose them for a special purpose and that their lives are "purpose driven." Having God personally enlist your services would make you very special. Having God call you to serve him would seem awesome. As well, assignments from God clearly qualify as important and special. Many Evangelicals perceive that God called them to fight against his enemies—what could be more important and special than that?

There is also a magical element to many Evangelical beliefs. I am not just talking about believing, for example, that Jesus walked on the Sea of Galilee or fed a multitude with five loaves of bread and two fish. I refer to Paul's belief that through the power of God he could know the thoughts of others. This allowed Paul to recognize that others had willfully rejected God's "clearly visible" qualities, defied his "righteous decrees," and had become filled with evil as a result. Paul understood that he had to fight against God's enemies, who were very powerful and "not of flesh and blood." Some Evangelicals similarly believe that God has given them abilities to identify false prophets or evil that threatens God's kingdom.

You can hear both of these elements in action when, for example, Evangelicals use the word "agenda," claiming to have insight into the homosexual agenda, the liberal agenda, the communist agenda, the atheist agenda, or the abortionist agenda (to name a few of God's enemies). Ascribing an agenda to a group of people they do not know not only requires the magical ability to channel their thoughts somehow; it also gives the enemy the appearance of greater power and organization than they would otherwise seemingly have and thus gives the Evangelical Christian a more important role as well. A suburban mother of two who votes a Democratic party ticket might not seem a very imposing foe, but if she schemes to propagate the liberal agenda, she clearly has more on her mind than her daughter's basketball practice. Further, when talking about the enemy's agendas, Evangelicals usually express no interest in confirming their beliefs about what these other people might be thinking with any evidence. In fact, they often will quote a passage like Romans 1:18–2:1* as biblical evidence that supports their view of human behavior.

Calling these beliefs grandiose seems fair, and it is fair to say that they have a magical or supernatural aspect as well. Similarly, paranoid schizophrenics—who receive guidance from beings other people cannot talk to or see—often think that someone chose them for special assignments. As well, paranoid schizophrenics often believe that they have evil and powerful enemies who plot against them—this feature provides the label "paranoid" in paranoid schizophrenic.

Let us try a thought experiment. Assume that we do not know whether the Evangelical God exists. Believers cannot demonstrate the reality of their claims—they do not have any better proof than does a man who claims he talks to Elvis. Their claims have no more validity than a man who says he just returned from an alien spacecraft. They have no more evidence than a man who channels his dead uncle. How are the spiritual neighborhoods of the Evangelical afterlife any different from those of the paranoid schizophrenic's delusion? How do the Evangelical beliefs—that God called them to combat his enemies—differ from the paranoid schizophrenic's belief that Elvis has revealed special assignments? If the Evangelical God does not exist—or even if we do not know whether the Evangelical God exists—then there is very little to distinguish the two sets of believers.

One difference, which we will build on throughout the book, concerns the difference between a typical Evangelical's sense of self and a typical paranoid schizophrenic's sense of self. We can easily understand how feeling worthless, toxic, and as good as dead might make fantasies of

---

* This passage is printed earlier in this chapter in the section, "Paul the Mind-Reader."

living with knowledge and power in another world appealing. Paul seems to have retreated into another world. He wanted no part of this world.

Evangelicals seem different, however. To be sure, they often become born-again during a low point in their lives. However, they do not see this as retreating from the world. Rather, they often view their conversion as confirmation that they have not lost their "mojo"—they have the smarts to see the clear truths of the Bible. As well, it often seems clear to them—as it seemed to me also—that they had it together all along. Rather than retreat, conversion often gives people a sense that they are *winners*. Now that they have joined the winning team, they have *less* desire to retreat and *more* desire to get back into the game.

Evangelicals often view their decision to pledge as a member of the Evangelical community and say the "Sinner's Prayer" as a smart choice. Add in eternal life as a bonus for pledging and the decision seems like a no-brainer.

In a sense, Evangelicals have made a smart choice by placing a heavy emphasis on Paul's doctrines and reasoning. After all, these smart Christians have accepted as truth a complex otherworldly set of beliefs. The vast majority make this decision quickly and with minimal or no reflection, just as I did. Accepting this belief as a good and correct choice, however, will not help when the honeymoon is over and things stop looking as clear as they did before. Paul helps with these crises of faith that many Evangelicals experience.

Evangelicals treat Paul—who uses paranoid schizophrenic reasoning in his letters—as an unassailable expert concerning their otherworldly beliefs. This unlikely marriage proves auspicious for Evangelicals. Simply put, we could think of paranoid schizophrenics as experts at maintaining complex otherworldly beliefs over long periods. Evangelicals lean very heavily on the schizophrenic-like reasoning style of the Apostle Paul.

Yet, while Paul had many traits and behaviors in common with paranoid schizophrenics, most Evangelical Christians do not. Undoubtedly, Evangelicals often use Paul's reasoning and explanations, but they use it differently than Paul did. Nevertheless, they remain faithful to Paul's Christ, even though they may not win any Oscars for convincingly acting like the Apostle Paul. In a way, adopting Pauline thinking comes with an extra credit reward. By remaining true to the disordered thinking of Paul, Evangelicals can misinterpret the evidence we have of the low attrition rate from Evangelical Christianity. They can conclude that this evidence further proves that they have it right—with little regard that others may find this conclusion unsupported by the evidence. They can dismiss the reasoning of nonbelievers entirely. With the disordered reasoning of Paul entrenched firmly, *only other Evangelical Christians have the privilege to determine truth.*

Unfixable Beliefs

Evangelicals, therefore, share with paranoid schizophrenics what psychiatrists call "unfixable beliefs." By "unfixable," I mean that any fallacies in the beliefs cannot be repaired. Let me give an example of a "fixable" belief. All of us have had delusions like believing in Santa Claus at some point. As children, many of our Santa delusions came complete with snow, reindeer, sleds, chimneys, and neatly wrapped gifts. Despite having these delusions, however, we eventually realized we had *false* beliefs. We learned new things and improved our judgments. We realized that Santa does not fit into our real world. We stopped believing Santa exists. Our belief was fixed.

In contrast, Evangelicals tend to remain unshakable in their faulty beliefs. As mentioned, Evangelicals have a remarkably low dropout rate. Indeed, it seems that heavily involved Evangelicals like pastors rarely leave the faith. After about five to ten years of heavy involvement, almost nobody leaves Evangelical Christianity. As well, people rarely become significantly less involved after significant involvement.

Consider this: What would it take to "fix" Evangelical beliefs? Let's try another thought experiment. Suppose we meet a schizophrenic man who claims Elvis speaks with him through his music. He tells us that Elvis told him—and therefore he knows—that the Dixie Chicks followed Jesus two thousand years ago in Galilee. Suppose we desired to persuade him that his claims contradicted the evidence. Where would we start? We know his mind has detached from reality somewhere in order to believe his delusion. Can we have any confidence that evidence will have any impact on his delusional thinking? What type of evidence, if any, might he find persuasive? If we brought the Dixie Chicks to visit him and explain that he was wrong, would he believe them? We have no idea how to frame this debate or hinge it to reality in a way that will reliably persuade this man.

Nonbelievers face much the same struggle with Evangelical Christians. Where do we begin? With carbon dating? With newly discovered manuscripts? With a catalog of inconsistencies within the

Bible? With improved translations? With personal testimony? I think not.

Does that make Evangelical beliefs unfixable? Yes, even though Evangelicals do not consider their beliefs unfixable because they see no need to fix them. But then, neither does the man who believes the Dixie Chicks lived two thousand years ago.

So: Evangelicals and paranoid schizophrenics have long-term beliefs in complex yet coherent systems with special roles, powers, and assignments that lie outside the physical world. Both hold beliefs that we cannot verify. Both hold unfixable beliefs. With Evangelicals, the rules of Hooks and Ladders ensure that their members' beliefs cannot change. Those who fix their beliefs, lose—as the rules clearly describe. As a result, Evangelicals and paranoid schizophrenics both display a remarkable resistance to changing their beliefs by reasoning.

Evangelical Autism

One Evangelical characteristic, though similar, slightly differs from the paranoid schizophrenic pattern. Many Evangelicals have a natural tendency toward autistic thinking. Realistically, this implies something different from the autistic thinking as classically described in schizophrenia.

Childhood autism has many complex characteristics that differ from traits of schizophrenic autism. What I refer to in regards to Evangelicals, in contrast, follows the classic description of autism as a trait and goes something like this:

> Abe is autistic. Abe, Bob, and Carl sit in the same room. Abe puts his toy truck in the toy box and shuts it. Bob leaves the room. Carl takes Abe's truck out of the box. Carl shuts the box and puts Abe's truck on a shelf. Bob comes back in the room and looks for Abe's truck in the toy box. Abe, being autistic, has no clue that Bob is unaware that Carl removed the truck from the box.

It seems that an autistic person's brain does not process information in a way allowing them to see things from another person's perspective. Essentially, they lack empathy. In the same way, Evangelicals have no idea when they say "Jesus" that others do not know that they have taken Jesus *out of the box*. Evangelicals have no clue that others do not know they do not mean the man from Galilee but rather the Jesus megastar Bible-God of their internal perceptions. This aspect of autism, which seems associated with a strong tendency to think concretely, causes serious communication problems with those outside the Evangelical community.

In schizophrenia, autism does not begin at birth or in early childhood necessarily. Rather, it describes a withdrawal from or loss of vital contact with the external world. Eugene Minkowski, perhaps the most influential man to characterize schizophrenia, describes this in his classic book *La schizophrénie.* He describes the loss of vital contact as the essence of schizophrenic autism. He considers this phenomenon the *trouble genérateur*—the initial trouble that generates schizophrenia.[21]

Schizophrenics become autistic, or significantly more autistic, as they lose contact with the external world and retreat into their delusional world. Someone inclined to have innate autistic traits, however, does not necessarily retreat from the external world. Rather, they often clearly see their spiritual world as real. They see this as accepting the truth of the real world.

Examples of this type of autistic thinking abound from Evangelicals. Perhaps the most common and most striking example is manifested in the way they see the Bible. Evangelicals seem to naturally embrace the following sentiment from Paul's letter to the Romans, which I have quoted several times before:

> For since the creation of the world God's invisible qualities—his eternal power and divine nature—have been clearly seen, being understood from what has been made, so that men are without excuse (Rom 1:20 NIV).

Many Evangelicals seem to decide, even before they become born-again, that they can clearly see that the Bible contains God's message to the world. They can clearly see that the Bible makes sense. From that day forward, it seems that many Evangelicals have no idea that others may not clearly see what they clearly see. Much like an autistic child, many Evangelicals seem to lack the capacity to comprehend that others do not view the Bible the same way they do. They seem comfortable thinking that all could clearly see what Evangelicals see if they opened their eyes to the truth. They seem comfortable believing that nonbelievers who have read the Bible must have lied or blocked out the true message of the Bible. In contrast to the often-disingenuous way they might say, "I know I am a worthless sinner," Evangelicals rarely seem anything but sincere when they say, "God tells us in his Word ..." They will often say something like this to an atheist, seemingly oblivious that an atheist does not believe the Bible is the word of God.

I have had many frustrating discussions with Evangelicals that include autistic thinking. Many Evangelicals seem to have difficulty comprehending that others do not see what they see. In fact, most Evangelicals with whom I discuss Christianity know that I do not believe God had anything to do with writing the Bible. Despite that, I have had conversations too many times to count that included something similar to this exchange:

Believer: "God explains to us in Ephesians that salvation comes through faith—and not works."

Billy: "I do not believe God said that."

Believer: "I thought you said you used to be a Christian. You must have heard Ephesians 2:8–9."

Billy: "I merely said that I do not believe God said that."

Believer: "I can show you that verse and prove it to you. I have my Bible with me. Do you have some crazy way of interpreting God's word differently—from ancient Greek? Did you figure out some way to twist the meaning, as you did when you claimed Paul called himself an abortion?"

Billy: "No, I simply do not believe that God had anything to do with writing Ephesians."

Believer: "I *never* said God wrote Ephesians—Paul wrote Ephesians—God inspired him. You are putting words into my mouth."

Billy: "You did say that, 'God explains to us in Ephesians'—and I merely told you I do not believe God had anything to do with the writing of Ephesians. If you had said, 'Paul explains to us in Ephesians,' I would agree with you. Do you know that I do not believe God had anything to do with writing any book in the Bible?"

Believer: "Come on, Billy! You just want to pick a fight. Stop acting like a jerk."

Far too many Evangelicals, like the believer who discussed the Bible with me, seem incapable of comprehending that others do not see things as they see them. They seem to truly believe that others actually do see things the same way they do. They seem to truly believe that others purposely choose to reject what they see. They seem to truly believe that some infidels go to great length to ignore what they see and rationalize away the truth of God's Word. They think non-Christians are just acting like jerks.

Hooks and Ladders Revisited

What does any of this have to do with the game of Hooks and Ladders? To sum up the previous sections, Paul's lack of identity and sense of utter worthlessness made him long to have Christ inhabit and control him. After ceding control to Christ, Paul became perfect. He cannot sin, he shares with the Almighty the ability to know others' thoughts, and God speaks through him. Thus, in Paul's mind, if someone rejects his theology that person has rejected the Creator. For Paul said in his letter to the Romans: "What may be known about God is plain … Since the creation of the world God's invisible qualities—his eternal power and divine nature—have been clearly seen" (Rom 1:19–20 NIV). Any condemnation of Paul or God must be willful and evil. Only those who recognize God's power and authority and who have given over their identity to God know the truth are pure—everyone else continues to exist as corrupt and toxic, as Paul had been before Christ took control.

Most Evangelical Christians, following Paul's example, believe they have an indwelling spirit that allows them to receive messages from God, as in the HOLYSPIRIT plug-in I described earlier. In essence, this spirit allows them to download messages from God properly and without corruption. They believe that only those who receive these downloaded messages can properly understand the Bible and the truth of the world around them. They believe that they are controlled by God and that they have an important role to play in fighting God's powerful enemies—enemies who are not controlled by God and reject his clearly seen truths.

With these beliefs girding Evangelical Christianity, it is not at all surprising that the rules of Hooks and Ladders developed as they did. Those controlled by Christ and guided by an indwelling Holy Spirit win. Those who have willfully ignored the truth deserve to lose. Now we have made our way back to familiar territory.

3. Becoming an Evangelical Christian

LET US RETURN TO THE PERSON who decided to say the "Sinner's Prayer" and accept Jesus as Lord and Savior. The soon-to-be born-again Christian usually has no idea of what will happen. The "unsaved" person will go through a step-by-step process that mirrors the schizophrenic processes described previously. In order to become saved, one must express feelings in common with people who lack a sense of self. Virtually all American Evangelical Christians take identity-shedding steps on the road to conversion. After all, if I believed Paul spoke for God, why would I want to hold onto the toxic, sinful nature of the old me when I could have a new, Christ-like nature? Why not leave the toxic, sinful nature behind and become born-again? Let us review the steps taken in the spiritual delivery room.

Step One: Problems with Confession

Earlier, I pointed out that almost all new converts to born-again Christianity recite a prayer that starts with admitting one's sins and making a confession. I gave a couple of examples, but how does this confessional prayer compare to a real confession? Imagine, for example, a man charged with cheating on a math test and then lying to his mother about it. We all know these observations to reflect reality:

- This man could never plead guilty to these crimes if he thought his confession would put him at risk of prolonged torture and death.
- If this man ever did confess, he would do so only after assurance that he would suffer little or no punishment.
- A true confession—where the confessor truly believed he should face torture and death for his deeds—would almost certainly provoke a tremendous outpouring of emotion.

Do people in real life confess minor transgressions and accept harsh punishment for them? For example, would the man confess to cheating on his math test if he faced eternal torture for cheating? Most would consider it excessive to sentence someone to a year in a prison for cheating on a math test. Most people reciting the "Sinner's Prayer" do not honestly believe they deserve a sentence of eternal torture for their transgressions, yet Evangelical Christianity requires them to believe that they do. So the first step to becoming born-again has unhinged from recognizable truths in the rest of the world.

Evangelicals may protest and point out that since Almighty God knows everything, a person cannot gain by denying guilt. Unfortunately, this does not alter the falseness of this typical born-again confession. With an omniscient God, the act of confessing one's sins becomes just that—an act! Confessing sins becomes pointless and phony.

Imagine a boy taking a cookie out of the cookie jar. His mother had forbidden him from taking a cookie. The boy does not know his mother sees him from another room. Now imagine him turning, cookie in hand, and seeing his mother, who says, "Son, confess that you wrongly took a cookie and I will not spank you." If he refuses to confess under these circumstances, his receiving a spanking may almost seem deserving since he has added foolishness to his guilt. However, by going through the act of confession, he can avoid a spanking.

To make matters worse, new converts do not believe God will do what born-again Christians claim he will do. For example, imagine four soldiers in the same foxhole in a fierce firestorm, one Catholic, one Mormon, one Muslim, and one who resisted the appeals of the other three to join their groups. Assume the three religious soldiers each say a similar prayer just before being annihilated by a grenade. They say, "Dear God, Creator of the Universe, I know I have let you down and sinned. I know I don't deserve forgiveness, but I pray you will forgive me." Let us further assume the unaffiliated soldier covered his bases—since allegedly, there are no atheists in foxholes. He started his prayer like this: "Dear God and Creator of the Universe, I admit I don't know which of my religious friends is right ..." Which of these four soldiers will God forgive, if any?

Most Evangelicals teach that God will not forgive any of these soldiers unless they asked Jesus to become their personal savior! In other words, Evangelicals do not actually believe God will do as the Bible claims, "If we confess our sins, he is faithful and just to forgive us our sins, and to cleanse us from all unrighteousness" (1 John 1:9 KJV).

Or, consider a man who committed murder walking into a courtroom and confessing to the judge that he murdered someone. He pleads for forgiveness and mercy. He expresses understanding that he deserves the death penalty for his murder. Imagine a judge telling him his confession did not count because he told the wrong judge! Furthermore, his confession will not stand because the judge hearing his confession was an activist Democrat! Despite how ridiculous this scenario already seems, we cannot stop here. Next, let us imagine the murderer now realizes he confessed to the wrong judge—as presumably people with *false gods* will realize when they meet the *true god* after they die—and says to the right judge, "Oops! I am truly sorry, Your Honor. I honestly did not know I confessed to the wrong judge. But regardless of who presides over my case, I freely confess and ask for forgiveness and mercy."

Now imagine the judge saying, "Sorry, buddy, your confession does not count in my courtroom anymore. You cannot plead for mercy now!"

What relevance can we ascertain from the "Sinner's Prayer" confession? After all, many people of many faiths pray to their gods and confess their sins. Do they receive forgiveness? For the most part, Evangelicals believe these people do not receive forgiveness. As a result, confession of sins has far less relevance than confessing to the correct god. That is the Evangelical position as expressed in Rule 1—*Evangelical Christians always win*. What happens to everyone else? They lose.

Of course, we have much more to deal with concerning this confession. Remarkably, Evangelicals claim we cannot avoid sin. They say we cannot separate sin from who we are. Nevertheless, despite having no power to avoid sin, the confessing sinner has to claim personal responsibility for his or her sin.

Some might argue these two claims contradict each other. For example, imagine a schoolboy whose father holds him down every morning to put on black-soled shoes with laces that the father ties with knots that the boy cannot remove. The father does this even on days he knows his son has gym class where the school forbids boys from wearing black-soled shoes with laces. If the gym teacher asks the boy, "Do you accept the responsibility and punishment for wearing black-soled shoes to my gym class?" What would we think if this boy responded, "It is my full responsibility, teacher. After all, I know I cannot wear black-soled shoes. My father straps me down every morning. He ties these shoes to my feet. I am worthless. I cannot figure out how to untie the knots and remove my shoes?"

Can people avoid sinning? Evangelicals claim people cannot avoid sinning. Should we feel guilty about things we cannot avoid? Could expressing guilt in something we cannot fix have moral implications? For example, why do we not acknowledge guilt and responsibility for our unavoidable skin color?

Let us go back to the example of the man who cheated on his math test and lied to his mother about it. Imagine him saying, "I had no control of my head and hand when I looked at my neighbor's paper and copied her answers onto my test. Therefore, I readily accept thy just punishment in the form of eternal torture." This adds another layer of incredibility to an already incredible confession. By accepting the belief that he deserves eternal damnation for an unfixable, sinful nature, he does not merely accept that this applies only to him. He must believe that *everyone's* core essence has no worth. He must believe that nobody can avoid corruption and that everybody deserves annihilation. But if he did not believe he would escape annihilation, it seems unlikely that he would accept this bleak view of human nature so easily.

At best, we might consider this confession on the road to salvation as a plea bargain. Quite simply, if God did not hand out tickets to heaven to people who confessed their sins, I doubt most born-again Christians would believe that their sins deserved eternal torture as just punishment.

Step Two: Problems with Forgiveness

After confessing their sins, new converts ask God to forgive them their sins. "Your word tells us, 'If we confess our sins, he is faithful and just to forgive us our sins, and to cleanse us from all unrighteousness.'" In this step, the sinner and the forgiver occupy the same delusional universe inside the same brain. The new convert assumes magical powers and authority not evident in our shared world. Furthermore, the person relinquishes his or her own identity and becomes merely an actor specially chosen by God, who controls all. The person stops feeling responsible for actions and behaviors that God allegedly controls.

Again, let us compare this Evangelical process of forgiveness to forgiveness in the real world. Let us say a boy named Johnny walks up near Bob and punches him very hard in the gut, making Bob vomit. After punching Bob, Johnny walks away. A few years later, Bob sees Johnny park his car. On the rear bumper of Johnny's car, Bob sees a bumper sticker that reads:

Christians aren't Perfect, Just Forgiven!

Somewhat shocked but a little amused, Bob musters the courage to confront Johnny. Bob asks, "Do you remember punching me in the gut a few years ago?"

We could anticipate a number of responses where Johnny accepts ownership and responsibility for his actions. For example, Johnny might say, "Yeah, I remember! You had just insulted my friend. You deserved worse than a punch in the gut." Alternatively, Johnny might say something like, "I sure do remember. I am *truly sorry* about that incident. Is there anything I can do to earn your forgiveness?"

Let us imagine Johnny asking for forgiveness as in the second answer. Bob decides and replies, "Yes, Johnny, I can forgive you and feel confident you are reformed if you remove that bumper sticker from your car."

Johnny protests, "But the sticker is true. I am now a Christian, a new person. God has forgiven my sins and changed my life."

Bob says, "Johnny, the sticker suggests you have delusional thinking. First, no one expects you to come remotely close to perfect, which your sticker implies. I would settle for less violent and creepy. Second, when you put the sticker on your car, I had not forgiven you! Your sticker is a lie!"

Johnny again protests, "It is not a lie. I confessed my sins to God in the name of Jesus, and he forgave me. If God has forgiven me, who are you to say I am not forgiven?" Has Johnny lied by placing the bumper sticker on his car, as Bob said?

Picture a little girl named Maggie going into an empty broom closet with a pair of scissors. She comes out twenty minutes later with her previously long hair cut jaggedly. Maggie says, "I cut my hair, but I only cut it because my imaginary friend, Lulu, told me to cut it. Lulu said it would look better cut. Lulu never lies. You cannot criticize my hair without criticizing Lulu. Only fools say in their heart Lulu does not exist."

Even though Maggie accepts that she physically cut her own hair, she claims that others should consider Lulu responsible. Lulu told her to cut her hair, and conveniently, Lulu has perfect judgment. In this example, it seems clear what might motivate Maggie to claim Lulu told her to cut her hair. After all, Lulu has special powers and characteristics that limit criticism of Maggie's actions. If Maggie's parents accept Lulu's existence, Maggie benefits. Even if her parents do not accept that "Lulu never lies," her parents may curse and malign Lulu's advice. This also benefits Maggie because she still escapes direct responsibility for her actions.

Even though Maggie—alone in the closet—claims ownership of her actions, she does not claim *Maggie* made the decision to cut *Maggie's* hair.

Thus, Lulu assumes responsibility as the agent directing Maggie's actions. However, if Lulu's competence and authority fail to earn respect, Maggie will have to answer questions like, "Why did you listen to your foolish friend Lulu?"

For the soon-to-be born-again Christian, God assumes responsibility for new converts. Indeed, we can easily imagine someone reciting the "Sinner's Prayer" alone in a closet like Maggie. When they come out, they likely believe that God forgave their sins. This transfer of agency seems so powerful that most Evangelicals seem confused when asked, "Given that you went into the closet alone, why do you think that anyone forgave you of anything?" The belief that God assumes responsibility for someone's beliefs and actions seems almost too obvious to recognize. For example, consider the abundance of common Evangelical sayings expressing relief in the ability to transfer agency to God. A few examples are:

- Lay your sins at the foot of the cross.
- What a friend we have in Jesus, all our sins and griefs to bear.
- Therefore, go and make disciples of all nations, baptizing them in the name of the father and of the son and of the Holy Spirit, and teaching them to obey everything I have commanded you.*

Evangelical Christians believe that God has real presence and performs real actions—100 percent of them. With ease and totality, Evangelicals relinquish their sense of responsibility. God assumes responsibility for their actions. They believe actions done in "service to the Lord" have immunity from common morals and laws. In their minds, they have *zero* personal responsibility for actions performed under the direction of their god.

Let us go back to the example of Johnny and Bob. Johnny, like many Evangelicals, flips back and forth between non-Evangelical thinking and Evangelical thinking. Nevertheless, when Johnny has his back up against a wall, he opts to give up control of his identity to his powerful friend, God. This is typical of many Evangelicals. They abandon their responsibility for their actions and take on the authority of their powerful friend. In the example, Johnny adopts God's authority and then gets to decide whether

* (Matt 28:19–20) This command is commonly called "The Great Commission."

he receives forgiveness. Johnny does not seem to realize that when he hit Bob in the gut, Bob retained the right to forgive Johnny.

Suppose that if Bob and Johnny cannot agree on a fair settlement, other people may help them settle a dispute. So, for example, if Bob says, "Let's go ask Dave if removing your sticker seems like a fair penalty for hitting me." Suppose Johnny agrees Dave will rule fairly, and Dave determines that Johnny should remove his sticker. Unless Johnny wants to appeal to other people, we usually consider this a valid and binding decision.

But Johnny's imaginary judge, God, has no utility for resolving disputes unless everyone agrees that he can do so. If Bob does not agree that Johnny's god can resolve the dispute, then Bob, in a sense, is not bound by God's decision as relayed by Johnny. In Hooks and Ladders, however, Bob must accept the decision. If he thinks he does not or demands some reason that he should, he has willfully rejected the truth and therefore loses. Bob's judgment does not count—unless he agrees with Johnny.

Bob called Johnny's sticker a lie. As lying hardly represents a Christian virtue, we might expect Johnny to take the charge of lying seriously. But if Johnny acts like a typical Evangelical, he will disregard the charge. He will probably remain oblivious that he has acted inconsistently.

Evangelicals detach themselves from ownership of the decision to forgive. They do not consider their feelings of forgiveness as a mental exercise or a state of mind. They view it as a real, otherworldly process that has real significance outside their own minds. For Evangelicals, when it comes to forgiveness, they claim, "God said it. I believe it. That settles it."

Evangelical forgiveness in this sense has lost value for social communication. For example, suppose a woman says, "Oh, I have wronged so many people in my years. I could never remember all of them. I could never make amends for all my sins. I am ashamed. I pray to God every day and ask him to forgive me. God knows my heart has changed, and I plead with him to remove the heavy burden I feel. I feel I can serve others more fully without such a heavy heart for my past sins." Here she uses *forgive* as a metaphor. This resonates with people and has value in social communication. She uses words like "heart," "burden," and even "God" metaphorically. She tries to convey that if we could see her thoughts and emotions, then we would realize she has changed. We would see a different attitude in her. Thus, this woman made her statement specifically to appeal to others for redemption. This person, in a sense, remains at the mercy of other people. She hopes others will accept her desire to feel forgiven as this will help her work more effectively in the future. She would probably find many people who were sympathetic to her plea. We usually accept forgiveness for wrongs a person cannot address directly.

However, Evangelicals do not use *forgive* metaphorically. Evangelicals do not have others in mind when they ask God for forgiveness. The Evangelical conception of forgiveness has virtually no social meaning—only personal. An Evangelical can go into a closet alone and ask God to forgive her. She can leave the closet thinking that God concretely erased her sins. Although she believes God commands her to sin no more, this also has no social context. This command remains strictly between her and God. The Evangelical meaning of forgiveness does not match any useful social definition of that word. As a result, Evangelicals do not feel obligated to gain forgiveness from others.*

In discussing unfixable ideas shared by Evangelical Christians, I described how many of us as American children believed in Santa Claus. Most children cannot think abstractly, and the use of words in an abstract or metaphorical way develops in most people (if at all) in their teen years. Children then cannot comprehend that adults may tell them about a make-believe person named Santa to add excitement to Christmas. It would not help to tell a child that adults use Santa's *Naughty and Nice* list as a metaphor and that Santa does not really have a list. Describing this to a child will do little to relieve her anxiety that Santa may have etched her name on the *Naughty* side of his list. Indeed, if the child thought Santa and Mommy disagreed about what "naughty" means, then too bad for Mommy! The child would probably care more about Santa's list.

Do Evangelicals use "forgive" in a concrete way? Yes, they do. Virtually every one of them will claim God concretely removed their sin from some sort of spiritual record book. They do not say when they ask God for forgiveness they feel *as if* God removed their sin from a record book. In the minds of Evangelicals, these become mental pictures. They

---

* This is not to say that Evangelicals never use the word "forgiveness" in a social way. For example, after the closet confession, the born-again Christian may seek redemption from others and may go and ask the many persons she has wronged for forgiveness. My point is that she does not have to do this to be "saved."

think of this in a tangible way. They often have a mental picture of God erasing their sins in the way children may have a mental picture of Santa Claus making his *Naughty-or-Nice* list.

In the same way that the child does not care what Mommy thinks about Santa's list, Evangelicals could not care less that others might not consider them forgiven. Like the child waiting for Santa at Christmas, Evangelicals concern themselves only with the list they imagine God keeps. This concrete thinking contributes greatly to Evangelicals' use of words in ways that have little or no value for social communication with people outside their community. To use a metaphor, it seems *as if* Evangelicals have no sense of what "as if" means.

The literalism inherited from Paul probably contributes to the use of forgiveness in this concrete sense. It is inherent in Hooks and Ladders.

Step Three: Problems with Accepting Jesus as Lord and Savior

Once the new converts have confessed their sins and asked God to forgive them, they accept the free gift of salvation and ask God to take control of their lives. There are many problems with this third part of the "Sinner's Prayer." Let us start with the concept of the "free gift."

When Is a Gift Free?

Let us revisit our friends Johnny and Bob. Johnny is the newly born-again Christian with the bumper sticker on his car.

Johnny: "Bob, I have this brand-new BMW car I want you to accept even though you don't deserve it."

Bob: "What happens if I decline your free gift to me, Johnny?"

Johnny: "If you decline my free gift, Bob, then I gouge your eyes out and feed them to hungry pigs, and I inflict you with continually festering sores over your entire body."

Bob: "Well, Johnny, that sure seems unpleasant. Tell me the catch. What are you going to expect me to do if I accept your supposedly free car?"

Johnny: "Well, Bob, I'll expect you to do everything I tell you to do. That's not so bad, though. You should *want* to do everything I tell you because I am a good guy."

Bob: "If I *have to do* everything you ask, how can you call this car a free gift?"

Johnny: "I didn't say you *have* to do everything I ask, I said you *will want to*."

Bob: "Well, you did say, Johnny, you would expect me to do everything you ask, which in my case would feel coerced as I'm quite confident that I do *not want* to do everything you tell me to do. Indeed, calling that car a gift and free seems manipulative."

Johnny: "You cannot call me manipulative because I am Johnny, and I make all the rules and decide all the definitions since you are essentially worthless, cowardly, empty, and dead. Even though you have free will, you need my will in order to even have a will."

Bob: "So let's get this straight. I have to choose between two options. However, you give me no choice. You tell me I have only enough will left in my worthless body to choose to die. If I choose to accept your gift, I cease existing. You have complete control over my abandoned corpse. Indeed, you claim I only have enough 'me' left to want you to be 'me' forever!"

At this point, Bob realizes Johnny has engaged him in a discussion of theology, not just a new BMW. Bob walks away in disgust. Johnny shakes his head, thinking, "Another person who willfully rejected a free gift. How can people be so blind?"

Let us look at the requirements for the free gift of salvation in Evangelical Christianity. Evangelicals believe they must give over complete control of their lives to Jesus. How could someone give up complete control of something and not consider that to be a cost of the gift? How could they consider it a gift at all? Why do they not consider this a deal or an exchange?

We have seen how Paul felt about this. He believed he had a toxic essence, no identity or self other than a worthless, sinful nature. He felt his very essence (what he and Evangelicals call "sin nature") gave him a negative value. He was better off dead, because with death he at least stopped corrupting things as he was under the control of sin. Because Paul felt this way, it is not surprising that he felt he gave up nothing by giving up control of his life. Only if a person lacks a sense of personal value could they conceive of this deal as a free gift.

For Evangelicals to make any logical sense of believing they received a free gift, they must think they do not own their own life. This logic does not work if a person simply thinks of life as miserable. People who feel they have a miserable existence may gladly give up their life for an eternal life of bliss. However, this constitutes an exchange, not a gift. Someone has to consider the value of their life as zero or negative to consider giving up control of their life a gift.

Let us evaluate this in real-world terms. The actions, behaviors, and relationships of people who believe they have no worth and a toxic essence can never result in a positive outcome. As a result, people that believe this way might draft a particular time during a person's life this way:

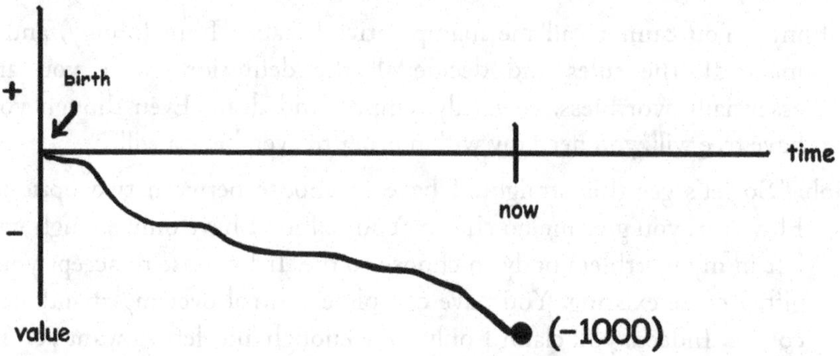

Evangelicals who believe everyone, apart from God, has a toxic sin nature consider that an unbeliever's life has a net negative value in a way that the above graph portrays. Let us assign the man represented by the graph an arbitrary number to denote his value, like –1000. If this man gives over control of his life to God, he may still believe that his toxicity can diminish the value of the work God does through him. It may make sense for him to believe that when he does not have enough faith then God cannot use him to his fullest potential. Regardless, if the man comes to believe God will make him a new creation and work through him productively, we might imagine him thinking differently about his value in the future.

Years after reaching a breaking point (at –1000 value points) and giving control to God, we might ask him to graph his life's value again:

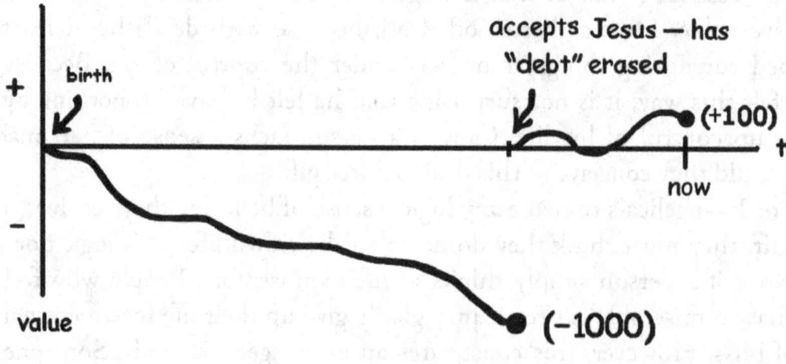

In this example, Evangelical logic makes sense. Indeed, even the ridiculous idea that someone can go into a closet come out with his sins forgiven makes sense. After all, we should all be glad that God forgave this man's sins. In this case, we might find reason to thank God for allowing this man to declare *moral bankruptcy*. Everybody benefits from this action because this man's value—let us say he measures his current value at +100, so even without his "debt erased" his value improves—would come out to –900 because, –1000 + 100 = –900.

If Jesus had not washed away this person's debt and paid the penalty for his sins, however, we might project this person's value would have continued to plummet. Perhaps having reached, let us say about –1500. Thus people with a toxic sense of self, like the man in this example, may think their value clearly improves after giving God control of their lives. In this example, the man has a net gain of +600.* For people who have a sense of unfixable worthlessness, they may clearly see that Jesus changes their lives for the better.

Consider these oft-quoted verses from Paul's letter to the Romans:

> For we know that our old self was crucified with him so that the body of sin might be done away with, that we should no longer be slaves to sin—because anyone who has died has been freed from sin.
>
> Now if we died with Christ, we believe that we will also live with him. For we know that since Christ was raised from the dead, he cannot die again; death no longer has mastery over him. The death he died, he died to sin once for all; but the life he lives, he lives to God.
>
> In the same way, count yourselves dead to sin but alive to God in Christ Jesus (Rom 6:6–11 NIV).

What does Evangelical Christianity have to say about a person who might consider their birth (the real one) a precious gift? Certainly, applying the word "gift" here seems reasonable. None of us did anything to merit birth. Thus, our physical birth truly represents a gift, as it did not come from works or good deeds. How could I consider an offer that requires giving up my life as free, if I see my life as valuable? When people feel their lives have positive value, they cannot accept the gift with no personal cost.

---

* Since –900 – (–1500) = 600. Evangelicals do not calculate their value and determine to become saved based on calculations like this. The point of this exercise is to add context to their rhetoric, which Evangelicals have in common once they become born-again.

Let us consider the graph of a man who feels his life has positive value. Let us suppose, however, things have not gone too well for this man. Because things have gone badly, he has considered giving his life to Christ. Here is the graph of this fictional man's value:

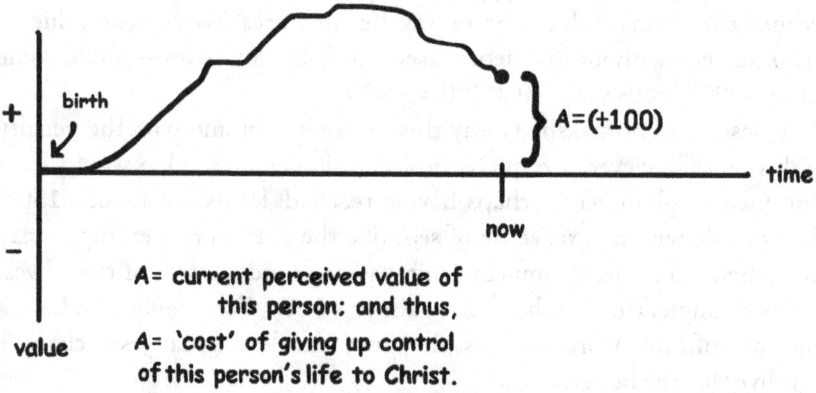

Let us give this man an arbitrary number of +100 value points. Some may argue this value means close to nothing compared to God's offer of eternal life. Arguably, with such a vast difference in value, we could think of God's offer as free. After all, who would not give up a penny to gain $1,000,000,000,000?

God as a Value-Added Partner

Undoubtedly, being a person who believes that she would gain substantially by incorporating God's unlimited resources, wisdom, and love into her life represents probably the most common way that Americans of all faiths look at their relationship with God. They view God as a deity who views them as a valuable people and who can help them become better people. Even many people I have met who label themselves as Evangelicals seem to have a sense of God like this.

I consider people who view God this way as people who have made God a *value-added partner* in their life. They treat God in the way that we might imagine a typical college student treating his or her parents. They treat God as old-fashioned, and with things going well they only visit a couple times a year, like at Christmas and Easter. Just like college students, however, they reliably come home when having problems. These people want God at their wedding, the birth of their children, or when facing a serious situation. As well, when they consider settling down, just like Mom and Dad, God no longer seems so backward. Neither does their church. Many feel this type of relationship with God seems perfectly natural, just as it does with their parents. They perceive the mixture of dependence and independence as steps to maturity. Indeed, they believe God would not approve of them remaining completely dependent on him.

In a similar way, value-added Christians rarely use the Bible or the opinion of Christian leaders as a primary source of motivation for their behavior or actions. For the most part, these Christians (even if they call themselves Evangelicals) usually claim ownership of their own thoughts, actions, and behaviors.

Unfortunately, no Evangelical doctrines support a value-added view of a relationship with God. Furthermore, within the Evangelical elite, finding a consistent, outspoken advocate of value-added theology proves difficult. Every Evangelical doctrine that comments on human worth without God's involvement clearly explains this as zero or subzero value.

Unfortunately, Evangelical culture practically forces everybody to use what I call "identity-dumping." In this identity-dumping culture, everyone talks as if they believe they have no inherent worth (whether they actually believe this or not). Because Evangelicals often find new converts at a low point in their lives, identity-dumping language proves easy to reinforce. From the point converts give their lives to Christ onward, they face relentless pressure to attribute every improvement in their situation to God. In addition, they have pressure to attribute every setback to their lack of faith or their sin nature. Many will readily accept any positive change in their life as evidence that God has worked through them.

Most people when confronting a decision to become born-again, who have had mostly successful lives, would likely experience an improvement in their situation regardless of what they decided to do. A common mistake people make concerns how they evaluate improvement. Although not intuitive, people who have had recent bad outcomes compared to normal will likely return to normal positive outcomes no matter what they do. Any method they pick to fix their problems will probably result in an improvement. For example, consider the man mentioned earlier who feels positively about his life but has had some recent hard times. In a sense, by recognizing his recent poor results, he has already made a decision to fix the problem. He has already taken the first step toward fixing the problem by deciding to try to fix it.

Now he has arrived at a decision about whether to become born-again. Regardless of what he chooses, he will most likely show improvement. Indeed, accurately predicting where this person will end up at some time in the future (let us use three years for this example) would likely involve a process like:

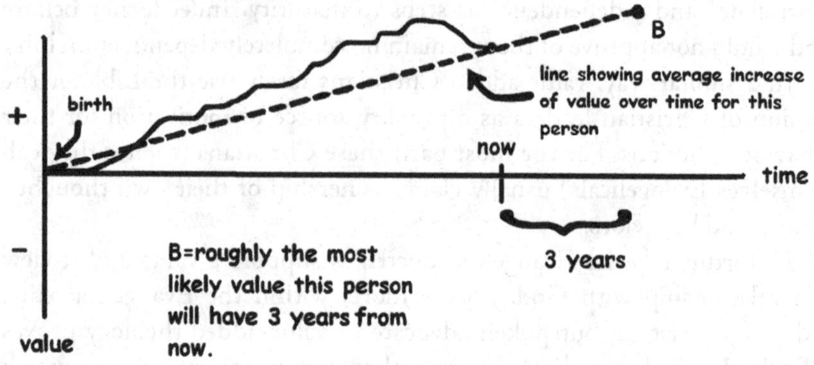

It seems common for people in the midst of things going poorly to feel that their downward spiral will continue indefinitely. That belief usually proves inaccurate, however. For many new Evangelicals, if they had relatively normal coping skills before becoming saved, they would likely find their situation improving—no matter what steps they took to improve things. However, in their new Evangelical communities they will be encouraged, if not compelled, to give credit for this improvement to God. As well, they will start saying (and believing) that they would have continued in their downward spiral without God. Furthermore, they will rarely consider that joining an organized and supportive community, whether Evangelical or not, would have improved their lives.

The most common evidence Evangelicals give for their belief in their god comes from their own, and other Evangelicals', changed life. They consider this evidence persuasive. However, their changed-life logic follows the rules of Hooks and Ladders. An Evangelical's thumb is always on the scale. If you define life before Christ as less than zero, you have nowhere to go but up afterward.

Suppose things go badly for the new Christian. Will believers attribute this to their decision to accept the gift of salvation? Of course not. Rule 2 is: *Evangelical Christians are always correct.* Poor results in a believer's life stem from sinning or perhaps from their doubting the truth of Christianity. Or they may simply lack a commitment to the Evangelical community. It could not possibly be due to any flaw in Evangelical Christianity itself. If someone suggests that perhaps it could, then that person will run afoul of Rule 3: *Only Evangelical Christians have the privilege to determine truth.*

4. Explanation Personal God

WE HAVE SEEN HOW EVANGELICAL CHRISTIANS tell the story of their conversion to Christianity and make it fit the facts of their lives. But more underlies the conversion picture than that. Evangelicals tell and listen to stories frequently about the times when God used strong emotions to bring people closer to him or as a tool to lead people to salvation. Most of the Evangelical Christians I have met ignore the possibility that their emotional state at the time they decided to become believers may have adversely affected their judgment about the decision to become believers. If their vulnerable emotional state at the time of conversion is taken into account at all, it is generally viewed as a positive factor, as something the Lord used to draw them to Christ.

Indeed, I am aware of only a few Evangelicals who have acknowledged that the feelings they may have had, like despair or fear, could have affected their judgment and made them more likely to accept false Evangelical claims. Yet, Evangelicals will mention the *positive* influence of these stressors and emotions when they have played a role in a person's decision to say the "Sinner's Prayer"—or a role in bringing a believer "closer to the Lord."

Many Evangelicals seek out for evangelism people who are experiencing stressful and highly emotional situations and have successfully persuaded many to convert during these times of emotional turmoil. Because of these successes, Evangelicals cannot entirely ignore the role that stressors and emotions have had in shaping their community. However, perhaps because they view the result as positive, Evangelicals seem willing to assume that a believer's reliance on emotions as a basis for belief is a good thing, even though in most areas of life the same Evangelicals would warn against the effects of strong emotions when making moral choices or other important decisions. From what I have seen, Evangelicals seem oblivious to this inconsistency.

In my experience, Evangelicals will often describe the emotions that influenced their decisions about their faith in rational terms. For example, they might say, "I was a mess, so giving my life to Christ made perfect sense," or say, "I realized I would never find *true* happiness apart from God." Thus, an emotional component becomes an integral part of most Evangelicals' rational basis for their belief. As a result, most Evangelicals consider it self-evident (and thus rational) to believe that God created humans to *feel* better when they depend on him, and when they have strong emotional attachments with Evangelical communities. Therefore, most Evangelicals take for granted that their church communities will focus on meeting their social and emotional needs—and many assume that they may have to go elsewhere to have their intellectual and physical needs met.

On an individual level, the same paradigm holds true for most Evangelicals. Beyond the benefits of membership in their Evangelical communities, most Evangelicals will describe the benefits of their personal faith primarily in emotional terms. They will describe how their feelings of joy, peace, contentment, security, and belonging have logically resulted from their personal relationships with God. Evangelicals describe these emotional benefits of faith as if they were self-evident. Similarly, Evangelicals take for granted that without their personal relationship with Christ, the emotional benefits of their faith would evaporate. Thus, Evangelicals *know*—and take for granted that nonbelievers understand—that without their personal relationships with Christ, their lives would have had more sadness, angst, despair, conflict, and instability. I do not know, and have never heard of, an Evangelical who does not view the comparative advantages of his or her own faith in this way.

I want to make it clear about what I am saying about Evangelicals, as it is critical to understanding the way Evangelicals view the benefits of their personal faith. First, Evangelicals, *without exception*, believe that they benefit from the personal relationships they have with Christ. As a result, no matter how much evidence may exist of dysfunction within the Evangelical community, for the individual, the benefits of a personal relationship with Christ do not change. Every Evangelical believes that he or she would have ended up more dysfunctional without a personal relationship with Christ. As well, every Evangelical believes that a person who has chosen to have a personal relationship with Christ has made the best of all choices, by far, to facilitate that person in becoming as compassionate, as neighborly, and as good of a citizen as possible. Evangelicals, however, do not distinguish themselves from others when they believe that they have made a good choice about how to conduct their lives. Many people have those same feelings whether their personal choice involved religion, politics, marriage or children. But Evangelicals can be distinguished from the rest of satisfied humanity because they believe the benefits of their faith are self-evident, and do not need evidence or explanation.

Not only do Evangelicals believe that they benefit from a personal relationship with Christ, they believe—once again, *without exception*—that the benefits of their personal relationships with Christ are *obvious* to any honest inquirer. I have never known, or heard of, an Evangelical who feels any need to explain any action he or she took in the name of the Lord, or any need to explain why nonbelievers should accept that applying Christian principles would lead to better results than applying other principles would. In other words, Evangelicals have a kind of autism about the benefits of a personal relationship with Christ—they see it as clearly beneficial, and they believe every honest observer sees it as beneficial, as well.

Evangelicals seem essentially incapable of even considering alternatives to the stories they tell themselves about the decision to become a Christian—alternatives that take into account the potential perils of making important judgments and decisions during times of stress or emotional instability. They seem incapable of considering that Evangelical faith may have made them less capable, less moral, and less neighborly than they might have been otherwise. They seem incapable of comprehending that many nonbelievers may *honestly* consider the actions they take as believers to be morally lacking and possibly even harmful. This lack of awareness about how others might perceive their actions seems to have given Evangelicals strong feelings of certainty about their beliefs. But their feelings of certainty come at a price in this case—the price of neglecting the possibility that they are not remaining in touch with the real world.

Before we move on, I want to make it clear, again, what I am saying about Evangelicals. I am not saying that Evangelicals are wrong just because they may have made decisions based on emotions, even important decisions. Nor am I saying that Evangelicals are wrong just because they failed to consider alternative explanations for how they arrived at their current beliefs, although that is part of it. I am saying that Evangelicals do not consider that they may have arrived at a poor decision in reliance on emotions, including feelings of fear, loneliness and despair before conversion. And I am saying that the feelings of certainty and relief they may have after conversion are too commonly mistaken as being credible evidence that their beliefs are based in fact and have a positive effect on them and on those with whom they come into contact. I am saying that Evangelicals persist in using these feelings of certainty to justify the decisions they made, after the fact, as being the result of cold hard reasoning and evidence.

AFTER THE FACT JUSTIFICATION

You may recall that most Christians accept Jesus as their personal savior before having much knowledge of the Bible. But even so, they will tell you that if someone could conclusively prove the Bible false, their personal relationship with Jesus would have no meaning. At the same time, many Evangelicals give the impression that they welcome fair-minded discussion. Many non-Evangelicals trust this impression and engage Evangelicals in discussion. For example, many nonbelievers have investigated the biblical and historical claims made by Evangelical Christians, and they have often concluded, as I have, that Evangelical claims have no basis in reality. They will then launch into the task of setting the record straight. *Surely,* they think, *sensible Evangelical Christians will acknowledge the lack of evidence for Evangelical Christian beliefs.* But this almost never happens. Why?

Few people engaging Evangelicals consider all the possible arguments for and against the Evangelical conception of Christianity. Most look at historical evidence exclusively and then try to determine whether Evangelical Christians have made reasonable conclusions about it. After concluding that Evangelicals have not made a persuasive case for their conclusions, critics will focus on the historical evidence in their confrontations with Evangelicals. In my experience, Evangelicals and their critics share one common belief: both groups believe that a thoughtful review of the historical record should lead to acceptance of their positions. Yet few consider the validity of conclusions Evangelicals have made based on the historical evidence that they consider facts. Few consider that even if all the historical evidence Evangelicals use to support their faith proved to be true, Evangelicals might have made erroneous conclusions based on that evidence. They may have made assumptions and drawn conclusions that are not supported by that historical evidence. In this chapter, we will look at Evangelical beliefs beyond the historical record.

Most Evangelical Christians link these two beliefs:

1. Historical evidence confirms that events described in the Bible—including the life, death, and resurrection accounts of Jesus—actually happened exactly as the Bible records.
2. Jesus, God's son, came to Earth to pay the penalty for our sins. This demonstration of love paved the way for us to have a personal relationship with Jesus.

Neglected by Evangelicals and their critics—a person's reasoning process could create problems regardless of whether his or her facts prove correct.

Like critics of Christianity, Evangelical apologists focus on showcasing the evidence for (1). Most contend that if they can persuade nonbelievers to agree with (1), then they have done enough to prove (2). People that agree with (1), Evangelicals contend, have all of the intellectual reasons necessary for accepting Jesus as their personal savior. Yet, even if Evangelicals could prove (1) true, (2) does not follow from that. Specifically, Evangelicals take for granted that if they can prove that the Bible describes historical events accurately, then their explanations for *why* those events happened logically follows from the same evidence. But we could think of many explanations where (1) proved true and (2) proved false. We will consider this possibility. More importantly, we will try to figure out why Evangelicals seem unaware that they automatically link (1) and (2) and how this affects their reasoning.

For example, many Evangelicals claim that God instills in all of us a longing to seek him. Evangelicals will describe a desire for purpose and meaning in their lives. They will say humans have a need to feel connected with God. Consider what Hugh Ross—an astrophysicist and reasonably well-known Christian author—wrote:

> Can we really know God, and know Him in a relational sort of way? We Christians often say that spiritual life is not about religion but about a relationship with our Creator and Savior. This declaration has a nice ring to it, especially to those who recognize relationships as life's core program, not just as interesting electives....
>
> We are especially eager—some would say desperate—to fulfill our longing for intimate, lasting relationships that allow us to know and be known, accept and be accepted, cherish and be cherished, all with a depth and breadth that grows through time.
>
> If God is a personal being, as the Bible says, what we have learned from human relationships should allow us to make some applications to build a relationship with Him. And what could be

> more desirable than an experiential connection with unlimited Love, Life, and Truth? We want it; so does He, according to the Bible ...
>
> He [God] has proven, again, his willingness to disclose himself for the sake of strengthening and deepening our relationship with Him and of drawing others to join us in that venture ...
>
> The test presented to Christians by these mysteries has been for us to honor Him as the Truth, whose name is also Teacher, and to respect each other as students. We know our assignment is to study, dialogue and discern, but instead we often dispute and divide.[1]

Ross fails to consider that the emotions created by his angst might influence his thinking. Most Evangelicals, like Ross, do not consider that their feelings may have shaped their thinking about God rather than the other way around. They usually accept with certainty and without considering any alternative explanation that God stamped feelings and desires on all humans. As we have just seen, they convince themselves that feeling "whole" after conversion confirms their beliefs. Their feelings confirm God's plan of inner peace through a relationship with Christ. Rather than view this as a potential bias, Evangelicals nearly always view personal desires and feelings as corroborating evidence for their beliefs. Why do so many people have strong emotions and longing for a god? For most Evangelicals, the only reasonable answer is:

> God created us in such a way that we cannot *feel* whole without him.

Nearly all Evangelicals have a strong sense of certainty that their feeling about God came from God. I use "certainty" in a particular way that marks an important problem with Evangelical thinking. In most cases, it is hard to be 100 percent certain about the reason why anything happened the way it did as long as you can imagine an alternative explanation. After all, just knowing of an alternate explanation creates some factor of doubt. For example, Evangelicals may claim they have *certainty* that Jesus rose from the dead and claim this provides the best explanation for his empty tomb. Even in this example, Evangelicals usually recognize at least two explanations for the empty tomb. For instance, they know some nonbelievers might believe that someone might have stolen Jesus' body from the tomb.

So how can we explain Jesus' empty tomb? Let us call the explanation of Jesus rising from the dead "Explanation R" and call someone stealing Jesus' body "Explanation S." Even though Evangelicals believe Explanation R provides a much better explanation than Explanation S, most know of alternate explanations like Explanation S and acknowledge a burden for their community to defend Explanation R against heresies like Explanation S.

What would happen, though, if people did not know—or were unable to conceive—of any alternate explanations for one of their beliefs? Well, most Evangelicals have only one explanation for how they interpret personal evidence of their decision to accept Jesus.

Explanation PG

When I was an Evangelical, preachers and apologists frequently presented straw man arguments attributed to skeptics of Christianity. For example, I have heard this one many times: "Some will say that grave robbers stole Jesus' body from the tomb. They might say Jesus had not died yet. These people will rationalize why they reject God's truth, no matter what the evidence shows." Most Evangelicals can recall a time when they heard or read something like this. They may have read something similar in an apologetic's book. For Evangelicals, explanations like this come up frequently as part of discussions on how to reach unbelievers. Most Evangelicals never hear or preach: "Some will say that your heart does not have Jesus there. Some might say your mind does not have the Holy Spirit in it. They may say you accepted a false belief at a time of weakness." Evangelicals rarely address this subject, if ever, in sermons or apologetic books.

Evangelicals never consider the possibility that their feelings and emotions about God may cloud their thinking. The following explanation makes sense to Evangelicals (let us call this "Explanation PG," where "PG" stands for "Personal God"). Thus:

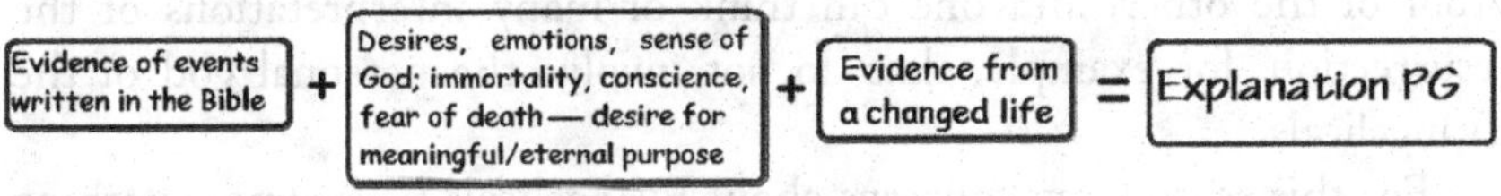

Explanation PG—God purposely planned historical events. God made us seek him. God made us long for him. God made us feel empty without him. God wants to have a relationship with us. God wants to change us and work through us. God wants us to depend on him. God purposely made human emotions. God instilled a sense of right and wrong in all of us. Evangelicals never consider a different explanation for all these things other than their personal god made them that way. As a result, they can feel 100 percent certain about this.

EXPLANATION PG EQUALS A TRUE SENSE OF CERTAINTY

Evangelicals do not really choose Explanation PG—they simply have no choice—because they cannot conceive of an alternative. Most Evangelicals have zero thoughts traveling their mind that cast doubt on Explanation PG. This oblivious single-mindedness colors virtually everything Evangelicals do, think, and feel. As a result, many Evangelicals simply have no way of deciphering any stimulus or information without filtering it through Explanation PG. Information that comes in weighs against this *certain* belief.

Very few Evangelicals seem to have a mental conception of this possibility:

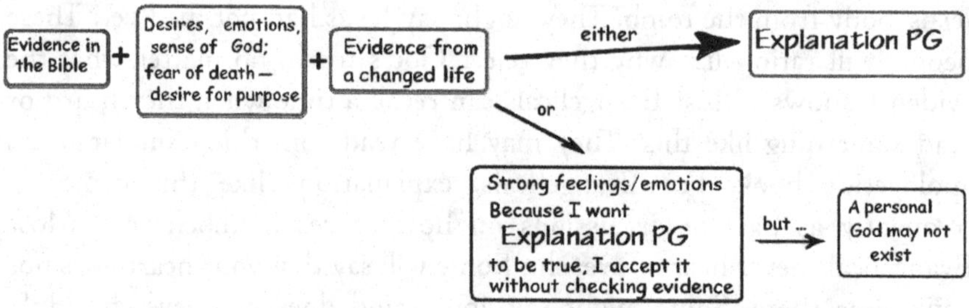

It may take further explanation to clarify what makes this problematic, so once again let us suppose for a moment that we could prove every detail about Jesus' life, death, and resurrection. As discussed, most Evangelicals would tell you that proof of these "facts" show conclusively that they are right about sin, salvation, and their personal relationship with Jesus. In short, they assume that proof of facts about Jesus is equivalent to proving Explanation PG. But this is not the case. Proof of one does not equal proof of the other, and one can think of many interpretations of the resurrection, for example, that do not involve the personal god of the Evangelicals.

For this reason, my concerns about Evangelicals have almost nothing to do with historical facts. My contentions about Evangelicals' disordered thinking would be valid regardless of what the historical evidence showed. Thus before Darwin, before access to historical records, before the discovery of DNA, and before the discovery of other evidence, the case against Evangelical Christianity already proved damning. Evangelicals seem to have no concept that other interpretations may explain these events better than Explanation PG, and they have no grounds for acting on their belief that Explanation PG represents the only possible explanation for biblical events.

GOD'S NETWORK/ALL USERS/BELIEVER'S FILE/MY PICTURES

I have a hunch that many will have arrived at this point in the book and not yet have a grasp on what I mean by considering an alternate explanation to Explanation PG. To help clarify this we need to think about the mental images we carry around with us. For example, someone with a huge oak tree in their back yard can likely conjure up a mental picture of that tree that resembles the mental picture of the tree that others have. The same holds true for mental pictures of friends and family. In contrast to mental pictures of friends and family, however, most of us realize that a person who has studied and works with oak trees—whom we might call an "oak tree expert"—will likely have a more accurate and precise mental picture of oak trees than others will have.

As well, if someone believes in a personal god, he or she likely has some mental pictures, albeit a little hazy, of God, Jesus, and the Holy Spirit. For example, Christians might mentally envision the Holy Spirit working through them as being similar to electricity. No one can see electricity, but most of us have a mental image of electricity traveling through wires, cords, and circuits. Even though invisible, most of us still think of our mental pictures of electricity as real. So Evangelical Christians, in the same way, may think of their mental concept of the Holy Spirit—though invisible—working in and around them as real. Most of them will have never thought about things without having these pictures in their mind. Because these pictures of the Holy Spirit exist in their minds in the same way that the picture of the oak tree does, the Holy Spirit pictures have become real to them, just like the oak tree. They do not question the reality of the Holy Spirit any more than they do the reality of the oak tree. Many Evangelicals live their entire lives without ever realizing that they cannot "clearly see" these mental pictures. They believe they see what they do not see. As well, they live their whole lives without realizing that unlike oak tree experts, Evangelical experts do not have any clearer or more consistent mental pictures of the Holy Spirit than others may have.

We need to address the mental pictures Evangelicals have of things that we cannot differentiate from nonexistent things. These things are invisible, just as electricity often is, but also undetectable, which differentiates them from electricity. When Evangelicals accept the reality of the invisible and undetectable subjects of the mental pictures he or she has (i.e., the Holy Spirit), then they *must* find a way to reconcile these mental pictures with their experiences.

Let's look at pictures to help clarify this point. My brother Tom has a very good knowledge of football. Imagine you and I had a conversation, and I told you something Tom told me:

It would be weird if you had responded:

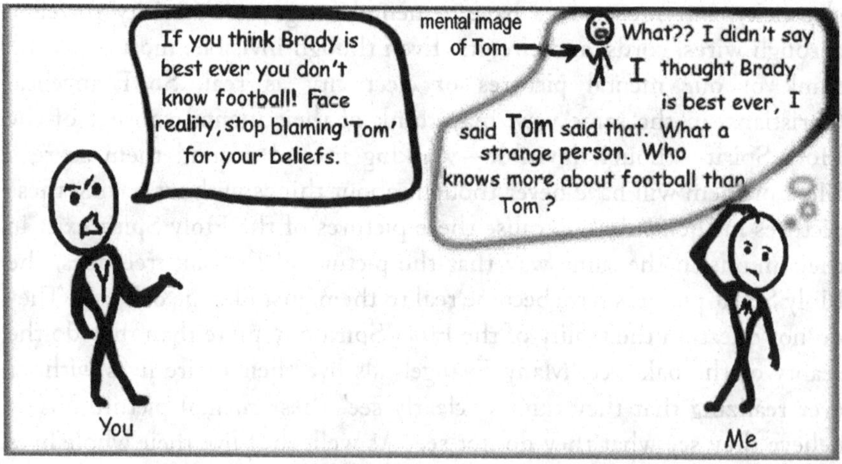

I have many mental images of my brother (too many—but we won't get into that). I have no reasonable way of evaluating what someone could mean by blaming me for what Tom said. When I tell someone Tom said something, I do not take responsibility for Tom's opinions. Nevertheless, suppose I ask you why you gave such a strange response, and you say, "I do not believe you have a brother." Now what do I do? On one hand, I could just write you off as an odd person and avoid you.

Let us suppose that I had had a conversation about Tom with a man who had made the same strange comments to me as the "You" character in the picture above. But years later I had crossed paths with him again and I overheard him talking to another man about buying a deli across the street from where an NFL football team had planned a new stadium. I overheard him saying that the deli was not making a profit, but if the team built the stadium, as they had planned, then he would probably do well financially. I also heard him say that if the team did not build the stadium, then he might lose his fortune.

Now, let us suppose that a few days before I saw this man again, I had talked with Tom about the same NFL team's plans to build a stadium that the man had mentioned. Tom had told me that—unknown to most—the team had serious financial problems, and that the team's owners had planned to scrap the plans for a new stadium.

Should I say anything to the man who had said he was thinking about buying the deli?

Realistically, if I did not tell him about what Tom had told me about the altered plans for a stadium, the man could lose his fortune. Even though I had had a weird conversation with him before about my brother Tom, could I have justified not telling him about what Tom had told me? Even though the man could suffer serious consequences if I chose not to tip him off that the team had scrapped their plans for a new stadium, the potential suffering he may have endured would have paled in comparison to the suffering he would have to endure if he spent eternity in hell.

Nevertheless, I would likely have felt obligated to give him the "gospel" I had heard from Tom that the team had planned to cancel their construction of a new stadium. So suppose I had told him about what Tom had told me, and he had said, "I told you before, I do not believe you have a brother. Furthermore, even if you have a brother, I doubt that he knows a darn thing about the team's plans for a new stadium, or the team's financial situation."

Confronted with that situation, how should I have dealt with this man? Should I have just left him alone to make a poor investment? Or should I have tried to convince him that Tom was real? If I had decided to convince the man that Tom was real, how should I have gone about doing that?

If I had tried to convince the man that Tom was real, I could have done many things, such as: let Tom and the man talk on the phone; shown the man family photos and articles about football that Tom had written; or presented the man with citations about Tom's financial dealings in pro football. I could have had friends who knew Tom speak with the man. Let us suppose I had done all that and the man still did not believe that what Tom had told me was true, and he did not believe that Tom was real. If I had cared enough about the man's financial affairs, then I could have still gone the extra mile and provided him with more proof of Tom's existence and more evidence of Tom's inside knowledge of professional football. I could have drummed up birth certificates and DNA tests or let him speak with our parents. I could have arranged for him to meet Tom and ask questions. For even the most skeptical people, if I had done all of those things, then that should have settled the matter.

What should I have done, however, if I had tried to provide the man with proof of Tom's existence and expertise, but I could not find any proof? Suppose I could not find Tom's phone number; I could not find any family photos; I could not ask my parents for proof about Tom because my parents had died; and I could not find Tom's birth certificate or any record of his birth. If I did not have any proof whatsoever of Tom's existence, what could I have done then?

Should I have doubted whether Tom existed? I probably would not have done that. With that scenario, even though I could not have proved that my brother Tom existed, I probably still would not have doubted his existence. Perhaps I would have thought: *That person makes me mad. I hope he pays dearly for willfully rejecting my gracious attempts to save him from financial ruin.*

Moving on, suppose many others started to question whether Tom existed. Should that have altered how I felt about the comments that the man had made to me about Tom? At that point, should I have considered the possibility that I did not have a brother named Tom? Should I have considered the possibility that I had delusions of a brother who did not actually exist?

It is at the endpoint of this scenario where I believe most Evangelicals interface with the rest of the world. They have many people saying that many of the important beings in Evangelicals' lives (e.g., God and the Holy Spirit) do not seem to exist. They have many people asking for sufficient evidence of Evangelicals' spiritual entities, and many people who say they do not believe Evangelicals have provided that evidence. Despite not having sufficient evidence of their spiritual entities, Evangelicals consider their spiritual entities real. They consider the Holy Spirit, for example, as real as I would probably have considered my brother Tom—even if I had not had sufficient evidence to satisfy skeptics that he was real. Beyond that, however, they consider the Holy Spirit as real as I consider my brother Tom, even when I have more than enough evidence to prove that Tom is real. They consider their evidence of the Holy Spirit to be just as compelling—but it is not.

CONFRONTING REALITY

Using my brother as a metaphor helps us begin to understand why Evangelicals respond to their critics in the ways that they do. Many well-meaning nonbelievers will present their reasons for rejecting Christian claims and will take Evangelicals at their word about embracing an interest in fair-minded discussions about Christianity, and Evangelical Christians often respond just as I did in the example above, much to the puzzlement of the nonbeliever. I have said before that these attempts by nonbelievers to set the record straight usually fail. It is because in order to start at common ground, Evangelicals would have to consider the evidence about their truths of the Bible that allowed for a mental picture of the world without their spiritual entities. Yet, they do not. Evangelicals do not doubt that their personal god exists any more than I doubt my brother exists. Anything an Evangelical says, thinks, or does conforms to this belief about a personal god.

Evangelical believers have a mental concept of how God downloads information through the Bible into their brains through the HOLYSPIRIT plug-in. Like electricity, the believer never questions this process or the realness of all this spiritual network wiring. As a result, the believer will say, "God tells us in his Word ..." They rarely say something like, "I think we should interpret this Bible passage to mean ... What do you think?" Just as my brother Tom was the source of my information about a new NFL stadium, the personal gods of Evangelicals provides information about what the Bible means. Evangelicals, for the most part, do not believe that they figured out or discovered this information on their own—or received it from solely natural sources. So, Evangelicals can feel very certain about what the Bible means since God has told them—and God knows all and has unlimited power and perfect judgment. Evangelicals can also be very certain that anyone who disagrees with them is wrong, since who dares to contradict God? Most Evangelicals believe that even hinting at questioning the facts Evangelicals attribute to God demonstrates a nearly pathologic, profound—and most importantly—unforgivable lack of judgment.

Many Evangelicals, and most of the highly committed ones, treat anyone who has openly criticized them as they would an intractably delinquent teenager. With an overwhelming air of superiority—and often pity—Evangelicals commonly view their critics as dangerously unpredictable. After all, Evangelicals consider critics of their God—like juvenile delinquents—to have already proven they have a problem. Many Evangelicals believe that a person who defies their God must have serious mental or emotional deficiencies—and ex-Evangelicals are considered worst of all. For example, they will often assume that a person with an average or higher than average intelligence who rejects Evangelical Christianity must have an extreme lack of insight and judgment—and an inability to plan for the future. Despite being intelligent, the person selfishly does "whatever feels good" or "satisfies the lusts of the flesh."

I could have an impeccable reputation as hard working, honest, brilliant, and consistent. For Evangelicals, however, a twelve-year-old believer would deserve more respect than I do, even in my field of expertise, just because I do not have the special HOLYSPIRIT plug-in. By characterizing nonbelievers as lacking judgment, Evangelicals have a very effective tool for reinforcing Hooks and Ladders Rules 2 and 3.

Years ago, as an Evangelical, I could not prove that my personal god existed. The Evangelicals I knew or read could not prove God existed either. Most of the Evangelicals I knew freely acknowledged they could not prove God existed, and as a result, I faced a moral dilemma. In those circumstances, I had no moral basis to act on my beliefs about my personal god, just as I would have no basis to act on my beliefs about my brother Tom if I could not prove he existed.

For example, the weight of my claims that I attributed to Tom came from Tom's credibility and reliability. Tom has no credibility beyond my own credibility if he does not exist. After all, some of my actions based on my Tom delusion may have harmed others. How could I know if something Tom told me might hurt someone else? I could not tell. For example, in the scenario about the NFL stadium and deli, I would have truly believed I was helping the man by relaying Tom's word. I could harm the man planning to buy the deli without knowing I harmed him, and even while thinking I was helping him.

In the same way, I realized I could no longer morally justify acting on my belief that God existed without proof. I realized that despite believing I would meet God in heaven after I died, I had no moral justification to act on my belief that nonbelievers would go to hell. How could I justify telling people they would go to hell for not believing in a God that I could not prove existed? How could I justify this any more than I could justify telling people I knew of a cure for cancer that I could not prove worked—even if I believed it would work? I realized that my and every other Evangelical's claims about God did not take on magical, supernatural qualities. I had no right to expect people to consider my beliefs about God to have any more credibility or reliability than my claims about other things.

Many nonbelievers feel that Evangelicals, at the very least, need to consider the way those of us who do not believe in their spiritual entities perceive the world. If believers considered the possibility that the images in their minds might not exist—or the true image might not have the characteristics of their mental pictures—they may understand why others often perceive their beliefs as delusional. They may understand that when they say that their personal god told them something, the rest of us hear that the believer said it, not God. They may understand when they claim a moral justification for actions based on the commands of a personal god it can come across as immoral, especially when the believers cannot justify doing those things themselves.

I might not want to consider whether I really have a brother, and Evangelicals might not want to consider whether they really have a personal god. Nonetheless, Evangelicals might benefit from realizing that many others cannot clearly see their invisible friends.

Evangelical Autism Revisited

As I explained in the first chapter, when Evangelicals assume others clearly see the mental pictures they see, they have autistic thinking. We can find examples of this type of autistic thinking throughout Evangelical Christianity, and I gave some examples earlier. Explanation PG is another of those mental pictures that Evangelicals believe nonbelievers can clearly see.

Every Evangelical pastor and leader has made sweeping claims that they seem to expect others to see as they see. For example, Billy Graham used to speak to entire stadiums packed with people and say something like this (taken from his Web site):

> God loves you and wants you to experience peace and life—abundant and eternal. The Bible says:
>
> > "We have peace with God through our Lord Jesus Christ" (Romans 5:1, NIV).
> >
> > "For God so loved the world that He gave His only begotten Son, that whoever believes in Him should not perish but have everlasting life" (John 3:16, NIV).
> >
> > "I have come that they may have life, and that they may have it more abundantly" (John 10:10, NIV).

> "For all have sinned and fall short of the glory of God" (Romans 3:23, NIV).
>
> "For the wages of sin is death, but the gift of God is eternal life in Christ Jesus our Lord" (Romans 6:23, NIV).
>
> People have tried in many ways to bridge this gap between themselves and God. The Bible says:
>
> "There is a way that seems right to a man, but in the end it leads to death" (Proverbs 14:12, NIV).
>
> "But your iniquities have separated you from your God; your sins have hidden his face from you, so that he will not hear" (Isaiah 59:2, NIV).
>
> The Bible says:
>
> "For Christ died for sins once for all, the righteous for the unrighteous, to bring you to God" (1 Peter 3:18, NIV).
>
> "But God demonstrates his own love for us in this: While we were still sinners, Christ died for us" (Romans 5:8, NIV).
>
> God has provided the only way. Each person must make a choice.... We must trust Jesus Christ as Lord and Savior and receive Him by personal invitation.[2]

Billy Graham uses his Web site in his crusades for evangelism. As he speaks to nonbelievers, we might reasonably assume that at least some of his audience does not know or accept that God inspired the writing of the Bible. Remarkably, Billy Graham does not make any effort to explain why or how he connects the Bible to his claim that it is God's Word. He seems to have taken this for granted and assumes that his listeners will do so as well.

Why does Billy Graham do this? It seems hard to imagine that Billy Graham would have failed to recognize the importance of this link. As well, it seems surprising that he thinks he has the liberty to make such a bold claim without any proof that the two are connected—or without even making an attempt to link the two. But if we consider that Dr. Graham believes in Explanation PG and has some measure of Evangelical autism, we can understand Dr. Graham's repeated oversight.

For example, if it were not for Explanation PG, this is how I would see and interpret Graham's altar call:

> Billy Graham has provided the only way. Each person must make a choice. You must trust Graham's interpretation of Jesus

> Christ as Lord and Savior. You should feel privileged that Graham came here to tell you how to avoid the eternal torture you deserve.
>
> Everybody has less value than Billy Graham has, unless that person has accepted a personal invitation to the salvation party. Because Graham is so special, he does not need to provide you with any evidence that the ancient writing that he quotes came from Almighty God directly.

Because Billy Graham, like most Evangelicals, seems to have believed in Explanation PG and clearly saw mental pictures of God's kingdom, he seems to have assumed that everyone else clearly saw those same mental pictures. He took for granted that those mental pictures represented real life in a meaningful way. So it seems he did not feel the need to explain that what he said came from God through the HOLYSPIRIT plug-in and not from himself—everyone should have clearly seen this, as well.

In another example, a person who knows my views on Evangelical Christianity sent me an e-mail that typifies this type of Evangelical autistic thinking. She knows that I believe Evangelicals misinterpret the thought and motives of nonbelievers (e.g., secular scientists). The woman, despite knowing my views well, thought I might find this compelling:

> God was sitting in heaven one day when a scientist said to him, "God, we don't need you anymore. Science has finally figured out a way to create life out of nothing—in other words, we can now do what you did in the beginning."
>
> "Oh, is that so? Explain ..." replies God.
>
> "Well," says the scientist, "we can take dirt and form it into the likeness of you and breathe life into it, thus creating man."
>
> "Well, that's very interesting ... show me."
>
> So, the scientist bends down to the earth and starts to mold the soil into the shape of a man.
>
> "No, no, no ..." interrupts God, "*Get your own dirt.*"[3]

Autistic thinking, combined with Explanation PG, ensures the integrity of Rule 3: *Only Evangelical Christians have the privilege to determine truth.* Far too many Evangelicals seem incapable of comprehending that others do not see things as they see them. They clearly see their spiritual world as a natural and seamless extension of the real world. They see this as accepting the truth about the real world, and they see others as refusing to acknowledge what is plainly in front of them.

So now you can understand the problems nonbelievers face when discussing matters of religion with Evangelical Christians. Evangelical

Christians accept Explanation PG and cannot conceive of another explanation for the same events. They filter everything they do and say through their understanding of the *real* world. For Evangelicals, the real world includes their judgments based on Explanation PG, which they clearly see. To the nonbeliever, the Evangelical Christian sounds delusional because they appear to attribute their own thoughts and desires to a nonexistent being. We cannot question or challenge this being. Even though the Evangelical appears to be fair-minded and welcoming of open debate, once the debate starts, the nonbeliever runs into Explanation PG and the dialogue shuts down.

When Explanation PG combines with Evangelical autism, discussion with nonbelievers becomes even more strained. Then, not only will the Evangelical not be able to conceive of an alternative to Explanation PG, he will assume that the nonbeliever standing in front of him also clearly sees Explanation PG. Because of the combination of the two misconceptions, the Evangelical believes that he knows what the nonbeliever is thinking and seeing, even when the nonbeliever says otherwise. This confounding issue proves challenging when discussing Christianity with Evangelicals. Evangelicals often clearly see the nonbeliever as an enemy combatant battling valiant Christian soldiers in a protracted supernatural war. Of course, as per Rule 1, Evangelicals know that God's army will remain victorious. This makes nonbelievers more than just enemies. It makes them *foolish* enemies.

Mind Reading—A Crucial Tool for Justifying Rule 3

I remain in awe of the way that virtually every Evangelical has easily dismissed the lifetime work of admittedly brilliant infidels. This ability to discount the opinions and reasoning of other people inevitably results from Evangelical autism, as I have described. Attributing an agenda to another person is an example of autism at work. It requires a belief that they, as Evangelicals, can know the thoughts of others. It requires mind reading.

Let me explain how this works. Most people feel they have what we can call, "immunity from errors of misidentification" when expressing their own thoughts. For example, if I say, "I like the color of orange. My favorite color is orange." I do not expect someone to tell me, "You liar—your favorite color must be something else. Who told you to say that you could have orange as a favorite color?" A comment like that seems too weird. It seems weird because most people grant immunity from errors of misidentification.

If I claim orange as my favorite color, most people generally consider that I have immunity from other people legitimately claiming that I have made an error. Some people with autistic thinking, however, do not grant others this type of immunity. Whether from a natural flaw of the brain or not, their claims suggest that they can read minds. They can know, better than I do, whether I *really* like orange. They trust their judgments about my thoughts more than my claims about my thoughts. They also believe their judgment about my thoughts should gain more respect from others than my claims about my thoughts.

Evangelical autism enables believers to do the same. As described in the preface, by attributing bad faith to doubting Christians, Evangelicals knock doubters down a few levels in the Hooks and Ladders game. Evangelical Christians, following Paul, also attribute all manner of evil behavior to nonbelievers. Evangelical Christians can do both of these things because of Explanation PG and Evangelical autism. They believe that doubting Christians and nonbelievers refuse to see what is clearly visible to the Evangelical Christian. Doubters and nonbelievers cannot—or will not—see what is real in their eyes, even though doubting Christians and nonbelievers alike may plainly express their sincerity about their beliefs. Most often, however, Evangelicals reject these claims. Evangelicals confirm the truth of their perception through Explanation PG. God has told them the thoughts and motivations of nonbelievers and doubting Christians.

As I described in regard to my brother Tom, we cannot ethically justify acting on the commands of a being we cannot prove exists. We have no way of knowing whether the messages we might relay have any basis in reality. We may harm others by acting on those messages even though we may intend to only do good. Evangelicals rarely examine the possibility that their rules, especially Rule 3, may prove impossible to implement without acting immorally. By claiming to know someone's inner thoughts and motives, Evangelicals have essentially become mind readers—and liars.

Of course, this kind of thinking gives Evangelicals a rhetorical leg up in discussions with non-Christians. Claiming to know that someone purposely and often maliciously set out to "bring down Christians" makes it easy for Evangelicals to dismiss a person's claims. By far and away, Evangelicals use mind reading more than any other method to reinforce Rule 3.

What recourse do we have when an Evangelical feels entitled to ignore, or cannot comprehend, that we know our own thoughts better than they do? We know that God does not implant information and thoughts in the brains of Evangelicals about others. Yet, it seems that Evangelicals feel their special providence includes their ability to truthfully describe other people's thoughts, feelings, and motivations. Evangelicals who have removed themselves this far from reality could justify anything.

Let me give you another example of these thought processes at work, taken from the writings of a well-respected Evangelical Christian, Bill Bright (1921–2003). He was a former president and the founder of Campus Crusade for Christ International, and he has introductory comments in Josh McDowell's book, *Evidence That Demands a Verdict*. This commentary has appeared in editions of this book for over thirty years. Bill Bright wrote:

> The evidence confirming the deity of the Lord Jesus Christ is overwhelmingly conclusive to any honest, objective seeker after truth. However, not all—not even the majority—of those whom I have spoken have accepted Him as their Savior and Lord. This is not because they were *unable* to believe—they were simply *unwilling* to believe! ... Well-known professing atheists, including Aldous Huxley and Bertrand Russell, have refused to come to intellectual grips with the basic historical facts concerning the birth, life, teachings, miracles, death and resurrection of Jesus of Nazareth.[4]

We have everything that we have just discussed right there. Bill Bright believed he knew the thoughts of the majority of people with whom he spoke, as well as the thoughts of writers and philosophers like Aldous Huxley and Bertrand Russell, whom he may never have met.[5] These nonbelievers were unwilling to acknowledge what he, Bill Bright, knew to be true and thus could not be "honest, objective seekers after truth." After all, the "evidence" was "overwhelmingly conclusive."

Comparing Evangelical thinking to the thought processes of people with mental challenges makes many people uncomfortable. If, however, an Evangelical Christian believes that Bright's comments describe the truth about these nonbelievers, then I know my conclusion about that person's thought processes has merit. I know with 100 percent certainty that Bright could not read minds. I know that Bright did not know whether nonbelievers were honest, objective seekers after the truth, and so his claims have no merit.

Nevertheless, Bill Bright's comments, in my experience, clearly reflect the sentiments of the average Evangelical.[6] I have had at least a hundred different Evangelicals tell me that they know my thoughts better than I do. Many have said flatly, "You are a liar. You never *honestly* examined the *truths* of the Bible, or you would not have turned your back on God." Most Evangelicals can calmly tell me they knew what I thought and felt better than I knew what I thought and felt as if I should accept—as *self-evident*—that their claims about my thoughts and feelings had more validity. Bill Bright did not know my thoughts better than I know my thoughts. Bill Bright did not have flawless insight into the minds of Aldous Huxley and Bertrand Russell, even though many Evangelical Christian leaders will tell you that he did and that they do as well. We can know with certainty that Evangelicals have no more knowledge about the thoughts of others than the rest of us.

Explanation PG and the Role of Personal Testimony

Evangelicals seem to have no problem accepting that every believer becomes an expert witness once saved. Indeed, Evangelicals feel wholeheartedly that valuable information comes from someone's "personal testimony." After all, it goes by the name "testimony," as if given at a trial! Evangelicals seem to have no doubt that their testimonies have value in making an effective case about the active role of their god in their lives. Whom do Evangelicals expect to convince with their testimonies? What information contained in their testimonies do they expect others to accept as credible evidence for their beliefs?

Evangelicals fall into the same logical loop that we saw in Billy Graham's altar call and in Bill Bright's introduction. They expect others to believe what they say in their testimonies because they know it is true. They see their own mental pictures of the Holy Spirit and *know* that the pictures represent reality. They know how they felt before and after their conversion and know that everyone else must feel similar longings that should lead them to accept Jesus. They know that there must be something wrong with people who reject their personal testimonies since they are so self-evidently correct. However, Evangelicals rank among the least reliable judges of the truth of their own personal testimonies.

A man named Marty once told me his doctor called him paranoid schizophrenic. I asked him what he thought about that diagnosis. He said, "Of course I'm paranoid! Brother, if someone slid thousands of cockroaches under your door every night, you would be paranoid too." I cannot argue with that. I despise cockroaches.

Suppose we decided to assemble a group of people to investigate Marty's claims about cockroaches. Suppose we had to pick people from a list of three billion adults. We number the list and give the top numbers to top investigators. We give the bottom numbers to unreliable investigators. We might imagine Marty's name appearing at a number like 2,999,642,239 out of 3,000,000,000. Marty's opinions about his claims have little use. Why do we think Marty is so unreliable? Marty accepts his belief that someone slides thousands of cockroaches under his door as evidence supporting that same belief.

Marty's testimony about Explanation Cockroaches has about as much meaning as Evangelicals' testimonies do about Explanation PG. To understand the reasons for this, we must return to schizophrenia.

At the beginning of this chapter, I said that most Evangelical Christians ignore the role that their own feelings and thought patterns play in their decision to become a believer. This failure of most Evangelicals to recognize the possibility that their feelings may have tainted the way they think about their feelings represents the point where most Evangelicals' thinking departs from reality.

The schism between thought and feeling is the feature that defines schizophrenia. In fact, the "split" in schizophrenia (split personalities) refers to the seeming lack of connection among thoughts, feelings, and reality.[7] Why do I call this typical aspect of Evangelical Christian thinking a split?

Consider a typical explanation of an event that lacks connection between thoughts and feelings. Imagine a young man who wears older, practical clothing, who never learned to dance, and who has trouble talking to women. He walks into a crowded, popular nightclub with an enormous dance floor and sees people dressed in the latest popular fashions. Now imagine this man sees two women at a nearby table looking toward him while whispering to each other and laughing. The young man immediately becomes convinced that these two women have singled him out for ridicule.

If this young man is capable of linking his thoughts and feelings, upon later reflection he will most likely determine that his discomfort when entering the nightclub may have provoked feelings that tainted his thinking when he interpreted what happened that night. He might think, "Those two women seemed to look, whisper, and laugh as if they were directing that at me. But I might have incorrectly interpreted those actions because I felt out of place in that club."

If the young man cannot effectively link his thoughts and feelings, as commonly happens with schizophrenia, he will not consider the possibility that his feelings influenced his interpretations. Because he has no capacity to link his thoughts and feelings, the only way he has to make sense of the women's action becomes: "Those two women did look at me and whisper, and laugh about me." To be sure, answers like this do not require someone to deny their feelings; the young man in the example recognizes his discomfort. Rather, they process their feelings in a disordered way. In this example, one might expect the young man lacking the normal connection between thought and feelings to explain, "Of course I felt out of place. You would feel out of place too if women laughed at you!"

To compare this to Evangelical thinking, we might ask an Evangelical, "Did you consider the possibility that your feelings may have influenced the way you interpreted Christian claims before you accepted Jesus as your personal savior?" Remarkably, few Evangelicals seem to view their feelings prior to their conversion as problematic or as having any influence on their decision to become a Christian. Just like the young man in the example above, who does not connect his thoughts and feelings effectively, Evangelicals will also perceive that their feelings around the time of conversion as logically resulting from normal traits that God instills in all of us. They will say something like, "When separated from God's love, of course I felt empty, insignificant, and alone. But I stopped trying to fake happiness. God had a plan for my life that I could not see because I spent all my time looking out for myself. I thought I did not need God. It took sinking to the level I sank before I realized how much I needed God." In other words, they say that they felt uneasy and insecure because they were being laughed at and do not consider that their feelings of unease and insecurity might have caused them to misinterpret what was going on in the world around them.

I have asked some Evangelicals directly, "Would you consider it *wrong*—or a *sin*—to consider the possibility that your feelings may have influenced the way you interpret the evidence for Christianity?" I have found that most Evangelicals seem to indicate that doubting the influence of God on their feelings would indicate weak faith, and perhaps even a sin. Evangelicals do not acknowledge the possibility that their strong feelings may have made them vulnerable to sloppy reasoning. It is completely missing from the stories that Evangelicals tell each other—

their personal testimonies. An Evangelical who admitted that Christianity looked good to her because she felt lonely, and going to church gave her something to do and a new set of friends, would immediately slide down a level or so in Hooks and Ladders.

PAUL'S THEOLOGY + "SINNER'S PRAYER" + EXPLANATION PG = HOOKS AND LADDERS

From Paul we understand that worthlessness triumphs in the believer. Sinful man cannot reliably do anything without God. Life is worth nothing without the gift of salvation. Anyone who rejects God does so willfully and in bad faith. They clearly see God's truth. Believers must accept everything their personal god tells them without question, as most cannot even envision any other alternative. They cannot think about the connection between their own thoughts and feelings, and yet they insist they can know the thoughts of other people better than those people do themselves. To the extent they cannot or will not consider a connection between their thoughts and feeling, Evangelicals' beliefs become unfixable.

5. Evangelical History and Hooks and Ladders

WHAT HAPPENS ONCE THE NEW EVANGELICAL CHRISTIAN prays the "Sinner's Prayer" and accepts Jesus into his or her heart? To answer this question, we must look at the Evangelical Community and Evangelical churches. Most Evangelical Christians do not live in a vacuum. Most Christians had another Christian "lead them to Christ." Consequently, most new converts have a strong relationship with a member of a local Evangelical church and feel compelled to attend the same church as their Christian mentor.

In my case, my mother, my two brothers, and I began to attend the same church as those who led us to Christ, and we joined the group of committed Christians at The Fellowship Center. It became a full-immersion experience. We not only attended on Sunday mornings, but we also went to youth groups and other events during the week. Immersed in church life, I had my first experiences with Hooks and Ladders, as I described in the first chapter.

Hooks and Ladders takes a group to play. It takes a group to operate the phantom hooks. It takes a group to explain how becoming a doubting Christian can lead to a loss of stature in their community. It takes a group to band together and to let the nonbelievers know that "it is not too late" to give their lives to Christ—and win Hooks and Ladders.

We have seen how an individual will adopt certain thought processes—indeed will *have* to adopt those processes—in order to become and remain an Evangelical. We have seen, in contrast, that the rules of Hooks and Ladders prevent the individual Evangelical Christian from trying to follow the teachings of Jesus independently. We have seen, as a result, that those thoughts necessarily involve acceptance of the rules of Hooks and Ladders, even if the individual remains unaware that he or she has done so. It is now time to look at the Evangelical community and its role in shaping and enforcing the rules of Hooks and Ladders.

Immediately, we run into problems. We cannot pin down Evangelicals easily. First, Evangelicals, despite what they may claim, cannot share identical delusional worlds. To some extent, each

Evangelical will add a personal spin to the standard. Consequently, Evangelicals display a wide range of opinions about what the board of Hooks and Ladders looks like. Because of this, and because the Evangelical community does not have a formal structure like the Catholic Church, it is easy for Evangelicals, when confronted with evidence of poor Evangelical behavior, to avoid dealing with the criticism by saying, "My church does not do that," or "I would not call them True Christians," for example.

Still, there are certain aspects of Evangelical Christianity that all Evangelicals share. So I will attempt to define what "Evangelical Christian" means—especially to the people whom the Evangelical community embraces as True Christians. Readers beware! Many Evangelicals can easily slip out of these knots. Evangelicals are good at redrawing the game board so that the hooks hold nothing and the ladders lead nowhere.

EVIDENCE OF COMPARATIVE ADVANTAGE

Before we can look at the current Evangelical community, we have to go back at least 250 years to sort out where Evangelicals came from. A brief summary of this history will provide context for many issues in this book.

American Protestants lack easily identifiable religious rituals. They also lack an extensive religious calendar and legalistic religious laws. As a result, they move easily in a secular culture, and there are few, if any, ways to distinguish them from secular people.

Two hundred years ago, Protestants promoted the values we now call "American values." Most American Protestants, and nearly all Evangelicals, approved of democracy over monarchy, simplicity over rituals and splendor, and "common sense" over legalism. Many Protestants, and most Evangelicals, demonstrated a disdain for the organized church and government. Hard work and discipline distinguished the committed Christian from others. American Protestants promoted personal responsibility and a belief that "all truth is God's truth." Many became motivated to uncover God's truths through properly applied scientific principles and reason.

Most American Protestants felt the Bible contained the infallible Word of God. However, they felt the individual could access the truths of the Bible without relying on church authorities to interpret the meaning for them—"the priesthood of all believers." They believed that God dealt with each of them individually. This inspired an earthly individualism and self-reliance. Protestants in America seemed to have an attitude of uncertainty about almost everything except their faith.

In the early years of the American republic, Evangelicals shared most of their views with other American Protestants. Evangelical Christianity itself grew out of a tradition called "Pietism." The cornerstone of Pietism is a personal relationship with God. Like the Pietists before them, Evangelicals stressed responsibility and self-control and believed Christian values could help establish and maintain social order. They had an optimistic view of human nature. They believed people had the potential to apply Christian standards to improve society.

For the Evangelical Protestant, conversion required a change in attitude that typically came from an emotional experience that appealed to the heart, not the mind. As we have seen, conversion remains an emotional experience. Evangelicals use the phrase, "Jesus came into my heart," not the awkward sounding, "Jesus came into my mind."

Evangelicals preached that, "once saved, always saved." However, this did not seem to provide the same assurance of salvation that structured religions provided. Evangelical Christians often have a feeling of uncertainty about whether they were *really* saved. This provided a useful glitch.

Many Evangelicals seemed to have a recurring doubt about whether they had valid conversion experiences. Thus, you will frequently hear stories about Evangelicals who "asked Jesus to come into their heart" many times before they felt confident in their salvation. Many pray, throughout their lives, for God to give them assurance of salvation. Some have "rededicated" their lives to Christ after a period of "backsliding." Indeed, many Evangelicals never entirely shake their anxiety about salvation. Many past Evangelicals' anxiety about salvation increased even further because there were few outward signs by which to identify American Protestants and Evangelicals.

Some Evangelicals overcompensated for this insecurity. They acted in a way that proved to others, as well as to themselves, their commitment to Christ. They woke up earlier, worked harder, volunteered more, and lived more simply. Evangelical Protestants acted considerately and cheerfully to show the world that their hearts had changed.

At the time of the American Revolution, the popular values of the Enlightenment matched most of the values of Evangelical Protestants. Both values challenged stale religious traditions and church governance. Both values rejected monarchies. Evangelical values added context to Enlightenment ideals. When motivated by a love for God, Evangelicals provided insurance for the Enlightenment ideals of reason, liberty, and freedom by implementing them for the "right reasons."

Evangelicals created a culture that thrived under America's new capitalist government. This success probably reinforced a belief that Protestant values represented the "right way" to live. Evangelicals, like Pietists, did not spend much money. They had money to invest, which they did. They also continued to work hard. This "Protestant work ethic" proved lucrative, but the ethics of personal piety safeguarded against excessive materialism.

It is fair to say that Evangelical Protestant values prevented America's young democracy from falling prey to a charismatic dictator. They promoted higher education and dedication to science. Most importantly, they prevented the rise of a government-sponsored church. However, the story does not end there.

Enlightenment

Undoubtedly, both the Enlightenment and the Romantic period that followed generated criticism of Christianity. For example, Enlightenment philosophers like Immanuel Kant argued that we could never prove a metaphysical position. Thus, questions like, "Is there a God?" or "Do we have free will?" will never have conclusive answers, according to Kant. This argument made the certainty of Christians' belief seem unjustifiable.

Around 1800, the Enlightenment became unfashionable. Intellectuals replaced what they saw as the dull and cold reasoning of the Enlightenment with a new set of artistic, soulful, and aesthetic ideals. The Romantic era began. Yet Romantics seemed even more critical of Christians than their Enlightenment predecessors did. Many viewed Christians as clinging to outdated creeds that stifled creativity. Many felt Christians were too rational, too much like the Enlightenment thinkers. How did Christians respond to the criticisms coming from both Enlightenment thinkers and the Romanticists?

Schleiermacher Persuasive in Blocking the Antibiotic of Reason

Enter Friedrich Schleiermacher, a Reformed (Calvinist) chaplain at a charity hospital in Berlin, Germany. Schleiermacher held to the traditions of Protestant Pietism and pledged devotion to God unapologetically. Despite his faith, Schleiermacher actively participated and thrived in a highbrow social group. His circle of friends included a number of avant-garde, early-German Romanticists. Schleiermacher labeled this group as "cultured despisers of religion."

The Romanticists in his group considered Schleiermacher an enigma. They had all freed themselves from organized religion. They could not understand how Schleiermacher could share many of their views but remain a dedicated Christian minister. On his birthday in 1797, his friends cornered him and made him promise to write a book explaining how he could remain a Christian. Two years later, Schleiermacher presented *On Religion: Speeches to Its Cultured Despisers* to his friends.[1]

Schleiermacher's defense of Christianity seems to have successfully changed the views of many of his "despiser" friends. They no longer viewed passionate religious convictions as a marker for someone who was automatically ignorant and uncool, to use a modern expression. In America, where "cool" presented less of a problem than it did in Europe, Schleiermacher's defense of Christianity was even more persuasive. His writing influenced many intellectuals in major American colleges and universities like Harvard, Yale, and Princeton. What did Schleiermacher write that seemed so compelling at the time?

Schleiermacher explained that his critics would never grasp his religion by using the tools of philosophy, science, and ethics. Schleiermacher felt that true religions stemmed from our innate feelings of "utter dependence on God." No human tool, he argued, such as science or philosophy, adequately described this religious feeling. He argued these limitations represented human limitations, not divine limitations.

Although Schleiermacher did not use this analogy, one could compare his defense somewhat to the often-heard commentary about love: "If you've never been in love before, you will not understand how I feel." In the same way, Schleiermacher explains:

> Of all that I praise, all that I feel to be the true work of religion, you would find little even in the sacred books. To the man who has not himself experienced it, it would only be an annoyance and a folly....
>
> If you have only given attention to these dogmas and opinions, therefore, you do not yet know religion itself, and what you despise is not it.[2]

Schleiermacher almost single-handedly silenced criticism of Christianity. With his *Speeches,* people no longer regarded faith as incompatible with science and reason. Most importantly, Schleiermacher ended an era where intellectuals treated Christians as ignorant. Indeed, intellectuals abruptly stopped treating Christians as inferiors.

Consider the culture of skepticism in America in the 1790s. Thomas Paine, for example, published the first part of his *Age of Reason* in 1794. Paine's book was a bestseller—despite containing a scathing attack of Christianity. The following quote from *Age of Reason* typifies some of the open disregard for Christianity many had at that time:

> Christian Mythologists bring the two ends of their fable together. They represent this virtuous and amiable man, Jesus Christ, to be at once both God and Man, and also the Son of God, celestially begotten, on purpose to be sacrificed, because they say that Eve in her longing had eaten an apple.
>
> Putting aside everything that might excite laughter by its absurdity, or detestation by its profaneness, and confining ourselves merely to an examination of the parts, it is impossible to conceive a story more derogatory to the Almighty, more inconsistent with his wisdom, more contradictory to his power, than this story is.[3]

Paine, at the time seemed highly regarded among college students. Consider what Lyman Beecher, a student at Yale in 1795, wrote about his peers that year:

> The college church was almost extinct. Most of the students were skeptical, and rowdies were plenty.
>
> That was the day of the infidelity of the Tom Paine school. Boys that dressed flax in the barn, as I used to, read Tom Paine and believed him; I read, and fought him all the way. Never had any propensity to infidelity. But most of the class before me were infidels, and called each other Voltaire, Rousseau, D Alembert, etc., etc.[4]

But Paine's *Age of Reason* probably marked the end of an era when such an aggressive attack of religious ideas could achieve bestseller status.

In 1795, Timothy Dwight, a grandson of the highly regarded theologian Jonathan Edwards, became president of Yale College. Dwight relentlessly defended Christianity. Initially, Dwight had limited success at converting his skeptical students. In his seventh year at Yale, however, a revival broke out and nearly a third of Yale's 230 students converted to Christianity.[5] To put this in perspective, even though Yale now has thousands of students, an evangelist that could successfully convert the same number of Yale students today (roughly 76), let alone a third of

Yale's student body, would achieve world renown! Dwight restored respectability for a Christian position at one of America's most prestigious colleges.

To have caused such a change in only seven years, Dwight must have profoundly influenced American culture. Yet Timothy Dwight and the Yale revival are largely forgotten today. Even at the time, academics hardly took notice of the Yale revival. Why did this remarkable event not generate even a yawn of criticism from the previously skeptical elite? Schleiermacher's arguments, even if not fully accepted, had by then permeated academic circles. His defense of religion may well have sparked a change in the tone directed toward Christians and in the respect given them.

In just a few short years, Christians rebounded from naïve and stupid to respectable in the mind of the elite. Indeed, by 1802 many felt that a commitment to Christ might provide someone with a beneficial perspective. Paine went from appealing to the *cool* people with a revolutionary spirit to symbolizing the elite's misguided hostility toward those with *faith*. This change in perspective has endured. Even now, over two hundred years later, many Americans automatically scorn someone for criticizing Christian beliefs.

Although it is hard to imagine now, in 1800 there were probably substantially fewer college graduates from every college or university in America and Europe combined than there are graduates this year from Ohio State University. Thus, it took only the softening of a few key academic elite to distance themselves from people like Thomas Paine.

Certainly today, Christianity has its critics. In fact, books critical of Christianity have become bestsellers in recent years, just as Paine's books did in the 1790s. However, personal faith remains largely off-limits to criticism. Schleiermacher deserves as much credit as anyone for this. He helped usher in an era where people of faith can participate in a tolerant public forum. Who knows what American history would be like if Schleiermacher did not get intellectuals and religious critics off the backs of Christians? Although today there is a rash of books (like this one) to challenge the prudence, ethics, and rationality of religious faith, I cannot help but think that Schleiermacher and his advocates delayed this process by two centuries.

Schleiermacher remains a very obscure historical figure. What may be surprising is that Evangelicals consider him the father of "Protestant liberal theology" and a heretic. Historians credit Schleiermacher with ushering in an era of liberal and tolerant theology. They credit his theology for shaping over a hundred years of religious thought, influencing Protestant religious teachings even today.

I take issue with the conventional view. Despite Schleiermacher's influence, strong pressures on religious orthodoxy already existed. The trend toward liberal theology, or the abandonment of Christianity altogether, was for many reasons inevitable. But Schleiermacher's defense of Christianity had the effect of lessening the criticism directed toward Evangelicals and fundamentalists. Even today, while certain fundamentalist claims may provoke some eye rolling, such as their claim that God inspired the King James Version of the Bible, they do not, or have not until recently, received the scathing response such a claim would have incited Thomas Paine to make. Schleiermacher, as much as anybody, made it seem uncool (and certainly uncivil) to attack someone for their religious faith. Evangelicals and fundamentalists have been the greatest beneficiaries of Schleiermacher's liberal theology.

Few, If Any, Atheists in the Eighteenth Century

One thing deserves mention. Kant, Schleiermacher, and others, like Thomas Jefferson, held a largely unquestioned belief in the existence of a creator. Before 1800, people had to explain how very complex animals and humans came into existence. Most people had limited exposure to the diversity of life on the earth. As a result, believing that everything just somehow appeared did not make much sense. Consequently, these thinkers usually assumed that everybody agreed in a creator of some sort. For this reason, atheists, as we think of them today, may not have existed. Yet despite nearly universal belief in a creator, many found Christianity untenable. They had no trouble reconciling the existence of an intelligent designer with a rejection of many of Christianity's other claims.

Around this same time, in the late eighteenth century, new discoveries and explanations seemed to hammer away at the Creation story told in Genesis. Before the nineteenth century, few doubted the earth's age numbered in the thousands of years. Around 1780, however, James Hutton first reasoned that the earth had existed for billions of years. After noticing that a 1,650-year-old Roman wall in Scotland had hardly eroded at all when compared to a nearby and nearly leveled volcano, he surmised that the volcano must have existed thousands of times longer than the Roman wall.* Other evidence continued to chip away at the Genesis account of creation. For example, dinosaurs were not discovered until the 1820s.†

Before these scientific discoveries, sound scholarship had already buried Evangelical claims about biblical authority. By the time Darwin described evolution in the mid-nineteenth century, atheism had already become a more viable position. Although many overestimate the importance of evolutionary theory, when seeing it as a first strike against biblical authority, it is entirely possible to consider evolution to be the final nail in the coffin of an already-moribund view. Indeed, what the advent of evolutionary theory seems to have done was to have bolstered many Christians' resolve to fight against the already well-established critics of their God. They lumped all of their critics in with the already vibrant and expanding ranks of "the godless atheists." The fight continues in Internet forums today.

Evangelicals inherited from Pietism a belief in the importance of a personal relationship with God. Like other American Protestants, they were suspicious of organized institutions and believed strongly in the importance of the individual. Although they were despised for their emotionalism by the Enlightenment generation, many granted them enhanced status through Schleiermacher's writings, which encouraged tolerance and respect for others' religious beliefs. All of these things set the stage for Hooks and Ladders—but it took recent events to create the game Evangelicals play today.

Definition of Evangelical

Now let us return to the contemporary Evangelical community. First, let us define what Evangelical Christianity means. This is an ambitious undertaking, as Evangelical Christianity spans many Protestant denominations with diverse views. George Barna, a respected Evangelical

---

* Hadrian's Wall, built by the Romans in 122 C.E., still stands in Scotland. Based on his suspicion about the earth's age given the erosion of the volcano and an assumption of *uniformitarianism,* Hutton concluded the earth could not be 5800 years old as Christian theologians had suggested. He concluded the age measured in *billions* of years.

† Reverend William Buckland is credited with the first scientific description of a dinosaur, Megalosaurus, based on a jawbone with teeth found in 1815 and described in 1824.

pollster, defines an Evangelical as a person who can affirm all of the following:

- Do you believe Jesus Christ lived a sinless life?
- Do you believe eternal salvation is possible only through grace, not works?
- Do you believe Christians have a personal responsibility to share their religious beliefs about Christ with non-Christians?
- Is your faith very important to your life today?
- Do you believe Satan is a real, living entity?
- Do you believe God is the all-knowing, all-powerful, perfect deity who created the universe and still rules it today?
- Do you believe the Bible is totally accurate in all that it teaches?

While some may require believers to make additional affirmations before they will consider them True Christians, the above points are an uncontroversial Evangelical baseline.

Battle for the Bible

Today, an Evangelical Christian must believe that the Bible has divine authority. This forms the basis for the last statement in Barna's description of the Evangelical. Yet, most Evangelicals have no idea that the specifics of this belief became an obsession, and most have never heard about the recent "Battle for the Bible," even though this battle played a huge role in shaping the current Evangelical community.

In the early 1970s, some Evangelical Christian leaders felt that too many biblical scholars believed the Bible had errors. The International Congress on World Evangelization, held in Lausanne, Switzerland, in 1974, addressed this issue. The congress, headed by Billy Graham, had 2300 attendees from 150 countries. This resulted in the *Lausanne Covenant*, which included a statement about the authority of the Bible as follows:

> We affirm the divine inspiration, truthfulness and authority of both Old and New Testament Scriptures in their entirety as the only written word of God, without error in all that it affirms, and the only infallible rule of faith and practice.[6]

This statement addresses the inerrancy (which means, "without errors") and authority of the Bible. At a minimum, most people (and certainly most Evangelicals) would not consider a person an Evangelical if they did not agree with a position at least as strong as the *Lausanne Covenant*. A person will certainly lose Hooks and Ladders if they believe that the *Lausanne Covenant* overstates the authority of the Bible.

But some of the most respected Evangelicals, people like theologian Francis Schaeffer, felt that Evangelicals needed an even stronger statement about inerrancy. It may not be immediately obvious why this is so. After all, the *Lausanne Covenant* affirms the divine "truthfulness ... of both Old and New Testament Scriptures," describes them as "without error," and refers to the Bible as "the only infallible rule of faith and practice." However, the more conservative theologians, like Dr. Schaeffer, realized that the *Lausanne Covenant* contained a possible loophole through which some Evangelicals could slip. The phrase "without error in all that it affirms" could be viewed as limiting the Bible's infallibility (and also its authority, as we shall see) to religious values and spiritual matters, instead of recognizing the Bible's infallibility in *all* areas of thought and experience, including history, science, politics, medicine, art, law, and any other topic you could imagine.

This loophole would allow a Christian claiming to be an Evangelical to recite the *Lausanne Covenant* with enthusiasm while believing, for example, that biblical passages involving astronomy had mistakenly described the way the world works. So the story in the book of Joshua, where the sun seems to revolve around the earth, for example, could have merely reflected the limited understanding of the scientifically undeveloped culture in which the Bible was written. Dr. Schaeffer thought that by opening a culturally based loophole for science, the *Lausanne Covenant* opened a loophole for other areas as well. As he explained:

> This problem can be seen in what has happened to the statement on Scripture in the Lausanne Covenant of 1974 ...
>
> Upon first reading, this seems to make a strong statement in support of the full authority of the Bible. But a problem has come up concerning the phrase "in all that it affirms." For many this is being used as a loophole....
>
> Those weakening the Bible in the area of history and where it touches the cosmos do so by saying these things in the Bible are

> *culturally oriented.* That is ... it only shows forth views held by the culture in the day in which that portion of the Bible was written ...
>
> But let us realize that one cannot begin such a process without going still further ... Now certain moral absolutes in the area of personal relationships given in the Bible are also said to be culturally oriented ...
>
> There is no end to this. The Bible is made to say only that which echoes the surrounding culture at our moment of history. *The Bible is bent to the culture instead of the Bible judging our society and culture* [all emphasis in original].
>
> Once men and women begin to go down the path of the existential methodology under the name of evangelicalism, the Bible is no longer the Word of God without error—each part may be eaten away step by step....
>
> Notice though what the primary problem was, and is: infiltration by a form of the world view which surrounds us, rather than the Bible being the unmovable base for judging the ever-shifting fallen culture. As evangelicals, we need to stand at the point of the call *not* to be infiltrated by this ever-shifting fallen culture which surrounds us, but rather judging that culture upon the basis of the Bible.[7]

Because of this perceived loophole, Dr. Schaeffer and other like-minded Evangelicals launched a campaign to make a more definitive statement about inerrancy.

International Council of Biblical Inerrancy (ICBI)

There were many who felt strongly that Evangelicals would head toward disaster unless they endorsed inerrancy strongly. By 1976, such concerns had gained enough steam to inspire a conference of those seeking to strengthen the Evangelical position on inerrancy. Dr. Jay Grimstead put together the International Council of Biblical Inerrancy (ICBI). This is what Dr. Grimstead recalls as the motivation to organize this council:

> Somebody should attempt to organize a national theological conference to deal with this battle for the inerrancy of the Bible and to expose the fallacies of the neo-orthodox false assumptions believed by so many Evangelicals at that time. What I visualized was something of a theological "army" of scholars who would take this thing into battle as a united team.[8]

CHICAGO STATEMENT OF BIBLICAL INERRANCY

The ICBI presented their culminating work in 1978 on what they called Reformation Sunday. Over three hundred prominent Evangelicals signed the council's conclusions, titled *The Chicago Statement of Biblical Inerrancy*.

This statement did not attempt to justify the belief of inerrancy based on evidence. In fact, it eliminated any possibility that evidence could exist to refute their position by simply denying the validity of contradictory evidence. Most of their doctrines are found in a section called "Affirmations and Denials." For example:

Article I.

We affirm that the Holy Scriptures are to be received as the authoritative Word of God.

We deny that the Scriptures receive their authority from the Church, tradition, or any other human source.

Article V.

We affirm that God's revelation in the Holy Scriptures was progressive.

We deny that later revelation, which may fulfill earlier revelation, ever corrects or contradicts it. We further deny that any normative revelation has been given since the completion of the New Testament writings.

Article VIII.

We affirm that God in His work of inspiration utilized the distinctive personalities and literary styles of the writers whom He had chosen and prepared.

We deny that God, in causing these writers to use the very words that He chose, overrode their personalities

Article XII.

We affirm that Scripture in its entirety is inerrant, being free from all falsehood, fraud, or deceit.

We deny that Biblical infallibility and inerrancy are limited to spiritual, religious, or redemptive themes, exclusive of assertions in the fields of history and science. We further deny that scientific hypotheses about earth history may properly be used to overturn the teaching of Scripture on creation and the flood.

Article XIV.

We affirm the unity and internal consistency of Scripture.
We deny that alleged errors and discrepancies that have not yet been resolved violate the truth claims of the Bible.

Article XVI.

We affirm that the doctrine of inerrancy has been integral to the Church's faith throughout its history.
We deny that inerrancy is a doctrine invented by scholastic Protestantism, or is a reactionary position postulated in response to negative higher criticism.[9]

NO DISSENT BY DECREE

The ICBI simply denied that anybody could rightly disagree with them and remain a True Christian. For example, we might consider it reasonable to figure out for ourselves whether the affirmations and denials in Article XVI were true. We could comb through historical documents and come to our own conclusions about this claim. But the ICBI rejects our right to do this. In fact, they reject anyone else's right or ability to do this, even though this particular affirmation has nothing to do with the truth of inerrancy.

The ICBI had no interest in supporting their beliefs on inerrancy with evidence or persuasive reasoning. They felt special enough to issue a decree that established truth, which one had to believe in order to be a True Christian, and they eliminated the possibility of dissent. In doing so, they removed the possibility of open dialogue within Evangelical Christianity about inerrancy.

ARE EVANGELICAL LIBERALS HARMFUL?

Let's back up a moment and think about what problem the ICBI wanted to solve with the *Chicago Statement*. After all, most Evangelicals already subscribed to the *Lausanne Covenant*, which affirmed "the truthfulness and authority" of the Bible "in [its] entirety as the only written word of God, without error ..." Certainly most Evangelical scholars shared the ICBI members' views of Jesus' death and resurrection, as well as their views of the path to salvation.

Yet the ICBI viewed these Evangelical scholars as heretics and labeled them "liberals." Could those liberal in interpreting the Bible, but conservative in virtually every other way, really threaten our entire civilization? The ICBI inerrantists thought so. With a perceived urgency, *The Chicago Statement on Biblical Inerrancy* became the line in the sand.

In a sense, this statement represented a declaration of war against those Evangelicals labeled as liberals. Inerrantists felt confronting liberal theologians about inerrancy represented the first battleground in the Battle for the Bible. The ICBI mobilized a theological army and set off to fight.

As the inerrantist leaders gained power, their ideas and doctrines trickled down to the Evangelical churches. Through pastors' sermons, Sunday school lessons, and books, the ICBI concept of inerrancy seeped into the average Evangelical churchgoer's consciousness, even though he or she likely had no idea of the battle raging behind the scenes. As defending inerrancy against its liberal detractors rose in importance among the Evangelical elite, matters like helping the poor, comforting the sick, and living a humble Christ-like life seemed faraway concerns. The issues that Jesus emphasized took a backseat to an issue with no practical significance for the average churchgoer.

Inerrancy Equals Authority

Let us assume we accept the ICBI's claim that the Bible contains no errors. Have they shown any evidence supporting their benefits of this view? As well, have they granted special meaning to the word "inerrancy" that does not otherwise exist?

The word "inerrancy" simply means "without error." Can we apply this word to anything that has no errors? For instance, we may be unaware of any errors in the laws of thermodynamics, but can we call laws of thermodynamics inerrant? Do inerrant things have special characteristics? For example, if I answered 100 percent of my calculus test questions correctly, does that make me inerrant in calculus? Would I deserve special, or even supernatural, consideration based on my inerrancy in calculus?

When its members wrote the *Chicago Statement*, the ICBI had more in mind for the Bible than simply establishing it as error free. After all, my receiving a 100 percent on my calculus test does not make me the king of calculus, and an error-free Bible does not necessarily have any special power either, aside from perhaps deserving more respect than a book riddled with mistakes. But the ICBI merged the concept of authority into its definition of inerrancy. If an inerrant Bible is also an authoritative Bible, then it starts to take on some power, even though that power does not derive from its inerrant status.

Interestingly, the first article in the ICBI's statement on inerrancy says nothing about inerrancy! It does, however, talk about authority. It reads:

> We affirm that the Holy Scriptures are to be received as the authoritative Word of God.
>
> We deny that the Scriptures receive their authority from the Church, tradition, or any other human source.

Just like magic—a creepy Ouija-board-like magic—inerrancy and authority are joined. Now, an error-free statement like 1+1+1=3 from outside the Bible becomes subordinate to a biblical claim that 1+1+1=1. Article I provides no evidence or even argument about inerrancy, but somehow we feel obligated to link inerrancy and authority. We are off to the races! Even a brief acknowledgment that the words "inerrancy" and "authority" have different meanings is lacking.

Perhaps the Bible's inerrancy naturally confers authority. But even if the Bible has no errors, what authority does the Bible have over a distant star, for example? As I said above, error-free books have more reliability than mistake-filled ones, but is that the same as being *authoritative*? Would a book's inerrancy make it authoritative only compared to other books? Could a book, even one divinely inspired, have authority over people? Alternatively, maybe the claim is that the error-free book itself tells us who or what has authority and we must assume that its designation is correct. None of these questions are answered; none are even mentioned or alluded to.

The ICBI felt it unnecessary to establish a link between the doctrine of inerrancy and biblical authority. And, indeed, it comes as no surprise that inerrantists glossed over their reasons for linking inerrancy and authority since these questions are hard to answer. But the inerrantists do leave the strong impression that because they believed in inerrancy, and were willing to mount a campaign to defend it, God has entrusted them with the special assignment to protect God's Word (from liberals, apparently) and execute God's will. Reading between the lines, the most important affirmation in the *Chicago Statement* was not about the Bible's inerrancy. It was not even about the Bible's authority over the lives of Evangelical Christians. It was about the authority that signers of the *Chicago Statement* and their allies would wield over the lives of Evangelical Christians. By drawing the line in the sand and launching their theological army of scholars, the ICBI members seized the power to decide who was in and who was out of the Evangelical fold.

Some have argued that this view of a few theologians thirty years ago has had little impact on the Evangelicals. That view is incorrect. The ICBI and similar groups have unabashedly implemented tactics of bullying and intimidation that continue to influence Evangelical Christianity.

Dr. Jay Grimstead, in recalling that time, describes Reformation Sunday as theological D-Day. He recounts the aftermath as follows:

> The net result was that there was an immediate reversal of who was in the "closet." Even though not many liberal Evangelical scholars really changed their position theologically, they knew that under this new theological climate we had created they would not be able to be as bold about their departure from inerrancy … Because of the visibility and success of the ICBI in its united and scholarly defense of inerrancy, many schools, churches, mission organizations, and some denominations began rethinking their doctrinal statements on Scripture. They realized that, because of the prevailing liberal theological "smog" most of their members had been breathing and because of the great confusion that reigned and the deliberate efforts of the liberalized Evangelicals within most ranks, they had to tighten up on their official statements on Scripture and require adherence to the orthodox view by their leadership and members.[10]

Grimstead seems unconcerned that we might consider this intimidation. Indeed he and others seem to have no problem with bullying and intimidation if it helped spread their beliefs. They view these as tools to accomplish their mission.

Agreeing to and signing Statements of Faith that affirmed belief in inerrancy became vital to survival in Evangelical Christian churches, schools, and seminaries. Some resisted this effort, but the resisters have suffered relentless pressure and intimidation. The original signers of the *Chicago Statement*, as well as other similar statements, read like a who's who in contemporary Evangelical Christianity.[11]

At this point, for a pastor or Christian leader to express doubt about inerrancy or authority would require great sacrifices. Certainly, some have stood up to the specific language of inerrancy. However, very strong support for biblical authority remains required to avoid constant harassment. An interested reader may wish to review the recent history of the Southern Baptist Convention, which illustrates this point.

In addition, Evangelicals would have a difficult time showing how their treatment of the Bible differs from their own definition of idolatry. The obsession with promoting this type of biblical inerrancy has had the effect of elevating the Bible to the status of God. In fact, the ICBI would have to pull out special magical powers to deny that it did not proclaim God is the Bible, and the Bible is God! The *Chicago Statement* promoted a Quadrinity—a godhead of four in one. Look at what it says in a section titled, "Exposition" and subtitled, "Authority: Christ and the Bible":

> By authenticating each other's authority, Christ and Scripture coalesce into a single fount of authority. The Biblically-interpreted Christ and the Christ-centered, Christ-proclaiming Bible are from this standpoint one. As from the fact of inspiration we infer that what Scripture says, God says, so from the revealed relation between Jesus Christ and Scripture we may equally declare that what Scripture says, Christ says.[12]

The Quadrinity replaces the Trinity. Inerrantists have added the Bible to the list of the godheads, alongside God the Father, the Son, and the Holy Ghost. Inerrantists gave the bibliocentric God of modern Evangelical Christians legitimate status.

In some cases, this reverence for God's Word is almost superstitious. Try to put a wet glass on a Bible in an Evangelical's home. In the movie *The Apostle*, a preacher sets a Bible in front of a tractor driven by another character. The tractor-driver is spooked by it as if it were a black cat or a broken mirror. Consider the preacher who takes his thick, black, leather-bound book, shakes it in the air, and tells us about the power of the Word of God. Does this preacher mean the same thing as when he discusses the power of God? Should we believe that power could emanate from the book he shakes?

For the signers of the *Chicago Statement*, holding up the Bible and shaking it does not mean much—unless it is shaken by the right person. After all, a liberal Christian or a Catholic priest, for example, can quote the Bible and shake it as well as anyone else can. Rather, it seems that these inerrantists wanted to ensure that everyone understood that they represented the only spiritually equipped people to interpret the holy book properly, which they elevated to the status of God.

Francis Schaeffer

Whether because of the ICBI's campaign of intimidation or simply because they heard it so often, most Evangelicals bought into the inerrantists' hype about the dangers of liberals. They accepted that Evangelical schools and seminaries had too many liberals, even if they had never met one in person. They believed liberalism and its fellow-travelers of humanism, communism, modernism, and post-modernism had infiltrated these schools. The label of "intellectual" usually described a person corrupted by one or all of these *isms*. Of course, Evangelical leaders admonished their community to avoid intellectuals at all costs.

Ironically, one of the people widely regarded as an intellectual by Evangelical Christians, Francis A. Schaeffer, was also one of the most strident and influential supporters of the *Chicago Statement* version of inerrancy. Although many outside of Evangelical Christianity are not familiar with his work, Francis Schaeffer did more than just about anyone else did to demonize the methods of those who displayed discomfort about the Bible's inerrancy. Schaeffer advocated considering proponents of inerrancy as immune from criticism, as described in Article XVI above. He viewed the Bible as absolute truth.

Schaeffer characterized inerrancy as the watershed issue for Evangelicals. He felt that the Christian community should confront those that did not affirm this belief. Schaeffer explained why he acted with urgency to address the inerrancy issue in his book with the none-too-subtle title, *The Great Evangelical Disaster*:

> Does inerrancy make a difference? Overwhelmingly; the difference is that with the Bible being what it is, God's Word and so absolute, God's objective truth, we do not need to be, and we should not be, caught in the ever-changing fallen cultures which surround us. Those who do not hold the inerrancy of Scripture do not have this high privilege. To some extent, they are at the mercy of the fallen, changing culture. And Scripture is thus bent to conform to the changing world spirit of the day, and they therefore have no solid authority upon which to judge and to resist the views and values of that changing, shifting world spirit.[13]

Among Evangelicals, Schaeffer has a reputation as a great Christian thinker. He first gained popular acclaim in 1976 after publishing the book and film series, *How Should We Then Live?* In them, he describes the philosophies of groups and societies dating back to the Roman Empire. Schaeffer concluded that these cultures failed. In contrast, Christianity, as experienced in the Western world, was a success. Moreover, to the extent that any non-Christian group or movement had success, its members had embraced the teachings of Christianity to some extent.

Schaeffer attributed the failure of the non-Christian societies he examined to a lack of absolutes. Schaeffer wrote:

> *If there are no absolutes by which to judge society, then society is absolute.* Society is left with one man or an elite filling the vacuum left by the loss of the Christian consensus which originally gave us form and freedom in Northern Europe and in the West.... Absolutes can be *this* today and *that* tomorrow.... Arbitrary absolutes can be handed down and there is no absolute by which to judge them.[14]

Schaeffer's reputation as an intellectual giant muted any reasonable dialogue about his views. Although he may not have been the one to introduce it, he certain popularized the concept that absolutes are essential to a successful society and culture, and that a society without absolutes will surely fall; a concept that has become a bedrock belief in Evangelical Christian circles.

To illustrate what can happen to a society that rejects absolutes, Schaeffer chose abortion as his flagship issue. He argued that a civilization that refused to prohibit abortion *absolutely* would fall into an ethical doom. He suggested that a society's acceptance of a situational ethic that allowed for abortions under some circumstances would inevitably lead to the society's acceptance of a right to kill children and a right to euthanasia. He painted a picture of a gruesome world where people would kill as a matter of their convenience and receive no punishment.

Of course, none of Schaeffer's predictions have come true.* But anyone familiar with Schaeffer's work will understand why the Terri Schiavo case became such a concern to Evangelicals and their governmental allies, and why Evangelicals have reacted so strongly to the anomalous Jack Kevorkian and stem cell research; any one of these might herald the ethical decay of Schaeffer's forecast.

Schaeffer's works have had a profound effect on the current Evangelical community. First, by using abortion as his central issue he succeeded in energizing Evangelical Christians to oppose abortion through political and social action. Even more importantly, he redefined the way Evangelical Christians saw themselves and the way they viewed and defined their enemies.

---

* Schaeffer's arguments employed reasoning that is familiar to many who have participated in competitive debate—the "slippery slope" argument combined with the "parade of horribles." When I was on the debate team in high school, for example, we would have fun trying to show that virtually anything could connect to a serious risk of nuclear war.

Schaeffer's account of modern Western civilization's downward slide pits Christians against all species of non-Christians. Following Schaeffer, Evangelicals use the labels "situational ethicist," "humanist," "relativist," "Darwinist," "communist," and "liberal" interchangeably to mean *the enemy,* although Schaeffer himself would have at least acknowledged the differences among those philosophies. Also following Schaeffer, Evangelicals use the word "absolute" synonymously with "biblical," even though other faiths and secular belief systems certainly have their own sets of absolutes. And, the label "Christian," when used by an Evangelical, usually means "born-again Christian"—that is, some variety of Evangelical or fundamentalist—and not Catholic, Mormon, or even liberal Protestant. Both the style of viewing non-Christians as enemies and the terminology flow from Schaeffer's commitment to inerrancy and authority. In fact, many Evangelicals may not even realize that these words and concepts have radically different meanings outside the Evangelical community.*

CHRISTIAN CONSENSUS

In the quotation from Schaeffer above, he uses the phrase, "Christian consensus" to describe the people who are *not* destined for ethical disaster and societal failure. The Christian consensus in his view is what gave Western civilization form and freedom. By Christian consensus, he meant "the group of people that believe in the inerrancy of the Bible as described in the *Chicago Statement.*" Schaeffer acknowledged freely, and many Evangelicals agree, that those who do not believe in inerrancy simply should remain excluded from all Christian groups past or present. He wrote:

> It must be understood that the new humanism and the new theology have no concept of true truth—absolute truth. Relativism has triumphed in the church as well as in the university and in society. The true Christian, however, is called upon not only to teach truth, but to practice truth in the midst of such relativism....
>
> This means, among other things, that after we have done all we can on a personal level, if the liberals in the church persist in their liberalism, they should come under discipline. Christianity is not just

* This has led to numerous misunderstandings between Evangelicals and non-Evangelicals. Although both may use the same word in an argument, that same word may have an entirely different meaning to each participant.

> doctrinal truth, but flaming truth.... Liberalism, on the other hand, is unfaithfulness; *it is spiritual adultery toward the divine Bridegroom.*[15]

Schaeffer, and the other inerrantists, fully intended to keep the Christian consensus free of dissenters. He simply defined everyone who did not agree with him as out of the Christian picture, and he suggests that people who disagree with him should be ejected and "come under discipline," as he put it. Schaeffer explained: "We not only believe in the existence of truth, but we believe we have the truth ... Christ and the Bible have given us this truth."[16] In this, he laid the groundwork for Rules 2 and 3 of Hooks and Ladders.

Schaeffer makes this casting out of fellow Christians easier for Evangelicals to stomach by explaining how liberal theologians have committed spiritual adultery. Schaeffer frequently discussed "confrontation with love." His picture of liberal theologians is not particularly gentle, however. He leaves us with a picture of liberals, caught with their pants down, fornicating with some sleazy fake-god whore.* Given that Schaeffer's inerrant Bible requires stoning adulterers (presumably in a loving manner), Schaeffer leaves no room for these non-inerrantists to contribute to the Christian consensus. Remember, many of these supposed liberals did not have a liberal bone in their body; they simply believed that the *Lausanne Covenant* was a strong enough expression of biblical inerrancy while agreeing with the majority of Evangelicals on everything else.

Evangelicals' move toward a more biblically fundamentalist position required no input whatsoever from non-Evangelicals and took place largely under the radar of non-Evangelical culture. Even though virtually everyone in the Evangelical church already believed in the inerrancy and authority of the Bible before the battle began, the new emphasis given to inerrancy (really inerrancy and authority linked together) and the mustering of an army, as the inerrantists intended, made enforcement of the new definition feasible.

---

* In this case, Schaeffer's terminology may be more of a Freudian slip. Perhaps he felt screwed by these so-called spiritual adulterers.

6. Evangelical Enforcement

AS WE HAVE SEEN, CONSERVATIVES' VICTORY in the Battle for the Bible had a profound effect on contemporary Evangelical belief. In order to avoid the loophole of relativity through which liberals supposedly allowed Christianity to slip, Evangelicals were now obligated to affirm their faith in new and more forceful ways. The Battle for the Bible spawned the writing and rewriting of Evangelical organizations' Statements of Faith. Most of these statements now require members to believe in inerrancy. Indeed, inerrancy usually appears first on the list of required beliefs even though some might think Jesus deserved top billing. Let us look at some specific examples.

BIBLICAL INERRANCY AND AUTHORITY IN STATEMENTS OF FAITH

In chapter 2, I mentioned Evangelism Explosion, a training program I attended that trained me in one method for sharing the Gospel with nonbelievers. During my training with Evangelism Explosion, we learned two questions to ask people:

1. Do you know for sure that you are going to be with God in heaven?
2. If God were to ask you, "Why should I let you into my heaven?" what would you say?[1]

After dealing with these answers, one may lead someone to receive the free gift of eternal life by asking them to pray the "Salvation Prayer." Evangelism Explosion also outlines the steps necessary to become a Christian. Here are the steps:

1. Transfer your trust from what you have been doing to what Christ has done for you on his cross.
2. Accept Christ as Savior—open the door to your heart and invite him in.[2]
3. Receive Jesus Christ as Lord—give him the driver's seat and control of your life, not the back seat.

4. Repent—be willing to turn from anything that is not pleasing to him. He will reveal himself to you as you grow in your relationship with him.[3]

If someone truly does these things and means them in his or her heart, then that person forever has the free gift of eternal life.

Nowhere on that list does it state that a new convert must believe the Bible has no errors or that it is authoritative. But guess what is first on the list in Evangelism Explosion's own Statement of Faith:

1. The Bible is the inspired, the only infallible, authoritative Word of God.

Relegated to the middle of the pack:

5. Eternal life is received by faith—that is, trusting in Jesus Christ alone for salvation.[4]

Evangelical Christians rarely mention what has become their most important doctrine—the inerrancy and authority of the Bible.

Evangelism Explosion is not unique. Most typical Evangelical Christian organizations or churches have similar statements. Let us look at the Statements of Faith from some of the most prominent and successful Evangelical congregations. Willow Creek, located in the Chicago suburbs, was one of the first megachurches and is often criticized as too liberal. (For example, Bill Clinton went there to ask forgiveness for his sins and the church leaders allowed him to address the congregation.) Yet in a section titled, "What We Believe" on their Web site, Willow Creek's first statement of belief is:

> The sole basis of our belief is the Bible, which is uniquely God-inspired, without error, and the final authority on all matters on which it bears.[5]

What about other churches? New Life Church in Colorado Springs, Colorado, has as its first Statement of Faith:

> Holy Bible: The Holy Bible, and only the Bible, is the authoritative Word of God. It alone is the final authority for determining all doctrinal truths. In its original writing, the Bible is inspired, infallible and inerrant.[6]

What about Saddleback Church in Lake Forest, California? To their credit, they do not give Bible inerrancy top billing. But still, in a section titled "What We Believe" they have:

> The Bible is God's word to all men. It was written by human authors, under the supernatural guidance of the Holy Spirit. It is the supreme source of truth for Christian beliefs and living. Because it is inspired by God, it is truth without any mixture of error.[7]

What about Lakewood Church in Houston, Texas? In a section titled "Our Beliefs," the first thing we read is:

> WE BELIEVE ... the entire Bible is inspired by God, without error and the authority on which we base our faith, conduct and doctrine.[8]

What about high profile Evangelical Christian organizations, like Billy Graham Evangelistic Association? The first bullet point in its Statement of Faith:

> The Bible to be the infallible Word of God, that it is His holy and inspired Word, and that it is of supreme and final authority.[9]

Does Billy mention this important issue, which he gives top billing in the Statement of Faith, in his Crusades? Nope.

I checked to see what the Statement of Faith of my alma mater, Wheaton College, has to say:

> WE BELIEVE that God has revealed Himself and His truth in the created order, in the Scriptures, and supremely in Jesus Christ; and that the Scriptures of the Old and New Testaments are verbally inspired by God and inerrant in the original writing, so that they are fully trustworthy and of supreme and final authority in all they say.[10]

Promise Keepers, an organization whose purpose is "introducing men to Jesus Christ as their Savior and Lord; and then helping them to grow as Christians," has a Statement of Faith that currently reads:

> 2. God uniquely revealed and inspired the Bible, so that it alone is God's Word written, hence the Holy Scriptures are the only inerrant authority for what we believe about God's moral law, salvation from sin and how we should live.[11]

In fact, the current version of the Promise Keepers' Statement of Faith is an excellent example of the influence that the *Chicago Statement* continues to have on the Evangelical community. In December of 2007—when I was confirming my sources and changing dead or altered hyperlinks—I found that Promise Keepers had changed its Statement of Faith from an earlier version to the version listed above. Why did they change it? I do not know for sure, but the earlier version followed the *Lausanne Covenant*:

2. The Bible is God's written Word.

   The Bible is the revealed Word of God, given in and through the words of human writers whom the Holy Spirit inspired and guided. The Bible is truthful in all that it affirms and without error as originally given by God. The Bible tells us what we need to know about God, His law, His salvation, and how we should live. The Bible is the only infallible rule of faith and life. It alone is the final authority establishing all Christian doctrine.[12]

I said above that the *Lausanne Covenant** represents the softest and most liberal interpretation that Evangelical communities would tolerate. Some people, including perhaps the people in charge of Promise Keepers, had this soft interpretation of biblical authority changed to the more rigorous present version.

Monolithia

Some may have felt in the previous sections that I made too much fuss over the issue of inerrancy and authority. Some may feel I have exaggerated people's concerns about the weakness of wording that leaves room for interpretation of biblical authority. Many insist Evangelical Christianity has "a big tent" and has room for many interpretations.

But Statements of Faith like those listed above, and like the *Chicago Statement* itself, do not leave room for dissent. Their writers did not intend for them to leave room for dissent. By placing inerrancy/authority front and center, Evangelical leaders circumscribed the issues on which Evangelicals can differ. They set the boundaries for who can claim the title of Evangelical Christian. More than anything else, the inerrantists established themselves as the people who had the divine duty to make

---

* For comparison, here is the *Lausanne Covenant*: "We affirm the divine inspiration, truthfulness and authority of both Old and New Testament Scriptures in their entirety as the only written word of God, without error in all that it affirms, and the only infallible rule of faith and practice. We also affirm the power of God's word to accomplish his purpose of salvation. The message of the Bible is addressed to all men and women. For God's revelation in Christ and in Scripture is unchangeable."

that determination. The Evangelicals' big tent may have enough room for disagreement over the stylistic aspects of Evangelical worship—hymns versus praise songs, organ music versus electric guitars—but it does not have room for true dissent about any matter of importance.

In addition, the creation of a formal Statement of Faith, especially one that includes inerrancy/authority, provided a powerful means of control over Evangelical beliefs. Let me make it clear what I mean by this. I am not suggesting that Willow Creek churchgoers have to line up every Sunday and swear allegiance to the Statement of Faith before they enter the sanctuary. However, Evangelical Christian groups usually require signing an oath that is very much like swearing allegiance for participation beyond just membership. These oaths tend to be more detailed than an Evangelical church's Statement of Faith. These examples—perhaps the advanced version of the Statements of Faith—show both the power of the formal statement itself and the power of inerrancy/authority as a tool of control. They serve as a mechanism for the enforcement of Rule 2: *Evangelicals are always correct.* Let's take a look at how this works among the Evangelicals who have the high privilege of determining truth.

Rule Enforcement 101—Isolate and Control

Doctrine: Scholars at Wheaton and Liberty

The recent controversy involving Wheaton philosophy professor Joshua Hochschild is a perfect example. Professor Hochschild converted to Catholicism while teaching at Wheaton. Although he told Wheaton administrators that he would sign Wheaton's Statement of Faith, he was dismissed from his position because a Catholic cannot "faithfully affirm" that the Bible is the "supreme and final authority."[13] More recently, Wheaton fired an English professor, Kent Gramm, after he and his wife divorced because their divorce in some way violated biblical standards.[14]

At Wheaton College, many professors have private beliefs that barely resemble core Evangelical Christian doctrines. For example, some of my science professors accepted most of the theory of evolution and believed the earth has existed for billions of years. Many considered evidence of fulfilled prophecy unreliable, and many rejected the claim that the Bible has no errors. Many considered common Evangelical views about the Second Coming of Jesus unsubstantiated in Scripture. Of course, not all of them felt that way—I have had conversations with Evangelical educators whose theological beliefs ranged from liberal—in comparison to their schools' doctrines—to conservative fundamentalist.

Despite this diversity among Evangelical scholars, it seems nearly impossible to find a public record of their diverse thoughts. For example, where do we find an Evangelical biologist who feels comfortable calling herself an expert in evolutionary biology? Where do we find an Evangelical biologist who will freely discuss the pitfalls of teaching creationism? Even though many biologists at Christian colleges believe in evolutionary theory, few speak out against teaching creationism.

In the same way, many professors privately do not believe the Bible is without errors. Yet it seems exceedingly unlikely one will ever publicly speak out against a belief in the inerrancy of the Bible. At least, I have not been able to find any such pronouncements. Why? Speaking out against inerrancy would end the Evangelical academic's career. Such an assertion would violate the terms of the school's Statement of Faith. Professors must sign a Statement of Faith to teach at Wheaton. If they do not sign it, or if their publicly expressed beliefs contradict the statement, they will not teach at Wheaton.[15] With a career hanging in the balance, a lack of public pronouncements against inerrancy seems understandable.

Of course, Wheaton could choose not to enforce the required beliefs. However, the Evangelical community *does* punish noncompliance. Over the last thirty years, Evangelicals have managed to rein in liberal views, just as Dr. Grimstead wanted. The witch-hunt against liberals has probably had a profound effect. Certainly, Wheaton has its own position as the "Harvard of Evangelical Christianity" to maintain—a reputation it would lose if it became too liberal or soft.

So, the Evangelical scholar has an untenable position with no escape. She cannot consider the evidence for and against inerrancy and leave with a different viewpoint. If a scholar, for example, felt convinced by the evidence that the Bible had errors, what could she do? She could simply choose not to tell anybody about her position and continue teaching and living her life as before. Her silence would not alter the message of the collective community. But she would be compelled to affirm a Statement of Faith she believed to be untrue.

But suppose this professor teaches at Wheaton and feels compelled to share her new conclusions about the Bible. What would happen if she told the president and board of trustees her new conclusions? This professor would have to leave Wheaton College.

How much energy do you think Wheaton's board members would expend before dismissing a professor like this? Would they carefully review and evaluate the professor's evidence and reconsider their own positions on inerrancy/authority? No, they would not. The professor could not save her job, no matter how compelling and reasonable her basis for disagreement with the doctrine of inerrancy. Through these enforceable Statements of Faith, Wheaton and other Evangelical schools—the brain trust of the Evangelical community—ensure their doctrines remain intact. While some may consider this type of enforcement essential to the protection of the faith and the maintenance of theological purity, it also ensures that faculty and students remain divorced from the reality the rest of us confront daily. Thanks to schools like Wheaton College, the most threatening and controversial subjects receive the least amount of attention from the brightest Evangelical scholars—the very people one would expect to be at the forefront of this kind of research.

Now let us consider an even more extreme example—Liberty University in Lynchburg, Virginia, which describes itself as, "the world's largest Evangelical university."[16] Liberty expects all its faculty members to endorse this doctrinal statement:

> We affirm that all things were created by God. Angels were created as ministering agents, though some, under the leadership of Satan, fell from their sinless state to become agents of evil. The universe was created in six historical days and is continuously sustained by God; thus it both reflects His glory and reveals His truth. Human beings were directly created, not evolved, in the very image of God.
>
> As reasoning moral agents, they are responsible under God for understanding and governing themselves and the world.[17]

Suppose, for example, that a chemist on Liberty's faculty is working on a new fossil-dating technique. Her preliminary data seems to have results that strongly contradict the claim that the universe came into existence in six days. We would fully expect the university board of trustees at least to remove funding or otherwise bring to a halt the scientist's research. Whether the board allowed the research to proceed or not, it would certainly expect the faculty to endorse the doctrines in the list. On the other hand, Liberty also has these faculty expectations:

> As faculty at Liberty University we are committed to the following ethical standards ...
>
> - Professional ...

- To continue to develop and grow by maintaining a regular program of research and study in order to stay current in our respective disciplines.
- To publish only with academic excellence and ethical integrity.[18]

We cannot consider Liberty's doctrinal statement coherent. Our chemist cannot simultaneously affirm the first set of doctrines and commit to "ethical integrity." Too much evidence contradicts the claim that God created everything in six days.* But even so, scientists have an obligation to leave open the possibility that further information will discredit previous conclusions. Indeed, ethical integrity seems to have fostered a culture that many regard as highly productive, including, apparently, the drafters of Liberty's statement.

The Liberty University professor is in the same situation as the Wheaton College professor. She cannot maintain a spirit of honest and open intellectual inquiry while also signing the Statement of Faith in good conscience. What do you suppose would happen if the Liberty chemist stuck to her guns and decided to publish the results of her research? Do you think that Liberty's board would allow her to continue to hold her position at Liberty while putting her name on a scientific paper that contradicted Liberty's official position that the "universe was created in six historical days?"

What should we expect from a group who cannot alter their collective beliefs? Do the rules of Hooks and Ladders seem so farfetched? You can see how Rules 2 and 3 work together and follow the Wheaton and Liberty models. Under Rule 3—*Only Evangelicals have the privilege to determine truth*—the board gets to decide which version of reality is correct, and under Rule 2—*Evangelicals are always correct*—they get to enforce it. If a professor has a view which calls the Evangelical view into question so that both his view and the board's views cannot both be correct, then he is no longer an Evangelical.† The board members, being Evangelicals themselves and following Paul and Explanation PG, will find

* In fact, Evangelicals increasingly acknowledge the absurdity of "young earth creation." For example, as of 1993 faculty members at Wheaton College removed from their Statement of Faith this clause: "Humans descended from an historical Adam & Eve, not from previously existing forms of life."

† Of course, he could still call himself an Evangelical; he just wouldn't be treated as one by the rest of the Evangelical community.

it easy to enforce doctrinal truths. They will be unable to conceive that the professor might have honestly reached a differing conclusion since everyone can clearly see the truth. The professor will join the ranks of sinners, those depraved people who plainly knew everything there was to be known about God, yet failed to glorify him.

Behavior: Students at Liberty University

Perhaps because of a belief in an omniscient God and a wholly lacking sense of self, Evangelical groups operate with an expectation that they need constant surveillance. For these same reasons, perhaps, they do not seem to mind it, and may even thrive, when they feel *herded*. After all, the theme of God as the Good Shepherd watching over his flock of believers appears over and over in the Bible. Because they expect correction from God when they step out of line, similar punishment from God's earthly surrogates seems appropriate. Within the Evangelical community, too few cues exist to remind the followers that they voluntarily chose to have their ideas and activities monitored. As a result, many have no concept of alternate ways to foster a safe and productive environment.

A particularly restrictive example of such a system of surveillance operates at Liberty University in Lynchburg, Virginia. Liberty expects its students to abide by a code of conduct. Its code prohibits students from smoking, drinking, or using illegal drugs.[19] It also contains a dress code for both men and women. Men's hair cannot reach below their eyebrows or ears, and no earrings or body piercings are allowed.[20] Women's skirts must be no shorter than the top of their knees, and shirts must have straps at least two inches wide.[21] Neither men nor women may wear hair or clothes "related to a counterculture," as determined by the Liberty Student Conduct Review Committee.[22] Offenses that may result in "administrative withdrawal" include abortion, participation in witchcraft, and "immorality," along with the more standard stealing, possession of drugs, and commission of felonies.[23]

Like many schools, Liberty's code relies not only on enforcement by school officials but also on enforcement by peers. It is an honor code, and students are expected to turn in their fellow disobedient students. Liberty does not keep this code a secret—any student attending Liberty University knows about it and voluntarily agrees to abide by its terms.

Of course, many schools have honor codes and expect their students to report other students for breaking the rules. In general, however, schools usually implement these codes under the pretense of protecting their students. Yet, only schools like Liberty seem to feel their students need protection from others who do things like kiss their girlfriend after dark or go to an R-rated movie.

Liberty University prides itself on its nationally ranked debate team. You might think that this shows a healthy appreciation for intellectual give-and-take and a respect for differing points of view, but you would be wrong. No matter what freedoms Liberty allows its debaters while in the arena, in real life the Liberty University code does not grant rights to their students that many people simply take for granted. For example, in 2004, Mel Gibson released his R-rated movie about the crucifixion of Jesus, *The Passion of the Christ*. Although Liberty does not allow its students to view R-rated movies, in this case it made an exception and not only allowed but also encouraged students to view the movie. Let us suppose a Liberty student considered the movie to have violated the Bible's second commandment in its depiction of Christ.* Our unwitting student (who has read the Liberty Code even less carefully than Joy, who should know better) decides to start a petition and organize a demonstration to challenge the administration's ruling. Bad move!

Liberty (yes, Liberty!) University students do not have the *liberty* to participate in an "unauthorized petition or demonstration."[24] Even though this creepy, Orwellian policy should make me outraged, I cannot seem to hold back a laugh when I think about it. It reminds me of the time someone asked Henry Ford if consumers could get one of his cars in different colors. Henry Ford famously responded, "The customer can have any color he wants so long as it's black." I imagine Liberty's board would respond similarly, perhaps saying, "Our students can protest anything they want as long as we approve." Apparently, the people of Liberty University view the concept of liberty differently than I do—and probably differently from most Americans.

The Portability of the Liberty Way

Students at Liberty University may congratulate themselves on acting more responsibly than students act at secular universities. Many simply assume that many view their belief in God as offensive, making *the Liberty Way* too restrictive for the ungodly community. Yet, many universities with religious affiliation operate seamlessly almost within the greater

* "Thou shalt not make unto thee any graven image, or any likeness of any thing that is in heaven above, or that is in the earth beneath, or that is in the water under the earth" (Exod 20:4 KJV).

secular community. For example, the students and board of directors at Notre Dame University—a Catholic university—obviously would not find a devotion to God offensive. Yet, many Evangelicals I know, possibly including the students at Liberty, perceive Notre Dame as secular. Indeed, many Evangelicals believe that compared to Evangelical colleges it is obvious that Notre Dame has a much higher incidence of decadent and sinful behavior. (Of course, they do not consider the signing of an oppressive and absurd Statement of Faith as sinful or immoral.) The greater Evangelical community—and probably Liberty students as well—view the differences in behavior as confirmation of the success of *the Liberty Way* and their restrictive environment.

It requires little thought, however, to break down this flawed reasoning. Suppose we scattered our Liberty University students throughout secular universities in the United States. Would people seriously have concerns that their behavior would suddenly become decadent? If the answer is yes, we might ask why. Is it because of the strength of Liberty's code or did the now-erring students choose Liberty simply because their convictions lacked enough strength to keep them in line? More than likely, though, our scattered Liberty students would behave about the same at any university. They would likely find a group of similarly conservative Christians that would provide them with the leadership and fellowship they would otherwise have had at Liberty.

Suppose we replaced the board of trustees at Notre Dame University with the board of trustees from Liberty University. Suppose they have the task of implanting the Liberty code at Notre Dame. I think that sounds fun. It would probably take around three minutes for the students who matriculated at Notre Dame to start organizing an effort to throw out the board of trustees. If that was unsuccessful, Notre Dame might find itself with substantially fewer students the next semester, either due to massive expulsions by the new board or massive transfers by the disgruntled students. For this reason, Evangelical systems, like Liberty University's, have a complete lack of portability. The *safe* environment they foster only works among Evangelicals playing Hooks and Ladders. Without the self-defining tools of Rules 2 and 3, the system falls apart.

Of course, the Liberty board, along with the Liberty students, might feel we should have expected such "lawless" and "godless" rejection of authority to prevail at Notre Dame. They may say the typical behavior of Notre Dame students corrupts our culture and society. Realistically, however, does anyone have a valid way of showing that our country suffers from the lawlessness and godlessness of Notre Dame University students as compared to the lawful and godly Liberty students?

Controlling behavior in this way may backfire as well. Take, for example, abortion. The Evangelical community has poured a lot of energy into fighting legalized abortion. Liberty University certainly strongly condemns abortion, but the Evangelical community may seriously sabotage its efforts to limit the numbers of abortions.

Imagine a Liberty University freshman who finds out that she is pregnant. She faces academic withdrawal if she (1) has an abortion, (2) is found to have engaged in immorality, or (3) is found to have spent the night with a student of the opposite sex. To her, it may appear easier to secretly have an abortion and confess to it years later than to deliver and care for a child that will surely result in her forced withdrawal from school as her pregnancy becomes obvious.

The Evangelical media may unwittingly confirm her choice. Christian radio, magazines, and sermons commonly report stories of now born-again women who had abortions in their pasts. Invariably, these women report feelings of remorse and longing for their unborn baby. Many of these testimonies involve women who have attended college and have married an upstanding Christian man. Most women waited until they developed a strong bond with someone before they confessed their dark secret. On the other hand, Christian radio rarely features the story of a teenage girl with a toddler, especially a teenage single parent or divorcee. What has happened to the girls who chose to have their babies? After all, how many single, teenage mothers went on to obtain a college education and marry an upstanding Christian man?

Many Evangelical parents unwittingly encourage abortion as well. For example, how many parents want their Christian son dating a twenty-three-year-old woman with a seven-year-old child? For a pregnant teenager, no choice will sit well with her church. If she chooses to have the baby, then all will know she had sinned by having premarital sex. This will certainly not endear her to Evangelical parents or possibly even to prospective Evangelical mates. With abortion, however, the girl has the option of hiding her sin from her church, where she can often maintain a high standing. The current structure of Evangelical Christianity inherently lacks the tools necessary to solve most problems. Evangelicals may actually function to worsen the problems they desire to solve.

Structure and Function of Evangelical Christianity

Evangelical beliefs also increase the risk of fostering extremism. To help explain this, I have relied on a concept I learned from the late Dr. David Bruce when I took physiology at Wheaton College. Most of us in the class had taken an anatomy class at the college prior to taking physiology. Highlighting the importance of the relationship between anatomy and physiology, Dr. Bruce wrote on the chalkboard:

Structure without function is a corpse.
Function without structure is a ghost.

The organism of the Evangelical community qualifies as a corpse.

The Corpse

What holds Evangelical Christianity together? We have seen how both the doctrine of inerrancy/authority itself and its inclusion in Statements of Faith operate to squelch disagreement among Evangelicals, largely by silencing the people who disagree with the rest of the Evangelical community or do not commit to the rules of Hooks and Ladders. For example, the Battle for the Bible I described in the previous chapter sparked an inquisition-like obsession with removing non-inerrantists from pulpits and schools. In extreme examples, as with the faculty at Wheaton and Liberty, believers face serious sanctions should they deviate from accepted doctrine.

Unlike the inquisitors of the Spanish Inquisition, Wheaton College trustees cannot publicly execute a professor for ending his or her support of inerrancy. Nonetheless, my professors' livelihood, tenure, and legacy hung on their ongoing support of the Wheaton Statement of Faith. Having professors sign this statement has no use outside of serving as a lynching tool. We might think of this as "inquisition-lite."

The inevitable result of such a system is an increase in extremism. Because a believer is either in or out, there can be little tolerance for ambiguity. Should a person claim a belief that might fall in a gray area, there will be significant effort devoted to sorting out the person's beliefs so he or she can be properly categorized.

There are other consequences as well. Alert readers may remember Marty from chapter 3, who believed that someone slipped thousands of cockroaches under his door every night. His Explanation Cockroach—his belief in his paranoid delusion—made him one of the last people we would want to consult if we wanted an honest opinion about cockroaches. Marty's expressed beliefs about cockroaches made him untrustworthy.

Now consider what would happen if other people had to sign Statements of Faith. Let us assume that U.S. Army officers had to sign a statement that said they believed in the superiority of U.S. battle tactics compared to other countries' battle tactics. Now, let us go find a captain serving in the army as a company commander. We might ask him, "How do you think U.S. battle tactics stack up compared to China's?" What a waste of time! Making this a requirement for service as an army officer would instantly make U.S. Army officers the least reliable people to give an honest answer about U.S. Army battle tactics. An officer would have a very strong motivation to stick with official policy if he was under threat of a court-martial.

Likewise, Evangelical pastors and scholars have given the least reliable opinions about biblical authority! I doubt the signers of the *Chicago Statement* lose much sleep over this problem, but we should. Evangelical leaders benefit from adherence to inerrancy/authority—they get to keep their jobs and the respect of their communities. Those same leaders risk trouble if they express beliefs that contradict those statements. As a result, we cannot trust their views on these issues. We have no way to figure out who may prove trustworthy. We might benefit from throwing everything they have written about Christian doctrines recently in the garbage!

Who decided that Evangelicals benefited from implementing lynching tools to punish the outliers who deviated from inerrancy/authority? Who would compel someone to push for a Statement of Faith requiring this belief? There is an obvious answer—the people who enforce the rules. Tough, aggressive, persistent, and intensely loyal* Evangelical leaders who are quick to denounce those who deviate

* We will see in the following chapter, however, that their loyalty shifts along with the base of power within the Church. As Billy Graham discovered, while pre-*Chicago Statement*, it might have been enough for Evangelical success to affirm the *Lausanne Covenant*, post-*Chicago Statement* Evangelical leaders risk ostracism and a loss of authority if he (and I do mean he) failed to affirm the more stringent version of inerrancy/authority. Many trace Dr. Graham's loss of stature within the Evangelical community to his failure to get behind the *Chicago Statement* fully (Baumgaertner 2007).

from accepted orthodoxy survive. They have become the "fittest." The culling of Evangelical leaders, however, remains hidden from public view. As a result, Evangelicals will continue to crank out leaders that have these same traits.

One trait includes a tacit mandate to monitor fellow Evangelicals for signs of liberalism, serving as if Evangelical FBI agents on the lookout for false prophets. For example, you can bet that bestselling Evangelical authors and megachurch pastors Joel Osteen and Rick Warren have many devoted Evangelicals watching their every move. Both have questionable alliances with liberals. Both have borderline liberal views. Sufficiently powerful Evangelicals can in effect excommunicate wayward Evangelicals simply by proclaiming they have liberal views.

Consider the example of Clark Pinnock. He is a longtime Evangelical insider and one of the signers of the *Chicago Statement*. Later in his life, he developed views such as "open theism," which is an attempt to combine God's omniscience with human free will, and "annihilationism," a belief that unbelievers would not suffer an eternity of torment.[25] His fellow *Chicago Statement* signer Norm Geisler, believing Pinnock to be soft on inerrancy, attempted to revoke Pinnock's membership in the Evangelical Theological Society. Pinnock saved his membership but remains a controversial figure within the Evangelical community. Pinnock's experiences provide an inside look at the process that keeps Evangelical leaders in line.

This is the power of Hooks and Ladders Rules 2 and 3. Despite lacking a Pope or other centralized authority, Evangelicals have managed to ensure a monolithic voice in matters of doctrine. No formal procedure is necessary; Evangelicals can unceremoniously lose True Christian status. Evangelical structures like seminaries, schools, and churches have the primary function of training people to carry on the coercion and intimidation that have come to define contemporary Evangelical culture. Evangelicals have effectively established a structure that rewards intense loyalty to their doctrines and encourages fighting against outside influences.

This structure requires the acquiescence of the entire Evangelical community, even though most Evangelicals may have only the faintest idea of what annihilationism is. The average Evangelical churchgoer may have defined a liberal quite differently than Francis Schaeffer or Norm Geisler would have. However, the intent of the leaders' message resonates quite clearly. Evangelical leaders preach that dangerous views and false teachings lurk around every corner. Evangelicals are prepared to believe this and look for signs of troublesome lurkers. To be sure, many average Evangelicals find some Evangelical leaders troubling and extreme. Unless these Evangelicals find a way, or the will, to challenge the authority of extreme members of their community, irrational extremists like Norm Geisler will maintain support for enforcement of their uncompromising, authoritarian, and aggressive positions.

Evangelical Christianity centers on a doctrine (*Chicago Statement* style inerrancy/authority) that most Evangelical church members do not know or fully understand. That doctrine has created an Evangelical structure that provides a rigid foundation but lacks any significant relevance to the average churchgoer. Evangelical Christianity, in many respects, provides a structure with no function other than maintaining its own existence; like a corpse, it just is.

THE DNA OF THE EVANGELICAL SYSTEM HAS FLAWS

Can a "good Christian" justify attending and supporting an Evangelical Christian church? Obviously, we would not expect an Evangelical pastor to ask this question of those attending his church. Surely, though, nonbelievers would like to know.

Some bright Christians have asked themselves the question even while failing to provide a comprehensive answer. For example, few people question the brilliance of Francis S. Collins, whom I quoted in the first chapter. Collins is a renowned geneticist, a Christian, and the author of *The Language of God*. Collins writes in much of the book about his own conversion to Christianity. He recognizes Christianity's long history of religious oppression and hypocrisy and implores us to:

> Look beyond the behavior of flawed humans in order to find the truth ... A real evaluation of the truth of faith depends upon looking at the clean, pure water, not at the rusty container.[26]

Collins uses an odd analogy. After all, with a bucket of water, the bucket represents the distinguishing character, not the water. It gives the water its shape, its color, and perhaps even its taste. Furthermore, wouldn't we naturally consider "flawed humans" to be part of the water as opposed to part of the container? What does "pure water" refer to in Collins's analogy? If he intended to refer to humans as rusty containers of the truth of faith, then his analogy becomes downright creepy. Despite his prowess as a geneticist, I have no doubt that Collins does not possess special visual powers to look beyond something we can all see and see something else that is not there. Although far from clear, let us assume "the rusty container" in Collins's analogy refers to Christian community structures—like the Catholic Church—and does not refer to individual flawed humans.

The analogy Collins uses seems inappropriate, regardless, when we use it to make an appeal about the truth of faith in Evangelical Christianity. We cannot separate the rusty bucket of oppression and unfixable delusions from Evangelical Christianity. Collins fails to recognize that the very nature and structure of the church could inherently promote harmful actions well beyond the behavior of flawed humans who inhabit the rusty bucket. Put a different way, the harms of Evangelical Christian organizations represent the expression of traits encoded in the DNA of Evangelical Christianity.

If presented to Collins this way, I venture, he would agree that removing these flaws from the clean, pure water might prove impossible without altering completely what Evangelical Christian means. The flawless water would be a completely different organism.

Most Evangelical communities have scathing criticism for the Catholic Church and its oppression of scientists like Galileo. Yet there is no evidence to suggest that modern Evangelicals behave with any less toxicity toward scientists whose ideas disagree with Evangelical teachings. Consider, for example, Evangelicals' treatment of astronomist Carl Sagan. In the late 1970s, Sagan hosted a popular television show, *Cosmos,* which highlighted scientific findings and research. He had a reputation as a thoughtful scientist. Few doubted his passion for science, and none doubted his scientific integrity. But you would never have guessed at any of these attributes had you learned of him solely through an Evangelical church. I remember how Evangelicals discussed Sagan and the psychotic murderer Charles Manson in the same breath and with the same derision. Evangelicals mocked him while expressing certainty that the earth was less than ten thousand years old. Despite his qualifications, Sagan could never have taught in an Evangelical school. Yet the compartmentalized Evangelical mind finds no parallels between the treatment of Sagan and the treatment of Galileo, and it may even congratulate the Evangelical community for never having operated an inquisition.

Let us discuss Francis Collins again. He gives us the opportunity to discuss Evangelical Christianity and science. Suppose we meet an Evangelical couple with four elementary school-aged children. They say that if all their children grow up to love the Lord and *serve* him as good Evangelical Christians, it will fulfill their greatest hope. Suppose we want to help this couple. We may encourage them to have their children pursue one of two career paths:

1. Steer them toward careers in science. Provide training that will allow them to become excellent scientists.
2. Teach them how to make counterfeit money. However, do not teach them how to avoid landing in prison.

Which career path should the Evangelical couple choose?

In reality, Francis Collins does not have much company. World-class scientists like Collins have one of the lowest conversion rates to Evangelical Christianity. As well, they have one of the highest rates of deconversion. Simply put, if parents had the same goals as the parents in our example, they should steer their children away from careers in science. Criminals have a much higher likelihood of living as True Christians throughout their lives.

7. Loyalty to Authority—The Hooks and Ladders Solution

WE HAVE SEEN THAT STATEMENTS OF FAITH serve the useful purpose of determining who should be disciplined by (in Francis Schaeffer's term) or cast out of the Evangelical community. Statements of Faith also help determine who stays in. The person who decides what goes in the Statement of Faith—and whether or not an Evangelical is living up to its standards—holds the most powerful position of all. Because of this power, these authorities command the respect of the Evangelical community and enjoy a privileged position within it. Evangelicals who fail to acknowledge the authority may find others have branded them as liberal and may find themselves losing Hooks and Ladders.

For this reason, many people have described the Evangelical community as authoritarian. And it is. The purging of liberals and the shoring up of Statements of Faith, however, does not tell the whole story. Before "Evangelical" became a household word, Protestant Christians who now fall under the umbrella of Evangelical referred to each other simply as "Christians." The specific affiliation or denomination of their church did not matter too much. You could hear these self-described "True Christians" talking then, much as Evangelicals I know speak now, about which churches "preached from the Word of God" and "were on fire for the Lord." My Evangelical friends referred to an excitement, or an energy, that "comes from the Holy Spirit when members of a church have *passion* for serving the Lord." In my experience, the difference between churches proved quite striking. This passion and energy proved quite compelling for me, and I imagine it does for most others as well.

Two hundred million Americans could claim the label "Evangelical Christian," but that would have little impact on who the Evangelicals considered Christians. Regardless of how many people claim to adhere to Evangelical Christianity in a poll, everybody who lives as a "committed Christian" knows that the number of *True Christians* is much smaller. To understand Evangelical Christianity fully, one must understand this characteristic difference among Protestant churchgoers. These True

Christians run the show, and they do not care too much for any label other than "Christian." Whether Methodist, Baptist, Lutheran, Episcopalian, or sometimes even Catholic, these Christians have a bond of loyalty to each other. True Christians only have loyalty to those who play Hooks and Ladders with the intention of winning.*

Everyone wants to play on the winning team. Evangelicals do as well. Therefore, they consider their choice to attend a church with a winner's mentality a smart decision that they consider their own choice. Indeed, they usually take full credit for their choice of church membership. Claiming ownership of a decision to join a church makes this a rarity for Evangelicals. Usually, when they do something that they consider good, they give all the credit to their Lord and Savior. In this context, it seems odd to consider Evangelicals as followers. Most Evangelicals do not identify with this label.

Yet, many have described Evangelicals as "authoritarian followers" who pledge blind allegiance to strong leaders. But such is not entirely the case. If it were, there could be no purges of liberal leaders, dissenting professors' jobs would be safe, and Clark Pinnock would have had nothing to worry about. Clearly more is going on.

This is where the interplay between Evangelicals' inner life and their community values comes to the fore. As we have seen, Evangelicals believing in an essentially worthless human condition maintain that God indwells them and communicates to them without human intermediaries.

Therefore, following Paul's lead, many Evangelicals maintain intense loyalty and obedience to their personal god. I do not mean by this that Evangelicals are all freethinkers, each going his or her own way and listening solely to the voice within. As I have described in the preceding chapters, Evangelicals have created a rigid, monolithic structure that defines the edges of permissible thought and behavior. So what happens when one Evangelical's personal god contradicts another Evangelical's personal god? That is where the rules of Hooks and Ladders come into play. In fact, it is why the rules of Hooks and Ladders were invented.

Because they have accepted the *Chicago Statement*'s vision of the Bible, modern Evangelicals have a high respect for church authority. At the

* Obviously, I have little respect for even the true Christians among Evangelical Christians. Yet, I have even less respect for those who go, week after week, to those "dead" churches. After all, these True Christians need only to look across the street at these "dead" churches to confirm that they have chosen a more excellent way.

same time, they have no loyalty to the individual people who hold those positions. The Battle for the Bible was essentially a war between two sets of people whose personal gods told them different things about inerrancy/authority. The victorious inerrant faction had a version of doctrine that allowed them to paint themselves as the only ones true to God's Word, and they had the aggressiveness to make their version stick. As long as a church leader can convince enough other people that he (and I do mean *he*) has the privilege to determine truth, that he is the Evangelical who is always correct, and that anyone's personal god who says otherwise is wrong, he will command the respect of Evangelicals.

Evangelicals, it seems, have less loyalty than one would think. Most do not have much loyalty to anyone except their personal god. To the extent that their personal god supports the rules of Hooks and Ladders, they remain loyal to the rules and the game—not to the players. If, perhaps, their personal god does not support the rules—oops!—a phantom hook lifts them up and removes them from the game. They no longer play Hooks and Ladders on the winning team.

The once-popular song "Hooked on a Feeling" may be a good title for describing the loyalty of True Christians. Practically every True Christian will balk at this title, as they seem to despise any claim that they base their actions on feelings. Yet, they understand fully that one Baptist church that seems "dead" may have exactly the same doctrines as a Baptist church that seems "on fire for the Lord." How do they differentiate True Christians from others? This can get tricky. Let's look at a couple of examples.

Cizik and Global Warming

Two examples may help make it clear how Evangelical loyalty to church authorities works. First, consider the Evangelical leader named Richard Cizik, who ~~is~~ *was* Vice President for Governmental Affairs at the National Association of Evangelicals (NAE). With members in sixty denominations and forty-five thousand churches, the NAE may have more members than any other Evangelical group.[1] Mr. Cizik, after weighing the evidence for and against global warming, concluded that global warming posed a serious threat to the world. He launched a public campaign to address this issue.

If Evangelicals loyally followed all their leaders, then we might expect them to have rallied behind Mr. Cizik and supported his campaign. This, of course, did not happen. A group of prominent Evangelicals wrote an open letter to the NAE.[2] Their personal gods did not tell them the same thing as Mr. Cizik's personal god. Here is some of what they wrote:

> Dr. L. Roy Taylor, Chairman of the Board March 1, 2007
> National Association of Evangelicals
>
> Dear Dr. Taylor:
>
> The issue that is dividing and demoralizing the NAE and its leaders is related to global warming, resulting from a relentless campaign orchestrated by a single individual in the Washington office, Richard Cizik ... While many of us consider Richard to be a friend, he regularly speaks without authorization for the entire organization and puts forward his own political opinions as scientific fact....
>
> The liberal media has given wide coverage to Cizik's views ... We have observed that Cizik and others are using the global warming controversy to shift the emphasis away from the great moral issues of our time ...
>
> We do oppose the efforts of Mr. Cizik and others to speak in a way that is divisive and dangerous ...
>
> Finally, Cizik's disturbing views seem to be contributing to growing confusion about the very term, "Evangelical" ... We believe some of that misunderstanding about Evangelicalism and its "conservative views on politics, economics and biblical morality" can be laid at Richard Cizik's door ...
>
> Richard Cizik also lacks this expertise ...
>
> We implore the NAE board to ensure that Mr. Cizik faithfully represents the policies and commitments of the organization ... If he cannot be trusted to articulate the views of American Evangelicals on environmental issues, then we respectfully suggest that he be encouraged to resign his position with the NAE.

How is that for loyalty! This letter gives testimony to a lack of interest in diversity within the Evangelical community. Personal gods do not have open minds. Why should they? They are gods. They do not accept controversy. *Problems have to go away.*

How could Cizik ever hope to change the minds of so many individual Evangelicals' (millions of them) personal gods? He couldn't. At best, he might rally Evangelicals whose personal gods already had told them the same things about global warming that his personal god told him.

Billy Graham Likes the Clintons—Including Hillary!

Let us look at another example. Can Billy Graham—considered by those outside the Evangelical community to be a model Evangelical—maintain the loyalty, obedience, and good will of Evangelicals? In a speech at his Flushing Meadows Crusade in New York, Graham addressed Bill Clinton, who sat on the stage. Graham displayed a sincere affection and admiration for Bill Clinton. He turned toward President Clinton and with a light-hearted and affectionate tone said:

> I told him before an audience that when he left the Presidency, he should be an Evangelist, because he has all those gifts, and he could leave his wife to run the country.[3]

Allegedly, this comment upset Franklin Graham, Billy's son and successor. Quite a few others who wrote to the Billy Graham Evangelistic Association shared Franklin's disapproval. Billy Graham's years of service could not overcome the many Evangelicals' personal gods. Apparently, many people could not accept that Billy Graham's kind words represented genuine affection. Nor could they accept that Billy Graham really meant what he said. Many Evangelicals seemed ready to throw Billy Graham off the Evangelical bus. Perhaps hoping to smooth things over, Franklin Graham said about his father's comments to Bill Clinton:

> Recently at my father's New York Crusade, he made comments in jest concerning the Clintons, which may have been misunderstood. My father, of course, was joking. President Clinton has the charisma, personality, and communication skills, but an evangelist has to have the call of God, which President Clinton obviously does not have, and my father understands that. For a long time, my father has refrained from endorsing political candidates and he certainly did not intend for his comments to be an endorsement for Senator Hillary Clinton.[4]

But it was not enough. For example, Rev. Rob Schenck, the president of National Clergy Council, attended the Flushing Meadows Crusade and wrote a letter titled, "Why I Walked Out on Billy Graham." Here are some excerpts:

> I have been a great admirer of Billy Graham for nearly 30 years. For 25 of those years, Dr. Graham was my role model in many ways as my ministry in preaching and evangelism developed. He set the gold standard for integrity, led the way in using technology to communicate the Gospel and stayed "on message," resisting trendy

> distractions by preaching only the simple Gospel for more than 60 years .
>
> Out of the shadows came a very familiar figure, but it wasn't Billy Graham—it was Bill Clinton!
>
> I was stunned. What were Bill and Hillary Clinton doing on the platform of a Billy Graham Crusade?
>
> When Dr. Graham was securely in the pulpit, he did indeed say some kind things about the Clintons, but instead of stopping there, he actually handed the microphone to the former president. That's when for me things went into a tail spin ...
>
> I was nauseated. But, it got worse ... [*At this point, Schenk described Billy Graham's comments to the Clintons.*] ...
>
> That's when I got up, turned away from the stage, and walked out. Now don't get me wrong, I didn't leave in a huff. I was more in a daze ...
>
> Of course, I'm not leaving Dr. Graham off the hook. He is after all, one of the top religious leaders in the world and a worldly-wise statesman. I'm simply giving him a little slack for being 86 years old, suffering from Parkinson's disease, prostate cancer, fluid build-up on his brain ... What I will say is that Dr. Graham and his organization allowed the Clintons to take this holy moment, this sacred hour, and once again soil it.
>
> The specter of Dr. Graham's departure from the world stage already had me in a sort of funk. But this was an even sadder spectacle; too sad for me, and I left. I never did hear Dr. Graham preach. I'd rather have his better days in my memories.[5]

Not even the most highly respected Evangelicals are immune. All Evangelicals must play Hooks and Ladders, whether they want to or not, and whether they think they are playing or not. A refusal to play means you lose.

It seems that almost anyone can lose the respect of Evangelicals. So why do they seem to have the appearance of unity and loyalty? We have merely made up the game of Hooks and Ladders as a metaphor, so loyalty to the game does not inspire Evangelicals. Evangelicals have enduring loyalty to the feelings of certainty they derive from their belief that God personally communicates with them. They have enduring loyalty to the Bible, which they believe is God's message to them. They have enduring loyalty to the authors of the Bible since they believe God inspired the authors to write it. Thus, you will never hear an Evangelical say, "After reading Galatians, I lost respect for the Apostle Paul."

Many Evangelicals maintain strongly that Christians do not *hear* God's voice. They recognize that if Evangelicals claimed they actually heard the voice of God in their heads, they have probably hallucinated. They associate hallucination with schizophrenia and do not believe they base their thinking on delusions and hallucinations. Yet, all Evangelicals consider the Bible to be God's Word. As well, they still describe the process of communication as God speaking to them or telling them what to do. For example, three of the most common phrases in Evangelical Christianity are (1) "God tells us in his Word ...," (2) "God spoke to me through his Word ...," and (3) "I answered the call of the Lord." All three give an impression that someone has listened to God talking. Should we consider this a hallucination?

It does not matter what we call the act of people who read the Bible and believe that they have read God's message to them. The difference between this and hearing voices is minimal and leads to the same result. Both claim to have received messages from a messenger that probably does not exist. And even if the messenger does exist, they both fail to demonstrate that the message actually came from the messenger. They both use language familiar to us as language used to describe written or oral communication. You may recall that I gave an example about my brother Tom and posed a scenario where I did not actually have a brother named Tom. What would people think if I read the *Meditations of Marcus Aurelius*, for example, and claimed that Tom had inspired Marcus Aurelius to write his meditations? What would they think if I said the book was "Tom's Word" and that when I am under a lot of stress, I turn to Tom's Word for guidance? In this context, would we call this delusion a hallucination? I do not know, but for simplicity, let's go ahead and give it that title.

Evangelicals have loyalty to the same kind of hallucinated messages from God when they read the Bible and turn to God's Word for guidance. It is easy to see why someone like Billy Graham can lose respect when he does something that runs counter to the messages Evangelicals receive from God's Word. Although many Evangelicals claim that they do not hear God's audible voice, *all* Evangelicals believe God communicates with them directly.[6] The vast majority of believers describe the Holy Spirit as an actual guide who implants thoughts or opens up some mental pathways for true discernment. Almost invariably, Evangelicals will say they could sense the presence of the Lord when they attended a church or gathering of True Christians with a passion for spreading the Gospel.

Few, if any, will attribute this sense to variations in commitment and enthusiasm that we witness commonly in other activities.

Even the relatively few Evangelicals who do not believe God operates locally or individually still believe they read God's message in the Bible and that it applies directly to them. Many Evangelicals turn to the Bible when they face problems that appear difficult to solve. Non-Evangelicals do not seem bothered by this. After all, many people turn to literature during troubling times for hope and inspiration. Evangelicals, however, have a larger agenda than gaining inspiration from reading a favorite Bible passage. They consider their reading to be God's communication to them, and they hope to discover God's plan for their life in the process.

Undoubtedly, Evangelical leaders influence how most Evangelicals interpret the Bible. Despite that influence, however, even the lowliest of Evangelicals believe that their marching orders come directly from God. Evangelicals will remain loyal to an Evangelical leader who tells them a consistent version of the messages that they received from the Word—or from the indwelling Holy Spirit. But they have almost no loyalty to any of God's messengers who distort, lead astray, or water down the true message that they believe came to them directly through God's Word. To be sure, people from many religions have more loyalty for their personal gods than they do for people. In a sense, Evangelicals make up a subset of these personal god loyalists whose personal gods have all singularly inspired the writing of an authoritative Bible.

Before we leave the topic of loyalty and authority behind, however, one matter deserves mention. Evangelical apologists spend an enormous amount of time and energy trying to prove that God inspired the writing of the Bible. They try to assure us—or, more realistically, assure their fellow believers—that Evangelicals base their beliefs about God's role in writing the Bible on sound reasoning and scholarship. Even if these apologists could make a convincing case for their belief (and they cannot), it would not alter one pesky detail: the majority of Evangelicals required *zero* evidence about the Bible's inspiration and validity before they said the "Sinner's Prayer."

Most Evangelicals—including most apologists, and I, before—never questioned or doubted that God inspired the Bible. We accepted this as true when our parents and churches told us about the Bible as small children. It never occurred to me, and nor does it seem to occur to most Christians, to question this belief. Nevertheless, one popular form of Evangelical testimony comes from those who declare that they were convinced of the truth of Evangelical claims only *after* making a scholarly assessment of those claims. I have never personally met anyone who did this. Even those who write about their pre-conversion assessments—as do well-known apologists Lee Strobel and Josh McDowell—do not provide compelling support for the truth of these claims. Remarkably, the overwhelming majority of Evangelicals take for granted as true a belief that has profound impact on their lives. Most remain unaware that they made this assumption entirely without any evidence.

Given that most Evangelicals have no insight into their uncritical acceptance of God's involvement in writing the Bible, it makes sense that they never consider or discuss what I consider as the most important question to direct at Evangelicals:

On what grounds *do you believe that God communicates to you?*

Evangelicals do not have a credible answer to this question—or at least not one that they choose to share with me or the rest of the world. Most Evangelicals, however, do not know or care that they base their life on a belief that they accepted without even a moment of reflection and to which they remain loyal. This incredible lack of insight probably helps a True Christian launch headlong into the disordered thinking required to sustain that belief without realizing where it all started.

Let us move on and review the some of the pitfalls that confront Evangelical Christians in their attempt to make sense of the world.

Authority Turned Inward

We have described the three rules of Hooks and Ladders and seen how they derive from the writings of Paul, the experience of conversion, and Explanation PG. We have also reviewed Evangelicals' interactions with the Bible and with church authorities. We have reviewed how Statements of Faith help enforce the rules of Hooks and Ladders, even when it means showing the door to long-revered Evangelical leaders. But we are not done with the story of Evangelical loyalty to authority.

AUTHORITIES

Deferring to authority poses many problems. As babies, we depend on adults. We have all had to follow authority. Many of us remain comfortable deferring to authority. Some of us, including many Evangelicals, prefer authorities to tell us what to do and how to live. At first glance, this might seem like a reasonable position, especially if God is the authority to whom we are submitting.

Further reflection on this position, however, paints a different picture. The most glaring problem with deferring to authority concerns the loss of the ability to provide trustworthy information. As we have seen above, the person who relies solely on Explanation PG is an untrustworthy source of information about whether Explanation PG is correct. In addition, as we have also seen, compelling a person to believe that there can only be one right answer, like the hypothetical U.S. Army captain compelled to sign a statement endorsing a belief that the U.S. Army has the best battle tactics in the world, becomes an unreliable source for information about the topic.

Deferring to an authority makes someone an unreliable source for interpreting the validity or wisdom of the authority's ideas and commands.

UNRELIABLE AS A PRESS SECRETARY

Examples that demonstrate this problem show up all the time. The week I wrote this section, President George W. Bush's former press secretary, Scott McClellan, provided such an example. Apparently, McClellan had given many press briefings during an on-going independent counsel investigation into the leak of the identity of an undercover CIA agent. After leaving the White House, McClellan wrote a book that includes these remarks:

> I stood at the White house briefing room podium in front of the glare of the klieg lights for the better part of two weeks and publicly exonerated two of the seniormost aides in the White House: Karl Rove and Scooter Libby. There was one problem. It was not true … I had unknowingly passed along false information.[7]

Could someone justifiably call Scott McClellan a liar? Personally, I think we can answer yes. But not everyone would agree with me, and this partially explains the attraction of authoritarianism. Most people will not expect McClellan to accept personal responsibility for unreliable and untrustworthy information passed along to him by his White House superiors since he was just doing his job and relaying his boss' words to the media. From that view, although McClellan passed along false information, which many people believed, he did not *lie*. What do we know about *any* statements McClellan made while under the authority of the White House? We have no idea whether they were truthful; it is entirely reasonable to lack confidence in the reliability of McClellan's other statements. If we had direct access to McClellan's sources, we still would not have a failsafe way of separating reliable statements from unreliable and untrustworthy statements. Bypassing the press secretary and going straight to his sources only removes one barrier that may prevent us from discovering or confirming the truth. Nonetheless, if we had access to McClellan's sources, then we would not have much need for him.

DEMONSTRATIONS OF LOYALTY

One problem facing the Evangelical players of Hooks and Ladders comes in deciding who is an Evangelical and therefore who can be trusted to know and love truth. Affirming a Statement of Faith written by True Christians helps, but the would-be True Christian could simply be mouthing the words or signing the form and not really care about truth. How do they know if a person, who claims to be a True Christian, really is a True Christian?

Quite simply, sometimes Evangelicals, just like the rest of us, do not have sufficient time to determine a person's loyalty through normal behavior. Nor do they have time to demonstrate loyalty to a superior through normal behavior. As a result, they often make use of a kind of shorthand for determining the True Christians. A superior may require a senseless behavior from someone to prove loyalty. As well, a person may believe an extreme act will prove loyalty to a superior. The risk of these types of displays involves the tendency to perceive these acts as good or beneficial.

THE EIGHT-YEAR-OLD QUEEN

I had an amusing encounter recently that helps demonstrate the above point. An eight-year-old girl in the hospital where I work found a blanket and wrapped it around her shoulders. She then proclaimed, "I am the Queen; all hail the Queen."

Amused, I asked her, "Your Majesty, I am your humble servant. What would you have me do?"

She thought about it for a minute and then said, "Go outside and find some dog poop; then eat it!"

This request, although amusing, would not shock anyone. After all, she could have said something like, "You look thirsty. Go in the refrigerator and get a Diet Coke." However, drinking a Diet Coke would not prove my willingness to submit to the authority of my young queen. No one in his or her right mind eats dog poop. If I obeyed her command to eat dog poop, nobody could doubt my loyalty to this self-anointed queen. Already at the age of eight, my new queen understood the type of request necessary to prove loyalty. Virtually every system based on authority requires similar demonstrations of sacrifice.

Clearly, God requires demonstrations of loyalty and commitment. Bible stories describe many difficult tasks God required of his chosen people. So too, Evangelicals expect loyalty to the authority of the Bible. Indeed, Evangelical Christians expect members to defend their faith against challenges to the Bible. For this reason, it is nearly impossible to achieve a position of respect in Evangelical churches without demonstrating tenacity and certainty about the authoritative Word of God.

Abraham's Loyalty

Evangelicals often tell the story of the biblical patriarch Abraham's loyalty to God (Gen 22:1–19). God asked Abraham to murder his son, Isaac. Abraham dutifully saddled up his donkey and prepared to sacrifice his son. Although Abraham stopped before he killed his son, he proved his loyalty to God satisfactorily.

Abraham claimed that God stopped him from killing his son, but Abraham's behavior would still look awful to a bystander. A bystander would likely consider Abraham dangerous unless the bystander also believed in Abraham's god. But, demonstrating a willingness to sacrifice one's own son when asked certainly shows loyalty to the person who asks. The very outrageousness of this behavior makes the test useful.

Today we would consider a man crazy if he claimed God told him to kill his son. As a result, Evangelicals do not ask other Evangelicals to kill people. Still, arduous and unreasonable tasks work the best for demonstrating loyalty. We have seen how professing a belief in inerrancy/authority helps sort the True Christians from the liberal pretenders. Let's take a look at some of the doctrines that similarly help determine who is sufficiently loyal.

Trinity

Belief in the Trinity makes so little sense, it helps Evangelicals prove loyalty when they profess to understand and accept this belief. Virtually everyone in the church has the same difficulty with this concept. Indeed, an enormous number of prayers by Evangelicals end in something like, "We pray these things in the name of your son, Jesus, Amen." If Jesus is the father and the father is the son, then why invoke them separately? Every human on earth thinks of a father and a son as two separate entities. We have no experience or experiences to help us reconcile the idea that they could be one person. What is the point? What benefit comes out of teaching that three separate entities equals one god? After all, most people who believe in God would have no problem with three separate gods. But Evangelicals act as though this concept has some mysterious importance and have made it a basis for sifting out true believers from false ones. Loyal Evangelicals accept the Trinity, which becomes a special measure of faith.

Many Evangelicals have no idea that the word Trinity does not appear in the Bible. Many similarly do not know that the concept of the Trinity was debated among early Christians and was not fully accepted as the orthodox position for several hundred years after the death of Christ. As well, they have little awareness that belief in one god, not three or more, is what distinguished Judaism from other religions. In fact, the Old Testament repeatedly stresses that there is only one manifestation of God. On the other hand, the New Testament, at least as read by Evangelicals, teaches that there are three manifestations of God. Many find this an irreconcilable contradiction. But Christians do not teach this concept as difficult or bizarre. They imply that the Holy Spirit will help Christians understand the concept.

Evangelical Christians often strain to try to justify their views of the Trinity. For example, in Hugh Ross' book, *Beyond the Cosmos,* he suggests that the Trinity makes sense if we realize that God occupies an extra-dimensional realm. Yet he fails to explain why it would be important to consider the Godhead as three-in-one in the first place. Dr. Ross gives many Bible verses to support his claim that God really is three-in-one. Yet he fails to justify why a person's reluctance to believe a concept that he agrees seems absurd in our three-dimensional world justifies that person's eternal damnation. Indeed, many have ceased investigating Christianity after finding that Christians' claims take the form of a mathematical absurdity, specifically that three equals one.*

Dr. Ross knows no more about dimensions or realms outside of our shared experience than we do. But he does a wonderful job of showing his

* Indeed, Islam teaches that there is only one God. Many believe that the extremely low conversion rate from Islam to Christianity stems from Muslim believers' difficulty in accepting the concept of the Trinity.

loyalty with his blabbering about these extra dimensions and so earns respect as a great man of faith.

JESUS, SIMULTANEOUSLY MAN AND GOD?

Let's take a look at another example. Most Evangelicals claim that Jesus was both fully human and fully divine. This does not make any sense. We do not know any human gods. If we did, we would know that they differed from us, and we would name them something else beside "human." We intuitively understand that "human" means "non-god person."

We should be in awe at how much scorn comes from Evangelicals when someone claims Jesus does not fit their definition of "fully human" if he was also "fully God." Quite obviously, however, we cannot compare our life to the life of Jesus if he was God, as we could if he were simply human like us. As God, Jesus would have experienced life on Earth quite differently than the rest of us mere mortals. If Jesus had a full complement of supernatural abilities while on Earth, then I have no context for evaluating his behavior. Did Jesus simply follow a script like an actor? If he did, then I would consider his achievements and his sacrifice meaningless and fraudulent. For example, did Jesus feel pain on the cross? I do not know the answer to this question if he had divine powers. However, if Jesus had the supernatural power attributed to God, and he did not turn off his pain during his torture and crucifixion, then I would consider his suffering masochistic and disturbing.

I would not consider it beneficial to me for a man (I am speaking now as if Jesus were a person like me) to allow himself to be tortured and murdered. I know what I would think of a man, who on a Thursday asked me to eat supper with him, because on Friday he intended to let people whip, beat, and kill him—and planned his massacre for *my* benefit ... since the beginning of time. I am confident most Evangelicals would feel as I would about this man; if he was fully human, then he was a profoundly disturbed human, one whom most of us would not leave alone with children, let alone read them stories about him at bedtime.

Evangelicals seem to believe that this act of a god in a person costume, following a pre-written script, somehow qualifies as a spontaneous and genuine sacrifice.* In fact, Evangelicals continue to insist that this description makes sense and that escape from eternal damnation hangs on the ability to accept this at face value. Requiring such a belief seems to help demonstrate loyalty to their personal god.

Evangelicals effectively crowd out the "fully man" Jesus in favor of the "fully God" version. Thus, when we ask an Evangelical, "What would Jesus do?" their answer often includes a verse or passage from the Bible that has nothing to do with Jesus. One may hear a quote from a verse in Ephesians or maybe even a passage from Deuteronomy. In the bestselling book *The Purpose Driven Life*, author and pastor Rick Warren never explains why he uses the whole Bible to describe Christ. His book contains a section titled, "You Were Created to Become Like Christ."[8] In that section, Warren has 130 biblical references. Yet only nineteen come from the Gospels, the part of the Bible that contains the words and acts of Christ. It would make more sense if he called this section "You Were Created to Become Like the Bible."

Warren, like most Evangelical Christians, thinks of Jesus and the Bible as the same and sees nothing wrong with attributing the entire Bible to Christ. Warren, like his fellow Evangelicals, may seem completely puzzled when other people consider this absurd. Still, despite Warren's liberal training at the suspect Fuller Theological Seminary, Warren has helped establish his membership in the Evangelical community. He has professed an absurd belief in Jesus as both fully God and fully man. As well, he did not seem to notice that when he wrote about being like Christ that he rarely referred to a human described in the Gospels named Jesus, but referred to the Quadrinity-Bible-God Jesus, as if this relationship did not need to be explained.

Talking to Evangelicals about concepts like the Trinity or the God/man nature of Jesus can be an exercise in frustration. First, as we have seen, they give words like human or one a different meaning than those same words have in the non-Evangelical universe. While many groups develop a language that favors certain words or concepts, most remain aware that talking with someone outside their group requires the use of common language.

Second, Evangelical Christians blame the Holy Spirit for their disordered thinking—or rather, they blame the Holy Spirit for a

---

* Interestingly, one of the distinguishing features of paranoid schizophrenia is the feeling that one is acting out a script where everything seems phony or fraudulent.

nonbeliever's lack of disordered thinking. In the Evangelical community, it is understood that the Holy Spirit imparts comprehension of difficult concepts to Christians. The reverse of this understanding, of course, is that those who say they have trouble with those concepts do not have the Holy Spirit guiding their thinking and therefore will never understand the concepts. Conversation between believers and nonbelievers can end right there.

Finally, many believe that God bestowed understanding of the Trinity and the God/man nature of Jesus upon them directly, as opposed to learning about it from another person or from any conscious thought or effort on their part. They do not perceive this *understanding* as something they own or achieved but rather as a gift from God. Thus, it is difficult for them to explain the concept to non-Evangelicals. Many of the ideas that Christians have about their faith they have never understood.

DAVID AND GOLIATH

For Evangelicals, God is both the originator of the Bible's message and the one who grants understanding to believers. As a result, Evangelicals may find differences in interpretations of the Bible disconcerting. In my experience, I found that the times I did not think the current Evangelical interpretations of Scripture made sense that others in my church considered me disloyal when I expressed my views openly. The particulars of my contention, for many, did not matter at all; merely expressing my views, as they told me, was disrespectful and disloyal. It did not matter, oftentimes, if the disagreement had little practical significance; Evangelicals found the fact of disagreement itself unnerving and a threat to their belief in the authoritative nature of the Word of God.

Let us look at the story of David and Goliath as an example. First Samuel 17 first tells us this well-known story. It is conventional wisdom that David needed God's help to defeat Goliath. However, is it possible that David could have had the advantage even without God's help?

Consider the scene as it appears in First Samuel. Goliath wore a bronze helmet with a coat of armor that weighed about 125 pounds. He had bronze on his legs and had a bronze javelin slung on his back. Goliath also carried a fifteen-pound sword. All told, Goliath's gear must have weighed about two hundred pounds. His mobility must have been terrible.

David, on the other hand, had excellent mobility. As well, he had a weapon that in skilled hands could accurately deliver incapacitating blows from a safe distance. David, we are told in First Samuel, had killed both a lion and a bear, and he was confident he could kill Goliath (1 Sam 17:34–36). It would seem that a young man with some skill at using a sling would fare much better than a nine-and-a-half-foot giant weighed down by heavy armor. In fact, if we were to try to re-create this battle, the most likely result of such a reenactment would suggest that David actually had an advantage over Goliath and that the outcome of the battle wasn't at all unexpected.

This hypothesis does not contradict the factual details in First Samuel 17, so there should be no problem with inerrancy. Nor does it detract from any core Christian doctrines, so the consideration of an alternative explanation should not carry with it the fear of going to hell. Despite this, I have found it difficult to find any Evangelical Christians willing to take the idea seriously. This is yet another example of the willingness to prove one's loyalty by accepting without question a belief that contradicts our basic understanding of the world.

Most Evangelicals seem acutely aware that having a differing view of something mundane like David and Goliath puts them at odds with Rule 2—*Evangelicals are always correct.* They seem to internalize the rules to shy away from positions considered controversial within the Evangelical community and avoid a penalty from phantom Hooks and Ladders.

Answer Books and Authoritarianism—In the Hands of God

How do Evangelicals know the right answer? How can they tell in advance what they should consider controversial? While the indwelling Holy Spirit might provide one answer to the question, there are other, more mundane explanations. We have seen how Statements of Faith help keep believers believing, but that is not the only way.

Before writing this book, I had a pet peeve—*answer books.* An answer book is a book written by an accepted Evangelical authority designed to do Evangelicals' theological thinking for them. Most of these answer books offer approved responses to common questions the Evangelical is likely to receive from nonbelievers about the meaning and validity of Christianity. From my experience, Evangelicals grant significant authority to answer books such as *Evidence That Demands a Verdict.* As I draw near to concluding this book, I still have a pet peeve—answer books!

Why? Developing reliable skills and methods to understand our world requires honesty. Primarily, a person must maintain scrupulous honesty with himself or herself. Relying on authorities, like an answer book, snuffs out the likelihood of scrupulous honesty.

A good way to develop honesty, ironically, may involve each of us writing an answer book. Most of us would have a different attitude if we had the final decision about answers in an answer book. We can imagine having terror in our hearts if we had to confront a task of writing an answer book that other people relied on. We would naturally become more careful and humble. We would likely have an attitude of uncertainty if someone told us we had made a mistake on an answer. In contrast, when we rely on other people's work—work deemed acceptable by people we respect—we may find ourselves being more arrogant in our support.

In addition, when we rely on answer books to do our thinking for us, we never learn to trust our own answers and may never learn the process that leads to the correct answer. For example, in many U.S. schools, children have calculators, teachers' editions, and parents to help them do their schoolwork, all of which have taken away many opportunities for children to solve problems on their own. Children who rely on these crutches may never learn to solve problems on their own in a situation where there is no answer book.

Evangelicals never consider the possibility that a heavy reliance on answer books may cause harm. They cannot consider this because they have accepted (most without question) that God has provided them with an eternally useful *super-answer book*. Thus, only a heretic would propose that leaning on God's Word could prevent one from learning to walk by causing overdependence on this crutch. Regular answer books, written by flesh-and-blood authorities, share in this respect.

Another result of reliance on authorities, including answer books written by authorities, is that most Evangelicals assume no responsibility for the actions they take in the name of their god. This group includes many Evangelical women. In Evangelical Christianity, women have a doctrinal obligation to assume a supportive and submissive role. Consequently, some Evangelical women will not defend their faith beyond a cursory level except to refer their questioner to answer books, usually answer books written by male Evangelical authorities. My wife, Brooke, who inspired this book, defended her faith to me (before we married) by telling me to read the Christian books (answer books) she had sent me. Like Brooke, many have never read the books they recommend! They feel no responsibility for the accuracy, scholarship, or integrity of the books they suggest others consult. Many Evangelical women have never thought through or discussed the topics they want us to discuss with their authorities—like their pastors.

Despite not taking personal responsibility for their beliefs, many Evangelical laypersons make good Christian soldiers. They have no difficulty confronting non-Christians, and they believe their boldness represents independent thought and genuine interest in an issue. If you engage in a discussion with one of these Christian soldiers, you may have no idea that the Christian's views lack any personal investigation or critical thinking. What I have found, with remarkably little variance, is that the Christian foot soldier has memorized an answer book which he or she may not understand. Although many Evangelicals perceive they play a vital role on a winning team—for the reasons stated—they have the characteristics of authoritarian followers.[9]

For example, consider an Evangelical Christian confronting his biology teacher. We might hear him spout off stuff about irreducible complexity, DNA, and carbon dating. He may also spout off a definition of the second law of thermodynamics and the reasons this makes a belief in evolution problematic. He may deviate from biology and tell his teacher about the different design characteristics of the Rocky Mountains as compared to Mount Rushmore. He may even say something about plate tectonics and flood geology. He often may have canned arguments, gleaned from an answer book or from a summary of an answer book, and he often will have not attempted to ensure the accuracy or reliability of these arguments.

The Evangelical foot soldier and the hapless biology teacher may end their conversation with mistaken impressions. The unsuspecting biology teacher may put this student in a league with the students who come to her office to discuss biology. She may think her Evangelical student reads about science in magazines, has every *Nova* episode on DVD, and pesters his parents to take him to science museums and fairs. After all, how many students who do not have a passion for biology confront their biology teachers to discuss things not covered in class? For his part, the Evangelical misinterprets his actions as evidence of effective debate skills and adequate knowledge. He may even walk away feeling quite pleased that he had the courage to stand up to the infidel. It will not cross his mind to walk down the hall of his school to sign up for the drama club—even though he has just pulled off a brilliant act. On the contrary, he may perceive his interaction as evidence that he has leadership potential.

Consider this example. I have asked many Evangelicals why they claim 100 percent certain knowledge that Jesus rose from the dead. I explain that the resurrection stories in the four Gospels seem inconsistent with each other. I have asked many Evangelicals about this for over twenty years. Yet, in only the last two years, I have heard this response from at least four of the Evangelicals who I have asked about the resurrection stories in the Gospels:

> Well, imagine that you are on a street corner and witness a car accident. Picture three other people in different places who also witnessed this accident. If you and the three others all wrote a report, would you expect your report to have the exact same details as the other three people? Will you agree that the resurrection stories are actually more credible because they differ in some details?
>
> After all, you would point out, in an instant, if all the Gospel accounts had the same details. You would say three of them copied the first Gospel. Some people refuse to believe the truth of God's Word no matter what.

Obviously, my four Evangelical friends did not come up with this same analogy by coincidence. Someone taught them this nifty little response. None of them admitted that they were simply reciting something they had heard or read, though. Nevertheless, I had a fresh reminder of why this method has appeal. Despite my warnings to others about Evangelicals using canned answers to hard questions, the first time I heard this answer I believed the speaker came up with it on her own.

But consider this. It should take even an average reader less than thirty minutes to read all four resurrection stories in the Gospels. This short time investment lets every reader become an expert of sorts. Thus, every Evangelical Christian should—within about an hour—be able to articulate how these differing resurrection stories fit together. They should not need to consult with a theologian or their pastor in order to formulate a response. But many do. The Evangelical community has vetted the Evangelical authority's answer. The response of an individual Evangelical might not pass muster with the Hooks and Ladders set if anyone were around to hear it. The authority's answer is the *safe* answer when playing Hooks and Ladders, and that is the answer the curious will get.

Can we feel confident that we grasp Evangelical thinking? Do Evangelicals really consider their authorities' answers the safe answer, or does this merely help us explain their behavior in a way that makes sense? Up until now, we have considered problems generally with answer books and submitting to authorities. Realistically, we could find similar examples of problems in almost any group. For example, Hugh Ross probably did not write his book to impress his personal god. He wrote it, more than likely, to impress other Christians. In most of the problems we have worked through so far, we can identify a motive for past behaviors and use this to make an informed prediction about future behaviors. We can attempt to predict the likelihood of Evangelicals fixing or minimizing these problems.

Ultimately, we want to know where Evangelicals get their answers and what kind of behavior should we anticipate when encountering or questioning them. As well, for their sake and our sake, we want to know what might happen in stressful or extreme situations. Could Evangelicals become more harmful to themselves and others?

8. Answers, Authorities, and Autism

WE HAVE SEEN HOW EVANGELICALS BEHAVE within their own community. Through the Battle for the Bible, we have seen how one set of Evangelicals waged war on another set. We have seen how Evangelical enclaves like Liberty University and Wheaton College enforce norms of behavior and thought within their metaphorical walls. We have also seen how the Evangelical community as a whole deals with those who deviate from accepted authority—like embracing environmental goals or accepting Evangelical enemies Bill and Hillary Clinton. At this point, you may be thinking, *Fine, I would never go to Wheaton College or attend a megachurch, so why should I care what Evangelicals do to each other?*

But Evangelicals do not live in a vacuum. As the first part of this young century has shown, Evangelical Christians have a powerful influence upon the culture and government of the most powerful nation on earth. Even when their influence is not at the high levels it achieved during the presidency of George W. Bush, it is still strong. Estimates vary, but as much as 25 percent of the U.S. population claims to believe in a decidedly Evangelical Christian worldview. So, it seems wise to understand what such a large part of the public believes and how those beliefs affect their behavior—not only toward each other, but toward the rest of us. That means looking at the question posed at the end of the last chapter. Can Evangelicals become harmful to themselves and others?

Pascal's Wager

If God does not exist, one will lose nothing by believing in him,
If God does exist, one will lose everything by not believing.

This statement, known as Pascal's Wager, claims to show that if someone believes in God, he or she has made a sensible choice. Indeed, Pascal's Wager surfaces at the end of many Christian apologetic arguments. Most Christians feel that their involvement in a Christian community has obvious comparative advantages. Most Christians take for granted that they have made a better choice by choosing a Christian life. At a minimum, they believe they have made a harmless choice.

But what happens when we ignore the possibility that choosing Christianity causes harm?

Have Evangelicals placed a safe bet? Do they come out as winners no matter what, as Pascal's Wager suggests? Does adopting the disordered thinking of Paul and living in the culture of Hooks and Ladders constitute a safe bet?

Let's look at the problems that can result from adopting the disordered thinking of Evangelical Christianity.

Following Authorities with Autism

Many outside the Evangelical community have formed opinions about Evangelicals based on limited information. Many outsiders, for example, have watched brief snippets of an Evangelical megachurch service on television on Sunday mornings. They may conclude that Evangelicals are obedient to their church authorities. They may conclude Evangelicals follow their pastors dutifully.

We could anticipate this impression. We can imagine an Evangelical outsider defending his judgment that Evangelicals behave as followers by saying, "You don't have to take my word for this. Watch it on television this Sunday … Where else can I go and find two thousand people seemingly in a trance and listening to one man? I doubt you will find an equivalent phenomenon anywhere else."

Does everybody agree with everything their pastor says in these churches? Of course not. So why don't they speak up and confront the pastor? Undoubtedly, most Evangelical readers will dismiss this analysis. Most will rationalize that if members want to confront their pastors, they should find a better time and place than in the middle of the sermon. That seems fair enough. However, do not expect to find a long line of people waiting to confront their pastor after the service. You will not find one. Evangelicals rarely confront their pastors. It does not matter that some may disagree with their pastor. The leaders and pastors control the message. Evangelicals bestow the responsibility for controlling the message and the agenda of their churches on their pastors and church leaders. The rest of the congregation follows them.

Yet most Evangelicals do not agree with this assessment. They do not consider their actions to be faithful obedience to their pastors. How can they have this belief when the evidence strongly suggests otherwise? Do not expect a cogent explanation of this. I do not have one. I do have an explanation, however, that requires ideas and entities outside our shared world to hold together. The minds of Evangelicals perceive their church as governed by an omnipresent, omnipotent being that spends every Sunday morning at their church working busily on the hearts and minds of those in attendance. Evangelicals will tell you readily that they follow Jesus, not their pastor. They will tell you their pastor answers to the Lord just as they do.

Do pastors have powers to control their congregations, as it appears they do on television? Consider this scenario. A megachurch has a guest preacher scheduled to give the sermon at the next Sunday morning service. Most of the congregation has never heard this preacher preach. As well, many in the congregation, caught up in their busy lives, do not know their regular pastor will not preach on Sunday morning until they arrive at church. When this visiting preacher gives his sermon, how will the congregants, unfamiliar and unprepared for the guest preacher, react? We can answer this question confidently. The thousands of people who attend that service will sit eerily still and silent, and few, if any, will confront this preacher regardless of what he says in his sermon.

Thousands of people will do nothing interactive every week all year long during the sermon—the main event of Sunday morning church services—sitting in silence for thirty minutes. What are they doing? The vast majority of Evangelicals believe that during the Sunday morning sermon they are listening to a message about or from God that will help them. Indeed, Evangelicals will use the word "message" synonymously with "sermon."

By interjecting a powerful external entity into their thinking, Evangelicals seem to lose the ability to use the word "follower" in the way that we use it most commonly. Let me give an analogy. Suppose I am an army infantry platoon leader. During a field exercise, my company commander gives me the operation order to secure a position at the top of Jersey Peak. The order details how the company will cross the ravine and traverse the southwest face of the hill to the peak. I have reviewed the maps and explored the terrain. My assessment leads me to conclude that a northwest approach would make more sense. I decide to confront my company commander (unlike most Evangelicals who disagree with their pastor). My company commander does not like my proposal and explains why he does not. I remain unconvinced and continue to believe the northwest approach has more merit. Nonetheless, nightfall comes and the company executes the mission. I lead my platoon up the southwest face as ordered.

I disagreed with my company commander, but I still executed his plan. What do we call this? The answer is simple. We call this *following*. I am a *follower*. Who am I following? I am following my company commander. It does not matter how I may think of this in my mind; in the end, I followed the orders of my company commander. To be sure, I could claim that I disagreed with my company commander and that I serve only Mary Tyler Moore—or Elvis—or Gaia, as she guided me across the treacherous southwest face—or Jesus. Evangelicals perceive their pastors as just another grunt trudging through life and following the same otherworldly commander. Regardless of what they may say, Evangelical Christians behave as classic authoritarian followers, because they obediently follow their earthly authorities. Furthermore, they characteristically scorn those who criticize or question their earthly authorities.

"That's a load of horse manure," one Evangelical said to me during a discussion about Evangelicals as authoritarian followers. He then added more details that are otherworldly to his description. He said, "We do not blindly follow our pastors. If our pastor did not preach from the Word of God boldly, we would get rid of him or go to another church. Each of us has different roles. God calls some to serve him as pastors—to shepherd a congregation. When we choose a pastor, we carefully consider each candidate. We consider candidates only if they have demonstrated a passion for preaching the gospel—who do not stray from the truth of the Bible. Before deciding, we take it to the Lord. We pray fervently for him to guide us in choosing the man that he has chosen for us."

Is that clear?

This man made a case passionately refuting my contention that Evangelicals behaved as authoritarian followers. To do so, he described a chain of command and a process that does not exist in the real world. Evangelicals behave as authoritarian followers of earthly authorities, but most of them believe they get their answers and orders from somewhere we cannot see and a place we cannot go.

We can count on Evangelicals following, without question, a person they believe God called to lead them. However, that means almost nothing. No person, place, or thing (including the Bible) will help us figure out whom an Evangelical will endorse. The history of inerrancy that we reviewed provides a good example. Turning to the Bible would not have provided a single clue about the importance of inerrancy to the Evangelical community. Remarkably, knowing a person's beliefs about salvation through Jesus Christ will not help us know which person an

Evangelical will follow. For example, pick out the leader that Evangelicals seem to believe God approved of the most: Jimmy Carter, Ronald Reagan, or Dick Cheney. Jimmy Carter, an outspoken, born-again Southern Baptist, ranks a distant third in this group—despite Dick Cheney working very hard to change that.

We know Evangelicals rely on answer books and follow certain authorities without question, but it is hard for us to get our minds around either one. Perhaps we need to stop trying to reason our way through an irrational thought process and instead look for patterns of behavior. With that in mind, what messages do Evangelicals have in common? It may seem reasonable to think that they hear similar messages because large groups listen to the same message their pastor gives on Sunday morning. Yet, despite these messages coming, in large measure, from God's Word, good luck finding Evangelicals who remember these sermons. Most cannot remember details of a sermon they heard just days ago. Few can give details of three or four sermons they heard in the last year. These messages from God do not stick in their brains anywhere near as well as their favorite television shows, for example.

Do we ever observe a consistent message? Yes, we do. Evangelicals in churches throughout the country know that a given Sunday morning service will look nearly identical to the service of the previous week and the service last year, and that next year's service will look nearly the same as well. Though not a spoken message, the message of consistency and stability comes through loud and clear.

But wait—repetitive, habitual, and monotonous behaviors are not common characteristics of paranoid schizophrenia, even if hearing voices and obeying the commands of unseen, otherworldly figures is. So this seems like a good place to part ways with any notion that we should expect Evangelicals to behave as paranoid schizophrenics do. The following page highlights some crucial differences.

Comparison of paranoid schizophrenic and Evangelical Christian behavior

Paranoid Schizophrenics	Evangelical Christians
Dynamic communication with external entities—missions, messages, voices change over time	**Static communication**—mission and message never changes; Bible fixed for eternity

Substance abuse and risky behavior—over 80 percent of schizophrenics smoke; also alcohol and illicit drug use common.	**No substance abuse**—smoking and risk-taking behaviors very rare
Hygiene neglected	**Clean and well groomed**
Synthetic and divergent—example: Paul uses Adam's sin, Abraham's faith, righteousness, and "seed" along with Jesus' death to piece his delusional world together	**Analytic and convergent**—with delusional world fixed mental focus converges. Example: Bible studies focus on one chapter or one verse. Evangelicals rarely, if ever, focus on broad comparisons or themes.
Separation of real and delusion world—may seem contrary to previous claims. Example: though Paul believes his spiritual world exists concretely, he does not want it to resemble this world. Yet, he creates rich metaphors from this world to describe his spiritual world.	**Integration of natural and supernatural**—Evangelicals seamlessly integrate natural and supernatural and consider them real in the same way. In contrast, Paul describes a very clear sense of separation between this world and his spiritual world.
Fantasy—Paranoid schizophrenics create complex and detailed delusional systems in their minds and seem drawn to ideas involving fantasy and magical thinking.	**Reality**—Evangelicals despise fantasy and magical thinking. They believe it takes sober serious thought in the "white hot light of day" to "clearly see the invisible qualities of God."*
Novelty—openness to new experiences and seekers of novel experiences; example: the itinerant preaching habits of Paul	**Routine**—characterized by repetitive and stereotyped behavior; new insights, novel interpretations of scripture, changing pastors frequently, and itinerant preachers unwelcome
Change in autism—autistic traits manifest or dramatically worsen in temporal proximity to other schizophrenic traits	**Autistic traits unchanged**—Most have always believed others see what they see. Examples: The Bible as God's message to humankind; the superior morals, love, and goodness of True Christians; homosexuality as unnatural.

* This separates Evangelicals from the more magical-thinking "charismatic" Christians who emphasize "the gifts of the Spirit."

Paranoia, disordered thinking	Paranoia, disordered thinking

This description of Evangelicals will feel right for many readers. The characteristic behaviors of paranoid schizophrenia do not describe the Evangelicals they know. Most agree with the characterization that most Evangelicals are habitual, disciplined, and ordinary. As some have said, "It is not that they aren't normal; they're too normal." The Evangelical traits I have described, of course, are generalizations that apply to Evangelicals and certainly not to everyone who might call themselves a born-again Christian.

These Evangelical traits have a lot in common with autism. By reflecting on Evangelical and American history, we can begin to make sense of this. Evangelicals in America live in the oldest constitutional democracy. They had a prominent place at the table during the establishment and early years of the nation. They can trace a rich history of success, productivity, and progress. We have reviewed how, for the most part, the Thomas Paines of the world have left Evangelicals alone for two hundred years. Many American Evangelicals come from suburban and rural communities and have experienced very little cultural diversity; in fact, many American Evangelicals come from some of the most isolated communities in an isolated country. Evangelicals attend churches that separate their church activities from their secular activities. In their communities, Evangelicals commonly have had the most success, and at this point, they have enjoyed a long heritage of success. So it should not seem too surprising that many Evangelicals lack the ability to see things as others may see them. They have had little exposure to other viewpoints and even less desire to look for them. Yet this seemingly insignificant and harmless mistake of Evangelical autism may generate more problems than we care to admit.

Can a simple mistake, as I once made when I assumed that God inspired the writing of the Bible, cause disordered thinking? It sure can. Indeed, most critics of Evangelical Christianity quickly recognize Evangelicals' ideas about the authority of the Bible—especially inerrancy—as their most vulnerable position. At the same time, however, if Evangelicals attempt to *fix* this position, their faith becomes threatened. Furthermore, it threatens their standing in their community and threatens, realistically, their whole way of life. They cannot fix this without changing everything. As a result, it seems understandable that threats to a position of inerrancy may have signaled an alarm in

Evangelicals. With Evangelicals representing arguably the oldest ruling class in the free world, it makes sense that they would call otherwise conservative theologians liberals if they threatened to uproot the Evangelical way of life. Evangelicals see their past and present as positive, successful, and *right*. They cannot see things, or do not want to see things, differently. Uncontested, isolated, and in charge for over two hundred years, Evangelicals understandably want things to stay the same—or better yet, return to the good old days.

This explanation does not help us understand why Evangelicals focus so much on Paul's writings. After all, Evangelicals now would probably not want a pastor who had a record like Paul's. Paul traveled all the time, he did not show up when he said he would, and continually he changed what he told his churches. So why do Evangelicals focus so heavily on Pauline theology?

I do not know the answer to this. It may have happened simply because they assumed the Pauline emphasis on sin and salvation to be truth in the same way they accept the Bible as the Word of God—uncritically. Regardless of how this came about, Pauline theology helps Evangelicals maintain the status quo. Pauline theology gives them a disordered reasoning that helps keep their way of life unfixable.

This still may not sit well with some. Some may wonder: if Evangelicals have schizophrenic-like reasoning, why don't Evangelicals act like schizophrenics?

We can resolve this conundrum easily. To help explain this, let's imagine taking a journey in Paul's brain when he was writing his letters. If Paul were a typical paranoid schizophrenic, his mind would have been racing—constantly racing through Scriptures and ideas to make all these concepts fit together: the Law, Jews, covenants, Gentiles, Jesus, circumcision, faith, sin, and worthlessness. Paul fit together pieces from Adam, Moses, and Abraham, the prophets, covenants, seeds, and revelation to keep his world hooked together. Unbiased readers of Paul's letters readily recognize changes in Paul's views of the same topics. His views became more complex, detailed, and elaborate over time. In other words, even though we could not fix or correct Paul's delusional thinking with reason and evidence, Paul's delusional world did not stay fixed but rather changed in complexity, scope, and detail over time. Here is an example that we reviewed in chapter 1:

> I must go on boasting. Although there is nothing to be gained, I will go on to visions and revelations from the Lord. I know a man in

> Christ who fourteen years ago was caught up to the third heaven. Whether it was in the body or out of the body I do not know—God knows (2 Cor 12:1–2 NIV).

This verse—which Evangelicals do not like to talk about—gives us insight into Paul's mind. He did not bother telling us what "third heaven" means and did not mention any details of the first two heavens either. Perhaps he believes we see what he saw and that it therefore needs no explanation. Nevertheless, he probably had a mental construct with at least three heavens. Regardless, we can imagine Paul's mind constantly adding detail and layers to his delusional world.

Now, imagine we take a snapshot of Paul's mind at a moment in time and write all the details of his delusional world down in a document. Let's call this document *The New Testament*. To be sure, we would have a complex delusional world that required disordered thinking to piece it all together. However, we no longer have to be in Paul's mind, where time did not stand still but kept marching on, leaving Paul's mind racing to hinge his world together better. Indeed, a snapshot of Paul's mind, as described in his letters, has become core Evangelical doctrine. Like taking one photo out of a photo album, Evangelicals treat Paul's theology as static and unchanging. Undoubtedly, Paul's video diary would tell a different story.

A feature in the computer program Adobe Photoshop can take two or more pictures, or put additions like text that a person may want on a poster, and do something called "MERGE DOWN." When a person chooses the MERGE DOWN feature, all the layers of the composite picture are merged into one layer. Like that feature, Evangelicals MERGE DOWN the layers of theology in the Bible and all the differences in thought throughout biblical history. They view the Bible as written as if by one mind and describing truth relevant for all time, to all people, absolute, eternal, first to last, last to first, beginning to end from the Alpha and Omega—to the glory of God who knew the end from the beginning. Our job, they believe, entails merely learning eternal Truths from the Bible, which they have merged down from multiple layers from multiple biblical sources into a single, perfect picture of Truth. We do not have to figure out what the different authors of the Bible—writing during different times and in different cultures—may have meant at the time they wrote. Evangelicals believe they can clearly see that the contents of all the books of the Bible had been determined before the authors who wrote them were born. More often than not, Evangelicals couldn't care less who might have written a particular book of the Bible, as they believe the authors were merely transcribing Truth that God told them to write down. Just as most people who receive a memo from a CEO of a company, for example, do not usually care which executive assistant may have typed the memo that day, neither do Evangelicals care too much who God's assistants were, especially since God, unlike many CEOs, made sure that his assistants did not have any mistakes in their transcriptions.

To the extent that Evangelicals acknowledge that the Bible is layered at all, they view this as God's unfolding of the layers of Truth over time, much like truth and knowledge are revealed to children throughout their schooling. Evangelicals, however, believe that God has finished revealing Truth, or at least that he has taken a break for the last two thousand years. They believe that when Jesus came to Earth and died, for example, he showed us, essentially, how all the layers that God had revealed throughout biblical history fit together into one perfect picture of Truth. Jesus came to Earth, they believe, so that *all* could know Truth, and so all could see this perfect, completed picture of Truth.

AUTHORITARIAN FOLLOWERS

Could we describe Evangelicals as authoritarian followers accurately? I suppose we could, but we could describe them more pointedly as individually committed to making things the way each of them thinks their personal god intended. People with personal gods that have enough in common with the gods described in Evangelical Statements of Faith believe their gods are all the same God. They clearly see that they all share the same personal god, who is "the one true God." Therefore, they see their way of life as *right* and believe the rest of us clearly see this as well—even when we explain to them that we do not see their way as right or even good. They will not describe people who do not agree with them as people who do not see the merits of their biblical interpretations, the merits of their culture, or the merits of their faith. Rather, they describe these people as people who deny Truth, people who fear Truth, or people who are still not ready fully to confront Truth. Individually, they will freely admit they live as followers of their personal god. And most of them will tell us that their personal gods had finished revealing Truth two thousand years ago when the book of Revelation was added to the Bible.[1]

As Evangelicals believe they have a completed copy of God's Truth, the Bible, we can expect them to stay conservative—or even ultra-conservative. They believe Truth does not change, as God does not change; people cannot negotiate, amend Truth, as God does not bend to the will of people. They do not even believe people can interpret the same Truth differently from the way, they believe, God intended for people to interpret his Truth. Evangelicals view this Truth as if it were God's orders to them, and will commonly say, "We are followers of Truth."

As well, Evangelicals often call themselves "ambassadors of Truth," and believe saying this should be understood to mean that they are God's ambassadors. They believe God wants them to obey him by serving as ambassadors of Truth and to share his Truth with people who do not have it. Many Evangelicals view American history as a glorious period where God's ambassadors had more freedom to spread Truth than during any other time or in any other place in human history. They view America's prosperity as a testament to the successes they have had spreading Truth and believe people recognize Evangelicals as appointed by God to not only share Truth but as the rightful protectors of Truth—as I have explained in the rules of Hooks and Ladders. Thus, if they sense their glory days slipping away, they may well consider this to be heralding the Apocalypse. They clearly see that a world that does not recognize Evangelical supremacy has lost its way. They will follow this Truth, wherever it may lead them.

For more on the sociology of these observations, you can consult the work of prominent research psychologist Bob Altemeyer, whose book *The Authoritarians* discusses some of these same ideas in detail.[2] Another book by Watergate figure John Dean, *Conservatives Without Conscience*,[3] addresses much of the same information. Both describe Evangelical communities as predominantly made up of people whom they describe as authoritarian followers. I am not alone in viewing Evangelicals this way.

But I have one beef with Altemeyer's views on authoritarian followers generally. The label "authoritarian followers," and Altemeyer's descriptions of them, make them sound weak, hapless, and unsuccessful. Perhaps this perspective is backward. For example, Eli Manning, the star quarterback for the Super Bowl XLII–champion New York Giants, may have followed his coach's instructions without question. This would make him an authoritarian follower. Will anyone ever think of him this way? Who cares? He is still the hotshot young quarterback who performed brilliantly and led his team to win the Super Bowl.

If becoming an authoritarian follower will help people win a Super Bowl and become superstars, many people will sign up—understandably. Indeed, Evangelicals have done this. They have signed on to one of the most successful teams in American history (hard to deny for even the most strident critics). They have signed on to win Hooks and Ladders, which has the greatest prize of all: eternal life. Everybody would sign up—if only it were true.

Sandbox Kings and Queens

Imagine playing in a sandbox with a little boy a few centuries ago in England. Although gifted for his age, this little boy still has the mind of a child. Later, he says that he speaks to his father every day, and his father often reminds him that he will have to save the world from evil empires some day. The boy tells you that his father ordained him to do this job in a special ceremony. Then, you find out that this boy's father died many years ago. You discover that this little boy's father had worn a crown and people recognized him as the king of England. Understandably, this boy expects you to treat him like a prince, which he thinks he is. However, the boy has become king of England, because his father, the previous king, has died. This boy believes you should do everything he says his father told him you should do. You try to reason with the boy at times and ask him if he will explain why he expects certain things from you. But this just makes the boy mad. He says, "I did not ask this of you; my father asked this of you. I, as just a little boy, would not claim to know the reasons that my wise father has for asking these things of you."

Now imagine an entire sandbox filled with crowned princes and princesses who all have dead fathers and commissions to do the work that their fathers asked of them. They all expect you to see how they have obtained the good graces of the ruling king and expect you to act accordingly. Although none of them has trouble sharing their royal opinions, none of them takes responsibility for the merits of the demand that they ask of you, nor do they take responsibility for treating you as inferiors. They all claim that their fathers, who have all died, told them what to do. As they see it, if you do not recognize their importance and their tight relationship with the king, then you have serious problems. Regardless, if you have a problem with them, they believe you should clearly recognize that you will have to take your concerns to the king, as they are clearly not the ones who have ordered you to do things—they are just following orders.

This sandbox analogy describes Evangelicals. Turning into their autistic worlds, they all believe God has a special purpose for them. The Evangelical sandbox comes with people enveloped in their own imaginary universe—filled with special assignments, characters, and animated non-things. They all have the power of their imaginary king. They all have the power of the king for all eternity *sans* responsibility.

It might seem obvious that a person who believes they have the power of a king without the responsibility of a king may have little hope of developing reasoning and judgment skills. Nevertheless, this does not seem obvious to most Evangelicals.

Having No Purpose with Purpose-Driven Thinking

Pastor Rick Warren's book, *The Purpose Driven Life,*[4] remains a perennial international bestseller among Evangelicals. Rick Warren, like virtually every Evangelical, believes that all people have a spiritual purpose. Here is how Warren describes it:

> What on earth am I here for? By the end of his journey, you will know God's purpose for your life and will understand the big picture—how all the pieces of your life together. Having this perspective will reduce your stress, simplify your decisions, increase your satisfaction, and, most importantly, prepare you for eternity....
>
> It is not about you.
>
> The purpose of your life is far greater than your own personal fulfillment, your peace of mind, or even your happiness. It is far greater than your family, your career, or even your wildest dreams and ambitions. If you want to know why you are placed on this planet, he must begin with God. You were born by his purpose and for his purpose.
>
> The search for the purpose of life has puzzled people for thousands of years. That is because we typically begin at the wrong starting point—ourselves. We ask self-centered questions like, "What do I want to be?" What should I do with my life? What are my goals, my ambitions, and my dreams for my future? But focusing on ourselves will never reveal our life's purpose.
>
> You were made for God, not vice versa, and life is about letting God use you for his purposes, not you using him for your own purpose....
>
> Fortunately, there is an alternative to speculation about the meaning and purpose of life. It's revelation. We can turn to what God has revealed about life in his Word. The easiest way to discover the purpose of an invention is to ask the creator of it. The same is true for discovering your life's purpose: Ask God ...
>
> God is not just a starting point in your life; he is the source of it.

> You discover your identity and purpose through a relationship with Jesus Christ....
>
> God was thinking of you long before you ever thought about him. His purpose for your life predates your conception. He planned it before you existed, without your input! ... You don't get to choose your own purpose.[5]

Not surprisingly, this over-determined and incoherent purpose-driven thinking generates quite a lot of angst for Evangelicals. As I am sure Rick Warren will attest, probably the most common question the average Evangelicals ask of their pastors and leaders is, "How can I know I'm doing God's will and living as he planned for my life?" After all, am I too presumptuous in surmising that if the average Evangelical had a clear knowledge of God's plan for their lives, Rick Warren's book would not fly out of bookstores?

TAUTOLOGY—FINDING A PURPOSE AFTER THE FACT

Problems with purpose-driven thinking are a byproduct of worthlessness. After all, if you have a purpose for living, you would seem to have worth. But think about this. A person who believes he or she has intrinsic value might find utility in working toward an internally motivated purpose. Indeed, most people find satisfaction from asking and answering these questions:

1. What are my goals?
2. What steps do I need to take to accomplish my goals?

Rick Warren describes these questions as self-centered, and assures his Evangelical readers that they will never discover their purpose by focusing on themselves. He claims God has determined your purpose without any input from you! You cannot give your input to determine your purpose, which—as we will review—creates serious problems with purpose-driven thinking.

As a result of this purpose-driven thinking, it becomes essentially a sin for Evangelicals to make any plans or have any goals other than discerning God's plan for their lives. Evangelicals believe that their actions apart from God have no value, and that they should behave like an actor, faithfully performing God's script. After all, Evangelicals believe they cannot add anything to God's script without screwing it up. God is a director, telling the Evangelical lead actor, "I want you to say, move, and emote exactly the way I tell you to act, without deviating from what I say." No improvisation, retooling, or negotiation is allowed. Seasoned

Evangelicals rarely consider the possibility that they may choose their own goals and still accomplish God's plan.

Evangelicals, even bright Evangelicals, accept this vision of God's plan even though it is completely tautological.* They seem not to notice that it requires a truckload of post-hoc (after-the-fact) justifications for it to make any sense.

Let's take a look at God's plan for the fictional Bob and Amy's lives. Bob finds Amy attractive and wants to marry her. Likewise, Amy finds Bob attractive and wants to marry him. Bob claims a personal relationship with Jesus. Amy goes to Catholic Mass twice a year and has not accepted Jesus as her personal savior. Bob leads Amy to the Lord, and she becomes an Evangelical Christian. Now both claim that God called them to do missionary work. Bob, Amy, their families, and their pastors conclude that it was God's plan for Bob and Amy to meet each other. In fact, everyone believes that, just as Pastor Warren describes, even before Bob and Amy were born God drew up the plan for them to meet.

On the other hand, consider this scenario. Amy goes to Catholic Mass twice a year and has not accepted Jesus as her personal savior, but she wants to marry Bob. Bob is attracted to Amy and wants to marry her. Bob witnesses to Amy and tries to lead her to the Lord so that she will become an Evangelical like him. However, Amy decides Bob's interpretation of the Bible does not make sense. She remains a minimally committed Catholic. Bob decides his desire to marry Amy represents his own selfish feelings and ends his relationship with her. He discusses his situation with his family and pastor. They all agree it was not God's plan for Bob to marry Amy. Years later, Bob meets and marries Susie, a devout born-again Christian. Bob claims that it was God's plan for him to marry Susie and that God brought Amy into his life to teach Bob to place his complete trust in God. God knows better than Bob does whom he should marry.

Of course, if Susie leaves Bob after she has an illicit affair with the garbage man, this was all part of God's plan for Bob's life too.

---

* Generally, I have tried to avoid using fancy words like "tautology" in this book as they rarely have clear meaning to most readers. The formal definition of a "tautology" is, "a propositional logic statement that can be inferred from any proposition." In other words, nothing can prove the statement false. Calling something a tautological statement means that the statement has no meaning and is a waste of time to make.

Do you see now what I mean by tautology and after-the-fact justifications? No matter what happens, it was God's plan. In the second example, if Bob had decided to marry Amy, the Catholic, and their marriage had ended after five years, it still would have been God's plan for Bob's life (and Amy's too, presumably). If Bob had married Catholic Amy and they remained happily married until they both died peacefully in their sleep at the age of ninety, then *that* would have been God's plan for Bob's life, although Amy's fiery afterlife in hell would be a big disappointment. It should be an obvious conclusion at this point that one does not convey any useful information when one's explanation tells us that what happened only makes sense when we realize God planned it that way.

Teleology—Finding a Purpose Where None May Exist

Purpose-driven thinking—even without a belief in worthlessness—can cause problems. Let's review how this type of reasoning can cause problems.

In philosophy, purpose-driven thinking goes by the name "teleology"—an argument from purpose—or the currently popular Evangelical term, "an argument from design." Evangelicals often overlay evidence with a need for a designer. Interpreting evidence and explaining it in terms of a designer's purpose, quite simply, has nothing to do with science.

Most with a modicum of scientific experience understand this fully. Consider this statement: each sperm *wants* to get to an egg and be the first to penetrate into the egg and fertilize it. This teleological statement deserves scorn. After all, how can anyone know or ever prove that a sperm wants anything? Even if it were true, this explanation brings us no closer to understanding what happens during conception.

The sperm example might seem relatively basic, but many teleological explanations require more subtle reasoning. For example, one may see someone squinting and holding their breath when they enter a bathroom. We might ask this person, "Why did you hold your breath when you went into the bathroom?" In a casual setting, an answer like, "I was afraid Bob made a mess of things in there. I had no desire to smell any evidence," might be completely adequate. For someone picky about scientific reasoning, this teleological explanation might seem like overreaching. He or she might answer, "I don't know why I held my breath and squinted. But I do know I have no desire to find out what Bob may have left in there for me to smell."

Why would this fall in the category of teleological reasoning? Because this person initially attributed a purpose (avoiding noxious smells) for his action (squinting and holding his breath) that may not accurately explain what happened. After all, how do we know he chose his actions? Can we exclude the possibility that his actions happened involuntarily? How can we know if he assigned a purpose only after someone told him of his action? Similarly, if someone were to say that God purposefully made us with these protective mechanisms, that explanation might also be inadequate. In this example, what purpose would God have for causing squinting?

Both tautological, after-the-fact reasoning and teleological, purpose-driven thinking give the illusion of an explanation without actually explaining anything. Even if God had a plan and purpose for each of our lives, explaining events and behaviors as doing God's will or fulfilling God's plan for one's life has minimal utility. Discerning God's will often ends up an exercise in assigning meaning to events after the fact. As a result, when someone commits to following God's will, this usually requires an enormous amount of teleological explanations of experiences and behaviors that may not have had any purpose at all when they occurred or may not have had at the time the purpose later attributed to them. Avoiding purpose-driven thinking allows some of us to consider other explanations for events, which may help us avoid the pitfall of thinking a purpose exists when it may not.

Evangelicals use "purpose" to explain how, when, where, and why things happen. When they do this, sit down and buckle up! Expect a wild, strange trip down Teleological Lane. However, do not expect to come out with a better understanding of anything except disordered thinking.

Purpose with Worthlessness

This brings us back to the added problems Evangelicals have with purpose-driven thinking when they believe Paul's Worthlessness Doctrine. To begin, Evangelicals run into problems by dismissing the possibility that God intended for us to have personal goals and desires that we come up with on our own.

Evangelical purpose-driven thinking requires many assumptions. We could imagine an adept computer programmer, for example, writing a program with different characters that have similar but unique parameters for their behavior. We can imagine a programmer running this program and enjoying watching his characters interact. What might pique this programmer's curiosity? If this programmer already knew what was going to happen, it is difficult to imagine him or her finding much enjoyment in watching the program run. But ever since some theologian decided that God had to be omniscient and omnipotent, most Christian groups have painted God into a nightmarish existence. Because God knows everything, he cannot create a world where he can enjoy watching his creation without knowing the outcome in advance. He already knows exactly what will happen for the rest of eternity.

With a belief in a God who knows the future, a person who claims this God intervenes in our lives take on dubious meaning. With Paul's Worthlessness Doctrine, no meaningful event in history can come about because of an individual or group's own initiative. God scripted all meaningful actions for all eternity. God already know what happens. Our job becomes figuring out how to download the GODSPLAN program into our brains. Then we will know God's plan for our lives. Because God knows the end of history at the beginning of history, every day becomes an unfolding of God's plan. Thus, every event and every story we have ever heard, God planned an eternity ago. They all must have a *purpose*. Consider the following events, which must have a divine purpose:

- Jesus' virgin birth—Purpose: to fulfill prophecy
- God became man—Purpose: to show us he loved us
- Jesus' crucifixion—Purpose: to pay the penalty for our sins
- Jesus' resurrection—Purpose: to show us he conquered death

It does not matter that throughout history senseless executions have happened. Did all those people fit into God's perfect plan? Of course, we can understand why people do not want to believe someone close to them died senselessly. For example, we can understand a parent whose child dies of cancer wanting to believe God had a purpose for the child's untimely death. Although understandable, assigning a purpose to an event that may have no purpose does not qualify as scholarly, or more importantly, correct.

But this purpose-driven thinking for Evangelicals has more problems than the average rationalization. It has profoundly schizophrenic-like characteristics. With this thinking so embedded in our culture, many do not recognize it right away. Let's take a closer look at how Evangelicals think of Jesus' death and resurrection and compare it to schizophrenic thinking.

One of the most commonly described characteristics of schizophrenic delusions includes a belief that demonstrates a profoundly diminished sense of ego boundaries. This often manifests itself in what is called a "referential delusion." If a man believes the anchor on the six-o'clock evening news on television is talking directly to him, for example, we would call this a referential delusion.[6]

Now let's look at how Evangelicals view Jesus' death and alleged resurrection. Many Evangelicals will claim euphorically, "Jesus allowed himself to undergo torture and crucifixion for me! God loves us so much that 'he sent his only begotten Son that whosever believeth in Him should not perish, but have everlasting life.'* Jesus died for me!"

So, what can we conclude from this? Even if all of the Evangelicals' facts proved correct—a first-century Jewish cleric put to death whose followers saw him alive after his death—becomes inseparably linked in their minds with a referential delusion. They cannot separate the details of this event from the reference to themselves, thinking, "Jesus died for me!"

Evangelicals do not behave any differently than the delusional schizophrenic man. For example, imagine a man who claimed Dan Rather spoke directly to him in a news broadcast in 1988. He may go to great length to find a recording of that broadcast to prove that he did not hallucinate when he saw Dan Rather's broadcast. He may say triumphantly, "See, I have the tape. I did not make it up. Here it is. It is very real." We, of course, would not be too impressed if this man showed up with a video tape of the broadcast that he claimed spoke directly to him. We know he has made a mistake—he has a referential delusion.

Similarly, Evangelicals believe that if they can prove Jesus lived two thousand years ago and died on a cross that we should conclude that *he died for them.* They make the same mistake as the schizophrenic man with referential delusions. They do not realize that they could show up with a DVD of the last supper and Jesus' crucifixion and that would not make their referential delusion any more real than the man who thinks Dan Rather spoke to him directly. Evangelicals, like schizophrenics, have a complete lack of insight that they have made these wild leaps with the information they have heard. They have no idea whatsoever that these events do not have a purpose that all can clearly see. They consider the details of Jesus' life recounted in the Gospels to be overwhelming evidence

---

* John 3:16 KJV (This is the most-quoted verse of the Bible, by far, among Evangelicals. Most Evangelically raised children know this verse before kindergarten.)

that the events described took place solely to demonstrate that God wants us to have a purpose for our lives. It seems to them crystal clear that these events prove that God wants us to give him control of our lives. What could be clearer? After all, proving that a cleric was unfairly put to death is the clear equivalent of proving that God wants us to accept him as Lord and Savior, right?

Ontology: Making Beliefs Fixed with Concrete Thinking

Ontology is boring! I consider most of these *ology* ideas dull, and ontology most of all. Ontology, after all, concerns *what kinds of things exist.* Figuring out which things exist, and which do not exist, should not be hard for a critical thinker. But wait—do critical thinkers exist?

People seem good at producing mental images and ideas that then seem to exist. For example, if you are reading this right now, are you conscious? Do you *have* consciousness? If so, could you *lose* your consciousness, and if *lost,* could you *regain* consciousness? If you are like most readers, you probably feel you have a clear understanding of what consciousness is—and feel you have it. If that seems true for you, please write down as clearly as possible what consciousness is.

People can easily start behaving as if a nonexistent thing exists without having any realization they do not have a clear idea of what the thing actually is. Nonexistent entities seem to crop up all the time and can prove difficult to identify. Consider how many people speak of the idea of "freedom," as if freedom had specific existence that we can have, give, lose, find, defend, attack, etc. Do we live in a free country? Can we bring freedom to the Middle East? Can fear cause someone to lose his or her freedom?

We can avoid ontological pitfalls with careful thought and by practicing statements like this: "I am fighting in the army to defend myself, my family, and my community. If my goal of staving off the invading army succeeds, I can return to my former way of life, where I felt free to pursue my own goals without interference." Statements like this avoid repeatedly using a word like freedom in a concrete way.

Let's turn back to our question—do critical thinkers exist? I highly doubt critical thinkers exist. It is unlikely that an autopsy, blood test, MRI scan, or anything else will ever reveal a "critical think," possessed only by "critical thinkers." Critical thinking is a verb, not a noun. A person is a critical thinker only when he or she is engaged in critical thinking, and not when simply being silly.

Just as critical thinking makes the most sense when describing how a person's brain may operate some of the time, we might think of a person having faith making the most sense when describing a person when they are being faithful. Through the magic of ontological thinking, however, this does not seem to describe how the Apostle Paul thought of faith. Paul describes faith as something that came after God revealed faith through Jesus Christ. Paul writes in Galatians:

> Before this faith came, we were held prisoners by the law, locked up until faith should be revealed. So the law was put in charge to lead us to Christ that we might be justified by faith. Now that faith has come, we are no longer under the supervision of the law (Gal 3:23–25 NIV).

Paul made faith a thing that a person must *have* in order to have eternal life. For Paul—and for Evangelicals who embrace Paul's views—a person must *have faith,* which does not describe a state of faithfulness. Interestingly, through the distortion of Paul's worthlessness, faith assumes a bizarre meaning. Paul's doctrine of faith says a person must have faith that God will save him or her despite falling short, lacking faith, or being unfaithful to God. Paul describes Jesus as his Lord and as a lord who does not want his servant to disobey him. However, Paul tells us repeatedly that people cannot avoid sinning, and people cannot avoid having sin control their life. In other words, Paul believes that a person has no way of avoiding doing things that Jesus would consider unfaithful. Nonetheless, most of the time Paul's ontological beliefs about faith did not influence his reasoning when he wrote about faith. Thus, his definition of what this faith is that he referred to frequently makes some sense. For example, Paul described faith in Jesus in Romans:

> "The word is near you; it is in your mouth and in your heart," that is, the word of faith we are proclaiming: That if you confess with your mouth, "Jesus is Lord," and believe in your heart that God raised him from the dead, you will be saved (Rom 10:8–9 NIV).

Paul's ontological views about faith, however, do create some problems. For example, virtually every Christian—Evangelical or not—considers Jesus to be the Lord and believes God raised him from the dead. Yet Evangelicals believe many of these Christians will not be saved. Why don't Evangelicals believe, as Paul states, other Christians will have eternal life after confessing and believing Jesus is Lord? Simply put, most non-Evangelical Christians do not have the *right kind* of faith in the view of most Evangelicals. For Evangelicals, the ontological faith that one must have for salvation trumps the faith that describes a state of faithfulness.

To give another example of the problems of ontology, consider this well-known verse from Paul's chapter about love:

> If I have a faith that can move mountains, but have not love, I am nothing (1 Cor 13:2 NIV).

Presumably, Paul must have thought the power from a faith that can "move mountains" came from God. Thus, if we apply Paul's doctrinal logic to a person who *has* this kind of faith, then the verse should end, "I am nothing—except *saved*."

However, Paul's ontological use of the concept of faith seems trivial in comparison to the ontological nightmare he creates when describing sin. Paul never uses the word sin as a description of behavior. Rather, he always uses it in a way that fits perfectly with the way we think of a nasty virus. Indeed, Paul even traced the origin of the sin virus back to Adam. Paul wrote that sin came into the world through Adam and infected everybody (Rom 5:14–19). Christ, like a virologist with the only antibiotic for an infection, came to save us from death through sin. Because Paul considered sin to have a vital role in the lives of everyone, his ontological beliefs about sin warped his reasoning and thinking about almost everything else—including his beliefs about salvation and eternal life.

This ontological view of sin, which Evangelicals embrace wholeheartedly, poses many problems. For one thing, we have no credible evidence that sin has a specific existence like a virus. Of course, since Evangelicals do not consider it a thing that has physical substance in our physical world, we cannot apply something like Koch's postulates to determine if sin exists the way Evangelicals think of it.[7] Nonetheless, Evangelicals act with strident certainty on their belief that sin is real. They seem to have no capacity to think of unacceptable behaviors differently than they think of a virulent disease. Thus, mass murder and stealing a pen from work both make a person a sinner, and people who have no interest in accepting Jesus are sinners whom Evangelicals describe as "controlled by sin"—rather than the more rational "people who commit sins." As well, Evangelicals do not attempt to describe sin in a way that we might consider logical if their premise proved correct. Thus, we will never hear a comment like this from an Evangelical: "We call nonbelievers sinners because nonbelievers do not try to stop sinning." Rather, they use the language of infectious disease and usually say, "They have chosen to live in sin." Since issues about behavior have a central role in nearly any discussion about religion and God, Evangelicals' disordered thinking about sin impacts almost every issue they confront. This makes effective dialogue with Evangelicals nearly impossible. They add layers of reasoning to things that exist and often confuse them with things that do not exist. With this mental clutter, many Evangelicals become virtually inaccessible to reason and evidence.

We have plenty of other choices if we want to find an idea to which Evangelicals assign ontological existence. The animation of truth may represent the most important of the other non-thing things. Truth helps support Rule 3 of Hooks and Ladders. Indeed, using Evangelical language, Rule 3 reads: Only Evangelical Christians *have* Truth.

9. Lack of Confidence and Disordered Thinking

WE HAVE SEEN THAT EVANGELICAL BELIEFS lead down some strange paths. The unfixable nature of some Evangelical beliefs makes communication between Evangelicals and nonbelievers difficult. In the popular work of Evangelical author Rick Warren, we can see some of these flawed thought patterns, while in Evangelical concepts of sin we can see others. But these are not the only problems with Evangelical thought.

Confidence

For almost any task, the best predictor of future success is past success. But, our understanding of past success is dependent on a comparison of our performance to that of others. For example, would Ellen Gandy, a thirteen-year-old swimmer from the Beckenham Swim Club, have felt confident if in 2005 she was entered to swim a 100-meter freestyle race in an international swim competition? More than likely she would not have felt too confident if Jodie Henry, Inge de Bruijn, and Natalie Coughlin, the three medal winners of the Athens 2004 Olympics, entered the same competition. After all, Ms. Gandy only swam the 100-meter freestyle in 58.54 seconds at the Cheestrings ASA Championships at Ponds Forge Sheffield in the summer of 2005. That time, although good for a thirteen-year-old girl, pales in comparison to Jodie Henry's gold medal-winning time of 53.84 seconds.

Perhaps, however, we could send Ms. Gandy back in time and give her a chance against less formidable competition. Maybe we could send her back and enter her into the 1924 Olympics—in the *men's* 100-meter freestyle competition. Johnny Weissmuller won the 100-meter race that year. Many trivia buffs know of Johnny Weissmuller as the man who played Tarzan in old movies. This poster boy of virility, however, might not have played Tarzan if he lost in the Olympics to a thirteen-year-old girl. Tarzan, it turns out, won the gold medal with a time of 59.0 seconds—crushing the second-place swimmer by more than two seconds!

Since two seconds seems like an eternity in swimming, Ellen Gandy would have would have almost certainly brought home at least the silver medal in the 1924 *men's* 100-meter Olympic competition. Yet I doubt Ellen Gandy knows that she swam faster than Tarzan did in the 1924 Olympic Games. By comparing herself to other elite swimmers, Ms. Gandy continued to improve and set a record for London girls in the 100-meter freestyle category by finishing in 57.23 seconds in the summer of 2007 at the age of fifteen.

Suppose we let Ms. Gandy know when she started swimming as a child that nothing she did would ever come even close to what others had done already. If her parents told her she had no hope of ever swimming better or faster than those who came before her, little Ellen Gandy might have never become an accomplished swimmer.

Evangelical parents and leaders, however, deliver a similar hopeless message every day. To be sure, they will claim otherwise. They may quote the Apostle Paul, who wrote,

> Do you not know that in a race all the runners run, but only one gets the prize? Run in such a way as to get the prize (1 Cor 9:24 NIV).

Yet an Evangelical can study Greek, Aramaic, history, philosophy, literature, and science. He or she could serve in a mission tending to the sick, changing bandages, plowing fields, harvesting grain, and feeding hungry children. This person could go to the ends of the earth working to improve understanding, enhancing cooperation, spreading goodwill, and sharing the gospel while living in squalor. All to no avail, since Paul says, "only one gets the prize," and Evangelicals believe firmly that no one can run a better race than the Apostles Paul, Luke, Mark, Matthew, Peter, John, and all the other New Testament writers. Evangelicals can do nothing to compete in the first-century Olympics in theology or service to the Lord.

Evangelicals have placed all-supreme knowledge of God in a box for all eternity—without any chance for improvement. So do not expect to find too many Evangelicals who know much about their Bible or biblical history. Most do not. Why should they? Tarzan always wins.

Hooks and Ladders Rule 1 may need amending: *Evangelicals always win, but they always lose to first-century New Testament authors.*

Confidence Corralled

Imagine an Evangelical parent telling a boy in first grade confronted with a homework assignment to write a complete sentence: "Young man, you have sinned against God. God will not accept your sinfulness. Your efforts and works without God have no value. Unless you confess your sins and ask God to forgive you and accept Jesus into your heart, your actions will not please God. Your efforts, corrupted by sin and the work of Satan, will lead you farther and farther away from the truths of God's Word. Young man, any sentence you write without the guidance of the indwelling Holy Spirit *will amount to nothing*. If you could write sentences like William Shakespeare tomorrow, what will that matter? What do you gain by having the skill to write like Shakespeare if, because of that, you do not accept your worthlessness? *You will rot in hell for all eternity* ... Are you ready to accept Jesus?"

Can we justify teaching someone they have no value? If we asked the first-grade boy—a few years later when he is in fifth-grade—how his day went in school, imagine what we would think if he said, "I am the least among the students in my class, I am worthless and corrupt, I am hopelessly bad, and I am like a walking abortion."

Most parents, including Evangelical parents, would consider a statement like this from a fifth grader an emergency. Most would go to great lengths to find a way to bring this child out of this mindset. We cannot imagine that this attitude has benefits for the child. Nevertheless, why not shout, "Praise the Lord! Our prodigious child has learned our Evangelical teachings at a very young age. Maybe he will be a great servant of the Lord, just like the Apostle Paul!" Somewhere between fifth-grade and adulthood, Evangelicals seem to believe that we should develop an understanding that nobody has value apart from God. After all, the highly venerated Apostle Paul said all the things our fictitious fifth-grader said, but rather than think the Apostle Paul needed a psychiatrist, Evangelicals consider him a great man of God.[1] Despite evidence to the contrary and actions that suggest otherwise, Evangelicals continue to view every person as worthless, just as Paul did.

Does the bleak outlook of the human condition have a negative impact on Evangelicals' creativity and confidence? Most Evangelicals probably do not think so. Neither do many others who have a false perception that Evangelicals fill their ranks with inbred and dim-witted people. From my vantage point, however, the answer is *yes*. Evangelical teachings about the rottenness of people seem to have taken a toll on the creativity and confidence of Evangelicals in general. Although difficult to prove and possibly confounded by other factors, Evangelicals produce remarkably few preeminent artists, writers, musicians, scientists, and innovators. Considering the number of talented and naturally gifted people I met at Wheaton College, I find this very disappointing.

We could go to my alma mater, Wheaton College, and find people who have confidence in their swimming ability. For example, we might find someone who expresses confidence they can learn how to swim. We might find another confident they can make the swim team, and yet another, perhaps, with confidence that they can win a 100-meter race at a district competition.

But you should not expect to find the same sort of confidence about theology. You will find a strange sort of comparison on that topic. It will seem as if they compete to prove they have less value than others. If there were such a thing as a theology team, its captain would have to show that he or she recognizes most fully how worthless and insignificant he or she is when compared to the surpassing greatness of Jesus, Paul, Peter, and the whole first-century lot of them. These giants of first-century Palestine did not just set the records two thousand years ago; they shattered them for all eternity. To win at Hooks and Ladders, one must stay permanently corralled within the perimeters set by two-thousand-year-old clerics.

Confidence in Failure: Do Evangelicals Quit to Win?

We understand instinctively that when we describe someone as fast, slow, smart, funny, compassionate, responsible, brilliant, or almost anything else, we base our judgments about that person on a comparison of their qualities and talents to those possessed by others. After all, if I claim I can run fast, nobody thinks I mean I can run faster than a Border Collie or a house cat.

Yet, Evangelicals spend an awful lot of time trying to convince themselves they can and should *stop* comparing themselves to others. Even so, with or without Christ controlling their lives, Evangelicals, like the rest of us, base what they know about themselves and virtually everything else by comparing themselves to others. Although they preach, "all things are possible through Jesus," they know that they will not run a three-minute mile. They will not learn to read a thousand pages of a book in one hour. They will not become conversant in a foreign language in a week. Just like the rest of us, Evangelicals know this by observing and processing information about others.

Evangelicals have not accepted that they do not have supernatural mental abilities. Thus they purposely ignore—and criticize scornfully—any attempt to compare their mental abilities to others. As a result, they do not have realistic boundaries of what they can expect from themselves and others. Too often Evangelicals believe they have abilities that have gone so far out of the boundaries of normal human ability that merely calling them outrageous does not convey how grossly inaccurate they have assessed their abilities.

This problem of ignoring clues about the limitations of the human condition often causes problems for Evangelicals. Their unrealistic expectations repeatedly generate crises of faith, anxiety, depression, and even despair when things do not work out as they expect. For instance, despite the age of puberty significantly dropping and the age of matrimony significantly rising, Evangelicals continue to consider premarital sex a serious sin. Evangelicals seem convinced that the Lord will give them strength to resist temptation, even though observation would suggest that suppressing sexual desires for many years can have a bad effect on people. Because they have ignored the experiences of others, Evangelicals often experience profound guilt if they "give in to their sinful nature" and have premarital sex. Conversely, other Evangelicals have experienced a crisis of faith, anger, or bewilderment when they "did what God asked me to do" and waited to have sex until after marriage. Some have not found a way to turn off their thoughts about sex as sin. They cannot shed the mental barriers they developed when single to help them resist temptation, even when trying to achieve the long-hoped-for intimacy of marriage. Because Evangelical expectations were wildly unrealistic at the outset of marriage, they are at greater risk in handling the problems that arise when or if the marriage fails.

The impact of believing that having faith imparts magical properties to believers affects the judgments of Evangelicals and puts all of us at risk. For example, retired Air Force Lt. General Patrick Caruana, an Evangelical Christian, explained:

> I am personally convinced … that the most important support that you and I can provide for our military men and women is continual and believing prayer.[2]

Caruana explains how we can "communicate with our Father, God, directly." Thus, Caruana believes, as do most Evangelicals, that rather than focus on money, equipment, logistics, human limitations, military history, contingencies, human rights, and principles, our *first priority* should be to provide our troops with "continual and believing prayer."

Just as Caruana does, many Evangelicals suspend their judgments about the potential limitations on human abilities. Instead of relying on observation of other people and their experiences, Evangelicals rely on a belief that God can give them supernatural abilities to have strength, endurance, certainty, and courage that exceeds any normal expectation. Believing they have special powers imparted to them from God, many Evangelicals may launch headlong into tasks (like wars) without taking into account that they, like the rest of us, make mistakes and exhibit human frailties. Evangelicals may forego the task of observing and analyzing others and replace it with prayer—believing they, in a sense, can run that mile in under three minutes—*if they only have enough faith*.

For this reason, Evangelicals' judgments and expectations offer them no support when it comes to making things happen in the real world. Their hooks are attached to a delusional universe and hold nothing.

He Changed My Life? Where's the Evidence?

By giving up control of their minds to God, Evangelicals have little use for others. They focus on otherworldly ideas to determine what they can and cannot do, and they turn to the Bible to determine what they should or should not do. They become less concerned about what others expect from them and what they can expect from others. Rather, they consider it a virtue to focus on what God thinks of them and what God expects of them. This process of turning inward that we see in Evangelicals is precisely what psychiatrists mean when they use the word autism to describe this aspect of schizophrenic behavior.

We have reviewed some pitfalls of autistic thinking in previous chapters. Let us review one of the most common. Earlier, we saw that Evangelicals, believing in Explanation PG, fail to see how their feelings might have influenced their decision to become an Evangelical. We also saw that, like Marty who used Explanation Cockroach to explain his paranoia, Evangelicals have no problem explaining the importance of their changed life as evidence that God is real.

"My father was the town drunk," Josh McDowell reports in his book in a chapter titled "He Changed My Life." Josh wrote,

> "Dad, I love you." I did not want to love that man, but I did. God's love had changed my heart ... Then he blurted out, "How can you love a father like me?" I said, "Dad, six months ago I hated you, I despised you ... But I have put my trust in Jesus Christ, received God's forgiveness, and He changed my life. I can't explain it all, Dad. But God has taken away my hatred for you and replaced it with love."[3]

Evangelicals have no problem questioning the validity of other people's claims of a changed life. For example, Mormons or Muslims might claim that God changed their lives. Evangelicals have no problem believing that someone duped the followers of these false gods into believing a nonexistent god changed their life. Evangelicals readily grasp the inadequacy of the changed-life argument. So why do they fail to question their own life-changing experiences? Why do they continue to forward their changed life tales as credible evidence for their god?

Let me give an example of a typical conversation. I will ask an Evangelical, "Why do you feel you have not fallen prey to a convincing falsehood that changed your life in the same way a Mormon or a cult member might have?" A typical answer usually goes something like this: "Because they did not place their trust in the one true God. The liberals tell us that we have many truths. They say what might be true for one person might not be true for someone else. They tell us we have many ways to experience God. However, God clearly tells us in the Bible, 'I am the Way, the Truth and the Life. No man cometh to the Father except through me.' So unless they believe in Jesus, I am afraid they will not gain eternal life."

I may ask the Evangelical if he or she considered that their changed life might have resulted from factors like those experienced by Mormons who have also had changed lives. If I do, I usually get an answer like, "Of course, at times I have had doubts. We all have doubts. However, I know that Jesus is real. I know that I will be with him in heaven someday." In my experience, Evangelical Christians very rarely consider that their personal experiences may have resulted from falsely believing their changed life came from God.

The more Christian education an Evangelical has the more likely we will find this bizarre reasoning. This should not seem odd. After all, believing that Jesus and the Holy Spirit dwell inside people has no basis in reality. As a result, we might expect to find that more knowledge and education requires more creative and convoluted ways to connect the knowledge to delusional beliefs.

Characteristic flaws in thought processes and reasoning tend to result from so much mental attention placed on otherworldly entities and ideas. Unhinged from reality and yet unfixable, Evangelicals often cannot make sense of the world any better than most paranoid schizophrenics.

Circumstantiality, Tangentiality, and Loose Associations

Like paranoid schizophrenics, Evangelicals use unfixable reasoning that employs circumstantiality, tangentiality, and loose associations. Psychiatrists use these terms to characterize the disordered thought processes of schizophrenics. I will give examples of how Evangelicals use this reasoning process and explain the meaning and relevance of these concepts along the way.

Evangelical Example of Circumstantiality

Two Evangelical scholars, Norman Geisler and Frank Turek, wrote a book called, *I Don't Have Enough Faith to Be an Atheist*. Presumably, the authors anticipated the title might attract atheist readers who did not share their beliefs. Despite knowing that, the very first paragraph of their book reads as follows:

> Religious skeptics believe that books like this one can't be trusted for objective information because such books are written by religious people who have an agenda. In fact, that is the way skeptics view the Bible—it is a biased book written by biased people. Their assessment may be true for some books about religion, but it is not true for them all. If it were, you couldn't trust anything you read concerning religion—including books written by atheists or skeptics—because every writer has a viewpoint on religion.[4]

In the first two sentences of their book, Geisler and Turek make judgments and conclusions without any evidence. In short order, Evangelicals like Geisler and Turek make a flurry of unsubstantiated judgments and conclusions, leaving someone attempting a sensible dialogue hamstrung with too many issues to confront at once. Furthermore, many people feel uncomfortable (like I do) making similar claims, so we do not respond with evidence-free claims of our own (at least not intentionally).

Geisler and Turek's introduction to a book supposedly about atheists does not even mention atheists. As well, they forward a generic argument about trusting people who have a religious agenda when they write. What does this have to do with atheism? Their conclusion has no relevance to their topic. Essentially, we can sum up their conclusion this way: Some people who have a religious agenda when they write may prove trustworthy. Does this have any relevance to their topic? Perhaps it does. However, Geisler and Turek did not explain why it does, but they did load their first paragraph with many issues that do not directly address their topic of faith and atheism.

Interestingly, Geisler has a reputation in the Evangelical community for being able to sniff out the logical fallacies in the arguments of nonbelievers. Yet he fails to have insight into the characteristics of his own arguments that parallel schizophrenic thinking. Indeed, the introductory comment of Geisler and Turek fits the description of what is known to psychiatrists as circumstantiality. Circumstantial thoughts delay reaching the point and over-include details and parenthetical remarks.[5] You can think of it as a form of changing the topic while failing to or perhaps even refusing to acknowledge the change. Geisler and Turek, who are ostensibly discussing atheism, shift the focus of their message to "trust us," while continuing to act as though they are still discussing the original topic.

What makes this unfixable? Geisler and Turek make it clear to fellow believers that religious skeptics essentially cannot be trusted. It says very clearly that skeptics cannot be trusted because, at the very least, they are wrong to have not found some religious books *trustworthy*. Can religious skeptics fix this by simply telling Geisler and Turek that they do not have preconceived notions about the trustworthiness of religious books? Maybe, but I don't think so.

TANGENTIALITY—INSPIRED VS. INSPIRED

Tangentiality is a dysfunctional thought process similar to circumstantiality; in some ways, it is a more disordered version of the same thing. Let me give you an example. In a broadcast of *Focus on the Family*, Dr. James Dobson introduced the planned show, which was taken from a 1982 lecture series given by Francis Schaeffer, titled "America's Moral Freefall." Dobson implied strongly that Schaeffer's warning about the morality of Americans more than twenty years ago has proven accurate. Rather than provide direct evidence for this conclusion, however, Dr. Dobson chose to focus on what he could never know or prove—Francis Schaeffer's relationship with God. Dr. Dobson concluded with this claim before Schaeffer's recording played:

> I truly believe he [Schaeffer] was inspired by God.[6]

Let us analyze this statement. First, I cannot imagine a bolder claim than Dobson's. He concluded that Almighty God, the Creator of the Universe, personally inspired a person to give a lecture series. This detail has minimal direct relation to Schaeffer's claims about America's moral freefall. However, as with schizophrenic-like circumstantiality, adding this irrelevant detail makes Schaeffer's views—and therefore Dobson's opinions of Schaeffer—unassailable. After all, if Schaeffer was inspired by God, who dares to challenge that endorsement? This makes Dobson's view of Schaeffer's claims unfixable in the same way that paranoid delusions are unfixable—evidence and reasoning will not have any impact on Dobson's beliefs.

Dobson's claims about Schaeffer's views as inspired by God, however, fall too far away from the topic he presented—America's moral freefall—to qualify as merely circumstantial. To be sure, if Dobson could somehow prove God specifically chose Schaeffer to give a divine message to the world, it would provide a good reason to listen to Schaeffer. It was clear from the context that Dobson considered it important to link Schaeffer's thoughts to the mind of God. Perhaps he thought this strengthened Schaeffer's claims. But Dobson's comments lead us far away from the issue of American morality and Schaeffer's qualifications to comment about it. This is a good example of tangentiality, which is the inability to have goal-oriented associations of thought.[7] The train of thought is not just diverted to another mental track; it is derailed.

People certainly say tangential things all the time, but this example has the characteristics of schizophrenic thinking for at least two reasons. First, Dobson did not say it as though he thought of his comment as tangential—and more than likely he would not consider it tangential if we asked him. Second, it is not correctable with reason or evidence. How would we go about even confronting Dobson on this matter in an attempt to fix his reasoning? For example, I called *Focus on the Family*'s headquarters and asked about this matter. A representative assured me that Dobson did not mean that Schaeffer's message was inspired in the same way that the Bible was inspired. They later wrote me:

> If after graduating from a Christian College and tuning in to *Focus on the Family* for thirty years you still don't understand that there are gradations and levels of meaning in the way Christians employ words like "inspiration," then there probably isn't much we can do to help you.[8]

What did Dobson mean when he used the word "inspired?" Who knows? He uses language with no useful meaning. No matter what *Focus on the Family* might mean by gradations and levels of meaning, Dobson refers to his personal god, the one he believes rules the universe. Dobson will not tolerate criticism of any gradation of his alleged communication from Almighty God. In making this announcement, Dobson made it clear that he would not and did not need to consider evidence that Schaeffer's comments lacked moral clarity.

In addition to tangentiality, Dobson's comment demonstrated yet another schizophrenic-like feature—a disconnection between the content and the emotional response to something. After all, Dobson chose to use the word "inspired" to describe Schaeffer; the same word Evangelicals use about God's role in the writing of the Bible! Where is the wow! Really! Stop the presses! Extra, extra, read all about it! Almighty God has seen fit to communicate to us directly through his servant Francis Schaeffer! Does Dobson truly believe that God inspired Schaeffer's message? That would qualify as the most awesome, fantastic, and glorious news of our lifetime. Should we add the God-inspired CD set to our God-inspired Bibles?

Indeed, this almost offhand comment of Dobson's packs a tremendous number of unsubstantiated claims. With one comment, he puts an *Approved by Almighty God* stamp on *all* of Schaeffer's claims. None are fixable. For example, I listened to Schaeffer's comments in "America's Moral Freefall" and concluded that that many of his comments were conclusory, inflammatory, and often blatantly wrong. He gave accounts of many people and groups of people in America that he could not have possibly known about with any reasonable certainty. But would I be able to present my concerns to Dobson and expect a reasoned discussion? No.

It is unlikely that Dobson or anyone who crowds issues with unfixable, tangential, and circumstantial reasoning will ever have the capacity to consider evidence critically.

Loose Associations: The Second Law of Thermodynamics

Here is the principle scientists call the Second Law of Thermodynamics: *In a closed system over time, entropy always increases.*

This observation, which has never been shown to be false in any situation, is known as a scientific law. A law in science has one use—to serve as a description of nature. A statement about the natural world can rise to the level of a scientific law only when the statement will explain the outcome of some aspect of nature every time—and only after results of observations and tests done in every conceivable way have affirmed it. A statement that only describes how something behaves most of the time in the same circumstances cannot become a scientific law.

EVANGELICALS AS NATURALISTS

Many Christian apologists have a fondness for the Second Law of Thermodynamics. They prefer to define it as, "things always move from order to disorder." These Evangelical apologists argue that a process of evolution would have violated the Second Law because it involves an increase in the orderliness and complexity of systems over time.

I could stop right here and point out the flaw with arguing that the Second Law has any practical value for evaluating evolutionary theory. Simply put, we could take a broad look at evolutionary theory and describe it as an increasingly efficient and flexible global process of harnessing energy from the *open* energy system that we live in. Because we live in an open energy system and the Second Law only describes what happens in a *closed* energy system, Evangelicals display illogical, if not disordered, thinking by suggesting that they can clearly see that evolution violates the Second Law of Thermodynamics.[9]

Despite the flaws in reasoning that Evangelicals display when applying the Second Law to evolution, I do not believe this shows conclusive evidence of the type of disordered thinking found in schizophrenic thinking. A more charitable view of Evangelical reasoning should take into account that very few people have a good grasp of the Second Law of Thermodynamics. Realistically, Evangelicals' misinterpretation and misapplication of this difficult concept does not set them apart from many people in other groups.

Nonetheless, when Evangelicals use the Second Law of Thermodynamics in defense of their beliefs they use disordered reasoning of the type called "loose association" by psychiatrists. Psychiatrists use the term when describing the most disordered examples of disordered reasoning. When a person's reasoning does not appear to have any connection to reality, psychiatrists label that person's reasoning as a loose association. For healthcare professionals, loose does not mean "weak." Rather, it means that the associations have unhinged from reality to the point where they do not even meet the low standards required to label them circumstantial or tangential. Many professionals will use the word "incoherent" and the phrase "loose association" interchangeably.

Because many people lack a thorough understanding of the Second Law of Thermodynamics, let's give Evangelicals a pass for loosely associating it with their criticism of evolution. But Evangelicals use the Second Law to form many other loose associations. Indeed, Evangelicals bring up the Second Law more than any other scientific law other than the law of gravity. (When I was an Evangelical, I found comfort in the Second Law as well. It fit my theology and worldview. A law that says things will continue to decay and that only God can restore order, complexity, and certainty gave me a sense that God created a world in such a way that we would discover scientific laws that validated his Word, which described a fallen and dying world.) Yet, Evangelicals have some serious questions to answer when they invoke the Second Law.

The Second Law applies to our shared physical universe. With scientific natural laws, by definition we incorporate every event that has ever happened in our shared universe into our understanding and descriptions. Thus, if someone believes in miracles, which are by definition supernatural, they cannot simultaneously believe in the Second Law of Thermodynamics.

However, with disordered thinking, Evangelicals can scoff at the naturalist. They can scratch their head and pretend they do not understand why someone does not accept their bold claims that death and decay can be reversed. They can tell us how a man physically died and then came back to life three days later. Then—without stopping to breathe—they will say that evolution could not have taken place because it violates the Second Law of Thermodynamics!

These Evangelical, part-time naturalists have memory lapses about Jesus. After all, if Jesus physically rose from the dead, then the Second Law of Thermodynamics no longer has the status of a natural law. Remember my definition of a scientific law: it must describe events or phenomena 100 percent of the time, not just most of the time. If an event ever happened that contradicts a description of nature, that description can never meet the criteria for the designation of "law." The laws of nature do not have special Holy Ghost-power immunity in the case of a miracle. As Evangelicals believe the physical resurrection of Jesus' dead body took place, then by definition they do not believe in the description of nature that entropy always increases.

It takes special Holy Ghost-power reasoning and discernment to bypass this issue and still consider the entropy description to be a scientific law. At one moment commenting about the "overwhelming evidence" for the resurrection of Jesus and the next moment arguing about the supreme position of the Second Law of Thermodynamics is a good example of a loose association.

We can and should call this an example of a loose association, a term generally reserved for the most disconnected kinds of reasoning. In fact, this association is so loose that it is essentially detached. This applies here because using the Second Law of Thermodynamics the way Evangelicals often do has no basis in reality and is incoherent. After all, it already takes disordered reasoning to believe with certainty that the evidence for the resurrection exceeds the evidence for evolution, especially when the quasi-entropy arguments are excluded—which many Evangelicals contend applies to both issues. Therefore, even if we charitably imply the best kind of reasoning to Evangelicals, open-minded people who do not exclude the possibility of miracles should conclude, "Evolution is a miracle!"

Although my mentors weren't among them, I've found that some Evangelicals are able to see the problem with using the Second Law to discredit evolutionary theory. But none seem to find a problem with believing in both the Second Law *and* the physical resurrection of Jesus. They are oblivious to the incoherence of this particular set of beliefs.

Why Do So Few Recognize the Schizophrenic Reasoning of Evangelicals?

Undoubtedly, calling Evangelicals incoherent and comparing their reasoning to that of crazy people requires crossing a line that many do not want to cross. Many people I have talked to seemed to have trouble even entertaining the idea that bright Evangelicals usually rely on incoherent arguments to defend their faith. Even those who have openly expressed their opposition to Evangelicals often tread with caution when making claims such as this. Given the caution of Evangelical opponents in calling out Evangelicals for their incoherent reasoning, it is easy to understand why Evangelicals themselves fail to recognize it.

Interpretive Charity

When Evangelicals use scientific principles and reason to defend their beliefs, it can be difficult to see the underlying flaws in their arguments. Many outsiders will charitably interpret such arguments, viewing them as part of a skillfully crafted plan to discredit reliance on science and reason without including God. For example, I sent an early draft of the section of this book about the Second Law to Dr. Richard Carrier, who graciously provided feedback on parts of the book. Dr. Carrier, a historian and naturalist, has had many dealings with Evangelicals who generally consider him thoughtful and bright despite his nearly wholesale rejection of Evangelical claims. More than likely, his willingness to practice interpretive charity and give Evangelicals the benefit of the doubt in his dealings with them has led to this unusual respect.

Dr. Carrier, after reading the early draft, expressed his concern that my analysis was uncharitable. Considering that I used my analysis to show how Evangelicals use the Second Law of Thermodynamics in a way that resembles the most disordered type of reasoning found in paranoid schizophrenia, I should have anticipated the possibility that he would consider my analysis uncharitable. But I did not. Nonetheless, his comments to me provide a good example of one of the challenges we face when confronting Evangelicals about their beliefs. Specifically, it provides a good example of how Evangelicals have socially engineered American culture in a way that makes effective communication between Evangelicals, ex-Evangelicals, liberal Evangelicals, and non-Evangelicals strained—or nonexistent.

Dr. Carrier wrote:

> When you argue, "As Evangelicals believe the physical resurrection of Jesus' dead body took place, then by definition, they do not believe in the explanation of nature that entropy always increases," etc. I think you are being uncharitable. Formally, their argument is called a reductio, "If naturalism is true, then (a) only evolution can explain life and (b) the second law always holds; but if the second law always holds, evolution cannot explain life; life exists; therefore naturalism is false." The first premise can be consistently held simultaneously with, "If naturalism is not true, then the second law doesn't always hold," (i.e., one can consistently believe miracles violate the second law and at the same time believe the second law cannot be violated if there are no miracles). Of course, neither the first nor the second premise is factually true. (The second law does not always hold on naturalism, and even when it does, evolution remains scientifically possible.) But that's not a logical error, but an empirical one—a product of ignorance rather than inconsistency, although in my opinion it is often a willing ignorance, (i.e., maintained even in the face of personal knowledge that the premises are false, or maintained without bothering to check if they are in fact true).

In order to treat Evangelicals fairly, Dr. Carrier remains consistent in his application of interpretive charity. He never participated in the Evangelical community, so maintaining his position of interpretive charity makes sense for him. He makes a case that suggests that an Evangelical position using the Second Law does not necessarily meet the criteria necessary to label it as incoherent. On the contrary, his charitable interpretation provides a way that Evangelicals could not only appear coherent; it makes their logic appear elegant.

Did I overlook this explanation? No, I did not. Why did Carrier's judgment catch me off guard? Well, despite having had many discussions with Evangelicals about their beliefs—including many involving the Second Law—I have had very few discussions about Christian beliefs with non-Evangelicals. Thus, from time to time I still fall victim to the Evangelical autism that plagues my reasoning. In this case, I assumed Dr. Carrier would clearly see that Evangelicals do not think through or discuss the logical links between the Second Law and their acceptance of miracles.

How do I know this? I know it because I never considered the link before discovering the absurdity of Evangelical Christianity for other reasons. Thus, despite having recognized the absurdity of applying the Second Law in arguments against evolution, it never crossed my mind that believing in the Second Law warranted an explanation for why I believed in Jesus' physical resurrection.

Reflecting on this oversight, I have to admit that I suffered from Evangelical autism—I assumed that everyone could clearly see that *my* God could perform acts unconstrained by natural laws. A smug apologist may use this admission to suggest that my oversight does not represent the majority of informed Evangelicals. You may recall, however, how in the United States Evangelicals target their evangelism toward people who already believe in a god, and they most often target self-identified Christians from other faith groups. On one level, Evangelicals can make a weak argument about naturalists like Carrier having "too much faith in science" because they accept evolutionary theory even though it violates the Second Law of Thermodynamics. This argument does not apply to most of the people Evangelicals confront—they believe in the God of Christianity. For example, many Evangelicals will confront a devoted Catholic who accepts the validity of evolutionary theory with the same vigor and the same arguments that they use when confronting a naturalist like Carrier.

In the past, Evangelicals used the Second Law as their trump card to defeat believers in evolution—and many still do today. In essence, they make the argument that no matter how much evidence piles up that remains consistent with evolutionary theory, only an ignorant person would believe it because evolution defies the Second Law. Evangelicals tell each other that nonbelievers do not have the same passion and commitment to reality-based thinking as they do. They convince each other that they have a responsibility to the world to promote reasoning and evidence as the best way to determine truth.

Through the magic of loose associations, Evangelical reasoning does not require any reasoning at all. Evangelicals do not have to discuss with each other how they came to believe in a Second Law-defying event like the resurrection. They do not have to explain the logical steps they have taken that make sense of their leap of faith. They never discuss, for example, how or why the natural evidence they have has surpassed a threshold that would lead a reasonable person to include a supernatural event like the resurrection as an explanation for those natural events. So, they can tell each other that nonbelievers foolishly believe in irrational theories like evolution. During my years as an Evangelical, when we met people who believed in evolutionary theory, we and the rest of the Evangelical community regarded them as ignorant and foolish—whether they believed in a god or not.

Evangelicals do not have one set of arguments for theists and another set for atheists. They regard all people who do not believe their truth as ignorant in the same way. They may stumble across an apologist who, for example, uses an argument like the one Dr. Carrier gave against a naturalist position. They might start to incorporate it into their own defense of creationism or intelligent design, perhaps teaching it to their high school Sunday school class. Invariably in my experience, Evangelicals fail to recognize that the strength of their arguments differs depending on the beliefs of the person they confront. Thus, an Evangelical who believes God made Eve using one of Adam's ribs will consider a Catholic and an atheist equally foolish for believing in evolution. Whether the Catholic believes in the Resurrection of Jesus and other natural law-defying miracles does not matter. Only a fool, they will tell each other, would believe something that so clearly (in their minds) violates the Second Law of Thermodynamics.

Most Evangelicals, and nearly every Evangelical apologist, claim that as a God-fearing Christian student becomes more knowledgeable of historical and scientific evidence, the student will have increasingly less difficulty accepting the claims of the Bible. If we wanted to put this in the terminology of mathematics, we could write this axiom: "As knowledge of the universe approaches totality, the distance of the leap of faith necessary to accept the claims of the Bible approaches zero."[10] Despite this Evangelical perception, do not expect to find an Evangelical who can give you specifics about how they made this determination. Furthermore, do not expect a coherent explanation of why Evangelicals feel comfortable pressuring potential new converts to make a decision about the certainty of Evangelical claims *before* they have any credible reason or evidence to do so. As well, do not expect a coherent explanation of a step-by-step process that may lead us to the same conclusions about Evangelical beliefs.

LIMITS OF INTERPRETIVE CHARITY

"What would this mean if Albert Einstein said it?" When filling in the blanks of an Evangelical's argument, a scientist would probably believe that attributing the kind of sophisticated logic that Albert Einstein used as charitable—and a sign of respect. And I am sure many Evangelicals would find this acceptable. Likewise, what does interpretive charity mean to a naturalist like Dr. Carrier? More than likely, a naturalist will consider attributing the logic and reasoning of the most competent naturalists to the Evangelical as the most charitable way to interpret what an Evangelical means. As an ex-Evangelical, however, my concept of interpretive charity leads me in a different direction. I would find it more relevant to ask, "What would this mean if Billy Graham said it?"

As an ex-Evangelical, I have found it frustrating and difficult to explain the consequences of Evangelicals accepting their beliefs as facts without having any conception that their personal relationship with God may not have any input from a real god. I tried to explain this in the "Explanation PG" chapter. Even if the merits of Explanation PG gain acceptance, however, will non-Evangelicals fully comprehend the implications of Explanation PG? As an ex-Evangelical, I have no reliable way of gauging the answer to this question with much accuracy.

Trying to figure out what nonbelievers understand about Evangelicals proves difficult and confounding. First, many nonbelievers have a difficult time empathizing with Evangelicals. They cannot competently think through a problem, for whatever reason, the way an Evangelical would. In some cases this is ironic, as I have met nonbelievers just as bound by their beliefs, whether they believe in *laissez-faire* capitalism or the goddess Gaia, so that they make the same kind of logical leaps as Evangelicals do. Some of them, I cannot help but think, would have made good God-fearing Christians if their lives had a different set of circumstances.

I know how Evangelicals think because I used to think as they do—I know how to play Hooks and Ladders. Since Evangelicals almost completely separate their communities from outsiders, figuring out what happens inside their communities proves difficult. Usually, neither the

Evangelical nor the unassuming outsider notices the vast chasm that separates their interpretations of the world. Based on my own past beliefs and based on my experiences in the Evangelical community, I am less constrained when interpreting Evangelical writings and arguments. But any outsider to the Evangelical community, lacking this personal experience, may feel more of a need to bend over backward and give Evangelicals the benefit of the doubt when engaging them.

Does applying interpretive charity rule out the possibility of labeling someone's reasoning as a loose association? Before trying to answer this, it may help if I provide an example of a typical loose association and explain how we can make that determination in a reasonably objective way.

Suppose a man with paranoid schizophrenia, who believes he is a CIA operative, looks around nervously when you say his name. He says, "You know how important the CIA considers my work. Stop calling me by that name."

You say, "Contrary to your claims, I do not know how important the CIA considers your work. For that matter, you have never explained why I should believe the CIA even knows you exist. Why should I believe you have an association with the CIA? Please tell me how I should have known how important the CIA considers your work and why I cannot say your real name."

This answer would qualify as a loose association: "I already explained this to you. I watch my neighbor's house across the street at exactly ten o'clock at night. Only the best operatives go through special training to detect and decode an encrypted light. If he turns his bedroom light out before 10:01 PM, I have to report for a mission at 10:32 PM."

If this man says nothing further, then we have too little information to coherently link his answer to the question. Nonetheless, labeling this as a loose association, rather than simply incoherent, represents a kind of interpretive charity. After all, we can easily imagine the CIA adopting a complex signaling process to alert their operatives about missions. Furthermore, we could imagine this man providing reasons about why this signal makes him believe that the signal came from the CIA. Some of his reasons may even persuade you that he may have an association with the CIA. However, this man did not provide any further information. His failure to explain his answer indicates a lack of insight. If he knew and explained that his answer did not fully answer the question, then most mental health professionals would not consider his reasoning disordered—his answer would not fall under the category of a loose association. In this example, however, the man does not demonstrate any awareness of his failure to answer the question sufficiently; he thinks that his explanation is enough.

Does this same kind of pattern show up in the reasoning of Evangelicals? The average Evangelical rarely uses a loose association to explain a belief. However, many average Evangelicals do not feel comfortable explaining the reasoning and logic of most of their Christian beliefs. Rather, they defer to Evangelical authorities to explain the reasoning and logic. Many Evangelicals will refer to books, articles, and other sources that they believe adequately explain how a person can believe their doctrines using reason and evidence. Probably no one has written more of those than Norman Geisler, who has volumes on inerrancy and apologetics to his credit. Yet riddled through Geisler's work, as well as that of other Evangelical apologists, we can find explanations that fail to address seemingly obvious questions.

Many of Geisler's explanations assume the reader already believes that the Bible is God's Word and continue from that premise. But Geisler never acknowledges that he accepted Evangelical claims *before* trying to find reasons to support his beliefs. On the contrary, he maintains that enough evidence exists to accept Evangelical beliefs without presupposing that Evangelical claims are true. But does he actually prove this? Or does he simply sneak his biblical presupposition in without acknowledging that he is doing it?

Let's look at an example from Geisler's contribution to the book entitled, *I Don't Have Enough Faith to Be an Atheist.* In this book, Geisler turns to the Second Law to explain why atheism requires too much faith for him to believe. Geisler starts by claiming that atheists do not believe in the Big Bang Theory.

Already we have problems with Geisler's claims. Is it true that atheists reject the Big Bang theory? How should we interpret Geisler's claim about atheists? After all, Geisler, as a contemporary of Carl Sagan knows all too well that Sagan, an outspoken atheist, almost single-handedly brought awareness and enthusiasm about the Big Bang to America on his show, *Cosmos.* Geisler knows that Evangelicals ridiculed Sagan for years and years. In addition, he knows that their ridicule came largely at the expense of Sagan's beliefs about the Big Bang! Furthermore, Geisler and Turek quote Sagan in this same book. So what should we call this blatantly false characterization of atheists by Geisler? Interpretive charity fails me here; I cannot think of any pleasant answers to this question. We have more than enough evidence to say he purposely lied in this case.

Moving on, Geisler then tries to make the case that if an atheist did not believe in the Big Bang, then the atheist would similarly have to reject the Second Law of Thermodynamics. (Of course, Geisler does not provide any source that proves this connection, and he probably does not have the skills to prove it himself. Furthermore, Geisler is probably wrong about this conclusion, although I will charitably leave this aside for the moment.) So why doesn't Geisler have enough faith to be an atheist? In part, he says, because atheists' beliefs require believing in events that violate the Second Law. Geisler quotes Sir Arthur Stanley Eddington to stress his point:

> The law that entropy always increases, holds, I think, the supreme position among the laws of Nature. If someone points out to you that your pet theory of the universe is in disagreement with Maxwell's equations—then so much the worse for Maxwell's equations. If it is found to be contradicted by observation—well, these experimentalists do bungle things sometimes. But if your theory is found to be against the second law of thermodynamics I can give you no hope; there is nothing for it but to collapse in deepest humiliation.[11]

Yet, Geisler never bothers to explain why his pet theory (that Jesus was raised physically after death)—an event which is surely against the Second Law of Thermodynamics—will not "collapse in deepest humiliation." For all I can tell, it never occurred to him even to try to explain this, anymore than it occurred to the CIA operative to explain how his neighbor's bedroom lighting proves that he is in contact with the spymasters. Indeed, by agreeing with the validity of Eddington's conclusions, Geisler introduces (unnecessarily) a very high hurdle to jump over to prove his pet theory. But Geisler fails to acknowledge that he will have to jump over this hurdle—the hurdle only applies to the pet theories of dimwitted atheists.

To be sure, Geisler could backpedal if asked about this in the future and provide an explanation like Carrier's. Indeed, he tangentially explains why his pet theory has immunity from collapse later in the book. But that does not matter. He did not provide it in the book where the omission sticks out glaringly for anyone who does not presuppose that only the miracles described in the Bible really happened and that Geisler's god performed them. Geisler contradicts his own claim—he does have enough faith to believe in something that requires believing events violated the Second Law—Evangelical Christianity.

So we have here an example of a loose association that calls into question Geisler's reasoning process. Although there might be a way to connect part one and part two—Carrier suggested one way—the connection is never made by Geisler, and the lack of a connection goes unnoticed or at least unremarked upon by his Evangelical readers.

On one hand, we could apply interpretive charity to provide answers to the questions Geisler left unanswered. On the other hand, we could explain how his oversight fits a characteristic pattern found in loose associations—a lack of awareness that he gave an insufficient explanation for his beliefs. In the end, we want know what thought process led Geisler to write what he did. Applying interpretive charity here runs the risk of inaccurately judging Geisler's thoughts at the time he wrote. But we do not have to become mind readers to label this section of the book as a loose association. On the contrary, we can simply conclude that Geisler's reasoning—complete with his oversight of not explaining his pet theory—has enough gaps in reasoning to warrant calling it a loose association.

As I said, I based my conclusion that Geisler's thought process is disordered, in part, on his omission of details that might indicate he even considered the gaps in his reasoning. Although I do not know for sure, I doubt Geisler omitted these things purposely. After all, he intended to persuade his readers that Christians use fewer faith-based theories than atheists do to hold their respective beliefs together. More than likely, he left gaps in his reasoning for the same reason I would have when I was an Evangelical. I would not have explained why my pet theory could violate the Second Law while maintaining that other pet theories could not because it would not have occurred to me that this needed any explanation.

The same theme runs through all of Geisler's, and every other apologist's, writings. They presuppose the "truth of the Bible" and try to retrofit reason and evidence to this belief. At the same time, they usually say that one can discover that Evangelicals have Truth based solely on reason and evidence. You may recall Bill Bright's comment: "The evidence confirming the deity of the Lord Jesus Christ is overwhelmingly conclusive to any honest, objective seeker after truth." Josh McDowell similarly refers to evidence that demands a verdict, rather than singing the praises of blind faith, and works strenuously to marshal such proof. Evangelicals construct elaborate palaces of reasoning and logic, which rest on their presupposition that the Bible is God's Word, but the presupposition itself, and the reasons for it, are never examined.

The most committed Evangelicals at my church and at Wheaton College made a ritual out of praising and patting each other on the back. Among men, their praises often gave the impression that if they had a fault at all, it was thinking too rationally and too logically. But do Evangelicals listen to, or even hear, people who have a different perspective about whether these Evangelical men have demonstrated a commitment to rational thinking?

Evangelical autism, paranoia, and otherworldly disordered thinking results in a profoundly isolated community. This often-underestimated side effect of Evangelical theology may not appear obvious at first glance. As I've pointed out, Evangelicals often seem to fit perfectly into modern American life—"almost too normal," in the words of my friend. Yet their reasoning has made them alien.

Because most people do not realize this, their experiences with Evangelicals take place on the Evangelical's terms—dictated by the absurd rules of Hooks and Ladders. This puts outsiders at a distinct disadvantage the moment they agree to engage Evangelicals without first committing to following through with a dialogue in a thorough and comprehensive way.

Suppose, for example, that you confront a group of people who all suffer from colorblindness. Because they all suffer from this condition, if they take the lead in framing the way a debate or discussion should proceed, they will leave out topics that have to do with differences in color. Since most issues do not require a person to have the ability to distinguish between different colors, these people may seem perfectly normal. When an issue, however, touches on something that requires an ability to distinguish color, these seemingly normal people will appear bizarre. Indeed, in this example, we would all agree that the first order of business in discussing color with a group of colorblind people would include a way of establishing colorblindness. Obviously, a group of colorblind people—who do not know they are colorblind—will not take the lead in discussing topics that require an ability to distinguish different colors.

Using the analogy of a colorblind group as a comparison to Evangelicals helps highlight one glaring problem non-Evangelicals have in their interactions with Evangelicals. Because Evangelicals leave their exclusive communities occasionally and engage non-Evangelicals in discussions, non-Evangelicals have a problem. If they wish to convey the flaws in an Evangelical's reasoning, they have little choice other than using issues that the Evangelical picked for discussion. Evangelicals never want to discuss the merits of believing in the inerrancy of the Bible or the merits of using the evidence of a changed life to support a belief in Evangelical doctrines. Just as colorblind people do not start discussions about colors, Evangelicals do not start conversations about Explanation PG or their reasons for believing that the Bible has no errors. In their discussions with Evangelicals, non-Evangelicals may find it more revealing to focus their attention on topics that Evangelicals never discuss with each other.

MAKING SENSE OF EVANGELICAL BLINDNESS

After I rejected Evangelical claims, the following question became glaringly obvious: "Why do Evangelical Christians accept biblical claims about miracles but reject others' claims about miracles?" Furthermore, it dawned on me that I did not know *any* Evangelical who ever seriously considered this question. Since my educational experience came as a science major, surrounded by brilliant people at the most prestigious Evangelical college, the complete lack of interest in answering this question spoke volumes. It became painfully clear to me that I had held many unsupportable beliefs based on my unexamined belief that Almighty God had inspired the writing of the Bible. Does this theme sound familiar?

Indeed, even after I found Evangelical claims that I could not accept, it still never occurred to me to examine the reasons that had led me to accept the Bible as God's Word in the first place. Somehow, back then I just *knew* that if I conducted a rigorous examination of biblical history, the sciences, and philosophy, it would strengthen my previously unexamined acceptance of the Bible. (Of course, I was wrong about this, but that is what I thought at the time.) Back then, I did not care that I accepted the Bible as God's Word before figuring out whether I could support it logically, historically, scientifically, or philosophically. A victim of Explanation PG, I simply *knew* I could find God's message to me, and all humankind, in the Bible. I never entertained the idea that my experiences—and the experiences of other True Christians—could have resulted from anything other than my personal god causing them. Furthermore, many of my Evangelical friends and I had objective evidence (by secular standards) that our brains worked fine, as many of us excelled in school and obtained high scores on standardized achievement tests like the SAT.

While I was an Evangelical, my brain did not consider any other possibilities for my changed life after accepting Jesus as my Lord and Savior, other than God's work in my life. It still haunts me to think about how many things I accepted as rational based on this unquestioned premise. It still haunts me to think how little insight I had that this unquestioned belief fundamentally influenced my rational thinking about anything that related to my belief in my personal god.

How did this belief alter my approach to problem solving and affect my rational thought process? Should I have spent time figuring out if the various reasonable explanations of my emotional conversion experiences had any validity? Other than the explanation that I believed—that my personal god came into my life and changed me—what other explanations did I consider? What other explanations *should* I have considered? After all, I already believed the only explanation that cast my character, intelligence, and emotional stability in a positive light. In order for me to consider any other explanation, I would have had to consider the possibility that I had made a foolish decision by accepting Jesus as my personal savior. Even worse, every other explanation would require me to consider the possibility that my life had become a series of foolish and mostly senseless exercises. I would have to accept the possibility, for example, that I had repeatedly deceived myself into believing God had answered my prayers. In other words, I would have had to have the capacity to believe that somehow I believed something far more foolish than the people we called fools (like atheists) believed, and that I had ingested healthy doses of self-deception. Apparently, my brain would only allow me to file one explanation for my experiences and beliefs—Explanation PG—into a folder labeled "Reasonable Explanations."

As a result, it made sense for me to not waste time investigating some things. If I had no rational mental pathway that could lead me to conclude that God did not inspire the writing of the Bible, for example, then how could I rationally justify spending time dwelling on this subject? Within the context of the mental short-circuitry of Explanation PG, rationally accepting the Bible as God's Word, despite minimal investigation, almost makes sense. With no valid alternative explanation to consider, spending time investigating the truth about the Bible sank to the bottom of my priority list, competing with things like traveling to France to investigate the truth about the existence of Paris.

The Rules of Hooks and Ladders and Loose Associations

If you go to your local Bible bookstore, you may find my claim that close to zero Evangelicals converted to Christianity *after* studying the evidence difficult to believe. Evangelicals have a fondness for authors who claim to have found God through reason and evidence. But, even if we tallied all the Evangelicals who make this claim, they would only make up a tiny fraction of a percent of all Evangelicals. Even worse, most of the people who make this claim have often grossly overestimated the value of their claims. After all, who cares what reasons a person has for making this decision if he (I do not know of any female writers to whom this applies) has not shown an ability to solve common problems? They have duped Evangelicals into believing their claims have merit (perhaps because they want to believe they have merit).

For example, Josh McDowell, the author of *Evidence That Demands a Verdict,* claims that he converted to Christianity from atheism after becoming persuaded by the evidence for Christianity. Yet, McDowell acknowledges that he had an emotional conversion experience. But he also has the gall to pass off his egotistical, irresponsible, binge-drinking early college years as representative of a typical atheist, and most Evangelicals I know have no problem comparing McDowell's atheism to accomplished and respected atheists like Richard Dawkins.

Or consider Lee Strobel, whose *The Case for* ... series of books have sold millions of copies. Strobel also passes himself off as a person persuaded by reason to convert to Christianity. When starting to write this book, I still had not read Strobel and anticipated Strobel explaining the process that led to his conversion. I had already had many Evangelicals tell me about him. Strobel never explained what evidence and reasoning led to his *intellectual* acceptance of Christian claims. On the contrary, after he converted to Christianity, he interviewed mostly well-known Evangelicals and explained why he found their arguments compelling. If Strobel, *before* converting, decided to examine the evidence for Christianity objectively, then we would expect to find a pile of evidence that Strobel had used to build his case against faith and Christ. In the end, Strobel has the same problem that every Evangelical I know has—he starts with the unshakable belief that the Bible is the Word of God and makes it clear that he converted to Christianity *before* he set out to make his case for faith.

The world has a constantly replenishing supply of brilliant, accomplished non-Evangelical men and women. So why does the reason and evidence of Evangelicals fail to compel more than a tiny fraction of them to convert to Christianity? Especially given that standard texts, on subjects like physics or history, that deal with topics forged with reason and evidence, easily gain wide international acceptance—including the acceptance of intellectuals and regular Evangelicals alike. These texts present data and evidence that few, if any, dispute. They slowly build on previously explained information and reasoning to form a coherent, rational, and interlocking set of principles and practices that leave little room for misinterpretation.

Although the most elite thinkers may find loopholes and flaws in these texts, it does not matter whether people study them in Beijing, China, or Tuscaloosa, Alabama. Both groups will interpret and apply them in basically the same way. Furthermore, the best texts identify controversial conclusions and acknowledge uncertainty. Every subject has controversy and uncertainty. As a result, even Evangelicals would consider Bill Bright's statement (which I quoted in chapter 3 and which comes from the introduction to *Evidence That Demands a Verdict*) to be hostile, uncharitable, and frankly ignorant—if it addressed a non-theological subject:

> The evidence confirming ... is overwhelmingly conclusive to any honest, objective seeker after truth.[12]

So how do Evangelicals get away with using tactics that would universally lead to ridicule and scorn in nearly every discipline except theology? I do not know for sure, but I highly suspect Evangelical autism. We do know that Evangelicals do not have a standard text explaining the reason and evidence for their beliefs. Of course, many will say there is a standard text—the Bible—as if they owned the only correct formula for interpreting the Bible. We also know they do not have anything that resembles a detailed and comprehensive step-by-step explanation that a nonbeliever could follow in order to understand the rationale behind their beliefs that leads up to that all-too-obscure leap of faith. They do not even have a source that bright outsiders could review and conclude that although they do not agree with Evangelical beliefs, they can at least understand how Evangelicals could rationally accept the explanation they present.

In contrast, the supposed sound reasoning of 100 percent of Evangelicals comes in the form of Explanation PG and is full of telepathy, mind-reading, fortune-telling, and magic—full of supernatural powers, special assignments, and perilous obstacles. Bill Bright's reading of others' minds, quoted above, describes only one problem with these claims. For example, why did McDowell put this at the beginning of his book? After all, the title, *Evidence That Demands a Verdict,* if written by a man who actually believed in the importance of weighing evidence *before* rendering a verdict, would have a hard time explaining why Bright's comments were included at all. Did Bright and McDowell believe that telling readers, especially Evangelical readers, that many nonbelievers would "willfully reject" their "overwhelmingly conclusive evidence" would entice people to read the book? With Bright's conclusory comments about nonbelievers in the beginning of McDowell's book, neither of them even faked respect for objectivity.

For nearly all of the Evangelicals I know—and for me, when I was an Evangelical—our beliefs did not stem from a verdict made *after* reviewing the evidence. Rather, for those of us who fancied ourselves reasonable, we had a verdict that demanded evidence. But the glare of this lie shone so brightly that even I, in my otherworldly, autistic state, could not ignore it. Why did we all memorize the same Bible verses? Why did we recite the same answers to difficult questions, often without any comprehension? Why did so few of us actually read books like *Evidence That Demands a Verdict* but still used them like reference books—only referring to the resources to find the answer to defend our faith when confronted with a difficult question? In other words, why did we act like a band of thieves rehearsing the bogus story we'd all tell if we were caught? But most importantly to me, why did we continue to act as though the stories we told had anything to do with our faith, even when it became obvious that outsiders had caught us red-handed? I felt like I was in a comedy of errors, part of the band of thieves stumbling repeatedly to make a fake alibi plausible. Evangelicals keep fumbling, but unlike thieves, they do not seem to ever grasp that their gig is up.

The vast majority of people who become Evangelical Christians did not ask for or require sufficient reasons or evidence before committing to Evangelical beliefs. But this alone does not discredit them; the claim that they apply reason and evidence to bolster their faith could still be true. However, because Evangelicals also commit to the rules of Hooks and Ladders, their claims cannot be considered credible. Evangelicals believe (and claim to know with certainty) that they will win Hooks and Ladders. They deny that they could ever have erred in interpreting or accepting what they claim came from God, and they categorically deny that non-Evangelicals could have truths that Evangelicals do not have. Evangelicals cannot explain how reason can grow and thrive in their culture—at least not without relying on telepathy and magic to explain how.

So what can we conclude about gifted people who consider the evidence for Christianity overwhelming and claim that only dishonest and subjective people could reject it? Even with interpretive charity, we have more than enough evidence to diagnose a lack of basic reasoning skills in this case. My association with the Evangelical community ended when I realized that even in my delusional Evangelical world, I simply did not have enough fairy dust, magic, and telepathic networking to hold my beliefs together.

Evangelicals make this type of hostile and bold claim all the time, even as they trip over their delusional stories like the thieves with the bad alibi. Taken at face value, Bright's statements cannot be linked to reality. Even so, despite their complete lack of coherence, Bright's statements clearly convey a message to Evangelicals.

What message is that? Remember, the rules of Hooks of Ladders represent a distillation of Evangelical principles and beliefs that Evangelicals hold. They want to hear their leaders affirm these principles, and successful leaders like Bright do so often. Can you figure out a more succinct and effective way to say, "We win, everyone else loses, and we are the only source of truthful information" than Bright did?

Kinder and Gentler Evangelicals

I would not have written this book if new Evangelical leaders had the same type of swashbuckling, tough-talking, and blunt message as Bill Bright; the type of message that prevailed when I converted. Rather, I felt compelled in part because of Evangelicals and non-Evangelicals loosening their guard with the relative rise of kinder and gentler Evangelical leaders. Rick Warren, who wrote *The Purpose Driven Life*, falls into that category. Yet, Warren communicates the exact same thing quickly in his book. In the first lines of his book, he wrote:

> This book is dedicated to you. Before you were born, God planned *this moment* in your life. It is no accident that you are holding this book. God *longs* for you to discover the life he created you to live.[13]

For most of the history of Christianity, Warren would have had to consider the risk of government and church officials declaring him a heretic and his claims heresy. Nonetheless, what reasonable assessment can we make about a man who tells us, without a hint of speculation, that he knows God's deepest desires—and that his message came from God—

and that God planned his and my meeting. Even Evangelicals, most of the time, doubt the mental competence of such a man. And so do I. Unlike Evangelicals, however, I do not hold Rick Warren to a different standard.

Warren does not leave any room for doubt about what he thinks of the book he wrote. He believes that before I was born, in order to satisfy God's longing for me to discover my purpose, God planned for me to read *The Purpose Driven Life*. This would make Warren very special—if only it were true. Warren ups the disordered-thinking meter on James Dobson, who believes a god inspired another man's work. Warren ditches the intermediary and declares that his book was simply an unfolding of God's ancient plan to help *me* discover *my* purpose. Warren does not seem the least bit aware that his claims are not clearly visible—and absurd. I feel comfortable calling Warren's book fantasy or fiction and welcome a debate about whether we can conclude this fairly. Rick Warren's claims have no obvious ties to reality. And if Warren believes that his book gives us facts or truth, then his beliefs too have no obvious connection to reality. Rick Warren has strayed so far from reality he probably does not have the ability to make competent judgments about many issues—including all the issues he writes about that have made him famous.

So, does this oracle of God, who claims to know God's feelings and plan for *your* life, have the soundness of mind necessary to comment about important issues in America? No, he does not! But since Warren gives the impression of a warm and cuddly man, the sheer magnitude of his grandiose, delusional thoughts goes almost unnoticed. At least the style of Bill Bright and people like Pat Robertson and James Dobson did not allow them to don sheep's clothing when explaining their warped renderings of reality. They let everyone know what they thought of nonbelievers—especially nonbelievers who heard their gospel and rejected their claims. Although often more grandiose and incoherent in their thinking, the kinder and gentler Evangelicals like Warren do not give the same impression. Rather, they come across as more humble and less grumpy than the old guard.

Compare, for example, the opening remarks in Warren's book to remarks in the introduction of Norman Geisler and Frank Turek's book, *I Don't Have Enough Faith to Be an Atheist:*

> We hope the evidence we present in this book will, in some small way, woo you to God.[14]

Even though I find Geisler's thinking in particular disordered and riddled with inexcusable conclusions (like labeling all atheists as Big Bang skeptics), he does maintain some humility. To his credit, he has meticulously attempted to explain why he believes as he does. Geisler, and most other member of the Evangelical old guard, have a sense of obligation to be prepared to answer tough questions when sharing their gospel. Evangelicals like Rick Warren do not. Indeed, Rick Warren will probably never write a bizarre document like *The Chicago Statement of Biblical Inerrancy*. Why go to all that trouble when he came simply declare that he speaks for God?

Purposely Driving People Out of the Evangelical Community

Rick Warren hosted a forum for presidential election candidates John McCain and Barack Obama at Saddleback Church in California, where he is the pastor. I heard and read many commentators refer to Rick Warren as a popular and highly respected pastor within the Evangelical community. What does that mean? Do Evangelicals respect Rick Warren?

We have already reviewed the dysfunctional rules of Hooks and Ladders that the Evangelical community enforces. Thus, we know that Evangelicals have no credible way to guarantee the veracity or quality of *any* of their claims. For instance, I do not respect Rick Warren. I know many ex-Evangelicals and many liberal Evangelicals who do not respect Rick Warren either. For that matter, many Evangelicals regard Rick Warren as a dangerous liberal and do not respect him. Were they included as part of the tally for the Evangelical community? If we allow the people who have reached the highest levels of Hooks and Ladders to decide who can be tallied, only the people they decide deserve the label True Christians would count.

Yet how do people like Rick Warren become highly respected in the Evangelical community? Evangelicals become highly respected by thriving in Hooks and Ladders, which requires enthusiastically endorsing and applying the rules of Hooks and Ladders. Embedded in seemingly benign statements like, "as Evangelical Christians we believe ..." in the context of Hooks and Ladders is an implicit understanding among Evangelicals that they have magical abilities to read minds and render flawless judgments.

So what do non-Evangelicals concede when they allow people like Rick Warren to claim they represent a group of people called "Evangelicals?" Right out of the gate, they validate one of their least reliable sources of information about Evangelical Christian culture. Simply stated, if you want to know about Evangelical Christianity do not expect to get much useful information from Rick Warren. In contrast, I am a good source of information about Evangelical Christianity. Joy Fuller is a good source. People chosen at random from a list of self-identified Evangelicals may prove useful as well. But not Evangelical leaders forged by playing the intense game of Hooks and Ladders. They have become the oligarchy of a community that supported the rules of Hooks and Ladders—and are therefore unreliable sources of information about their community's intentions and beliefs.

If we want to know what life is like in Cuba, would Fidel Castro's claims have more credibility than a man who recently defected from Cuba? If we want to know what happens inside a cult, would we ask the cult's leader? Would we ask someone in the cult? Would we ask someone who has left the cult? If we asked all of them, who would we expect to give the most reliable information? People intuitively know the answers to these questions.

So far, I have avoided playing the expert card, but I will play it here. I know that Evangelicals use incoherent reasoning as I have described. I know that there is no credible way to explain their sloppy reasoning, even though hindsight and interpretive charity might enable me to supply one. I know that coherent explanations do not exist in the minds of the overwhelming majority of Evangelicals. I know this because I never realized that I could not coherently explain my positions while I was an Evangelical, and neither could any of the Evangelicals I knew.

10. Associating Freedom with Slavery, Censorship, and Surveillance

THREE HUNDRED OF THE MOST HIGHLY REGARDED EVANGELICALS met in Chicago in 1977 to draft and sign *The Chicago Statement on Biblical Inerrancy*. Despite the sense of urgency that brought them together, I doubt any of them realized they had written what I would contend has become the first draft of the Constitution of the American Evangelical Empire.

The push to promote inerrancy and other Evangelical truths came at a time when mass media and information technology exploded. As a result, a church tucked away in the woods or a small seminary could not as easily escape the scrutiny of the self-anointed Evangelical elites, as either may have previously. As well, with cable television, the extended reach of national retail chains, and syndicated radio programs, even members of isolated rural churches had easy access to Evangelical mass media. With an Evangelical community informed by the same small group of Evangelicals that dominated Evangelical mass media, seminaries and colleges that did not place emphasis on issues as inerrancy, could no longer fly under the Evangelical radar screen. Churches, colleges, and seminaries had to adopt the agenda set by nationally recognized Evangelical leaders. If they did not, then they risked alienating and losing many members of their communities. Thus, the *Chicago Statement* Evangelicals did not have to try to build an empire from the ground up. On the contrary, and by their own admission, they bullied already-existing churches, schools, and seminaries into signing on to their doctrines of certainty.

Although relatively few in number, Evangelical inerrantists forged a federation of diverse and often isolated Protestant groups into one group under the umbrella of Evangelicalism. These inerrantists proved as effective as any group of corporate executives in defining and shaping their brand. They focused their attention on groups that shared core Protestant beliefs about the authority of Scripture, salvation, and the deity of Jesus, even though these groups often had seemingly irreconcilable differences in areas outside their core beliefs. Inerrantists sent out a rallying cry for all believers to join the most important battle in history—the Battle for the Bible. Many groups put aside their differences and joined the Battle for the Bible, and over time, people branded these newly assembled inerrantists Evangelical Christians.

At the level of the local church, the battle did not involve too much struggle. Either churches complied with the rules of Hooks and Ladders, or they did not comply. If they did not comply, rank and file Christians who considered themselves soldiers in the Battle for the Bible passed the word along to their compatriots. It did not take long for every Bible-believing Christian to find out which churches to avoid. The hard-fought battles, however, occurred on Protestant Christian college and seminary campuses. Schools could easily advertise as Bible-believing institutions while harboring some liberal professors who did not share the inerrantists' belief about the Bible. It is easy to see where the inerrantists won; they won on every campus that Evangelicals now consider acceptable for an Evangelical Christian student to attend. Today, Evangelicals (who have become the same as inerrantists, for all practical purposes) depend on these schools to maintain the integrity of the Evangelical/inerrantist brand. Each school may have its own unique denominational quality, but for a school to be included under the umbrella of Evangelical Christianity, it has to have the same certainty about biblical authority.

Even though for many Evangelicals the urgency of this battle has ended, their army has not disbanded. The battleground has not changed—it remains on Evangelical campuses. Many warriors still monitor these schools and report insurgents to Evangelical leaders who still have the power to clean house. Having lost most of their militaristic rhetoric, however, the people who define and enforce the rules for groups that play Hooks and Ladders function much like a professional sports league. Like a sports league, the self-anointed executives of the inerrantists' league have the primary responsibility of defining the rules for the game and the rules for the league. In this sense, the similarity between Evangelicals and the National Football League, for example, is quite striking. As convenient shorthand to use while making this comparison, I will refer to the league of inerrantist Evangelicals as the American Hooks and Ladders League (AHLL).

Here is an example of a typical conversation that may help explain this comparison:

Bob asks, "Amy, do you know anything about Calvin College?"

Amy says, "I know a few things about Calvin, Bob. I know it is a Christian college."

Bob asks, "Is Calvin non-denominational?"

Amy says, "Not even close. I think they are Christian Reformed. They believe in a bunch of old and outdated Dutch creeds."

When Amy calls Calvin College a "Christian college," she means that Calvin has met the requirements for participation in the AHLL. The term "Christian" in this sense refers to the groups in the AHLL only. Therefore, a professor at Calvin can feel confident that she can go to any other AHLL group and have them introduce and treat her as a fellow Christian. But just as a Dallas Cowboy football player may believe the Chicago Bears have outdated team rules and lack the talent that the Cowboys have, the same concept applies in the AHLL. Amy can freely criticize Calvin's Dutch creeds as long as she does not cross the line and question Calvin's "Christian" status. Only the inerrantists who made themselves the executives of the AHLL get to decide whether a church or a college can join or stay in the AHLL. However, like the executives of a sports league, the inerrantists who operate the AHLL do not micromanage churches and schools. They put most of their efforts into marketing, safeguarding, and acting as gatekeepers for their brand.

A person does not have to listen to inerrantist leaders for too long before realizing these leaders act as if they should have the exclusive rights to using the title "Christian" and the exclusive rights to define the meaning of "Christmas," which is their analogous Super Bowl. Most importantly, these leaders believe they deserve recognition as the only rightful interpreters of the Bible. People or groups who so much as question how the inerrantists have interpreted the Bible have committed the ultimate heresy in the AHLL. The AHLL has a zero-tolerance policy for anyone who challenges the inerrantists' abilities to determine truth.

The principles of the AHLL have nothing in common with the principles of freedom and democracy that fueled the American Revolution. The AHLL operates under the rules of Hooks and Ladders. As a result, the AHLL functions like a separate country. In fact, the structures, laws, practices, and principles of the United States and the

AHLL have almost nothing in common—they are linked together only through a shared department of motor vehicles.*

Evangelicals have capitalized on the odd paradox inherent in a country set up to foster an attitude of uncertainty through checks and balances and limits on power. The United States jealously guards the rights of individuals who disagree with American principles. Thus, American Evangelicals can and should feel entitled to reject American principles, knowing that they will be able to do so with impunity. So far, so good.

But Evangelicals have not stopped there. Americans who support the principles of freedom and democracy have never had to confront a group as powerful as the AHLL, which capitalizes on religious immunity from supporting the rights of others in their communities. Because of this loophole in the American structure of government, and a number of other factors, Evangelicals have established a potent empire based on certainty. Evangelicals take full advantage of laws protecting religious groups, which give them special immunity to laws that other groups or individual must obey. But how can a community that claims to cherish the benefits of a free society also opt out of keeping the laws established by that free society? Evangelicals can easily explain away this apparent contradiction. To understand how, perhaps we should deconstruct what freedom means when Evangelicals use that word.

The Theology of Freedom through Slavery

Far from representing a traditional American understanding of freedom, Evangelicals apply a very different meaning of freedom to themselves. For Evangelicals, freedom means they have no obligation to support, defend, or even acknowledge anyone else's rights. It means that God has *freed* them from any obligation to treat nonbelievers with dignity, respect, or

---

* I am not building a case that American Evangelicals have a grand plan to create a theocracy. On the contrary, if you have read from the beginning, then you probably realize that *I don't have enough faith* to believe that Evangelicals have the skills necessary to launch and maintain a plan of that magnitude. Instead, I compare the AHLL to a parasite. A successful parasite cannot kill its host, and it has to have a way to prevent its host from digesting it. The most established Evangelicals seem to understand this. They scoff at dominionists (a fringe group of Evangelicals who want to make the USA a theocracy), and they ridicule people who consider dominionists a serious threat.

compassion. After all, people unwilling to believe, who have rejected the truth in favor of immorality, have freely chosen to accept disease, famine, strife, calamity, death, and eternal damnation. Evangelicals do not express guilt or consider their actions un-American if they limit the rights of nonbelievers. On the contrary, they claim their actions show moral values and patriotism.

Suppose a gay couple wants to get married or wants to record a civil union with the county clerk. Will most freedom-loving Evangelical Americans support their right to choose this path for their lives? No. Then why do American Evangelicals claim to defend freedom? Evangelicals have a very limited view of freedom. It boils down to this: you have the freedom to choose whether or not you want your name written in God's will—and if you choose to have your name included in his will, only then do you become entitled to the rights reserved for the Body of Christ. Evangelicals support your right to choose Truth, your right to worship the Lord and Savior, Jesus Christ, and your right to accept Jesus as your personal savior and Lord. Do you have the right to love another person who brings joy, fulfillment, and happiness into your life? Not if that other person happens to have the same sexual organs as you do, according to Evangelicals. It simply does not matter what the Declaration of Independence says about your unalienable rights—you do not have the right to live in sin.

What does "freedom" mean to Evangelicals? How can a person become free? Let's review a disordered reasoning process that any Evangelical Theology 101 curriculum should include. If a person accepts this line of reasoning, they should have no problems endorsing the rules of Hooks and Ladders. The reasoning goes like this:

I. Freedom means freedom from:

  A. Sin: "It is for freedom that Christ has set us free" (Gal 5:1 NIV). "You, my brothers, were called to be free" (Gal 5:13 NIV). "You have been set free from sin and have become slaves to righteousness" (Rom 6:18 NIV).
  B. The law and human judgment: "The man without the Spirit does not accept the things that come from the Spirit of God, for they are foolishness to him, and he cannot understand them, because they are spiritually discerned. The spiritual man makes judgments about all things, but he himself is not subject to any man's judgment" (1 Cor 2:14–5 NIV). "Now that faith has come, we are no longer under the supervision of

the law" (Gal 3: 25 NIV). "If you are led by the Spirit, you are not under law" (Gal 5:18 NIV).

II. Steps to gain freedom:

A. Through salvation: "All of us who were baptized into Christ Jesus were baptized into his death ... We should no longer be slaves to sin—because anyone who has died has been freed from sin" (Rom 6:3, 6–7 NIV).

B. Knowing truth: "And ye shall know the truth, and the truth shall make you free" (John 8:32 KJV).

1. Where can a person find truth? The Bible, which is Truth
2. Can nonbelievers find Truth in the Bible? No, see (I.b.) above

III. Are people who willingly reject Truth free? No, they are slaves to sin.

How do the tenets of Evangelical theology line up with the American system of government? They have nothing in common. Evangelicals unabashedly proclaim that God's laws take precedence over man's laws. For many Evangelicals this means that they have total immunity from any American laws that do not coincide with their views of God's laws.

What lies at the core of the un-American values of Evangelicals? As mentioned earlier, Evangelicals have—dare I say—an unholy addiction to certainty. What could provide a better high than this?

> If God is for us, who can be against us? ... Who will bring any charge against those whom God has chosen? It is God who justifies. Who is he that condemns? Christ Jesus ... is interceding for us (Rom 8:31–4 NIV).

Because of this certainty, Evangelicals have a biblical license to change American politics and government to support their beliefs. They do this without regard for whether their methods or behaviors meet American standards and values. Holding to their untenable certainty, however, means that justifying their belief takes precedence over everything else, and it means they must maintain their certainty at all costs. Thus, it helps Evangelicals to have the consistently inconsistent Apostle Paul (and others) to turn to when they need to alter their message. When the law or authorities disagree with them, Evangelicals can point to Bible verses like the ones above. When they have laws and authorities that agree with their position, Evangelicals have Bible verses that express how God wants his followers to obey authority. Evangelicals can use these passages to call into question the patriotism of dissenters and protestors with all the gravitas of Scripture. For example:

> Everyone must submit himself to the governing authorities, for there is no authority except that which God has established. The authorities that exist have been established by God. Consequently, he who rebels against the authority is rebelling against what God has instituted, and those who do so will bring judgment on themselves (Rom 13:1–2 NIV).

Few students of the American Constitution would disagree that the founding fathers, more than anything else, tried to ensure that America would not become a place where a few people could use the powers of the government to impose their certainties or beliefs on the many. Thus, no nobles, clerics, religious groups, or rogue agents have the right to circumvent the procedures set in place to ensure the equal rights of all citizens. Simply put, the founding fathers could not have made it clearer that simply because you believe you have the right god does not mean that you have more rights than people whom you believe serve the wrong god or no god at all.

Although I have tried to compare Evangelical rules to a game, the theology behind Hooks and Ladders makes this comparison somewhat invalid. Unlike other games, a person cannot play Hooks and Ladders without already declaring assurance of victory. This puts Evangelicals on morally shaky ground when it comes to evangelism. They cannot deny the tangible value of getting others to join their game. After all, any conversion means *saving* another person from eternal suffering. Who would have the gall to question the love of a person who rescues people from certain destruction and leads them to victory?

To be sure, some Evangelicals argue that showing Christian love, compassion, and the ethics of Jesus will work better than manipulation and deception at winning converts. But these Evangelicals cannot deny that their doctrines do not differentiate between converts from *principled* methods and *unprincipled* methods. And at the end of the day, their defense of honorable methods only describes a disagreement over strategy with other Evangelicals. To the extent that Evangelicals keep score at all, their most valuable players bring the highest numbers of people to salvation.

Many Evangelicals support almost any means necessary to win souls for Jesus. These Evangelicals have firm support in the teachings of Paul. For example, Paul wrote,

> It is true that some preach Christ out of envy and rivalry, but others out of goodwill ... But what does it matter? The important thing is that in every way, whether from false motives or true, Christ is preached (Philippians 1:15, 18 NIV).

Likewise, Paul made it clear that he considered deception a virtue if it was used for the purpose of evangelism. He wrote,

> Though I am free and belong to no man, I make myself a slave to everyone, to win as many as possible. To the Jews I became like a Jew, to win the Jews. To those under the law I became like one under the law ... to win those under the law. To those not having the law I became like one not having the law ... to win those not having the law. To the weak I became weak, to win the weak. I have become all things to all men so that by all possible means I might save some (1 Cor 9:19–22 NIV).

Furthermore, Paul makes it clear that adhering to the principles of a Christian life has no intrinsic value apart from the reward of eternal life. He wrote,

> If Christ has not been raised, your faith is futile; you are still in your sins ... If only for this life we have hope in Christ, we are to be pitied more than all men (1 Cor 15:17–19 NIV).

Few students of the Constitution would deny, as well, that in order for the American system to work most effectively, a critical mass of the population has to agree with the principles of the Constitution. Yet, Evangelicals do not agree with these principles whatsoever, and they have plenty of biblical teachings to keep any potential believers in American principles at bay. For example, Evangelicals wholeheartedly endorse this sentiment from Paul:

> Do not be yoked together with unbelievers. For what do righteousness and wickedness have in common? Or what fellowship can light have with darkness? What harmony is there between Christ and Belial? What does a believer have in common with an unbeliever? What agreement is there between the temple of God and idols (2 Cor 6:14–16 NIV)?

Indeed, because of verses like these, Evangelicals, in their communities, do not have to provide any evidence that:

unbeliever = wicked = agent of darkness = idol worshiper

Can a person who believes that this loose association came from the mouth of God participate in a representative democracy effectively?

Part of Evangelicals' definition of freedom includes believing they belong to the freest and most blessed community in the world. They have all the rights and privileges, they believe, that come with living as God's chosen people. They believe they follow the rightful ruler of heaven and earth, the King of kings and Lord of lords, Jesus Christ. They believe everyone should have the opportunity to share this kingdom with them. And this leads them to claim they share our goals for a free society. With their altered definition of freedom, however, this means our government and our laws should remove any obstacle that may hinder or discourage people from sharing the Gospel. They should remove any obstacle that may hinder or discourage anyone from hearing the Gospel or from joining a community of believers. But whether inside or out of the Evangelical community, according to Evangelicals, a person cannot have life, liberty, or true happiness without becoming a believer. A person must be born again to live at all—physically, spiritual, and eternally. Only believers have *true* freedom. Only believers have *true* happiness.

A Glimmer of Hope in the Theology of Hope

We have discussed how Evangelicals require unyielding certainty about many things, including certainty about the Bible's divine authority. Evangelicals do maintain an attitude of uncertainty, however, about one thing. They have an extreme reluctance to label someone as "hopelessly lost." They will hold out hope that someday even the most caustic nonbeliever may someday seek forgiveness and become a believer. This serves Evangelicals well, and they deserve credit for it. This unyielding hope for nonbelievers often makes Evangelicals compassionate, responsible, and long-suffering neighbors and friends. When confronted with routine situations, which do not have any religious implications, Evangelicals often provide us with an excellent model for behavior in a free society.

I have given reasons why I believe a person who tries to play Hooks and Ladders will have problems. Many people, however, will not recognize these as problems, or they will not agree individual Evangelicals have a problem. As well, people will continue to encounter Evangelicals whom they regard as model citizens. As a result, many people will probably continue to scoff at the idea that Evangelical Christianity could pose any harm. So let's set aside issues related to individual Evangelicals for the rest of this chapter. Let's take a look at "the rusty bucket" of Evangelical Christianity, as Dr. Francis Collins called it in his book, *The Language of God*. Let's look at the AHLL, the league without a headquarters or an earthly commissioner.

Does the AHLL pose a threat to our free and democratic society, even if individual Evangelicals do not?

In the World but Not of It

It may not seem possible that Evangelical Christian communities avoid ever teaching about or discussing freedom and democracy—especially when they seem to talk about these qualities all the time. To be sure, most of them, and nearly all Evangelical leaders, assure us they believe in freedom and democracy. But their positions of certainty, and their considerable lack of empathy make their support for freedom and democracy a near impossibility. Even after all these years, I still am not sure what Evangelicals mean when they use these words. And I have not met an Evangelical yet who can explain what these words mean in a coherent way. I explained the theological positions Evangelicals have about freedom earlier in the chapter, but I do not think many people will find that explanation satisfactory, as the theological description of freedom that Evangelicals have runs counter to a traditional American understanding of freedom.

If Evangelical Christians do not mean freedom in the traditional American sense of the word, what do they mean when they use this word? On some level, Christian freedom means acknowledging that people like Norm Geisler, Josh McDowell, Billy Graham, James Dobson, et cetera, are not only great Christians but great freedom-loving Americans. Failure to acknowledge this means one does not want to be free. In essence, one does not want freedom if one does not want to play Hooks and Ladders.

Who gets to decide all of this? People anointed as leaders from the group that already believes it, of course. Thus they can say, for example, that it was white Christians who worked to free the slaves, even though many white Christians worked their asses off to prevent it—and, more importantly, despite nearly 100 percent of African Americans supporting freedom from slavery. But the points of view of people like African Americans has had no effect on those Evangelicals who do not mean freedom in the Enlightenment sense. They mean freedom in the sense of a freedom of choice about whether or not you want to play Hooks and Ladders, where the only correct version of the game is the white American Evangelical Christian version.

Geisler and Turek, in *I Don't Have Enough Faith to Be an Atheist,* provide a good example of a description of this type of Evangelical freedom:

> One beauty of God's creation is this: if you're not willing to accept Christianity, then you're free to reject it. This freedom to make choices—even the freedom to reject truth—is what makes us moral creatures … For if the Bible is true, then God has provided each of us with the opportunity to make an eternal choice to either accept him or reject him. And in order to ensure that our choice is truly free, he puts us in an environment that is filled with evidence of his existence, but without his *direct* presence—a presence so powerful that it could overwhelm our freedom and thus negate our ability to reject him. In other words, *God has provided enough evidence in this life to convince anyone willing to believe, yet he has also left some ambiguity so as not to compel the unwilling* … That's why C. S. Lewis wrote, "the Irresistible and the Indisputable are the two weapons which the very nature of [God's] scheme forbids Him to use. Merely to over-ride a human will (as His felt presence in any but the faintest and most mitigated degree would certainly do) would be for Him useless. He cannot ravish. He can only woo."[1]

Unfortunately, we have to sift through some disordered reasoning, especially circumstantial reasoning, before attempting to figure out what this passage means. For example, what does "freedom to reject truth" mean? Does it mean that you are free to reject the overwhelming evidence that the Bible contains a long list of errors, inconsistencies, and morally abhorrent teachings? No, it does not. Does it mean that Evangelicals support your freedom to choose how you live your life *after* you reject their claims? No, it does not.

Why isn't this quote in a section on theology? It is not because many of the beliefs that Evangelicals have, like this one, simply use theological language to make a case for their philosophical and social preferences. Here, for example, Geisler and Turek ignore the possibility of placing the evidence for their claims on a sliding scale going from "almost certainly true" to "almost certainly false," with some claims falling in the "too close to call" category. Only people who have completely accepted, or completely rejected, claims rate a mention. Geisler and Turek dismiss people with an attitude of uncertainty. Who cares what these "empty-minded" people think? Since Geisler and Turek belong to a community of people who cherish certainty as they do, this argument makes sense to most of the people in their community.

Can they support this argument with evidence from the Bible? Far from it! Even when they have shrouded their after-the-fact reasoning in theological dress, it does not work. They claim that a person's will—a person's freedom to reject God—would be lost in God's direct presence. In all but the "faintest and most mitigated degree," God would foster "a presence so powerful that it could overwhelm our freedom and thus negate our ability to reject him." One may wonder if Geisler, Turek, and C. S. Lewis read their Evangelical handbook. Evangelicals unequivocally believe Jesus is God—and believe Jesus was God when he lived on Earth as a man. They unequivocally do not believe that Jesus' presence negated anyone's ability to reject him in the least. They firmly believe that many people in Jesus' presence *did* reject him.

Geisler and Turek make a common Evangelical argument in defense of their preference for an attitude of certainty. Their arguments, however, do not jive with their own interpretations of the story of Jesus' life in the Bible. But since the Evangelical community has almost completely rooted out everyone with an attitude of uncertainty, don't expect Evangelicals to call out the authors of this ridiculous argument.

Evangelicals generally do not support others' right to do anything that violates their Evangelical sensibilities, no matter how much this view differs from constitutional principles. For example, a disproportionate percentage of American Evangelicals support a constitutional amendment that would outlaw burning the American flag. Clearly, this would limit people's freedom of expression and has no obvious connection to Evangelical theology. Nevertheless, outspoken support for such an amendment would most likely increase a person's social standing among Evangelical elites.

Evangelical Society: A Parasite That Feeds on a Steady Diet of Evangelicals

Whereas nonbelievers fifty years ago may have looked at the churches dotting the landscape as adding character to our communities, many do not anymore. Many people I have talked to who find Evangelical leaders offensive, for example, have told me they no longer regard the churches they see as charming. Rather, they see buildings that may harbor the same sort of hate-mongering Evangelicals they may have seen on TV. Yet, many of the people I know who speak out the most passionately against the intolerant and extreme views of Evangelical leaders are Evangelicals. "Yeah, too many of those guys give Christians a bad name, and they seem to have forgotten what Jesus teaches us. But we are not like that at my church." I have heard some version of this too many times to count. Yet, somehow, that fifty-year-old model of Evangelicals as a group of people congregating on Sunday mornings to encourage one another to lead good Christian lives has largely vanished.

Even the most strident defenders of inerrancy usually do not believe inerrancy plays more than a minor role in defining a True Christian. On an individual level, Evangelicals do not consider their endorsement of inerrancy or, more importantly, their endorsement of an attitude of certainty, to be a crucial aspect of their Christian faith. Wheaton College has a typical example of this in the conclusion of its *Community Covenant*, which all Wheaton students, professors, and staff must sign. The *Covenant* reads,

> We, the Wheaton College community, desire to be a covenant community of Christians marked by integrity, responsible freedom, and dynamic, Christ-like love, a place where the name of Jesus Christ is honored in all we do.

Almost every Evangelical will say that they strive to become more like Jesus Christ, and that other goals rank far below this in importance. Most people, Christian or not, do not take issue with this goal. But as I explained in chapter 6, an investigation of churches would probably find substantial evidence showing that the inerrantists' parasite has sunk its teeth into virtually anything Evangelical.

I doubt the three hundred Evangelicals that assembled in Chicago in 1977 had any idea what would happen if their plans succeeded. They turned a mildly toxic attitude of certainty into a virulent strain of certainty called "inerrancy." Many of the Evangelicals with whom I have discussed my arguments about inerrancy have had a similar response. They recognize the focus on inerrancy as a scourge, but they do not know what to think or do about it. They, as did many who signed on to inerrancy in the beginning (like Billy Graham and Clark Pinnock), recognize that inerrancy has taken on a life of its own. They look at it as a person might look at a destructive parasite infesting their body. They wish they could kill it but do not know if they should feed it instead. Many

Evangelicals recognize that killing inerrancy could easily kill Evangelical Christianity altogether, so they try to make the best of this situation and hope that somehow the parasite will die.[2] They will keep praying for a miracle.

As a parasite, the AHLL needs to feed off our free society in order to survive. And as a parasite, AHLL has many safeguards to ensure our society will not digest it. Indeed, AHLL has only one obvious function—ensuring that Evangelicals maintain a separate identity from the rest of society. Maintaining a separate identity, however, does not come easy, and the AHLL has to get its steady diet from somewhere. Ironically, most of the AHLL parasite's diet comes from feeding off American Protestant Christians. For example, Wheaton College has no problem including Joy and me in their statistics of graduates who went on to obtain graduate degrees in law and medicine. We help them make their case that Wheaton provides an education that compares favorably with an Ivy League education, for instance. But do not expect Wheaton to put Joy's or my name in a list of their graduates, invite us to teach there, or to contribute in any way whatsoever at Wheaton. They have chewed up and digested what they needed from us in order to sustain their reputation, and then they spit us out.

As a testament to Wheaton's effectiveness at removing dissenting voices from its part of the Evangelical community, everybody to whom I have shown this book, non-Evangelicals included, takes it for granted that Wheaton College will not consider this book as part of the diverse body of work produced by their graduates. People seem to have Wheaton figured out about this, and there is plenty of evidence to support their assumptions. For example, Wheaton's promotional literature on the Internet (www.wheaton.edu) and elsewhere will often contain a list of Wheaton's more noteworthy graduates. An interested reader will easily find evangelist, Billy Graham, former Republican Speaker of the U.S. House of Representatives Dennis Hastert, and former U.S. Senator and ambassador, Republican Dan Coats, listed in Wheaton's materials. Good luck trying to find the name of Congressman Jim McDermott on the list—he is a Democrat who currently serves as a Representative from the state of Washington.

At times, Wheaton's lack of recognition of notable graduates seems downright spooky. I do not mean spooky in the way that perhaps Wes Craven, a famous filmmaker and a graduate of Wheaton, might have meant in his movie, *Nightmare on Elm Street.* I mean spooky in more of a *Twilight Zone* sense of the word. In that sense, Wheaton College rarely mentions many highly influential Evangelicals who graduated from there. For example, Josh McDowell, whom I would contend has had more influence on the Evangelical community than even Billy Graham has had in the last thirty years, graduated from Wheaton. Wheaton rarely includes McDowell's name in its list of notable graduates.

I have mentioned another notable graduate, Norman Geisler, many times in this book. He has left too many marks on Evangelical culture to erase. Geisler's prodigious list of distinctly Evangelical accomplishments probably rivals that of any other living person's, yet Wheaton rarely mentions him. Why? I know firsthand that many people at Wheaton believe that McDowell and Geisler have done more to damage than improve Wheaton's reputation as a school that provides an excellent education. I find it spooky that Wheaton is at best ambivalent about its many graduates who go on to become highly successful at doing exactly what Wheaton claims it hope its graduates will do. I hope to shed some light on why Wheaton might do this in the next chapter.

In America, a person who was born in a hospital in Wyoming or any other state has the same rights and privileges as any other American, whether we approve of him or her or not. Evangelicals do not have anything like this in their communities. They have turned the American system upside down. People who have lived their whole lives in Evangelical families, attended Evangelical churches and schools, and spent much of their lives preaching the Gospel of Jesus to everyone they knew still do not have secure membership in the AHLL. The AHLL reserves the right to kick anyone out at any time, and the right to deny responsibility for the actions of people whom they unceremoniously dismiss from their communities. The system they use to define who has membership in their community—beyond just un-American—is just plain spooky. Like a science fiction movie, they can take a member who they regarded highly last year and erase him or her from the membership rolls this year. They can then claim that the now unwelcome person was not actually a *true* member of their community last year either. In essence, the AHLL maintains historical records of the members of their community written in pencil, so they can erase any person's name at any time if that suits their purposes. This helps the AHLL ignore its failures. It can morph into a new parasite that looks and acts differently, and its members simply declare that the newly morphed parasite we see now looks and acts the same as the parasite that we saw previously. I gave an example of this in the first chapter when I explained how Evangelicals in one generation could believe that rock 'n' roll music was "satanic" and accept it completely in the next, while believing that the Evangelical community remained in possession of the complete Truth at all times.

EVANGELICALS' FAILURE TO SUPPORT FREEDOM AND DEMOCRACY

During most presidential election years, Wheaton College holds a mock election for students. In 1964, over 90 percent of Wheaton students voted for the Republican candidate, Barry Goldwater, in the college's mock election. It was hardly a surprise, as Wheaton students had always supported the Republican candidate in every recorded mock election, and in almost every presidential election recorded, the Republican candidate received at least 90 percent of the student vote. (This remarkable statistic might seem like something that people at an elite college would want to look into and discuss formally. But this topic did not come up too often when I was there. When it did, students who did not vote Republican brought it up informally, usually expressing how their political views made them feel disenfranchised from the community.)

Wheaton College students often boast about Wheaton's founder, Jonathan Blanchard, whose name seems almost inseparable from the title, "staunch abolitionist." Yet in 1964, when Barry Goldwater defined his candidacy by his opposition to the Civil Rights Act, Wheaton students still voted overwhelmingly for Goldwater in the school's straw poll. And, despite Wheaton's distinction as a college that fought to end slavery in the previous century, Evangelicals at Wheaton (and Evangelicals throughout the country) abstained from getting involved in the Civil Rights Movement during the 1960s.

If you listened to Evangelicals talk now, you would think that if they had lived in the sixties they would have joined the fight against racism. Some have convinced themselves that they would have peacefully weathered the abuses from white protestors while walking in the freedom marches side by side with African Americans and singing the praises of Martin Luther King, Jr.

Would Evangelicals have supported a Republican candidate who voted enthusiastically in favor of the Civil Rights Act as much as they did Goldwater? At Wheaton College, I think we can safely say they would have supported a pro-civil rights candidate just as much. So why did they so willingly take up the banner of racial discrimination? I do not know for sure, and I do not think anyone does. Regardless of the reason, Evangelicals stayed loyal to the Republican Party and did not seem to wince when racist southern voters threw their support behind Republican candidates in national elections.

Realistically, however, Evangelicals did not just haplessly throw their support to just any Republican. Evangelicals at the time (and to this day) despise those they view as radical. Regardless of what Evangelicals may say now, Evangelicals lumped the most ardent civil rights supporters in with radicals that did drugs, promoted sexual experimentation, protested against the Vietnam War, and condoned interracial relationships. To the extent that these radicals also supported the Civil Rights Movement, Evangelicals would have nothing to do with it. Evangelicals did not attempt to separate the Civil Rights Movement from the radical agenda of the extreme left. They did not weigh in when people questioned whether the leaders of the Civil Rights Movement had backing from communists, for example. By throwing their support behind anti-civil rights leaders, Evangelicals tacitly endorsed racial discrimination.

Have Evangelicals admitted that they did not do enough to usher in civil rights and probably contributed to racial discrimination? Have they provided any explanation of how they intend to prevent this from happening again? Have they attempted to seek forgiveness and atonement for the harms their past behavior may have caused to others?

You may recall that Evangelicals have a special way to atone for their pasts and have their memories erased. They simply think forgiveness, without uttering a word, a magical process takes place, and their past transgressions melt away. Often because Evangelicals represent the socially dominant class in their communities, their hypocrisy goes unnoticed. When Evangelicals consider God has forgiven them, it violates their cultural norms to bring up already-forgiven sins. They can simply will away problems by denying they exist. Like magic, again, Evangelicals can (and often do) say, "Some people who called themselves Christians discriminated against black people. But we think that is a sin, and the people that used to be like that have asked God to forgive them. As Evangelicals, we have some challenges with prejudice just like everyone else, but we are not racist." Just like that—*poof*—racism goes away. But not so fast.

Let's look a little closer at Evangelicals and their support of Barry Goldwater. One state came close to Wheaton's percentage of people who voted for Goldwater—Mississippi. Mississippi reported that 87 percent of their voters cast their ballots for Goldwater. How did this happen? After all, in 1964 African Americans made up 40 percent of Mississippi's population. They did not vote for Goldwater. In fact, African Americans most likely did not vote at all, thanks to Mississippi's voting rules. No matter how they remember it today, in 1964 Evangelicals voted like (white) Mississippi, ground zero for some of the most shameful and least freedom-loving moments in U.S. history.

You may think it is unfair to tag today's Evangelicals with the sins of their predecessors. But it is still true today—Evangelicals vote like (white) Mississippi. Mississippi, like some of its fellow southern states, still has laws on the books that operate in a discriminatory manner to disenfranchise African American voters. Do you hear white American Evangelical preachers and leaders—the values voters—expose the oppressive practices in many of the states, like Mississippi, where white Evangelicals make up a large percentage of the population? Of course not. They need the six electoral votes that Mississippi brings to the table.

Since the Fifteenth Amendment to the Constitution finally honored the right of African American (men) to vote, Mississippi has had the highest percentage of African Americans in the country (which in the 2000 census was 36 percent). Since the 1964 election, more than 90 percent of African Americans in Mississippi have voted for the Democratic candidate for president. Thus, it would seem likely that in close presidential elections that Mississippi's electoral votes would go to the Democratic candidate. Since 1964, with the exception of Jimmy Carter in 1976, however, no Democratic candidate has even come close to carrying Mississippi. Although Mississippi no longer has laws on the books that outright prohibit African American Mississippians from voting, the election results show that time after time, African Americans are still not voting in the numbers one would expect through the application of simple math.

Evangelicals apply interpretive charity to people who agree with them, although it might be more accurate to call this looking the other way. Despite Mississippi's long history of racial oppression—on full display in 1964—Evangelical leaders will charitably interpret the motivation of white voters in Mississippi who support the same candidates as they do. Despite the appearance of racism and a history of shady election practices there, most Evangelical leaders have no interest in investigating or overseeing these elections to ensure that their fellow Americans can fairly exercise their right to vote. They will often take offense at the mere suggestion that election results have even the appearance of racial discrimination. After all, Evangelicals know that God has forgiven other Evangelicals for past racism, and as the Bible says, God has removed their sins from his record book. Thus, just as God forgives and forgets it is politically correct within the Evangelical community to have total amnesia about Evangelicals' past sins of racism.

Undoubtedly, Evangelicals will generally welcome an African American into their fold. As a result, when others interpret some actions taken by Evangelicals as racist, they will say, "We warmly welcome African Americans in our churches. See, we have moved beyond our racist past." But all that shows is that they have no clue about racism. They mean that they will accept African Americans who live, think, and worship exactly as they do. They do not understand that racial equality means that white people do not get to be the gatekeepers for blackness, for racism, or for the honor of "true American" status. They will claim that Evangelicals have the best qualifications for determining what constitutes a patriotic American because they uphold the tradition of linking American values with Mom, baseball, and apple pie. They do not view this type of claim as racist, even though it is.

Evangelicals will welcome African Americans into their communities, but their sociology has to fit. Regardless, Evangelicals do not rein in their members who make absurd, racist statements. For example, almost every Evangelical I know, or have ever heard, derides African Americans for voting in such high percentages for Democratic candidates. But do not expect Evangelicals to deride white Evangelicals for voting en masse for Republican presidential candidates. (In the 2004 presidential election, 78 percent of self-identified white Evangelicals voted for George W. Bush—and we can have confidence that a much higher percentage of people heralded as True Christians by the Hooks and Ladders set voted for Bush.)

Occasionally, I have heard Evangelicals acknowledge that they have underemphasized the value of racial equality and civil rights in promoting freedom and democracy. Almost all of them, however, expressed their full commitment to values they consider more important—values other than freedom and democracy.

Freedom of the Press?

A baby born in America could live his or her entire life without ever leaving the controlled environment of the Evangelical empire of Hooks and Ladders. Starting as a child, a person could have socialized only with other Evangelicals, attended only Evangelical schools, read only books screened and censored by the Evangelical certaintists, and consumed only news from Evangelical media. Yet, Evangelicals do not set up their own neighborhoods, as the Amish do, for example. Nevertheless, we might expect that Evangelicals, who often insist that they are the most patriotic of all patriotic Americans, would apply the principles of the American

Constitution within their isolated and separate communities. And occasionally they do. Some Evangelicals, for example, forged their reputation as "great Americans" by speaking out against the human rights violations of communist countries.

This is ironic when you consider that the tight control Evangelicals have on speech and media within their communities is parallel to the restrictions of the former Soviet Union. Evangelicals have a viselike grip on what a person can say or believe, even to the extent that they regulate uncertainty. Books, movies, music, art, theater, sermons, and even reporting in bulletins, periodicals, and the traditionally uber-independent college newspapers all go through hardcore censors in the Evangelical community. Even a mild defiance of these restrictions brings down the full force of Hooks and Ladders disapproval.

At the same time, Evangelicals complain about the liberal bias of the secular media, which usually means that non-Evangelical media fails to report the heavily censored version of events found in Evangelical media.

Evangelicals can discriminate against anyone they want—and they do exactly that. Of course, they could simply deny this—an easy thing to get away with when they completely control their own media. But don't expect them to open their doors to the scrutiny of others. Rick Warren, for example, felt that his congregation had the right to scrutinize presidential candidates in a forum at his church. But did Warren ever weather a similar vetting process? Would he willingly allow a non-Evangelical reporter, for example, to follow him around and ask tough questions? If so, would he agree to publish the findings of this reporter in the church's newsletter or bulletin? What about as part of a Christian radio program, or even in a book or article that members could buy in their Christian bookstore?

Do Evangelicals have anything that resembles due process? No. Evangelicals do not even have church-run courts like Catholics and Mormons have. Do Evangelicals have the right to peacefully assemble or protest? No, as we mentioned, even at "Liberty U." Evangelicals do not honor this liberty. Shrouded in theology, Evangelicals practice gender, race, political, and social discrimination. They even wholeheartedly support cruel and unusual punishment. Although Evangelicals expect graduates of their schools to enjoy all the rights and privileges that graduates of secular schools enjoy, they openly scorn the academic principles that mirror the American principles of freedom and transparency. They scoff at peer review, and through their Statements of Faith, they put a stranglehold on objectivity.

Evangelicals have committed to an Orwellian social hierarchy where Evangelicals have the exalted position as the "most equal" group in our society. Because of Evangelical autism, they can "fellowship together" with other Evangelicals and reassure each other that everyone can clearly see that they have superior morals, better work ethics, and more constructive behaviors. With Evangelical autism, they whitewash their views of outsiders and consider their positions clear-eyed and rational.

Evangelical Leaders Function as Oracles of Truth Rather Than as Representatives

Evangelicals behave as the most equal class of people when they participate in discussions about the truths of the Bible. They do not hold their leaders accountable to represent them in fair and vigorous debate. Rather, Evangelical culture has evolved in a way that holds their leaders accountable to *explain* to others when outsiders have distorted the truth. As a result, Evangelicals choose leaders, not based on their ability to stand out in a sea of diverse media and points of view, but based on their ability to squelch or censor opposing media.

For many Evangelicals, they believe their communities should work to silence the people they call "false prophets." Even ones who give lip service to the benefits of a free press and free speech do not believe their leaders should lift a finger to defend the rights of someone who disagrees with them. Suppose, for example, that a church member wrote a book that criticized Rick Warren's book *The Purpose Driven Life*. Most Evangelicals I know believe their pastor should not allow their church bookstores to sell such a book—even though the members could simply choose not to buy or read the book. Many of these same people, however, could be counted on to show up and protest the censorship of a secular bookstore, for instance, if the bookstore chose not to sell *The Purpose Driven Life*.

For example, presidential candidate, Barack Obama, in a speech before the Call to Renewal organization on June 28, 2006, said,

> Even if we did have only Christians in our midst, if we expelled every non-Christian from the United States of America, whose Christianity would we teach in the schools? Would it be James Dobson's, or Al Sharpton's? Which passages of Scripture should guide our public policy? Should we go with Leviticus, which suggests slavery is okay and that eating shellfish is an abomination? Or we could go with Deuteronomy, which suggests stoning your child if he

> strays from the faith. Or should we just stick to the Sermon on the Mount—a passage that is so radical that it's doubtful that our own defense department would survive its application?

Some may consider this a reasonable appeal to discuss the validity of various interpretations of the Bible and their role in a pluralistic country like America. Some may consider this a challenge to freedom-loving Evangelicals, asking them to put their interpretations of Scripture alongside those of Al Sharpton's, for example, and encourage an open debate about the merits of each.

Evangelicals who have committed to the rules of Hooks and Ladders and have pledged to defend Truth in their Statements of Faith have no reason to discuss the validity of their biblical interpretations. They already know that they have the only *correct* interpretation of the Bible. For example, James Dobson commented about Obama's speech in his radio broadcast of *Focus on the Family* on June 24, 2008. He said,

> I think he's deliberately distorting the traditional understanding of the Bible to fit his own worldview—his own confused theology.

In other words, Evangelicals like Dobson will often claim they do not have problems with other Christians like Obama because of his skin color or because of cultural differences. They will claim they have problems with others who everyone can clearly see "distort traditional understanding of the Bible" and have a "confused theology." As a result, they will not regard their censorship of opposing views as a form of racism, for example. Like Dobson, most Evangelicals will claim that they have no problems with African Americans who believe in truth. How could anyone accuse Dobson of racism? After all, Evangelicals committed to Hooks and Ladders will claim Dobson has the courage to point out when someone distorts truth for his or her own selfish purposes—regardless of the infidel's skin color.

Combining Evangelical autism with their cultural amnesia, Evangelicals can clearly see that respected Evangelical leaders like Dobson deserve more respect than anyone who disagrees with them. And that translates to exclusive shelf space in their bookstores to sell their interpretations of the Bible, among other things.

Evangelical leaders, who have exclusive access to Evangelical media, not only use these media to prop themselves up, they will also often use these channels to put outsiders down. Yet, I have *never* heard an Evangelical in any medium express the slightest interest in allowing the targets of their put-downs a chance to defend themselves using Evangelical media. For instance, in the same broadcast of *Focus on the Family,* the host of the broadcast, Tom Minnery, expressed outrage that Obama compared Dobson to the well-known civil rights leader and African American Christian minister, Rev. Al Sharpton. Minnery said,

> He has compared you somehow as being on the right what Al Sharpton is on the left. Al Sharpton achieved his notoriety in the 1980s and '90s by engaging in racial bigotry, and many people have called him "a black racist." And he is somehow equating you with that and racial bigotry.

Round and round we go with the circular reasoning entrenched in Evangelical culture. Minnery doesn't just call Sharpton a racist, but a "black racist." Yet, Minnery never explains what separates a "black racist" from a "racist"—and how we can make such a distinction without considering a person's race. Minnery never explains that he himself counts as one of the "many people" who call Sharpton a black racist. Minnery suggests that everyone can clearly see that a person has no way of equating Dobson's spotless record on racial issues with Sharpton's extensive record of "racial bigotry." Regardless, Minnery has made it clear that he does not believe that the Rev. Al Sharpton has earned the right to have his voice heard in the Evangelical community in the way that Dr. Dobson has.

To be sure, many Evangelicals would disagree with Dobson and Minnery's assessments of Obama and Sharpton. But many of them would pat themselves on the back for their kinder and gentler position. Regardless, should we trust these kinder and gentler Evangelicals to endorse American principles of freedom and democracy? Do they have a commitment to remove their community's censorship? Many non-Evangelicals seem to think so. If non-Evangelicals find fault with less extreme Evangelicals at all, they take them to task for providing cover for the extreme members of their community like Dobson and Minnery. Non-Evangelicals look to kinder and gentler Evangelicals to open Evangelical media to more voices and to temper the extreme message coming out of the Evangelical community.

The conventional wisdom about kinder and gentler Evangelicals, however, merely stokes the flames of Evangelical autism and anti-American Evangelical principles. Although many Evangelicals advocate reining in the dogmatic and intolerant rhetoric of the more extreme Evangelical leaders, this does not mean they advocate opening up discussion about Truth to everyone. Like disagreements among peers in the House of Lords, kinder and gentler Evangelicals never so much as suggest that their views should come under scrutiny in the House of Commons. On the contrary, it takes a healthy dose of Evangelical autism to disagree with the prevailing message of the Evangelical community and remain an Evangelical Christian. In essence, Evangelicals who scoff at Evangelical extremists essentially say, "Even though I have a different viewpoint than the current Evangelical leaders, everyone should clearly see that I am right."

These "tolerant" Evangelicals leave no doubt about who should have the responsibility in our society to determine the truth—they should. They have just as much commitment to the rules of Hooks and Ladders as the "intolerant" Evangelicals have. Either way, African American Evangelicals like Barack Obama, (even more) liberal Christians, Catholics, and all the other godforsaken people in the country have no say in matters of truth—the kinder, gentler Evangelicals have the best qualifications for determining Truth. Just ask them.

The Case of Dr. Gramm: An Example of Evangelical Surveillance

You may recall the story about Kent Gramm, the English professor who was fired by Wheaton College after he and his wife divorced. In my copy of Wheaton's alumni news magazine (Autumn 2008), Wheaton College's president, Duane Litfin, wrote an article (p. 68) about Professor Gramm's firing. Litfin never mentions Gramm's name in the article, and at the outset he says, "No such firing occurred." He never explained what did occur. Gramm had chosen not to discuss the terms of his divorce with Wheaton's administrators—to determine whether the divorce fell within appropriate Scriptural parameters for divorce. According to news reports, Wheaton officials made it clear to Professor Gramm that if he did not disclose the nature of his divorce to them, then they would fire him. Rather than discuss his personal life with Wheaton officials, Gramm chose to resign.

Litfin explained how Wheaton justified asking Dr. Gramm, or others, to divulge intimate details of his personal life to Wheaton officials. He wrote,

> In joining Wheaton College, all of us make ourselves accountable back to this community for the historic Christian standards spelled out in the covenant. Accountability is thus built into our membership. To opt out of one's accountability is by definition to

> opt out of one's membership; to choose membership is inherently to express a willingness to live accountably.

Litfin used language in his article that has many features in common with the language of Evangelical autism. Litfin never explained who would decide whether a member of Wheaton's community had breached the covenant. He failed to explain that membership inherently means submitting to essentially nameless and unregulated authorities of the community. But more importantly, Litfin's comments about the "Christian standards spelled out in the covenant" leaves little room for doubt about how he regarded those standards. He never as much as hinted at the possibility that people may have chosen to "opt out of membership" because Wheaton's standards did not sufficiently meet their new and more demanding set of standards. For the Evangelicals I know, the mere suggestion that a set of non-Christian standards (or a different set of Christian standards) could exist that might lead to a better society never seems to cross their minds, just as Explanation PG excludes any consideration of an alternate explanation of post-conversion events.

Most Evangelicals give the impression that schools like Wheaton do support American principles of freedom and democracy. They often give the impression that schools like Wheaton stand out in comparison to secular institutions because their community members have chosen a tougher road than everyone else has. For example, Dr. Litfin wrote,

> The biblical standards spelled out in our Community Covenant no longer have much resonance in our secularized culture. Moreover, the corporate implications of living as a Christian are largely lost on our obsessively individualistic generation.

Evangelicals have released themselves as a group from almost all other responsibilities as Americans. They can engineer their communities socially, racially, and economically without regard for the laws that "our obsessively individualistic generation" and secular culture have to obey. For instance, Dr. Gramm should not have to worry about what the board at Wheaton College thinks about his divorce. The state of Illinois prohibits employers from discriminating against a person because of his or her marital status. Although the Community Covenant prohibits the members of the community from doing anything illegal, at Wheaton College, the covenant's laws take precedence over the laws of the state.

Did Litfin bother to address the most glaring controversial issue concerning Dr. Gramm's dismissal—whether Wheaton had chosen to disregard Illinois law? No, he did not.

Let's look at some implications of Wheaton's policy on divorce that demonstrates a lack of empathy for others. Suppose a Professor X had his marriage end in divorce, and Wheaton had asked him to explain why he had divorced his wife. But he had not decided yet whether he would discuss the reasons for his divorce with Wheaton officials. Now suppose he sought advice from someone who did not have Evangelical autism and could empathize with others.

What would an empathetic person advise Professor X to do? Without knowing any other details of Professor X's case, an empathetic person could not simply tell him that one of the choices he had was better than the other choice. Nevertheless, it would only take a short time for an empathetic person, even without ever speaking to Professor X, to realize that Wheaton's demands went far beyond the scope of the Community Covenant. Consider the following issues, any of which might have left the professor unsure whether he should tell Wheaton officials about his divorce:

- Professor X could have a problem with impotence, and his wife decided to divorce him because of it.
- His wife could have had an affair that she had since ended and had asked Professor X not to disclose this to anyone because she was not emotionally prepared to deal with the fallout of such a revelation in their community.
- His wife could have had an affair with someone who did business with Wheaton who would suffer financial hardship if Wheaton terminated its contract with the man or woman.
- His wife could have had an affair with a woman, and she feared that her co-workers, who were mostly conservative Christians, would ostracize her or potentially ruin her career if they found out about her affair.
- The professor could have had an affair with a student, who had already promised to leave Wheaton at the end of the semester, and the professor did not believe it was in the student's best interest to have his or her name revealed to Wheaton officials.
- The professor could have engaged in frequent sex with multiple partners before marrying and before becoming a Christian, and only recently found out he was HIV positive. When he had told his wife about it, she decided to leave him.

Of course, an empathic person could come up with many other possible scenarios that would run the gamut from things of an intimate personal nature to scenarios that involved people who had not signed the Community Covenant.

Wheaton officials, who function in a characteristically autistic manner, might defend themselves by saying that the professor should not be worried about sharing sensitive personal matters with them since they would keep his information strictly confidential. With autistic reasoning, this might make sense. But with empathetic reasoning it does not. Wheaton officials do not get to decide for Professor X whether he feels comfortable or not with sharing intimate personal information with them.

Similarly, did Dr. Litfin, or any Wheaton official in Dr. Gramm's case, ever mention that Wheaton's enforcement of its divorce policy could affect people outside the community? No, they did not. Did they show respect for Dr. Gramm's privacy by acknowledging that his divorce may have met Wheaton's standards, but he may have chosen not to share the details of his divorce for personal reasons? No, they did not.

THE BOTTOM LINE

If a person advocates that the Evangelical community should draft a constitution patterned after the constitution of the United States, then that person advocates something alien and unacceptable to American Evangelical Christians. Yet, many non-Evangelicals who have serious concerns about Evangelical Christianity still take Evangelicals at their word when they claim they believe in the value of a constitutional democracy like ours. Despite what Evangelicals say, however, their actions reveal how hard they work to insulate themselves and their communities from the effects of a constitutional democracy. Indeed, Evangelicals have become the most un-American and unpatriotic group with political influence in America.

In America, we are so free we let people pursue happiness by creating their own mini-Taliban states if that's what they want to do. If they want to think they can mind read and want to set up a thought police for their voluntary—for the most part—members, it's not a problem. Evangelicals have taken advantage of these freedoms. But despite setting up a mini-theocracy (aka the Covenant Community) in their backyards, Evangelicals pretend that they have established a free society. Yet they leech off a free society to make an unfree society. Judging from the unfree societies that Evangelicals set up when they get the chance, if they ran the entire country, then the rest of us would not have the same freedoms we have extended to them. Furthermore, if Evangelicals took control of the entire country and we chose to opt out of their dominant culture and set up our own mini-cultures, just as they have done, then Evangelicals have already demonstrated that they would have no problem excluding and ostracizing us. They have demonstrated their acceptance of treating us as unworthy to participate in the decisions that govern their communities. Back to my earlier question: Is it possible that Evangelicals cause harm? I think we can answer yes.

11. The Absence of Something

MANY LOOK AT WHEATON COLLEGE AS A STANDARD-BEARER of the Evangelical community. Therefore, we can look at this prototypical Evangelical community to figure out what makes Evangelical communities distinctive. For example, could we accurately describe Wheaton College as merely a community of committed Christians who have freely assembled? Most of the people I know from Wheaton would consider this an accurate description. Most people would say that Wheaton's community had a unique quality because most people there had a personal relationship with Jesus Christ and a commitment to Christian values and that this had a far greater impact on Wheaton's community than the community's practice of requiring affirmation of certitude about beliefs like inerrancy. They would say that this same logic applies to most other Evangelical communities as well.

Most of the Evangelicals I have known took for granted that Wheaton's distinctiveness had little, if anything, to do with a position of certainty. But most did not have evidence for their assumptions; they accepted the nature and source of Evangelical distinctiveness as a matter of faith. Is there something more than faith to go by? Does the evidence support their conclusions about the distinctive nature of the Evangelical community? Can we figure out what makes Wheaton distinctive?

We could look at the evidence from our physical world—the kind of evidence we use in courtrooms—and decide if this evidence supports the assumptions that most people from Wheaton have made. So let's examine the evidence to see if we can determine the most accurate way to describe Wheaton's community to people who do not know anything about Wheaton. Consider these facts:

- Members of Wheaton College's community refer to their community as an Evangelical Christian community and as one of many Evangelical Christian communities.
- All members of Wheaton College's community sign a covenant that states the following, "We believe these biblical

standards will show themselves in a distinctly Christian way of life."[1] Similarly, they believe that other Evangelical communities will show (or should show) the distinctly Christian way of life that they refer to in their covenant.

- Wheaton College does not have ties to other communities that may have overlapping or competing interests with Evangelicals. As such, Wheaton's distinctive Christian attributes are distinctly Evangelical.

Looking at this evidence, what are the attributes of Wheaton's community that are most distinctly Evangelical? In other words, which attributes will show up in similarly situated Evangelical Christian communities but not show up commonly in other communities?

Now imagine a jury asked to arrive at a verdict about whether an unknown community resembles Wheaton. The jury will be asked to decide whether we are more likely to find an Evangelical community like Wheaton's by identifying the community as one of these two things:

1. a group of freely assembled Christians who consider Jesus Christ their savior and who have committed to work together to live Christ-like lives and pursue academic excellence
2. a group where some members have to affirm a set of beliefs with certainty, including a belief that the Bible is inerrant and authoritative

As we will see, a reasonable jury would have to conclude that choice number 2 more closely describes Wheaton.

Evangelicals Have No Associations with Many Christian Communities

Does a person's personal relationship with Jesus have a significant impact on his or her choice of, or acceptance into, a school like Wheaton? Most would say it did, and undoubtedly, it does to some extent, but not as much as people at Wheaton usually believe. After all, many people have said that their personal relationship with Jesus is important, if not the most important, thing in their life. For example, Bill and Hillary Clinton, Al Gore, Barack Obama and his mentor the Reverend Jeremiah Wright, the Pope, lesbian Presbyterian ministers and their congregations, seemingly 90 percent of elite athletes, and even many rap music artists would say that their personal relationship with Jesus has had great impact on their lives. Yet, at best, a small fraction of them would ever consider going to Wheaton College— and Wheaton would only consider an even smaller fraction of them for admission.

Some Evangelicals may say that the list of believers I gave do not share Evangelical beliefs about salvation and other important doctrines. They may argue that these people are not True Christians, or that they have distorted the truths of the Bible. But Evangelicals, using the rules of Hooks and Ladders, will not get off their own phantom hook so easily. Even if we granted that Evangelicals had the unique ability to determine truth, Evangelicals would still have to explain what the deal breaker is that keeps many other Christians out of their communities.

Let's look at a man whose doctrinal beliefs line-up nearly perfectly with those of Evangelicals. Former President Jimmy Carter, a professed born-again Christian and a Southern Baptist until October 2000, has not been in the good graces of Evangelicals for over thirty years. Why not? Evangelicals certainly support his decision to accept Jesus as his personal savior. Carter's theological positions about his own salvation are in lockstep with the teachings of Evangelicals. Indeed, more people throughout the world have a sense of what "born-again Christian" means because of Carter than because of probably anybody else in history. Although acknowledging that he is not perfect, few would doubt Carter's claim that he has tried to pattern his life after Jesus. So, do Evangelicals consider former President Jimmy Carter acceptable for membership in their community of believers? Would Carter, for example, meet the standards necessary to become a professor at Wheaton College? No, he would not.

Simply put, even Bible believing born-again Christians like Carter cannot obtain membership at places like Wheaton College if they refuse to follow the rules of Hooks and Ladders. Carter, for example, refused to accept that, as the result of his relationship with Jesus, he somehow had special powers to know whom God would or would not admit into heaven. For example, he criticized the Southern Baptist Convention, in 1997, when some convention leaders characterized Mormons as non-Christians. He said,

> Too many leaders now, I think, in the Southern Baptist Convention and in other conventions, are trying to act as the Pharisees did, who were condemned by Christ, in trying to define who can and who cannot be considered an acceptable person in the eyes of God. In other words, they're making judgments on behalf of God. I think that's wrong.[2]

Mormons (who officially call themselves "The Church of Jesus Christ of Latter-day Saints") regard Jesus as their savior and consider themselves Christians. In order to comply with the rules of Hooks and Ladders, however, an Evangelical Christian would have to make it clear to others that regardless of what Mormons claim, they are wrong, and will face eternity in hell unless they become True Christians.

I do not know how Carter justifies his stance on Mormons, but perhaps he does not feel comfortable dismissing what the Bible says about this matter. You may recall from chapter 8, Paul wrote, "If you confess with your mouth, 'Jesus is Lord,' and believe in your heart that God raised him from the dead, you will be saved" (Rom 10:9 NIV). Regardless of his reasons, Carter refused to acknowledge the legitimacy of Rule 2 of Hooks and Ladders—Evangelicals are always correct.

Jimmy Carter publicly ended his sixty-five year association with the Southern Baptist Convention (SBC) in 2000. Here is some of Carter's explanation for his decision,

> Over the years, leaders of the convention have adopted an increasingly rigid creed ...These premises have become mandatory criteria that must be accepted by employees, by members of committees who control the convention's affairs and by professors who teach in the SBC-owned seminaries. Obviously, this can have a far-reaching and permanent effect ... Most disturbing has been the convention's recent decision to remove Jesus Christ, through his words, deeds and personal inspiration, as the ultimate interpreter of the Holy Scriptures ... This leaves open making the pastors or executives of the SBC the ultimate interpreters.[3]

His explanation suggests he did not agree with Rule 3 of Hooks and Ladders: Only Evangelical Christians have the privilege to determine truth. Moreover, he had reservations, as I do, about the "far-reaching and permanent effect" of requiring people to affirm a "rigid creed."

As an ex-president, with the most military experience of any president since Eisenhower, Carter probably knows as much as anyone else does about the perils of committing to a rigid creed or agreement. But Carter's concern about a practical matter (rather than a theological matter) would exclude him from a teaching position at Wheaton College and most other Evangelical schools.

To be sure, we would find that a subset of the people who consider Jesus their savior and have committed to living Christ-like attend Wheaton or teach there. However, even if we only considered the subset of the subset—those Christians who consider themselves born-again and who share most of Wheaton's theological beliefs, it still would not seem to help us distinguish Wheaton College from other non-Evangelical groups. Too many people and communities from this set of Christians either would not, or could not, join an Evangelical community like Wheaton College.

DOES WHEATON STAND OUT BECAUSE OF ITS ACADEMIC EXCELLENCE?

Many Evangelicals I know believe places like Wheaton have attracted some of the best Christian minds in the world. As such, they believe that Wheaton has a set of biblical standards that have resulted from two thousand years of scholarship, scrutiny, and refinement. They have contended that unmatched academic excellence in "distinctly Christian" subjects distinguishes Wheaton from other communities. One person described it to me this way, "Excellence may distinguish Wheaton from other Christian groups in the same way that the NBA [National Basketball Association] distinguishes professional basketball players from others who play basketball. Suppose an NBA basketball team always uses a triangle offense, which distinguishes them from other teams. Wouldn't you agree that the team is more distinctive because they have professional players rather than because they use a triangle offense? In the same way, Wheaton's emphasis on inerrancy does not distinguish them as much as their history of excellence in theology and their excellence in maintaining a vibrant academic Christian community. After all, people don't call it 'the Harvard of Evangelical Christian colleges' for nothing."

When I went to Wheaton, I wanted to believe Wheaton stood out because of its tradition of excellence. Most of us gave Harvard its just due and acknowledged that Wheaton did not quite match Harvard's tradition of excellence. Nevertheless, we believed that people would consider that Wheaton belonged in the same league of academically excellent colleges as Harvard, even if Wheaton had not reached Harvard's vaunted status. So, returning to the analogy of the greater Evangelical community as the AHLL, we believed the best schools from the AHLL had earned the right to compete with schools from the Ivy League.

Could Wheaton make a credible case that it offers an education that has anything in common with the education offered at Harvard? No, it could not. Wheaton offers an education that falls far short of the education offered at Harvard. Most people, however, fail to recognize how Wheaton's academic standards have fallen far behind the academic standards of the best secular schools.

If Wheaton offers such an inferior education, why do they have so many accomplished and successful graduates in almost every field? Let's return to my friend's basketball analogy. Suppose a school wanted to attract as many talented pro-basketball prospects as possible and suppose people have compared the school's basketball program to Duke University's program—one of the best basketball programs in the country. Just as Wheaton has convinced students that a Wheaton education compares favorably to a Harvard education, this school convinces some top basketball prospects that the school's basketball program compares favorably to Duke's program. If we visited this school and watched the students play basketball, we could easily imagine this school could have some impressive players. Some, we might even surmise, have so much talent that eventually they will play in the NBA.

But just because a school has enough good players to put an excellent team on the court, does not mean the school puts its best players on the court. It does not mean they teach the players the best way to play basketball either. More importantly, with enough good players at the school, some of them will probably succeed at basketball—even if the school has a terrible basketball program. Merely judging the future success of the players who went to the school does not really tell us about the quality of the team the school puts on the court, nor does it tell us much about how well the school cultivates players. The only thing we really know is that the school attracts good basketball players.

Suppose the school benches or expels most of their best players and teaches their players an outdated way of playing. Now suppose the school's team refuses to play teams like Duke but always wins against teams with a similar basketball philosophy. This same logic applies to Wheaton. Some of their students could have gained admission to schools like Harvard and rubbed elbows with the best and brightest. Many of them will have success in all areas of their lives. So on some level I agree with my friend; Wheaton has distinguished itself with its ability to attract many bright and capable students. Many students have gone on to have success on par with graduates from Ivy League schools—even in areas of academics.

Regardless of the success of Wheaton's graduates, the question about what distinguishes Wheaton's community from others remains. But I would pose the question differently: could Wheaton's distinction have resulted from falling far short of an acceptable minimal standard of academic excellence? I will return to this question below.

COMMON MISCONCEPTIONS ABOUT EVANGELICALS

Before addressing the question of the source of Evangelical distinctiveness, I need to correct what I think may be a common misconception of Evangelicals. Many non-Evangelicals have the wrong impression of Evangelicals, believing them to require a pledge of fealty to a lengthy laundry list of theological minutiae. So when I have explained my disappointment in Wheaton to others, many people have asked me, "What did you expect when you went to a religious school that required a rigid set of beliefs?" In reality, however, I expected the opposite of what I found. I expected Wheaton to live up to its Evangelical heritage as a place that welcomed people who shared a personal relationship with Jesus but who had a wide range of views on controversial issues. I expected Wheaton to continue to resist becoming yet another denomination with a creed that excluded other Christians because of disagreements about issues that had no bearing on whether a person was a born-again Christian. For example, I was surprised that Wheaton would not have allowed former President Jimmy Carter to teach at Wheaton.

After reading what I thought would be the final edit of this book, I realized that my original characterization of Evangelicals as certaintists who demand loyalty and my discussion of Statements of Faith could easily support this incorrect understanding or mislead readers into believing it to be true. So let me explain Evangelical attitudes more clearly.

Every Evangelical Christian I know believes that a person can become a born-again Christian even if he or she believes the Bible may have errors. As well, most Evangelicals I know would say, "I am a Christian," if someone asked, "What religion are you?" Evangelicals have historically taken pride in avoiding divisive Protestant denominational politics. Many prefer calling themselves "non-denominational," even when they have attended churches all their lives of a particular denomination. Evangelicals also know that Evangelical colleges, like Wheaton College, avoid having any denominational affiliation. Evangelicals typically believe that *any* born-again Christian should feel welcome in an Evangelical community and do not think too highly of subscribing to a specific denominational creed. I did not when I was an Evangelical.

Quite simply, Evangelicals regard themselves as the most tolerant of all Protestant groups. They typically scoff at schools that require affirmation of a specific denominational creed almost as much as most non-Evangelicals would. Likewise, they believe an Evangelical college would welcome *any* born-again Christian into their community, as long as that person met the college's academic standards. I believed those things when I went to Wheaton—so did most of the people I knew there. So I did not expect to encounter what I did at Wheaton—deception, an attitude of certainty, and intellectual black holes.

Deception in Evangelical Communities

So what makes Wheaton distinctly Evangelical? Evangelical Christian communities, especially colleges and seminaries, have developed comprehensive strategies to ensure that only believers with an attitude of certainty join them. I have explained how such communities use Statements of Faith, which emphasize inerrancy/authority, to accomplish this. Schools like Wheaton, however, did not (and at the time of this writing, do not) bother to explain this to their students or alumni. Simply put, many (if not almost all) of the students at Wheaton had no idea how the cancer of inerrancy continued to grow and thrive at their college.

Even after I realized that my belief in Evangelical claims was foolish, I still had a difficult time figuring out what made Wheaton so different. It wasn't until I found out, by chance (or through the machinations of Satan, as some Evangelicals would put it) that Wheaton required all professors to affirm a Statement of Faith, which has at its core the concept of inerrancy/authority, that I began to realize why Wheaton did not live up to my expectations.

A Lack of Diversity: Deceived by What We Could Plainly See

With every student's (possibly unwitting) blessing, Wheaton College officially excludes professors who will not affirm Wheaton's Statement of Faith. As a result, Wheaton requires its professors to affirm beliefs, like inerrancy, that go far beyond what a typical Wheaton student would consider necessary for inclusion in Wheaton's community of born-again Christians. As students at Wheaton, we did not have to affirm the Statement of Faith. I never knew that my professors did. I certainly did not have any idea of what this meant for my education. So, maybe people at places like Wheaton simply have no idea that their community has a problem, any more than I did.

There are other reasons for an inability to see the problem. It never occurred to me when I was filling out college applications how few Evangelical colleges, unlike many Catholic or Mormon universities, for example, had a diverse student body. Nearly every Evangelical college had close to 100 percent born-again Christian students.* This was true at Wheaton, as well. Yet, Wheaton had promised us they would provide a competitive college-level education. I have my doubts whether Wheaton, or anywhere else, could provide a competitive education with a student body that has so little diversity.

Because of the lack of diversity in our communities, I now realize that I may have misinterpreted the reason why Evangelicals seemed more committed to their beliefs than people from other faith groups. Lacking any challenge to our beliefs, while having them reinforced by nearly everyone we knew, made us different. However, I would have said then, and many say now, that our strength of commitment came from God. I would have said that our beliefs could stand up to intense scrutiny, which made it easy for us to commit to them. I feel foolish now that I realize that I could not have it both ways. Either we had beliefs that could stand up to intense scrutiny, in which case we should not have to exclude others who had opposing viewpoints, or our beliefs could not stand up to intense scrutiny, in which case it made sense to exclude people with opposing viewpoints from the college.

The Invisible Line in the Sand and the Covert Battle for the Bible

I started Wheaton in the early 1980s, at the age of eighteen. As a future Wheaton Army ROTC graduate and U.S. Army officer, I had as much interest in a good fight as anyone. So imagine my excitement starting at Wheaton College and going to one of the front lines in the Battle for the Bible. I went to Wheaton at the best time possible for a warrior, when the Battle for the Bible still raged, but all signs pointed to a decisive victory soon. Unfortunately, Wheaton College did not send any of us the memo about how the Battle for the Bible continued to rage at its campus and how the inerrantists were using Wheaton as a command post.

After leaving Wheaton, I still could not make sense of why people there seemed to lack any interest in learning about or discussing the most controversial issues facing Evangelicals. Then one day I stumbled across information about inerrancy and the Battle for the Bible. (First, I had to

---

* Actually, I could not think of any Evangelical college with a diverse student population. One person explained to me that people often refer to Pepperdine University in Malibu, California, as an Evangelical university. Even so, when I mentioned this to the Evangelicals I know, nearly all of them said they never considered Pepperdine to be Evangelical.

look up the word inerrancy in my dictionary, as I did not know if it meant what I thought it did.) I read about how, on the issue of inerrancy, Wheaton College had boldly drawn a "line in the sand" (as you may recall, inerrantist Francis Schaeffer called it that). I read about the fierce battle that waged in the halls of the very places where I went to my classes at Wheaton. I read about gallantry, courage, and Bible-believing Christians taking a stand. Most striking of all, I read about how these true Christians smoked out the liberals in their midst, who hid behind closed doors and secretly discussed their liberal beliefs about the Bible. I read how these liberals had a disdain for true believers who believed God's Holy Bible could not have errors. I read how bold Christians *exposed* these liberals in the white-hot light of day for all to see. I read how the white-hot light of day allowed people to see the true colors of these liberals. I read how the inerrantists' exposure of these liberals gave true Christians (which included me during the time referenced) the opportunity to see how phony, wrong, and dangerous these liberals were.

By the time I read this, years after leaving Wheaton, I had already realized how many odd paradoxical beliefs Evangelicals had. I knew they believed that only slaves of Christ could have true freedom. I knew that students at Liberty University had fewer liberties than students did at nearly every other university in the world. Nevertheless, what I read about these "bold" inerrantists did shock me. After all, I stood in the middle of their battlefield. I had a perfect vantage point to witness how the inerrantists took liberals to task. Not only did what I read imply that I should have had a front row seat to witness this Battle for the Bible; it also implied that my peers and I took part in the battle. Paradoxically, the inerrantists had rebuked liberals in the Battle for the Bible so boldly, so courageously, and so publicly that all of us missed it. I do not know of one person who attended Wheaton before, after, or with me who had any clue whatsoever about the "line in the sand" drawn on the issue of inerrancy at Wheaton. They all admitted they did not know about this when they were students, and most of them still did not know about it until I told them—all these years later.

The vast majority of Wheaton students and alumni I have talked to did not know that our professors had to affirm the Statement of Faith every year. They did know, however, that professors had to sign the Community Covenant (titled, "Statement of Responsibilities" at the time). But this only alluded to, but did not have specifics about, biblical inerrancy and authority. Of the people I know who did have some vague recollection of professors having to affirm the Statement of Faith, none of them knew that the clause on biblical inerrancy and authority was based on *The Chicago Statement on Biblical Inerrancy*. None of the Wheaton people that I know had ever heard of the *Chicago Statement*. Some did not know what the word inerrancy meant. No one I knew could recall having discussed or studied the evidence for and against biblical inerrancy. The vast majority of students and alumni who attended Wheaton did not know that Wheaton placed such harsh restrictions on our professors. They did not know that Wheaton made it nearly impossible for professors to suggest any uncertainty about the divine authority of the Bible at all—in whole or in part.

Before I went to Wheaton, I already had familiarity with the rules of Hooks and Ladders. So on a campus where everyone else had similar experiences, none of us questioned the merits of our rules. If I heard of ex-Christians who claimed they no longer believed in our Christian God, I thought it was obvious that they had serious problems and that they did not belong at Wheaton. After all, I wanted *intelligent* professors with academic freedom, not ones who foolishly believed our God did not exist. Nevertheless, somehow most of my peers and I supported the idea of academic freedom. I believed, for example, that giving people academic freedom would allow them to develop new or strengthened beliefs in God and the Bible. So it never occurred to me for a moment that officials at Wheaton did not share our commitment to academic freedom because they assured me that they did. But they did not.

A Distinctive Society of Certainty

What are the implications of creating a society that requires certainty from a group of people? Even more importantly, what are the implications of requiring certainty from a group of people who have already demonstrated some measure of autistic thinking? Understanding the implications of requiring certainty will help to grasp how places like Wheaton could have so many unexplained holes in their communities' renderings of reality. It will aid in understanding why people at places like Wheaton seem oblivious to their biggest problems.

Some might expect that people who have ended up on Wheaton's side of the fence on key controversial issues would easily distinguish the Wheaton-like people from others—and especially from nonbelievers. But as I have pointed out, many people at Wheaton do not know the first thing about the theological issues that otherwise distinguish Wheaton from other places on paper. Ultimately, I think that the reason people cannot see the most glaringly obvious distinction of Wheaton's community because it is the absence of something. Only after time does it become apparent that at Wheaton nobody seems to pay the slightest bit of attention to the most controversial and significant beliefs that define its community and their worldview. It takes awhile to realize that at this vaunted Evangelical college, the more relevant and controversial an issue is, the more it is ignored.

Intellectual Black Holes in Evangelical Society

I asked earlier whether Wheaton's distinctiveness could be attributed to its *lack* of academic excellence, instead of its status as the Harvard of Evangelicals. You will probably not be surprised to learn that I believe it can be, but let me explain why. A society based on certainty ultimately ends up with gaps in its knowledge—what I will refer to as black holes. I have already explained the most important Evangelical black hole—Explanation PG. In a sense, the gap in Evangelicals' thinking with regard to Explanation PG is like a black hole.

Humans have only recently discovered black holes. People have speculated that knowledge of black holes existed ever since Albert Einstein published his theories, but it remained unclear if they really did for a long time after that. Because black holes have such a strong gravitational pull, not even light can escape from them. Black holes suck in anything that comes close to them, and those things become invisible. In a sense, those things cease to exist. The same could be said of ideas or beliefs that lie outside of Evangelicals' realm of certainty. For example, Evangelicals treat the possibility that God did not inspire the writing of the Bible as if it were nonexistent. Indeed Evangelicals will treat any new proposal about the writing of the Bible in the same way. Any proposal that implies the Bible was not divinely inspired cannot be entertained, cannot be imagined, and for all purposes does not exist in Evangelical communities.

An Evangelical who believes the Bible may have some errors is flirting with danger at the edge of this Evangelical black hole. Evangelicals do not seem to have restriction on acknowledging or remarking about a Christian who doubts inerrancy. On some level, an Evangelical has the latitude to weigh the non-inerrantist's evidence against that of the inerrantists, and even has some latitude to have uncertainty about his or her position on the issue. But suppose someone suggests, as I have in this book, that it seems highly doubtful that any god inspired the Apostle Paul to write his letters. At places like Wheaton College, it will appear as if this kind of idea and the people who would forward such an idea have vanished from existence. It would appear as if they had fallen into an Evangelical black hole.

BLACK HOLE SUNDAYS

Understanding how Evangelicals create and maintain their black holes at different levels in their community will go a long way toward helping us understand them. Let's start by looking at a typical example at the local church level. I remember my pastor telling us this story:

> One day, a professor at a local university noticed a group of Christians sitting in a circle outside. They all had their Bibles open. They met at the university every week for a Bible study. This made the professor curious, so he went to talk to them. Eventually, the professor asked, "You don't really believe that stuff in the Bible is true, do you? It is nothing but a collection of fictional stories."
>
> One of the Christians answered, "We don't just believe the Bible is true, we know it is. We know it is God's word, and he wants you to know that too."
>
> The professor responded, "What about the story where God supposedly parted the Red Sea so that Moses could lead the Jews across it? After all, anybody could walk across the Red Sea, and most scientists believe it could not have been more than two feet deep even when Moses allegedly led them across thousands of years ago. Do you really think that is a miracle?"
>
> Then one of women in the Bible study shouted, "Praise the Lord! Isn't God wonderful?"
>
> The professor said, "What are you talking about? I just explained to you why one of your Bible's miracle stories is not a miracle at all. Why are you shouting, 'Praise the Lord,' about that?"
>
> The woman answered, "Because I just learned about how God drowned the entire Egyptian Army in just two feet of water."

Many of the people in my church roared with laughter after this punch line. I suspect that my pastor had hoped for this response. Virtually everyone appeared amused by the story. None, however, seemed to consider for a moment that this woman had acted foolishly and her response was immature. One the contrary, at the local church level, an attitude of uncertainty is itself a black hole for Evangelicals. In this story, for example, did my church members support a deliberate and systematic way of handling this professor's assertions? No, they did not. But, neither did they explain why they did not. An open-minded approach was like a black hole—that option simply did not exist. For the same reason, people took an attitude of certainty for granted, so my pastor did not need to defend it. My pastor, for example, never said something like, "I believe this woman did the right thing when she did not give this professor's assertions any credence. I think this is better than adding this professor's explanation to a list of possible explanations and dealing with it that way. I always believe utter certainty is best."

I have told this same story to other Evangelicals who usually laugh and acknowledge that this story would bring laughter to the congregations at their churches. I have asked them to explain to me why they think the woman's response deserved praise or laughter. None has so much as suggested to me that the woman's blind acceptance of the Bible as truth could lead to problems.

Consider this story, however, which shows how many Evangelicals feel differently about the same kind of foolishness when it does not involve the Bible. One woman in my church called her husband because her car stopped working well. She barely had enough power to drive her car into the church parking lot. She asked her friends to pray with her about the car before her husband arrived. The woman and her friends prayed that the car, which she relied on to do the Lord's work, would continue to run.

Later, the woman's husband came to the church and checked the car. He started it and drove it. It worked just fine. He came into the church and told his wife he could not find any problem with the car. She said, "Praise the Lord! I will have to tell the other women about how God has answered our prayers. I knew he would."

The husband asked her to describe the problems she had with the car. She said, "Well, it didn't accelerate as much when I stepped on the gas. It also had a strange smell and steam coming from under the hood."

The husband nodded and said, "OK. That makes sense. On hot summer days like today, honey, you have to make sure the car does not overheat."

The woman replied, "The car could not have overheated, sweetheart, because I had the air conditioner on and if anything it was too chilly in there."

The husband shook his head in disbelief and walked away. He knew that the air conditioner runs off the engine. The engine works harder and becomes hotter when the air conditioner runs. An engine will overheat more easily with the air conditioner turned on. Apparently, this man did not find his wife's foolishness and ignorance too funny. To be sure, members of my church found this story amusing. But when they laughed at the wife's response, they laughed for a different reason. They laughed because they found her foolishness and ignorance funny—even if pathetic.

But Evangelicals would not see the parallels between the two stories. As I've explained earlier, Evangelicals seem completely normal as long as you are discussing something unrelated to evangelicalism, like car repair. But when you get close to any topic touching on evangelicalism, the rules of Hooks and Ladders kick in and you are in black hole territory.

Black Holes at the Center of Evangelical Storms

I have already discussed at length how the issue of inerrancy created a storm that resulted in the Battle for the Bible. As well, I have discussed how that battle, and the issue of inerrancy, did not seem to exist at Wheaton College. Nobody could accuse Evangelicals of ignoring the issue of inerrancy or treating it like a black hole. Yet, at one of the epicenters of the inerrancy debate, and at one of the most important battlefields in the Battle for the Bible, Wheaton College, inerrancy and the Battle for the Bible were black holes.

Similarly, nobody could accuse Evangelicals of shying away from the controversy they have stirred up in the debate about evolution and creation. Once again, however, this debate would seem like a black hole to many observers at Wheaton College. Despite a belief in creation being one of the most recognizably distinctive beliefs of Evangelicals, most of my peers and I did not think that Wheaton's science department had much impact on Wheaton's Evangelical image. Some of my peers at Wheaton and I, as well, felt that some departments had too many professors whose Evangelical biases may have affected their abilities to teach effectively. Most of us, however, did not think an Evangelical bias had a wide enough scope to affect most of the professors in the science departments.

Ironically, because Wheaton's theology does not have too much impact on most subjects in science, it makes it much easier to pinpoint what distinguished Wheaton's science department from other schools—at least on paper. During my time at Wheaton, every one of my professors signed the Statement of Faith affirming they believed with *certainty* that every human on the face of the earth had descended from Adam and Eve, whom God created from dust and ribs respectively. What could be more distinctive than that? After all, leaving aside the unscientific nature of the belief itself, I would like to know how my professors justified, as scientists, signing *anything* that could compromise their objectivity.

If my professors had affirmed that they believed God *probably* created Adam and Eve, from whom we all descended, then that would have distinguished them from the vast majority of scientists in the world. For scientists to affirm certainty about the matter, however, is mind numbing. After all, as accomplished scientists, they must have had logical reasons and truckloads of evidence to justify their affirmations, right? One might have expected them to use sophisticated scientific tools that they had at their disposal in their investigations about evolution and creation before determining that Adam and Eve *certainly* must have existed. Surely, they must have had a way of explaining in exquisite scientific detail how the evidence confirmed—beyond a reasonable doubt—their beliefs about Adam and Eve.

Imagine, I had a rare opportunity to learn from a cadre of well-respected scientists who all had a *distinctly Christian* and certain belief about the validity of the Adam and Eve story in Genesis. Some people might surmise that I know, or at least know where to find, some of the best arguments in support of creation science. But I do not. I do not remember discussing evolution or creation even one time with my professors at Wheaton. I do not remember one lecture on the subject. We simply did not discuss the very thing that made Wheaton's science departments so distinctive. Can you believe it? Wheaton probably had the most prestigious Evangelical Christian science faculty in the world at the time. All of them had rejected a scientific theory that most other scientists considered valid. Yet, I heard nothing about it—and it was not because we were all too busy fighting in the Battle for the Bible.

I do not believe my science professors thought autistically, but I also don't think they gave enough thought to the impact that their affirmations would have on all of us. Collectively, the science department functioned as if housing only autistic people who never seemed to notice, and rarely commented on, the raging debate about the origin of humans. At that time, nearly every Evangelical could hear the din generated from evolution and creation debates around the country, but none of it emanated from one of the most prestigious communities of Evangelical scientists. As a result, I would have to say that the lack of discussion about evolution and creation—while at the Harvard of Evangelical Christian colleges—was the most distinctive part of my science education at Wheaton.

Intellectual Black Holes: Not Just Science

I recently received an e-mail from Wheaton describing its new Medical Sciences Project and asking me for a contribution. I wrote the project director, Brian Gardner, and explained to him why I did not feel comfortable contributing to the project. He graciously wrote back and offered to send me a book, titled *Not Just Science*. This book, published in 2005, was edited by and was largely written by Wheaton professors. He thought this book might interest me and wrote, "It explains better than I could Wheaton's philosophy of science as it relates to Christian faith."[4]

Gardner and I have this in common; we both believe *Not Just Science* explains Wheaton's philosophy of science better than either of us could. I doubt we agree as to why. I consider it a remarkable achievement in fitting-square-peg-into-round-hole-ology. After reading the work of many of the contributors, it seemed as if they were engaged in an exercise to see how close they could get to one of Wheaton's black holes without falling in. None of the contributors whose jobs depended on their ongoing affirmation of a statement of faith bothered to mention that they had signed one. So *full disclosure* is not a part of Wheaton's philosophy of science.

Beyond just failing to disclose the limitations placed on most of them by their schools, the book's editors did not feel that the ethical issues surrounding schools that require affirmation of a statement of faith merited inclusion in their book. Yet, many people have serious ethical concerns about statements of faith and the implications they have for the ability of schools that require them to operate effectively. This concern comes not just from non-Christians but from Evangelicals as well.[5] Indeed, in the years before the book's publication, many groups and organizations added or expanded policies that required people to disclose their "conflicts of interest." One might almost call those years a "Full Disclosure Revolution."

One of the primary objectives of *Not Just Science* is to specifically address the role of Christians in the scientific community. Failing to address the statements of faith that the authors and editors are required to affirm as a condition of their employment places a glaring absence—a seeming black hole—at the heart of the book. Understandably, when Evangelicals omit discussions about difficult issues, they can gloss over the issue as if it did not matter. Thus, an unwitting reader (a student considering going to Wheaton, for example), may assume that the issue does not matter, or any controversy has already been settled. Here is an example where one of the editors of *Not Just Science*, E. David Cook, gives the impression that the book's contributors have addressed important controversial issues. He wrote,

> The reader has been able to walk with the practicing scientists as they have encountered the crucial questions that arise as scientific work is conducted. These scientists have not tried to avoid the difficult areas or issues; rather, they have honestly and professionally shown how scientific work and Christianity are not in conflict but are intertwined and mutually enhance each other.[6]

Thus, a student who reads *Not Just Science* may assume that nobody questions the legitimacy of science programs at Evangelical schools that require professors to affirm a statement of faith. After all, if this were controversial, the contributors of *Not Just Science* would not have avoided the issue in a book designed to question whether scientific work and Christianity are in conflict.

As well, the contributors of *Not Just Science* have written an entire book without acknowledging that the vast majority of scientists believe that Christians have not forwarded a useful scientific explanation of how life began. The contributors simply ignore the thoughts and points of view of most of the scientists in the world. But bad habits and tortuous reasoning often result in faulty logic, and I found plenty of faulty logic in *Not Just Science*. So let's look at a few examples.

One of my chemistry professors, Dr. Larry Funck, wrote a chapter titled, "The Creation of Life: Charting When, Where, and How?" Dr. Funck wrote,

> The question of the origin of information is viewed by many as being the most crucial in origin of life science. Manfred Eigen, a prominent origin of life theorist, says, "Our task is to find an algorithm, a natural law that leads to the origin of information."[7]

I was especially surprised to read this passage because of an important lesson I learned from Dr. Funck. One day while I was struggling to learn quantum mechanics, Dr. Funck told me, "Billy, you have to understand that some of this stuff you won't understand. Just try to keep track of things that are there without creating things that aren't there—and make a note of things you are not sure about either way."

I remember this comment because it was initially as confusing to me as quantum mechanics was. But later I understood, so I started to label things or concepts that I did not understand with nonsense words like "zog" or "pog." Once I understood them, I started referring to them with their proper name. I continue to use this tool even today. I realized that many of the things that I had labeled zogs did not exist, except as ideas or explanations. In other words, they were nonexistent entities to which I gave a silly name so that I would not assign physical attributes to them mistakenly, as Evangelicals do with the word "sin."

Dr. Funck planted the seed that started me thinking about the pitfall of using ontological and concrete thinking, as I discussed in chapter 8. I remember Dr. Funck chuckled when I told him about how I started to label things "zogs" when I wasn't sure what they were, and how often my zogs turned out to be nothing at all.

So I am a little skeptical that Dr. Funck takes what he wrote seriously. I have to wonder if Dr. Funck has merely written as if he were a reporter, without discriminating between credible and absurd ideas. After all, Dr. Funck knows as well as anyone else that "information" is a zog, and as a zog, "origin of information" is also a zog.[8] Nonexistent entities cannot be found and they do not have origins. It does not matter how many intelligent design scientists click their heels together at the same time, they will not find "intelligent design," "information," or "origin of information." Or as I would put it, thanks to Dr. Funck's tutelage, they will not find zogs, pogs, or sogs. They will always remain, as they are—nonexistent.[9]

As if he were a reporter, Dr. Funck briefly reviewed aspects of most of the common Christian positions on the origin of life. He mentioned everything from "young earth creationism" (p. 219), to "evolutionary creationism" (p. 220), which runs the gamut from creation in six days less than ten thousand years ago to essentially unqualified endorsement of the theory of evolution. Did Dr. Funck take the opportunity in this book to give others, including non-scientists, an accomplished scientist's perspective? For example, I would have taken the opportunity to say something like, "If you say that you believe the earth is less than ten thousand years old, you will sound like a fool in the scientific community. Here is why …" Dr. Funck did not do this, put rather wrote,

> "Regardless of the position taken, a thinking Christian should be open to and tolerant of opposing views held by other people of faith." (p. 221)

What does this mean? I doubt Dr. Funck really thinks Christians should be intolerant of the opposing views of people without faith. I suspect Dr.

Funck likely did not consider, one way or the other, how thinking Christians should handle the opposing views of people without faith. He has likely fallen victim to Evangelical autism over the years and simply avoids going too close to this Evangelical black hole. Nevertheless, I think he has exhibited Evangelical autism here. Because, if we merely stick to "people of faith," I believe I know to whom Dr. Funck refers—the "people of faith" are other Evangelical Christians. He probably does not mean people belonging to Mormon, Catholic, or other distinctly non-Evangelical Christian faith groups—and more than likely his Evangelical readers interpret "people of faith" to mean only "people of Evangelical Christian faith."

Although Dr. Funck suggests tolerance for even absurd beliefs like young earth creationism, we have no idea how much tolerance he thinks Christians should have for non-Christians. But whether he wrote out of a kind of autism or not, Dr. Funck needs to explain why he has contributed to a book where some of his Wheaton College colleagues made so many scurrilous and unsubstantiated claims about others. For example, two of his colleagues from the theology department, Vincent E. Bacote and Stephen R. Spencer, wrote,

> To understand the wonders of this created order in ever-increasing detail without being moved to humbly adore the Creator is not only willful sin, but also an intellectual failure. Learning about this world that does not result in worship of the providential Creator-God profoundly misunderstands the world.[10]

My humble professor, Dr. Funck, did not feel comfortable explaining to young earth creationists that they had absurd beliefs. Yet, he apparently did not mind his colleagues calling people like me willingly sinful intellectual failures who misunderstand the world. Although, we do not know which set of people Bacote and Spencer believe have "profoundly misunderst[ood] the world," I think it is safe to assume they intended to insult people and not merely a particular style of worship in their poorly worded sentence. They have personified so many nonexistent entities, however, that I may have assumed too much. For example, the title of their chapter, "What Are the Theological Implications for Natural Science?" personifies "natural science." This elevation of natural science to an entity with human qualities persists throughout the chapter, including a comical (though sad) chapter subheading titled, "Should the natural sciences consider themselves a stewardship?" Bacote and Spencer may as well speculate about the answer to this question. The "natural sciences" will probably not give an answer about what they should or should not "consider themselves."

I have not included this analysis simply to scold a professor to whom I am indebted. Rather, I want to underscore a larger point. Evangelicals, who have a distinctly authoritarian culture that requires loyalty to members of the community, often fail to see how their authoritarian culture functions much like the authoritarian cultures they rightfully despise. The mafia or the former Soviet Union, for example, has used similar authoritarian models. For these authoritarian systems to work, some members of the group must operate as thugs, doing the dirty work for the cultural elite. Do Evangelicals have thugs? Yes, they do. Bacote and Spencer, and people like Josh McDowell, operate as the thugs of Evangelical Christianity. Most non-Evangelicals do not realize this, but then neither do people like Dr. Funck who see the enforcers every day.

Having a reasoned discussion with the thugs of Evangelical Christianity like Bacote and Spencer will seem like an exercise in futility, just as would a similar conversation with a mafia thug. They do not seem to be able to put a coherent thought together, but they mete out virulent insults with ease. Meanwhile, people like Dr. Funck act as if they do not have any responsibility for the actions of these thugs; but they do. Bacote and Spencer do not get the kind of leverage they have to make the kinds of muscular insults they have made from a god or the Bible. They get whatever leverage they have from people like Dr. Funck and other kinder, gentler, possibly smarter Evangelicals. In essence, few would read what people like Bacote and Spencer write, and they would not have a chapter in a supposedly scholarly book, without the backing of people who may deserve some credibility. Indeed, the thugs of Evangelical culture have few worries that they will run afoul of the rules of Hooks and Ladders by spewing insults at nonbelievers. Regardless of how virulent Bacote and Spencer's remarks are, they do not have to worry that they will garner anything but praise from Hooks and Ladders officials.

Just as other authoritarian regimes develop their own language and mores, so have Evangelicals. As a result, some of the things Evangelicals say might not make sense without first understanding where a person stands in the Hooks and Ladders pecking order. Science professors, for example, do not rank very highly in the pecking order, so decoding what they say may not be easy.

Consider this example. Dean E. Arnold, an anthropology professor at Wheaton College, wrote a chapter in *Not Just Science* in which he discusses scientific evidence that he believed should influence the way

Christians view the story of Adam and Eve. Professor Arnold suggested that few archeologists dispute that people lived in the New World (North and South America) at least 23,535 years ago. However, he notes that few of the Bible scholars who believe in a literal, Biblical Adam and Eve would place the first humans as existing much before the year 10,000 B.C.E. Using this portion of the Genesis story, Arnold explains why it is difficult to argue for an earlier date for Adam and Eve's existence:

> Eve ... conceived, and bare Cain ... And she again bare his brother Abel. And Abel was a keeper of sheep, but Cain was a tiller of the ground (Gen 4:1–2 KJV).

The Genesis story leaves no doubt that Eve gave birth to Cain and Abel. Similarly, the Genesis story leaves little room to doubt that Adam and Eve's sons, Cain and Abel, lived as agriculturists. Yet, there is no evidence of human agriculturalists on earth before about 8,000 B.C.E.

For Christians who believe all humans descended from Adam and Eve, as Arnold explained, this presents a problem. On one hand, a person could believe that humans from North America did not descend from Adam and Eve, and therefore—from a biblical standpoint—Native Americans would not have the human qualities that descendents of Adam and Eve have. Obviously, many would take issue with this belief (including the Evangelicals who have Native American heritage).

On the other hand, a person could believe that the story of the fall of Adam and Eve was intended as a metaphor explaining how all humanity has fallen from God's good graces. Thus, a person could believe that the Genesis story did not describe two real people. Professor Arnold suggests that he does not accept this belief about Adam and Eve. He wrote, "The biblical text ... suggests that Adam was a real historical person rather than a metaphor for humanity."[11]

It would seem that this puts Professor Arnold in a pickle. He as much as admitted that he did not believe the traditional Adam and Eve story. He did not seem to question the validity of the scientific research that placed humans in the New World before most would date God's creation of Adam and Eve. As well, he flatly rejected the possibility that people from the New World were not just as human as anyone else is.

How did Professor Arnold reconcile a belief in the Adam and Eve story with his knowledge of evidence that places humans living in the New World before Adam and Eve could have reasonably come into existence? He wrote,

> We are driven to an earlier date for the creation of Adam, one ... no later than ... 35,000 BC [B.C.E.] when the cultural capability of modern humans first began. Such a "pushing back" of the date for creation of the first truly human couple seems scientifically possible, since they probably were not all agriculturalists. In any event, a "late" Adam of 10,000 BC [B.C.E.] violates the biblical doctrine of the unity of humanity.[12]

Arnold stepped about as close to an Evangelical black hole as I have ever witnessed without falling into it. He wrote unequivocally that believing Adam and Eve lived no earlier than the year 10,000 B.C.E. was unacceptable in the light of scientific evidence of humans living in the New World before that. It would seem, based on Professor Arnold's conclusions, that Christian faith that includes a belief in a historical Adam and Eve and scientific knowledge of human origins are incompatible, unless one makes adjustments to the Bible story, such as assuming its reports of the first family's agricultural livelihood are incorrect. But Arnold concluded otherwise. He wrote,

> Relating a scientific view of human origins with a view that takes the Bible seriously is fraught with difficulties. There are no ultimate answers without raising issues of integration to a level that places authority of in our minds rather than faith in the God who created humans in His image. There are no final answers to be advanced with greater certainty about exactly what the Scriptures or science say that seems merited under the circumstances. It would seem better to speak tentatively and then live in faith in the resulting tension. Having said that, however, Christian faith and scientific knowledge of human origins are not incompatible.[13]

He did not adequately explain how he arrived at his conclusion, but at least he acknowledged uncertainty. He did not explain, for example, how his signing of Wheaton's Statement of Faith fit with his call to "speak tentatively," as there is nothing tentative about the claims made in Wheaton's statement. How could he both sign Wheaton's statement and claim he was not compromising his dedication to scientific knowledge?

Regardless, his conclusions leave us with an unsettling view of the origin of humans, and he left us with a sense that he did not believe a satisfying endpoint was close at hand. As a result, Professor Arnold introduced questions that may never have satisfying answers. This does not make him a good candidate for a leadership role in a group of people who cherish certainty above everything else.

Concluding that the authors of Genesis must have intended for us to think of the Adam and Eve story as metaphorical would be one way to resolve the "resulting tension" to which Professor Arnold alludes. As a professor at Wheaton College, Arnold no longer had to affirm a belief in a historical Adam and Eve, as Wheaton dropped that clause from their Statement of Faith in 1993. With that in mind, would the editors of *Not Just Science* have asked Professor Arnold to contribute to their book if he had concluded that the Adam and Eve story did not seem compatible with scientific knowledge? Would they have asked him to contribute to their book if they suspected he would conclude that Christians who believed that God created Adam and Eve had no rational way to reconcile their beliefs with current scientific knowledge?

In other words, could an anthropology professor from Wheaton have just as easily concluded these two things:

1. Adam and Eve were almost certainly not historical figures.
2. People who believed God created Adam and Eve had not yet forwarded an explanation for their beliefs that deserved respect from the scientific community?

In order to answer this question, a person would have to look beyond Wheaton's Statement of Faith and its Community Covenant. Although Wheaton no longer requires its professors to affirm a belief in a historical Adam and Eve, that does not mean it will tolerate professors who do not consider this belief rational.

Consider what happened to Alex Bolyanatz at Wheaton College. Professor Bolyanatz, an assistant professor of anthropology at Wheaton in the spring of 2000, taught his classes the theory of evolution, in keeping with the standards of his academic field. He apparently gave little credence to creationism when he lectured on human origins. Based on the recommendation of Wheaton's provost, Stanton L. Jones, who sat in on some of Professor Bolyanatz's lectures, Wheaton decided not to renew the professor's contract after the 2000–2001 academic year. Mr. Jones wrote Professor Bolyanatz a memorandum stating that although Wheaton did not require its professors to advocate creationism, it did expect them to treat creationism with respect.[14]

What did other faculty at Wheaton think about this decision? Some may believe that at Evangelical colleges the opinions and judgments of respected professors, such as Professors Funck and Arnold, would carry some weight in the decision-making process. In Alex Bolyanatz's case, for instance, the Faculty Personnel Committee unanimously recommended that Wheaton renew his contract.[15] However, even if the opinions of faculty peers are respected, they do not have the final say. Officials like Provost Jones, who enforce the Rules of Hooks and Ladders, have the power to overrule them

So, could a Wheaton professor have contributed to *Not Just Science* and suggested that a belief in Adam and Eve was not a belief that deserved much credence? It seems highly unlikely that such a contributor could have come from Wheaton. Based on Alex Bolyanatz's case, even if one did, that professor would not remain at Wheaton for too long.

In light of Professor Bolyanatz's dismissal from Wheaton, it becomes more obvious that Professor Arnold's conclusions put him on the precipice of an Evangelical black hole. After all, he flatly rejected the beliefs of young earth creationists who believe God created Adam and Eve around or later than 10,000 B.C.E. Does this mean that Wheaton officials have decided that professors no longer have to treat young earth creationists' beliefs with respect anymore?

AN ODD PARADOX: POPULAR INERRANTISTS ARE LIKE BLACK HOLES AT EVANGELICAL COLLEGES

Back in chapter 4, we discussed how inerrantists have decided who can serve as referees for Hooks and Ladders. But figuring out how they have maintained this power proves less obvious. For example, who decided that Wheaton's provost, Stanton Jones, deserved to have that job? After all, Evangelical colleges do not maintain a panel of inerrantists who could weigh in on decisions like this.

The answer does not seem too complex when taking into account the authoritarian nature of the Evangelical community. Just as most authoritarian cultures ultimately establish an unwritten pecking order that the people within that culture implicitly understand, so have Evangelicals. As a result, members of an elite small group of self-congratulating inerrantists have established themselves as the standard by which to judge all other Evangelicals. In fairness to Evangelical inerrantists, however, they have not assumed power through purposeful intimidation or unbridled lust for power. At the same time, however, their lack of an overt desire for power may have made their tight control of the Evangelical community less obvious over the years—to insiders and outsiders alike.

So do the inerrantists who control the Evangelical community have names? Yes, they do. As well, one person in particular, Josh McDowell, will almost undoubtedly go down in history as the godfather of Evangelical academic communities over the last two or three decades. Simply put, Josh McDowell's book *Evidence That Demands a Verdict* (hereafter, "*ETDAV*") probably sits on nearly as many Evangelical bookshelves as the Bible. Although books like Rick Warren's *Purpose Driven Life* might be a close runner-up to McDowell's work, *ETDAV* is often the only Christian book of an intellectual or academic nature that Evangelicals own. As well, many Evangelicals have seen a version of *ETDAV* sitting on the shelves of their church or Christian bookstores for over thirty years—and have never seen a book that challenges the claims made in *ETDAV*. Indeed, of Evangelicals I know, most of those, who did not attend an Evangelical college, believe that *ETDAV* has strong arguments that support their Christian beliefs, and that those arguments have withstood the test of time. Many have pointed out that nobody has successfully discredited McDowell's claims in *ETDAV* as evidence for the strength of these arguments. Many will defer to *ETDAV* as a work where a person could go to find formal intellectual explanations for many of their own beliefs. No other work comes even close to *ETDAV* in this capacity.

Many of these same Evangelicals continue to believe *mistakenly* that Evangelical and non-Evangelical scholars acknowledge the intellectual muscularity of inerrantists like McDowell. Individually, these *errant* Evangelicals do not have much power, but collectively they do. They write the checks to colleges like Wheaton. When they do, they expect their children to get a proper Christian education. This means they expect Evangelical colleges to train young Christians to understand and accept the same biblical truths that smart and sensible Evangelical intellectuals like McDowell have so masterfully proven to be true.

How does one become the next Josh McDowell or a member of the inner circle of intellectual Evangelical inerrantists? Few people make the list of highly regarded Evangelical inerrantists, and in order for a newcomer to make the list, he or she needs the approval of those already on the list.

Who is on the list, and who are the gatekeepers? Most of the people on the list do not work as clergy or full-time scholars, but rather as essentially itinerant apologists. For example, before they died, a list of inerrantist gatekeepers included the names of Francis Schaeffer and Bill Bright, who I have referenced many times already. Others like Lee Strobel, William Lane Craig, and even Rick Warren have replaced their names on the list, while others like Ravi Zacharias, Luis Palau, John MacArthur, James Dobson, Norm Geisler, and Josh McDowell have kept their names high on the list for the last three decades.

Even though Evangelical elites, just as the elites in most authoritarian cultures, show respect for each other and appear generous with their support and praise of other Evangelicals, that does not mean they are looking for new people to add to their list of elites. Even though they all pat each other on the back, most of them are shamelessly self-promoting. Returning to the AHLL analogy, most popular Evangelical inerrantists operate like team owners in the AHLL. They do not want to give control of their team to anyone else, nor do they want too many teams competing against them. As well, they consider their team the best. As a result, Evangelical elites will rarely admit that even Josh McDowell holds much sway in their communities, even though the evidence of his influence is nothing short of overwhelming.

What do Evangelical scholars think of the works of most of the popular Evangelicals like Josh McDowell? After only a short time at Wheaton, I realized that most Evangelical scholars do not think too highly of popular Evangelical leaders. Popular Evangelical leaders have notably few contributions to books or articles that Evangelical scholars hope others will take seriously, as they hoped others would accept *Not Just Science* as a serious and scholarly work. Indeed, by reading the writings of professors from schools like Wheaton College, one would have a hard time finding *any* reference to the Evangelicals who control and shape Evangelical culture. It may seem as though they do not even exist. As I mentioned previously, despite McDowell's unquestionable influence on Evangelical culture, Wheaton rarely includes him in a list of notable graduates. I do not ever remember his name, his books, or his contributions to Evangelical thought and culture ever coming up when I was there, and I doubt McDowell comes up very often now. Remarkably, Josh McDowell has become an Evangelical black hole there.

Undoubtedly, Evangelical scholars who have done serious, credible work would like to believe their contributions have helped shape Evangelical thought and culture. Their contributions have probably had some impact, as the gradual movement away from a belief that Earth is less than ten thousand years old, for example, indicates. However, the dismissal of Professor Bolyanatz from Wheaton, despite a faculty that unanimously recommended him for contract renewal, gives a good indication of just how little influence credible Evangelical scholars have.

Popular Evangelical leaders like Josh McDowell, whom most Evangelical scholars would regard as intellectual lightweights, have influenced Evangelical culture far more than people who are regarded as having more intellectual heft. To be sure, talented members of many groups will lament how people have misguided appreciation for less-talented members in their group. For Evangelicals, who have an isolated community and censored media, however, this has more consequences. At schools like Wheaton, Evangelical intellectual lightweights decide who deserves membership in the fraternity of Evangelical scholars. They make scholars affirm statements of faith that outline the beliefs of the most popular (even if intellectually unworthy) Evangelicals.

Suppose that the American Medical Association, for example, had depended on the editors and contributors of *Prevention* magazine to set the agenda and to determine the qualifications for membership for the association. Essentially, Evangelical scholars have done this. They have accepted that amateurs will have control of their fraternity of Evangelical scholars, and they have ceded control of the message they convey to others to people who do not share their expertise—to people whom these scholars regard as mostly unworthy for consideration as their intellectual peers.

Evangelical intellectuals like Drs. Arnold or Funck will not ever enjoy McDowell's popularity or power in the Evangelical community. People like McDowell are the ones who write the Statements of Faith and the ones who enforce the rules of Hooks and Ladders. But, in a sense, the intellectuals have their revenge—when they disappear the McDowell's from Wheaton.

The cultural peculiarities of Evangelicals, however, can prove disconcerting to non-Evangelicals. People who wish to confront Evangelicals, for example, might think that arming themselves with anti-McDowell material would be a good idea. But that material won't work against the subset of intellectuals who disdain him. Many Evangelical intellectuals will not take any credit or blame for the views of McDowell that have become widely accepted in the Evangelical community. Regardless, Drs. Arnold and Funck, as others, deserve some of the blame for the acceptance of views like the ones expressed in McDowell's work because they enable the people who forward these views when they affirm one of the Evangelicals' Statements of Faith.

When Evangelicals fail to acknowledge or discuss how their society has become increasingly authoritarian, where authorities did not come to power through a democratic process or because of merit, they help mask their antipathy toward two of America's most highly regarded principles—freedom and democracy.

12. The End Game

WE HAVE LOOKED AT EVANGELICALS' FOUNDING DOCUMENTS, from the New Testament letters of Paul to much more recent statements of faith. We have examined the inner lives of Evangelicals. We have seen how Evangelicals act within their own communities and within the culture as a whole. Now we will consider why Evangelicals remain Evangelicals and what might encourage them to leave. As well, we will take a look at ways of dealing with Evangelicals that others have tried or recommended and try to decide how they measure up when applying the lessons learned so far.

(A)Typical Example

Brooke is the person who inspired me to write this book. I met Brooke shortly after she began exploring the world outside of her Evangelical community. We often spoke about Christianity, God, and faith, and I told her about my many concerns about her faith.

Having little exposure to non-Christians, Brooke did not know that others did not have the same deference and respect for her Christian authorities that she did. Many Evangelicals never figure out that their Christian authorities do not garner much respect outside their church communities, though some gradually figure this out. When Brooke had to confront her views about her authorities, however, it was neither gradual nor gentle.

One day I received a box from Brooke. Although I knew to expect the unexpected from her, it did not prevent the nausea I felt as I opened the box she sent me. Inside I found answer books by Christian leaders I knew she considered intellectual and strong, some of which I have already mentioned in these pages:

- *Evidence That Demands a Verdict,* by Josh McDowell;
- *I Don't Have Enough Faith to Be an Atheist,* by Norm Geisler and Frank Turek;
- *The Purpose Driven Life,* by Rick Warren; and

- *The Case for Christ,* by Lee Strobel
- *The Case for Faith,* by Lee Strobel.

Brooke had not actually read the books she sent me; she simply trusted her Christian family patriarchs. Still, she hoped these books would inspire me to join her Evangelical family.

If you have followed me this far, you can probably guess that I was not so inspired. Following is an example from one of the authors in Brooke's package—Norm Geisler. Geisler was instrumental in writing the *Chicago Statement,* and you may recall from chapter 6 his involvement in calling Clark Pinnock's Christian credentials into question and trying to have him drummed out of the Evangelical Theological Society. Consider this comment by Geisler about an Arabic race, as chronicled by Lee Strobel in his very popular book, *A Case for Faith*:

> He [Geisler] began, "Listen, Lee, they were far from innocent. *Far* from it. These were not nice people. In fact, they were utterly and totally depraved. Their mission was to destroy Israel. In other words, to commit genocide. As if that weren't evil enough, think what was hanging in the balance. The Israelites were the chosen people through whom God would bring salvation to the entire world through Jesus Christ ...
>
> The destruction of their nation was necessitated by the gravity of their sin ... Had some hardcore remnant survived, they might have resumed their aggression against the Israelites and God's plan. These were a persistent and vicious and warring people ...
>
> They wanted to wipe every last one of the Israelites off the face of the earth. God could have dealt with them through a natural disaster like a flood ..."
>
> "But the children," I [Strobel] protested, "Why did innocent children need to be killed?"
>
> "Let's keep in mind," he [Geisler] said, "that technically nobody is truly innocent. We are all born with sin...."
>
> "In this thoroughly evil and violent and depraved culture, there was **no hope for those children**. This nation was so polluted that it was like gangrene that was taking over a person's leg, and God had to amputate the leg or the gangrene would spread and there wouldn't be anything left. In a sense, **God's action was an act of mercy** [bold emphasis added]."[1]

I know this: Geisler and Jesus have almost nothing in common. But far more disturbing to me than a man spewing crazed nonsense is the reaction of Strobel and the rest of the Evangelical community to Geisler's disturbing comments. Strobel felt this rant would persuade nonbelievers to become saved! And Strobel's book comes complete with glowing reviews from Evangelical big shots like Ravi Zacharias, Luis Palau, and Bill Bright.

Comments like Geisler's do not seem to generate a whisper of concern from Evangelicals. How can Evangelicals ignore or even support Geisler in his hatemongering? Even more to the point, how could Evangelicals think that reading a passage like this would persuade a non-Evangelical to pray the "Sinner's Prayer" and join their community? For one thing, like Brooke they may not have read the answer books they push on others, simply bowing to authority and the Evangelical consensus. As we have seen in previous chapters, the Evangelical community has a structure that accords power to those who are in the position to determine God's Word, even as it tears down those leaders who are insufficiently orthodox.

Evangelicals have a canon of answer books deemed okay to use for evangelism. The books that seem to receive a blessing from True Christians rarely deal with topics that Evangelicals consider controversial. Alternatively, perhaps, an Evangelical can recommend a book from a popular pastor with a well-known message and style. Regardless, Evangelicals do not expect to find anything new, provocative, or challenging in these books. They fully expect their popular books to say what they already know but cannot articulate as well as a book's author can. So why read them? Furthermore, why investigate the claims expressed in these books? After all, a True Christian has already done the heavy lifting of thinking through difficult theological questions. Evangelicals rarely seem concerned that their lack of diligence will put them at risk of accidentally straying into doubt or heresy within their community.

Fortunately, Brooke did not try to rationalize or make excuses for her Christian authorities after she finally read what they wrote. When confronted abruptly with the problems from the books and from the message of her authorities, she realized she could never again view her authorities in the same way. Brooke felt, as Joy and I did, that each authority required scrutiny. She could no longer automatically rubberstamp someone solely based on that person's acceptance by her Christian community. To be sure, Brooke did not make this transition overnight. As well, her transition included feelings of loss and disappointment. With Brooke, simply having someone point out the problems within her community initiated her transition. Would this approach work for most other Evangelicals? In my experience, the answer is *no*. Moreover, I have rarely found in other Evangelicals the open-mindedness that Brooke displayed. Why do Evangelical communities seem to have such a small percentage of people like Brooke?

Brooke's empathy and compassion for people may hold the key to the answer. You may recall from the discussion about autism that the distinguishing trait of autism manifests itself as a lack of empathy—as a lack of ability or desire to see what others see. Writing this book has led me to conclude that autistic thinking lies at the root of the disordered thinking of Evangelicals. Thus, Evangelicals reading Strobel's book—or as in Strobel's case, listening to Geisler discuss genocide—have so completely adopted Pauline thinking that they see nothing wrong with the slaughter of an entire race. Do you remember how Paul described people who did not accept as truth what Paul clearly saw as truth? They were "filled with every kind of wickedness, evil, greed and depravity." They were "full of envy, murder, strife, deceit and malice." They were "gossips, slanderers, God-haters, insolent, arrogant and boastful ... senseless, faithless, heartless, ruthless." And what was to be their fate? They "deserved death" and "the wrath of God is being revealed from heaven against them" (Rom 1:18–2:1 NIV). In other words, those kids had it coming.

Evangelicals can view Strobel's conversation with Geisler as an aid to the conversion of non-Christians because they truly believe that the rest of the world sees what they clearly see. Only *bad* people get hurt; who could object to that?

Reading what Brooke sent me was the catalyst that finally motivated me to begin writing this book. That was when I began to ask myself how it was that Evangelical Christians, people who were otherwise intelligent, earnest, and decent, could continue to support an enterprise that so plainly involved disordered thinking and questionable moral judgments about other people. I began to wonder how I could encourage her and other Evangelicals to leave.

An Addiction to Certainty Fuels Evangelical Autism

As with Explanation PG, most Evangelicals have never considered for a moment that their emphasis on having blessed assurance may have caused harm. Because most Evangelicals have never considered this, when they assemble, they have essentially formed a group that has autism about the merits of certainty. As a group, they virtually have no capacity to empathize with others who do not share their passion for certainty. Even worse, if some people have some insight into this problem with certainty, they will not last long in Evangelical communities. By enforcing the rules of Hooks and Ladders, Evangelical communities marginalize or remove people who empathize with people who have an attitude of uncertainty.

Certainty, in the true sense of the word, is essentially synonymous with autism. A person who has certainty about a particular issue and remains unaffected by the thoughts, feelings, and points of view of others on that issue, behaves autistically. An Evangelical leader who enters a room full of skeptics, for example, will often come out and proudly announce that his beliefs have remained the same—that the skeptics did not affect him at all.

Most Evangelicals do not have the same sort of affliction as people who have had autism since childhood. To act autistically, they must suppress or deny the natural desire that they have to empathize with others. Many people would find it difficult to imagine, for example, going into a room full of people who all had the same point of view on an issue—no matter how absurd the view was—and leave unaffected. When people remain unaffected by the thoughts, feelings, and points of view of others, their stolid response would have the same characteristics as typical autistic behavior. This lack of typical empathy does not have to come from an uncommonly found biochemical mechanism; it can be intentionally acquired as a learned response (or lack of response) when confronted by the thoughts, feelings, and points of view or others.

Some evidence suggests that a sense of certainty provokes a feeling of pleasure like an addiction in most, if not all, humans. For example, Dr. Richard Burton, a neurologist, has written a book called *On Being Certain*. In the book, he explains that when our brains produce a sense of certainty, there is no obvious neurological link between this sensation and rational thought. He has described "being certain" as nothing more than a pleasurable feeling that has little correlation with reality.

Despite a lack of significant formal research on the subject, my experiences with Evangelicals has led me to speculate that some people may crave certainty to the extent that it becomes like an addiction—where they crave certainty even when it may not be in their best interest to do so. Regardless, most people already accept that a link between a feeling of certainty and addiction exists—but most have a different way of describing certainty. That is merely semantics. After all, the often-discussed prevalence of addicts in "denial" is really just a backward way of saying that addicts are often *certain* that they are not addicts.

To be sure, most Evangelicals dispute my contention that certainty causes harm. But the evidence presented so far in this book (with more evidence to come), more than anything else, highlights the scourge of certainty. It leads to disordered thinking, ineffective problem solving, and most importantly, a lack of empathy for others. Furthermore, the benefits of an attitude of *un*certainty are well established. Many believe, as the late physicist Richard Feynman did, that in order for a scientific community to function effectively, it has to cultivate scientists who have an attitude of uncertainty. Feynman described this as "a kind of scientific morality."[2] In appendix B, "The Hyperbolic Road," I discuss the advantages of an attitude of uncertainty in further detail.

One interesting aspect of Evangelical culture is the relatively low percentage of people who have addictions to drugs, alcohol, or nicotine. Not surprisingly, most Evangelicals will express their certainty that this means their attitude of certainty fosters "clean and healthy living." Ironically, many of them use the language of addicts to describe how this works. They will say something like, "When you are high on Jesus, you don't need drugs or alcohol to make you feel better." As well, I have heard too many Evangelicals to count rationalize their addiction to certainty by comparing it to other addictions. Using that same kind of warped logic that addicts have commonly used, they will say something like, "If Jesus did not save me from despair—if I was not a Christian—I would be an alcoholic or addicted to something else."

Undeniably, Evangelical Christianity has saved many people from an addiction to something more destructive than their certainty. But even if addiction to certainty has less harmful effects than addiction to alcohol, for example, the harmful effects of certainty are clear and well established. When referring to Evangelicals who lack insight about the harms of their certainty, it seems wrong to call this "denial," even though it is. In my experiences with Evangelicals who have an addiction to certainty, nothing makes them appear more euphoric as when they discuss the benefits of their certainty. For example, they may say, "I don't doubt that my God is alive and well for a second. Ever since the Holy Spirit filled my heart with the peace and joy that comes from knowing I will spend eternity in heaven with Jesus, I have never doubted him. I know God wants you to experience the joy and peace that I have. He will give that to you too, if you let him." People familiar with Evangelicals will recognize this as a version of a refrain they have heard many times. Expressing certainty about certainty is an integral part of Evangelical culture.

Lastly, a link between addiction and autistic behavior is more than just speculative. Most people will have increased levels of chemicals that stimulate pleasure receptors in the brain when they interact with others. Alternately, the same response does not manifest in many people with autism. Researchers have found that many people with autism have elevated levels of chemicals that stimulate pleasure centers of the brain all the time. This has led some to speculate that some people with autism may not have to depend on social interaction in order to feel euphoric, as most of us do. A drug that doctors use to treat addictions to narcotics and addictions to alcohol, naltrexone, works by blocking the euphoric response addicts get from those drugs and alcohol. Doctors have used naltrexone to treat patients with autism with some success.[3] They theorize that if the euphoric response is blocked, people with autism will seek out social interactions to get their euphoric feeling back. Even if this treatment does not ultimately prove effective, however, the autistic effects of addiction manifest all the time, and people are all too familiar with them. Inappropriate responses to social cues and a lack of empathy characterize most addictions, whether from an addiction to something sedating (as are narcotics) or something stimulating (as cocaine or nicotine).[4]

Evangelicals have essentially outlawed uncertainty in their communities. We have reviewed the central role of certainty in the "Sinner's Prayer" and Explanation PG. Once Evangelicals have become saved, only doubt or disbelief can separate them from the gift of eternal life. Evangelicals make it explicit that if believers have doubts, even if understandable some of the time, they cannot allow their doubts to take hold. They must work to exorcise these doubts from their minds. They must try to regain their feeling of "blessed assurance."

How I Exchanged Blessed Assurance for Uncertainty

"Would you please check the X-ray chest on him?" The senior resident on our team, Shefali, asked me this one day during my internal medicine rotation at the hospital as a third year medical student.

I answered, "I will gladly check if you promise to stop calling it an 'X-ray chest,' which sounds too weird. We either call it a 'chest X-ray' or occasionally an 'X-ray *of the* chest' in this country." She told me we had too much work to do, so we did not have time for grammar lessons.

Before my impromptu grammar lesson, I had hoped we would have had less work to do that day. Another intern on our team, Shahida, had returned that day after recovering from an operation for a ruptured appendix. By about noon that day, however, Shadida did not feel well and went home. Before she left, she told me, "Billy, I feel too much under the weather to stay today."

I told her, "Please, don't worry about it. Go home." I probably did not hide my frustration with Shahida too well. I did not look forward to doing more work, but I did not hold that against her. Rather, I felt frustrated that Shahida had said she had to leave because she still felt "under the weather." Only a few weeks before that day, she asked a man who came to the hospital with an infection in his leg if he felt "under the weather." The man gave her a puzzled look. Shahida had asked him that to find out if he had fevers, aches, fatigue, or any other symptoms that might have suggested the man's infection had spread to his blood. I explained to Shahida that when we say, "under the weather," in the United States, we usually mean some sort of respiratory infection. I explained to her how people felt that exposure to cold or damp weather put people at risk of catching a cold, the flu, bronchitis, sinusitis, or pneumonia. People with one of these infections, I explained, might say they felt "under the weather." I explained that the man probably did not understand why she cared if he had a cold when he came to the hospital with an infection in his leg.

Before starting her internship, Shahida had never lived outside of Bangladesh, although she spoke English very well. When she started her internship, I helped her understand our culture and phrases we used commonly in the United States that she might not have learned taking English classes in Bangladesh. In exchange, she introduced me to her culture, religion, cuisine, and customs. We had fun.

But that day, Shahida had forgotten what I said about the phrase "under the weather." So when Shefali, who had gone to medical school in India, called a chest X-ray an "X-ray chest," I did not find it as charming as I did the first time she called it that. We had residents from Bangladesh, India, Pakistan, Egypt, Syria, Germany, Italy, and Argentina. On that day, I did not want to hear about any of those places. I did not want to hear about anyone's culture, religion, or customs. I did not want to debate whether playing cricket took more skill than playing baseball. I did not want to hear another foreigner explain to me why we have so many fat people in America.

I had empathy fatigue. I wanted to go home and watch baseball, eat cheeseburgers, and perhaps play a game of Monopoly with other Americans. Had I still believed in Evangelical Christianity, I would have found relief in my local church.

Even though I no longer had a church to go to, I had no problem finding people who agreed with me about how much better Americans were than foreign medical graduates. Many people cheerfully agreed with me that we had to put up with people like Shadida who did not have the common sense, intelligence, or enough of an interest in becoming a proud American, as any decent person should want. I have to admit, it felt like I had come home after a long journey, and it felt good. I enjoyed sinking my teeth into a cheeseburger dripping with ketchup that did not have the un-American smell of curry. I enjoyed the time I spent playing softball with people who actually knew how to throw overhand. Most of all, I enjoyed knowing that I had figured out my foreign medical graduates, and if they did not want to try to be like me, then too bad for them.

Before coming down from my patriotic high, I realized how energetic I felt because of it. Despite rarely getting enough sleep and working too many hours, I could not wait to get home and fire up the grill and cook a cheeseburger, for example. I even couldn't wait to get home and mow the lawn—what could be more American than that?

I could not stay cocooned in my own comfort zone for too long. After my frustration passed, I realized how much I had learned from people like Shahida. I realized over time how much harder she had worked to incorporate phrases like "under the weather" into her conversation so that she could communicate better. I realized that if Shahida had not tried to improve her language skills by incorporating commonly used phrases, her misuse of them would not have frustrated me.

Shahida had provided me with a way of looking at my own culture from the perspective of an outsider. She had taught me things about my own culture that I probably would have missed without learning about her perspective. For example, I had heard many people throughout my life emphasize that I needed to dress warmly on cold days in order to prevent infection. But heeding their advice probably did not help me avoid getting respiratory infections. Had people advised me to avoid rubbing my eyes without washing my hands first, I probably would have had fewer infections throughout the years. People introduce respiratory infections into their bodies by rubbing their eyes and nose with their own dirty hands far more often than they do by going out in the cold underdressed. Shahida's misuse of the phrase, "under the weather," helped me realize that phrases like this may have reinforced our cultural misconceptions about the role of cold and damp weather in causing respiratory infections.

In hindsight, I realized that I had a familiar but disturbing pattern to my behavior. When I had failed the most miserably in my attempts to empathize with others, as I had failed with Shefali and Shahida, I tended to retreat to a world with familiar certainties. I used my failures as an excuse to get high on my certainties in order to feel better about myself—as my certainty at the time was that Americans were the greatest people the world has ever known. Rather than accept my failures or try to improve, I did the opposite. I reveled in my autism. Looking back, also, I realized that my attempts to empathize might have never succeeded. It was unlikely that I would have ever understood or comprehended the behavior of Shefali and Shahida fully, for example. I could never really walk a mile in their shoes. Furthermore, I knew I did not want to walk a mile in their shoes. Ultimately, I had an unsettling feeling of uncertainty, and I felt incompetent. I did not like those feelings as much as I liked my feelings of power and competence during my patriotic fervor.

After a few experiences like this in medical school, I finally made a clean break with Evangelical Christianity. I had already made an intellectual clean break with Evangelical Christianity years before at Wheaton. Yet, I still felt Christians had an interest in living decent, moral lives, as I still did. At the same time, however, I did not feel that my Christian friends or I knew the best way to achieve our goals. I realized why I felt this way when I reread one of Jesus' most familiar parables.

The Good Samaritan, and Learning to Deal with an Addiction to Certainty

Here is the parable known as "The Good Samaritan," attributed to Jesus from the Gospel of Luke:

> A man was going down from Jerusalem to Jericho, when he fell into the hands of robbers. They stripped him of his clothes, beat him and went away, leaving him half dead. A priest happened to be going down the same road, and when he saw the man, he passed by on the other side. So too, a Levite, when he came to the place and saw him, passed by on the other side. But a Samaritan, as he traveled, came where the man was; and when he saw him, he took pity on him. He went to him and bandaged his wounds, pouring on oil and wine. Then he put the man on his own donkey, took him to an inn and took care of him. The next day he took out two silver coins and gave them to the innkeeper. "Look after him," he said, "and when I

return, I will reimburse you for any extra expense you may have" (Luke 10:30–35 NIV).

Most people assume, as I did, that the point of the parable was to show the love and kindness of a man who came from a group—Samaritans—that Jews hated in first-century Palestine. I had always thought that we should recognize the Good Samaritan as the main character in the parable, but I have my doubts now.

Not all of us have a donkey, two silver coins to spare, or the ability to treat and bandage wounds. On the other hand, all of us, at one time or another will essentially lie on the side of the road helplessly. We will have no choice about whether someone comes by, scrapes us off the side of the road, and takes care of us. We won't have the ability to force, persuade, or even discourage someone from helping us. We will all confront times when other people we do not understand, cannot control, and may never see again, affect our lives. Perhaps the only thing we can control to some degree is what neighborhood we are in when we end up crumpled and helpless on the side of the road. Choosing the right neighborhood would increase our chances of having a "neighbor" that we love and respect stop and help us. Yet, who are our neighbors?

After rereading the parable, I realized that as an Evangelical, I had tried to help do what we could never do. We wanted to surround ourselves with people who were just like us, and wanted to persuade others who were not like us to become like us. We wanted the world to become one big happy neighborhood filled with born-again Christians, which will never happen. I realized that no matter how hard we might have tried, we would eventually confront times where we would lie helplessly on the side of the road, would have to rely on others to tend to our wounds and tend to our needs. Jesus told this parable to explain to us who these neighbors are and to remind us that we cannot be sure that we won't end up by the side of the road.

When I was an Evangelical, our neighbors were atheists, Catholics, gays, liberals, poor, blacks, Islamic fundamentalists, communists, fascists, and every other kind of person who was otherwise unsuitable to join our covenant communities. Even if we did not think too highly of these supposedly unsuitable neighbors, we might feel differently when an otherwise unsuitable person scraped us off the road and took care of us—just as the Good Samaritan did for the half-dead Jewish man on the side of the road. Just as the half-dead Jewish man, however, we would not have any control whatsoever whether an unsuitable person, or anyone else, actually stopped to help us.

As Evangelicals believe God made every person in his image, perhaps they should have faith that someone who God made in his image will stop and help them if they need help someday—even if that person does not profess faith in Jesus. Perhaps they should have faith that they can live happy and fulfilled lives even though they might not have control of everything in their lives, have lives full of uncertainty, and lives without *blessed assurance*.

By Evangelical Standards, Requiring Certainty and Discouraging Empathy Is Sinful

It might seem odd that Evangelical churches would provide relief from interactions that may require empathy. After all, Jesus told his followers that they only really need to know two commandments (Matt 22:37–40). The second greatest of the two commandments, attributed to Jesus in the Bible, is, "Thou shalt love thy neighbor as thyself" (Matt 22:39 KJV). As we have seen, however, Evangelical communities have done more than just discourage empathy in their churches; they have outlawed it.

You may recall from chapter 2 that a lack of empathy is one way to describe autism. I gave an example of three boys, Abe, Bob, and Carl. Abe, having autism, did not know that the other boys did not know what he knew. Even when Carl left the room they played in, Abe thought Carl knew everything that happened in the room while he was gone. But suppose Carl left the room and never came back. Abe would probably never ask where Carl went or ask what Carl was doing. Unless Abe wanted or needed something from Carl, it is unlikely that Abe would give any indication that he ever knew a boy named Carl.

Because people with autism lack empathy, the hallmarks of autism involve issues related to social interactions. In particular, autistic people do not seem to comprehend fully that other people have their own thoughts, feelings, points of view, and plans. Thus, they have far less accuracy and precision compared to others when they predict what others may do or say in different social situations. For example, suppose Abe likes to play with toy trucks and Carl joins Abe in a room during playtime to play with Abe's trucks. Later, Carl stands up to leave the room. Before he leaves, he says, "I don't like playing with your trucks, Abe. I want to go to my room to play with my new blocks."

Suppose that the next day during playtime we found Abe in the same room as the day before playing with his trucks. But Carl does not join him on that day. Suppose we asked Abe at that time, "What do you think Carl is doing right now?" Abe's autism would make it unlikely that he would give us the most logical answer, "I think Carl is in his room playing with his new blocks." Indeed, if Abe consistently came up with answers like this, he would not have autism.

Autistic thinking leads to a number of paradoxes that can confuse people with developed social interaction skills. Specifically, people with the least empathy (and thus the most autism), often believe they have more empathy than others do. For example, suppose we asked Abe, "Do you think Carl likes playing with trucks?" Abe will likely say Carl does like playing with trucks, even though Carl said he did not. As Abe's ability to separate Carl's thoughts and feelings from his own decreases, his confidence in his ability to assess Carl's interest in playing with trucks, paradoxically, will likely increase. A person who does not know Carl, and who has not figured out that Abe has autism, will often incorrectly assume that Abe's confidence in knowing Carl's interests stems from knowledge of, and experiences with, Carl.

Identifying Autistic Behavior in Evangelicals

Let's put this paradox of autism in the context of Hooks and Ladders and Evangelical autism. As the amount of empathy for nonbelievers in an Evangelical community decreases, the confidence they have in their abilities to read the minds of nonbelievers, and their abilities to assess truth, increases. We have seen how Evangelical communities reward people who have certitude about other people's thoughts and feelings, and have certitude about knowing Truth. Putting this together, Evangelicals select leaders who have comparatively more autistic traits (and thus less empathy) than others do. As a result, their leaders will have more difficulty obeying Jesus' second greatest commandment, "Thou shalt love thy neighbor as thyself," than others do. Despite have difficulty obeying this commandment, Evangelical leaders will often claim that they do obey Jesus' commandment as well, if not better, than others do.

I have already given many examples where Evangelical leaders have confidently, yet incorrectly, characterized other people's thoughts, feelings, and beliefs. But let's look at a recent example. Many people consider Rick Warren more empathetic than most other Evangelical leaders. Some have pointed to his contributions to help fight the AIDS epidemic as an example of his concern for others, including people who contracted HIV and AIDS from gay relationships. To be sure, Warren deserves credit for his contributions toward fighting the AIDS epidemic. But does that mean that his concerns about AIDS victims stemmed from having empathy for homosexuals? Did Warren slip through the cracks in the Evangelical community and rise to prominence despite having developed empathy?

Many people, especially gays and lesbians, criticized Rick Warren for comments he made in an interview with Beliefnet's Steven Waldman. In that interview, Warren implied that allowing for gay marriage was equivalent to allowing brothers and sisters to marry and equivalent to allowing pedophiles to marry children.[5] Warren had advocated for a ballot measure in California, Prop 8, which could reverse a California Supreme Court decision that made gay marriage legal. Warren's comments about gay marriage came after Waldman asked him to clarify his positions on gay partnerships like civil unions. After Warren read a transcript of the interview, he wrote some clarifications about what he had said and asked Beliefnet to include his clarifications with their transcripts of the interview.

Warren's clarifications give us the opportunity to look at Warren's beliefs about homosexuals using his own carefully chosen words. Here are two examples of what Warren wrote:

> If ... homosexuals or anyone else think they are smarter than God and chooses [sic] to disobey God's sexual instructions, it is not the US government's role to take away their choice....
>
> Much of this debate is not really about civil rights, but a desire for approval. What they [homosexuals] desire is approval and validation from those who disagree with them, and they are willing to force it by law if necessary. Any disapproval is quickly labeled "hate speech."[6]

Do Warren's comments suggest that he had empathy for the thoughts, feelings, and beliefs of homosexuals? No, they do not. Rather, his comments strongly suggest he has autistic thinking. For example, does he know any homosexuals who "think they are smarter than God"? I doubt Warren could find even one homosexual who claims to be smarter than God. Similarly, would most homosexuals tell us they "chose to disobey God's sexual instructions" when they decided to enter into a homosexual relationship? How many people does Warren know who would claim that their support for legalizing gay marriage "is not really about civil rights," but rather about gaining "approval and validation from those who disagree" with a homosexual lifestyle?

Warren has badly misjudged the thoughts, feelings, and points of view of people who support gay marriages. His comments strongly suggest he has little, if any, empathy for people who support gay marriages. Just like an autistic person, Warren seems completely unaware that he does not get to decide the thoughts, feelings, and points of view of other people for them. Not only has Warren failed to predict what proponents of gay marriage would say or do accurately, he has given his assessments as if they were facts.

Beyond just misjudging the thoughts, feelings, and points of view of others, Warren displays other characteristics of autistic thinking. First, Warren has grossly overestimated other people's desire for his approval. For example, I support legalizing gay marriage, and I believe it is a civil rights issue. Everyone I know who supports legalizing gay marriage believes it is *primarily* a civil rights issue. At the same time, I do not know one person who cares a whit whether Warren approves of homosexuals or not. Imagine, for example, a gay couple who had a wedding that many of their friends and family attended. Does it seem at all likely that the couple decided to marry because they wanted to "force" people like Rick Warren to approve of and validate their relationship?

Next, Warren does not seem to understand that he does not get to decide what others think and feel about what he says or does. So when people tell Warren that they consider his words and actions hateful, he does not seem to take their thoughts and feelings into consideration. Rather, he dismissed their overt social cues about his behavior as "hate speech." Once again, he does seem to notice the obvious, which is that people really do consider him hateful.

If Warren had even a tiny amount of empathy, he would likely have at least offered an empathetic explanation for his remarks. Most people who pick up on social cues do this naturally. Let's suppose, for example, Warren said something like, "If I were a homosexual man who did not know anything about me, I could see how I might consider the comments that I made hateful." People who give a typical empathetic response like this usually describe how they have tried to imagine what they would think if they were in the shoes of another person. They attempt to validate the thoughts, feelings, and points of view of another person. Warren does not appear to have done that. A person who does not acknowledge and validate other people's thoughts, feelings, and points of view lacks empathy. Since we know Warren acknowledges the validity of his own thoughts, feelings, and points of view, he has failed to follow Jesus' second greatest commandment. He does not love his homosexual neighbors as he does himself.

WHY LEAVE?

I have explained why certainty is pleasurable to the point of being addictive. I have also explained how certainty and Evangelical autism are intertwined. So why would an Evangelical ever leave the church and leave those feelings behind in order to share in the world of people he or she may well believe to be depraved? It isn't easy.

But that isn't the only reason that Evangelicals stay. It is unreasonable to think that anyone could leave Evangelical Christianity without taking years to establish a separate identity. It takes years to overcome the fear of committing *soul murder* and feel comfortable that life has meaning outside of playing Hooks and Ladders. The sense of worthlessness that comes with Evangelical Christianity provides the glue that holds the board of Hooks and Ladders together.

Thanks to Paul's Worthlessness Doctrine, Evangelical Christians cannot ever outgrow their need for God. Thus, Paul's historically unrivaled self-loathing actually has a survival benefit of sorts. Pauline theology leaves Christians chronically and hopelessly dependent on God. More than likely, without first confronting the Evangelical doctrine of worthlessness, a person probably will not have the capacity to think through issues concerning faith without using disordered thinking.

However, effectively confronting worthlessness takes work and willpower (the very things Evangelicals are told cannot bring salvation). A doctrine of worthlessness inoculates a community against any challenges. If you truly believe that you are nothing but a walking abortion unless you surrender control of your mind space, how do you ever gather the will and the strength to question your situation?

Family Values

Worthlessness and Evangelical autism are not all that keeps Hooks and Ladders players in the game. Evangelical Christianity offers practical answers to one of the biggest questions many people face: "How do I raise my kids?" Following a period of relative hedonism, it is no surprise that many young Evangelical couples seem to rededicate their lives to Christ or find Jesus shortly after they marry or have a child. Confronted with the responsibility of raising children, they often rely on the church to provide them with more structure in their lives.

Most families in contemporary America have detached from their extended families, and many Evangelical Christian churches have positioned themselves to serve as a surrogate extended family. More than anything else, Evangelical Christianity considers the business of raising a family critically important.

Evangelicals have amassed a coordinated system that could rival the space program in scope, depth, and resources. For example, Evangelicals have confronted the evidence that their divorce rates match the divorce rates of non-Evangelicals. Many churches have developed programs and counseling to help couples confront sexual issues—despite a traditional reluctance to talk about sex. Evangelicals today can enlist a number of groups to help address problems that even fifteen to twenty years ago they rarely mentioned aloud. Just as Evangelicals have responded quickly to deal with previously neglected issues like sexual intimacy, they have proven they can respond quickly to problems that may surface in the future. For example, many churches and church run organizations already have sophisticated programs that help people overcome an addiction to Internet pornography.

The church also provides a venue in which to raise kids. Along with instilling Christian values and a healthy fear of God, the church also provides ready-made friends for children, and parents can be sure that these playmates come from "good Christian families." The Evangelical church provides a sounding board about child-rearing issues and marital problems. Sometimes churches even offer formal counseling. Many churches now have gymnasiums and recreational facilities that function much like a community center for children and families. As well, many churches offer summer camps and vacation Bible schools. Sometimes, churches have a yearlong list of programs that help relieve the burdens of child rearing faced by Evangelical parents.

Many people regard Dr. James Dobson as the most influential Evangelical Christian leader in the United States. Yet he does not hail from the ranks of the clergy. He practiced as a clinical child psychologist and hosts the popular radio broadcast, *Focus on the Family*. In its early years, *Focus on the Family* did precisely that; it focused heavily on providing guidance for raising children. Dobson claimed that he based his child-rearing methods on biblical principles. He has many books that deal exclusively with raising children and other family issues, such as the perennial favorite, *Dare to Discipline*. Many non-Evangelicals would be astounded to learn of the volume of letters and phone calls Dobson and his ministry receive, many of them asking for help with a particular family issue. Clearly, Dobson tapped into an unmet need.

Parenting, in this country at any rate, provokes fear, uncertainty, and doubt. Evangelical Christians, more than any other group, have tried to address this need. Evangelicals have a potent and seemingly effective child-rearing system in that Evangelical Christian communities have become an impressive repository of resources and information dealing with everything from coping with a grandparent who has dementia to practical advice about how to manage temper tantrums in a grocery store. You can even find advice on treating and preventing diaper rash.

Consider the success of Dobson's book, *Dare to Discipline*. This book served as both a guidebook for parents and a rebuttal to the 1960s style of permissive parenting. As might be expected from the title, Dobson's book tends toward the authoritarian. Some may disagree with his logic and methods of reasoning. However, Dobson made his book remarkably scientific for a book intended as an aid to parents. To his credit, he provided clinical evidence for his views, and he characterized the evidence, methods, and conclusions drawn by others with opposing views. He used a reasoned approach to dismantle their findings and conclusions. For those with an authoritarian worldview, Evangelical Christians may rightfully claim their system provides the most scientific, responsive, and comprehensive guidelines for living in this manner.

Even among those who are not natural authoritarians, the church, especially the Evangelical church, provides a strong example of child-rearing. In fact, it is so successful that many people may not be aware that other options exist. For example, I've heard parents say something like, "I went to Catholic school and used to go to Mass every Sunday, but I stopped going when I realized how hypocritically the church operates. Our priest, for example, had an affair with the elementary school secretary. He still performs Mass at a parish in Iowa. I do not believe you have to go to church to be a good Christian. I can worship God in my own way at home. Nevertheless, I want my son to go to church and catechism. I want him to learn about God and values. Even though I do not go to church anymore, I think it is important for me to expose my son to church. I do not want him growing up thinking there is no God. He needs to learn the difference between right and wrong." This story fits a familiar pattern that I have heard repeatedly: (1) a bad experience at church; (2) a loss of faith or trust in the church; and (3) a reluctant admission that the parents will have to send their child to church as this is "best for the child."

Reasoning like this leads many people to assume that even caring atheists should want their children raised in a religious tradition. To some extent, *any* religious tradition will do. Using this logic, Islamic fundamentalists provide their children with a moral code, even if flawed, and a belief in God, even if not the *right* one, as far as many Americans are concerned. Even though Evangelicals flatly disapprove of Islamic fundamentalists, they still perceive Islamic parenting as an attempt to raise children the *right* way. On the other hand, they believe that an atheist must be raising his or her children without any sense of right and wrong and saddling an innocent child with the depressing belief that nothingness awaits them after they die. They believe that even an atheist could not want to treat a child with such cruelty.

Given these beliefs, a Christian family may feel perfectly comfortable asking an atheist-raised child to go to church with them. However, they might find it appalling if atheist parents asked if they could discuss the merits of atheism with the church-going family's child. Yet commonly these parents would not consider a Muslim parent's request to take their child to their mosque as offensive. The atheist's request will seem more troubling, even if they say no to both the atheist and the Muslim parents. As well, when a person who claims to be not very religious marries someone who comes from a specific religious tradition, it seems to be a foregone conclusion that this couple will raise their children in the tradition of the more religious parent.

Many nonbelievers have simply not devoted significant effort toward providing parents with nonreligious and non-authoritarian resources to assist them in raising their children. For example, both theists, like Al Gore in *The Assault on Reason*, and atheists have recently banded together to counter authoritarian religion with an appeal that might be aptly condensed to, "reason is better." "We can all have a better life if we apply reason, critical thinking, and respect for credible evidence," seems to be the mantra. While they can point to successes like our constitutional democracy and accomplishments like sending a man to the moon as evidence of reason's superiority, these reason lovers seem to suggest that we should simply have faith that applying these same principles to raising a family will achieve better outcomes than the authoritarian methods advocated by Dobson. An Evangelical parent could easily turn the table on our scientific thinkers and say, "Show me the evidence!"

In summary, Evangelicals provide an incredible amount of resources to help parents raise children. Where does one go to find a comparable book to *Dare to Discipline?* Where do we find practical methods for raising children? What sort of programs comes close to matching those offered by Evangelicals? When leaving the fold, how can we compensate for the loss of community unity offered by Evangelicals? Of course there are answers, but even a skilled researcher, much less a harried parent, might find it difficult to assemble this information, whereas Evangelicals make it easy. Given the enormously important task of raising children, why would someone change their views and leave this security? Any argument for change that ignores this elephant in the living room will likely achieve only limited success.

The (Dis)Advantages of Community

The Da Vinci Code

Many Evangelicals spend their lives saturated by the Evangelical community. Their friends, families, neighbors, co-workers, and even the owners and employees of the stores where they shop may be Evangelicals. American Evangelicals have created an alternate universe in which they can awaken to the sound of Christian radio, watch Christian cable TV channels, surf Christian Web sites, and read Christian books and magazines. It is possible for an Evangelical to avoid encountering serious critics of their faith and their principles.

What do Evangelicals learn from their Christian media? In many cases, they will hear that they are in imminent danger from the numerous enemies of God, such as atheists, liberals, feminists, gay people, and Democrats. This culture of fear and paranoia leaves many Evangelicals insulated and understandably suspicious of the people they have been told over and over again are out to get them. Cocooned within the Evangelical community, they may continue to think and act in dysfunctional ways as long as they lack experiences and contact with others who may have a better way to live.

Many outsiders have little understanding of the victims of this indoctrination. They do not take the time necessary to gain the trust of Evangelicals. Admittedly, this can be an arduous task since those within the community demonize outsiders. But even those outsiders who have an interest in engaging Evangelicals and are willing to invest the time and patience often go about it in the wrong way.

Most people who try to reach out to Evangelicals do so with a spirit of tolerance and cooperation, displayed as a sign of their benevolence and moral goodness. Indeed, they will often chastise a person who makes a critical remark directed at Evangelicals. These outsiders may not consider how an Evangelical, especially one surrounded by the Christian community, may perceive such a gesture. Within the Evangelical community, many treat tolerance and open-mindedness with scorn—and as a sign of moral weakness and a lack of commitment to Evangelical principles. After all, we have seen the way that the inerrantists treated their liberal colleagues.

In contrast, the Evangelical community rarely admonishes its least tolerant members. Some churches carry this to an extreme and even encourage hatred, although they most likely will not call it by that name.* In many churches, members can launch scathing attacks against someone, even another church member, without repercussion as long as it is done in the right way. For example, an intolerant member may call someone else a heretic, a false prophet, a fool, an agent of Satan, or simply dangerous. Many churches will do nothing about a member like this. Few will dissuade them by saying, for example, "You'll have to answer to God for your actions." You may recall from chapter 11, for example, how the virulent insults of Evangelical thugs Bacote and Spencer were not only tolerated, they were included in the scholarly book *Not Just Science,* written by Evangelicals.

Consider the Evangelical community's response to the film *The Da Vinci Code,* which was originally a novel involving several secret societies, hidden treasures, and themes from Christian history. Its release gave rise to a flurry of activity in the Evangelical community. Evangelical books, sermons, Sunday school classes, and online forums refuted the claims made in what was plainly a work of fiction. (Of course, in an odd attempt to make order out of disordered thinking, we will find the Evangelical books that refute this fictional narrative in the *nonfiction* aisle.) Evangelicals attacked the author's credibility, morals, and character. Author Dan Brown knows by now where Evangelicals think he will spend eternity.

---

* Or if they do, they may refer to this practice as "hating the sin, but loving the sinner." As the target of some of this "love," I can assure you that it is hard to distinguish from the practice of "hating the sin *and* the sinner."

Was this Evangelical response effective? Nope. Evangelicals provided free advertisement, buzz, and credibility. The sheer magnitude of the Evangelical response has helped line Dan Brown's pockets with money. After all, who spends so much energy going after a known loser or incompetent? Even though many Evangelicals boycotted the movie, we may well wonder if the book would have ever become a movie if Evangelicals did not make such a fuss over it. Indeed, other people, seeing Dan Brown's success, may feel encouraged to write similar books of fiction with Christian themes. An author who can get under the skin of Evangelicals may find such writing lucrative.

Could we call the Evangelical response to *The Da Vinci Code* disordered or abnormal? Yes. The Evangelical response to this fictional account is so overblown as to seem bizarre and disturbed.* Indeed, Evangelicals seem to have invented a controversy and created a target audience of *Code* believers. But the pervasiveness of this response in the Evangelical community seems normal to the people inside.

The paranoia of Evangelicals, however, has the effect of keeping people in the community fearful of outsiders while seeming completely normal to those within. By the community depicting outsiders, especially outsiders who display the un-Evangelical values of open-mindedness and tolerance, as enemies of God who are out to destroy the church, community members are discouraged from considering alternative ways of thinking through problems. Outsiders end up alienating the people they are trying to reach despite—and perhaps because of—demonstrating their good will.

Called to Serve—Evangelical Authorities are Not the Fittest

When most people evaluate the Evangelical community, they assume it shares similar characteristics with other groups they have encountered. In those groups, the most competent, reasonable, and resourceful people within the community become its leaders. So when they perceive problems with Evangelical Christianity, they confront Evangelical leaders. Although we can understand readily why people may make this

---

* To be sure, some may believe that *The Da Vinci Code* was falsely labeled "fiction." But people who believe this most likely have problems of a different sort, far beyond what Evangelicals address in counter *Code* material.

assumption, it is a mistake. As with the autistic thinking of Rick Warren, for example, Evangelical leaders often have less capacity than other Evangelicals do to make rational and empathetic decisions.

We have talked already about who becomes an Evangelical leader. But we can add to our list an additional trait of Evangelical leaders—a remarkable ability to never change their minds. Evangelical leaders often become leaders because they have mastered the ability to remain unfixable. When the inerrantists ushered in their doctrine, they ushered out an attitude of uncertainty. In a sense, the inerrantists have ushered in an Age of Certainty. Evangelicals expect certainty about all Evangelical doctrines. Like many people who fear uncertainty, they desire repetition. Just as the three-year-old who has watched the same DVD twenty times would be horrified if an altered scene appeared or if the ending changed on their next viewing, many Evangelicals hate a new script.

Indeed, it is quite remarkable how consistent and cliché laden are the ways in which Evangelical pastors and leaders answer questions. For example, consider a question like, "Will you please describe for me how you came to be the senior pastor at ...?" We can consistently expect answers containing these clichés:

- "God called me to serve him when I was ..."
- "I answered God's call."
- "I poured through/devoured/searched God's Word"
- "Of course, when God calls you to serve, you don't say no!"
- "God's plan for my life"
- "Opportunity to serve the Lord"
- "The Word of God tells us ..."
- "If God can use me ..."
- "Shepherd his flock"

If these pastors' answers had intrinsic merit, we would expect Evangelicals in other professions to give similar answers. For example, Evangelical Christian dentists would have answered God's call to dentistry. They would have followed God's plan for their life. They should discuss their opportunity to serve the Lord as a dentist. We would expect to hear, "when God calls you to serve him as a dentist, you don't say no." Even most Evangelical Christians would probably tell a dentist that answered this way to cut the crap and tell us why you *really* went into dentistry.

Instead of these clichés, we expect an answer like, "Well, I was pretty good at science, and when I was thinking about applying to medical school my uncle described the absurd length of time and the long hours of medical residencies, so I applied to dental school instead." An Evangelical Christian dentist who gives you an answer like this is more likely to take personal responsibility when he or she botches a filling or misses a diagnosis that should have been made instead of pawning the mistake off as God's will.

Evangelical leadership requires resistance to change more than problem-solving ability. Many nonbelievers seek out Evangelical leaders to enlist their support in solving problems they share or in ironing out differences. Yet, Evangelical leaders, oftentimes, have leadership roles because they have demonstrated that they will not change—or the more appealing sounding—they will not give in to nonbelievers. As a result, the rules of Hooks and Ladders are unlikely to change when many of the most disordered thinkers have the most influence in the community. To the extent that outsiders direct their efforts toward discussing concerns about Evangelicals at the leaders of the community, the rest of the Evangelical community may suffer.

Conclusions, and Comparisons to Other Conclusions

In chapter 3, when we discussed the "Sinner's Prayer," I mentioned the process of identity dumping that occurs once a new convert accepts Jesus as his or her personal savior. Evangelicals do this when they claim that Christ or the Holy Spirit lives in them and acts through them. When this happens, we run into serious problems.

Our free and cooperative society requires faith in others. We need enough people to take personal responsibility for their uncoerced expressed ideas, actions, and behaviors. This type of social contract, however, takes for granted that enough people will have a strong sense of personal identity to be able to accept such responsibility. If you lack a personal identity, you will not be able to claim your actions as your own effectively. This is a problem where Evangelicals are concerned. Most Evangelical leaders of the United States claim they are servants of Jesus Christ. These Evangelicals will not take personal responsibility for actions that they believe their Lord requires of them, even when those actions hurt others or run counter to outsiders' basic understanding of a free society and human dignity.

Why do we tolerate this identity-dumping behavior? Why do we tolerate it, especially, when Evangelicals usually claim they want the same things that their personal god wants from them? They invariably claim that they consider the same behaviors wrong that their personal gods consider wrong. Therefore, Evangelicals should have no problem taking personal responsibility for their comments and behaviors. They should have no problem answering questions like, "Why do you think Mother Teresa deserves to spend eternity in hell?" or "How do you justify your position that homosexuals should not serve in the military?" without giving an answer that we would expect from a press secretary. We can move the conversation forward if we confront Evangelicals and refuse to allow them to dump their identities and blame their dysfunctional behaviors on their personal gods. Why would we talk to them as if their made-up identities deserved recognition?

DEBATE ABOUT DEBATE

Does it make sense to use reasoning to persuade people with poor reasoning skills to change? Many people who wish to engage Evangelicals do not directly address the fears and insecurities that Evangelicals have. As a result, we might benefit from downplaying academic issues, including the perennial favorite, evolution. Frankly, the focus on academic issues has had disappointing results because it plays directly into the Evangelical sense of paranoia and persecution.

"Attacking Christians has become a cottage industry," Joe Scarborough reported recently. Scarborough is a former Florida congressional representative and the host of a news-related program on MSNBC. Indeed, Evangelicals may believe reasonably that many of the recent books like *The End of Faith*, by Sam Harris, *The God Delusion*, by Richard Dawkins, and *Breaking the Spell*, by Daniel Dennett, targeted them.

It is possible that some people might read these books and change their mind about their religious faith, but such books are unlikely to have any effect on the average Evangelical. Most Evangelicals do not feel the slightest bit compelled to read these books. Instead, these books strengthen Evangelical beliefs that they are a persecuted minority. They provide evidence of an attack and fuel Evangelical efforts to fight these new enemies. These books, which largely promote atheism, make Evangelicals and many others very nervous. Their authors, along with many people, are outspoken against faith or belief in a god generally and argue in essence that we should replace faith with non-faith.

It is my suggestion that placing less emphasis on cramming information into the minds of Evangelicals and more emphasis on what happens to information once it enters the minds of Evangelicals would probably work better. I have shown how disordered Evangelical thought processes are. Even the most stringently logical argument will have no sway with people who have serious flaws in the way they think. In the essay at the end of the book titled, "The Hyperbolic Road," I hope to begin a discussion about emphasizing a better way to think through problems that an Evangelical may find more effective than their current reasoning process.

STOP IMMUNITY

How do my proposals differ from others? For example, Daniel Dennett, in *Breaking the Spell,* calls for the application of scientific reasoning to test religious beliefs and behaviors. My proposals do not conflict with Dennett's proposal, although I feel addressing the problems of Evangelicals requires a more fundamental starting point.[7]

A first step toward any reasonable communication would require Evangelicals to accept personal agency for their actions and beliefs. Evangelicals rarely claim their personal thoughts brought them to say something like, "God tells us in his Word ..." Indeed, most claim their sin nature restricts them from understanding the truth, just as anyone's does, no matter how clearly visible it may be. Without having God's truth revealed or otherwise inserted into their minds they would not know it. In order to break the spell on Evangelicals, we have to cut into the line of mental telepathy between them and their god. But how do we cut through a line that does not exist?

DOES DAWKINS MAKE A CONVINCING CASE AGAINST DELUSIONS?

Why do some many people who have problems with specific religious groups like Evangelicals couch their arguments and direct them at people of faith generally?

Richard Dawkins, for example, seems to focus more attention on Evangelicals than on most other faith groups. Yet he suggests that a God delusion poses problems of similar severity across *all* faith groups. He argues, for example, that assigning a religious label to a child at birth has harmful consequences and suggests that we do not label children in other ways.[8] Thus, we should not say, "This baby is a Catholic baby" or "This baby is a Mormon baby," for example. He argues that we should present the evidence about God and let the children come to their own conclusions.

Does Dawkins truly believe we do not assign children other labels? Surely Dawkins has realized that his parents and others most likely labeled him a "British baby," for example. It is hard to imagine that people would (or even could) stop labeling children. Dawkins falls short of demonstrating that religious labeling is harmful. He fails to consider the possibility that the evidence may suggest religious labeling has benefits.

Consider a hypothetical scenario where we analyze the life of a sixteen-year-old boy born and raised in Kearney, Nebraska. The boy's parents went to the University of Nebraska, work as fourth-generation farmers, and usually attend the local Lutheran church. He would have many labels like Nebraskan, American, and—given the overwhelming popularity of the University of Nebraska's football team—a Cornhusker football fan. Would Dawkins find labeling the boy when he was a child as a "little Cornhusker baby" harmful?

This common interest in college football among Nebraskans provides a platform where friends, acquaintances, and even strangers can discuss a relatively non-controversial topic. Any Nebraskan can feel safe asking anyone else in Nebraska a simple question like, "How about those Huskers?" You are going to get unrehearsed answers to your friendly question.

I wrote this section on September 22, 2007, before the Nebraska Cornhuskers, ranked sixteenth in the country, played first-ranked University of Southern California (USC) in Lincoln, Nebraska. Using the Huskers as a springboard to start a conversation, potentially useful information could have been gained about a new acquaintance. Consider what answers like these would have revealed:

> "I think they can win. They play in Lincoln this year, and Nebraska Cornhusker fans are the best in the world. Hopefully they can inspire the team to a victory."
>
> "The Huskers suck! Just because I lived my whole life in Nebraska, I do not know why that means I should robotically pull for the Huskers. The Huskers suck; the whole state sucks."
>
> "You mean that game where the college and sports broadcasters make millions of dollars off kids that they don't pay, don't educate, and then exploit?"

Discussions about a game or competition of mutual interest bring strangers together. The benefits do not stop there. Consider this same game. After the game (Nebraska lost badly), I heard an ESPN reporter comment about how Nebraskans are too nice! At a favorite post-game hangout in Lincoln, he reported on Cornhusker fans congratulating USC fans. Nebraskans fanatically support their team while maintaining good sportsmanship. This likely contributed to the decision of some USC fans to make the trip to Nebraska.

Is Religious Labeling Different?

In my experience growing up mostly in Midwestern suburbs, over 95 percent of the people I knew would call themselves Christian. What does this mean?

What would it mean if we ran into our sixteen-year-old boy from Nebraska and he said, "I am Lutheran"? Based on my experiences living in Nebraska, a boy telling me this would not have helped me know very much about him. A boy might call himself a Lutheran even if he never read one book of the Bible. Indeed, very limited knowledge of the Bible was probably the norm for self-identified Lutheran boys when I lived there. As well, a typical Lutheran boy had minimal interest in church or church activities. Perhaps because most neighborhoods had little religious diversity in Nebraska, people spent very little time discussing or thinking about religious issues. Nevertheless, when I lived in Nebraska, when a boy claimed he was a Lutheran, his admission did not mean he agreed with Lutheran theology. Culturally, people did not find it unacceptable if a boy called himself Lutheran while holding a skeptical view of his church—and if he did not believe that his fellow churchgoers had the ability to judge truth better than anyone else did.

I do not mean to pick on Lutherans. When I was growing up Catholic, it was normal for Catholics to be uninterested in most religious topics. That remains true among many American Catholics, who often have little regard for what the Pope has to say, even on topics the church deems important, like the use of birth control. They often consider the Bible, church creeds, and traditions unreliable and outdated and do not study them. I have even had a few people tell me, "I'm a Catholic, but I'm not sure I believe in God."

Sadly, for those of us concerned about the harms of extreme beliefs, this creates a predicament. On one hand, a majority of Americans who call themselves Christian share a concern about overzealous and extreme religious behavior. On the other hand, these Christians feel *normal*. These *normal* people perceive those that warn about the dangers of faith to be just as crazy as the religious extremists. After all, their Christianity has had a limited, benign, but still-vital role in their culture and identity.

We may benefit from peeling delusions based in worthlessness away from other delusions. The delusional, evidence-free zone of Evangelical Christianity has the snakes that alarm people. If we exposed the Catholic delusional world, for example, we would find an entirely different can of worms to address.

It may seem odd that in a book that compares Evangelical thinking to that of paranoid schizophrenics that I would berate someone for focusing on delusions. The strong association of delusions with schizophrenia is in this way unfortunate. Schizophrenics' disordered thinking fuels their delusion, which makes the delusions become increasingly complex and unfixable. It is the disordered thinking which distinguishes paranoid schizophrenics—not the delusions.

The spotlight stays off issues that are more serious when we focus on whether God exists and whether believing in a god is delusional. This draws attention away from a more significant question—a question Evangelicals cannot answer adequately:

On what grounds do you believe that a god communicates to you?

Recognizing That Evangelicals Lack the Capacity to Love Their Enemies

After hundreds of conversations, I know all too well that a majority of Evangelical Christians have no interest in learning a new language. Evangelicals avoid loving their enemies. Despite Evangelical rhetoric about how they mimic Jesus, an emphasis on empathy has no place in their faith.

I have countless examples of Evangelical Christians' unwillingness to look at issues from a different perspective. For me, it is clear that an author with a political agenda penned the New Testament book known as The Acts of the Apostles. I have asked (and at times pleaded) with dozens of Evangelicals to explain to me why Acts is not fiction. I explain to them that they will have a better understanding of my position if they review Acts the way I have. I outline a simple process that led me to my conclusions about Acts and ask if they would consider following the same process. I leave the door wide open to have them persuade me that I am wrong. I point out that no Evangelical has ever so much as responded to my request. I stress that I may find a thoughtfully different perspective persuasive. I have never had anyone take me up on this offer.

Here is my outline of this process. First, I point out that many Evangelicals date books of the New Testament based in part on their dating of Acts. For example, our old friend and Evangelical apologist, Geisler, dates many books of the New Testament based on his conclusion that Acts was written around 62 C.E. Here is a partial list of Geisler's rationale for his dates, from *I Don't Have Enough Faith to be an Atheist*:

> 1. Acts ends abruptly with Paul under house arrest in Rome.
> 2. Paul was executed sometime during the reign of Nero, which ended in AD 68 [C.E.]. And we know from Josephus that James was killed in 62 [C.E.]. So we can conclude, beyond a reasonable doubt, that the book of Acts was written before 62 [C.E.].[9]

Geisler contends that Luke, the supposed author or Acts, would have recorded these events. He smugly writes, "If you're still not convinced, consider this modern parallel: suppose someone wrote a book recording the events surrounding the main figures of the Civil Rights Movement in the 1960s ... If the book ends with Martin Luther King, Jr.—the very leader of the movement—still alive, when would you conclude that the book was written?"[10] Even though this comes in the form of a question, neither Geisler nor virtually any other Evangelical Christian cares about the answer. For simplicity, consider a theoretical book that I could write in 2007. I could decide to write with the intent of giving people a feel for how someone might have viewed the Civil Rights Movement forty years ago. Martin Luther King, Jr., would still have been alive, and ending the book that way might help convey the anxieties and the hope that many likely felt in 1967.

After I review the typical Evangelical rationale for an early date of Acts, I ask this: "What would a book look like if written for a political motive? For example, Romans destroyed Jerusalem and the temple in 70 C.E. Romans seemed more hostile to the Jewish people than others did. Romans likely associated Christians with Jews, who had a reputation as troublemakers. Suppose you lived at about 100 C.E. and wanted to present Christians as a community that Romans might consider an asset for their empire. What might you expect from that book? The author of Acts gives me the strong impression that he had motives for his book beyond just recording history. Will you read *Acts* in one sitting and explain to me where my thinking has gone awry? If nothing else, you will understand me better."

I have *never* had an Evangelical Christian take me up on this offer or any others. Nonetheless, let us briefly review what we might expect from someone with political motives writing a book like Acts. Suppose the author's motive was to make a case that Christians were helpful, productive, and loyal citizens of the Roman Empire. How would she make this case?

First, we would expect the author to distance Christians from Jews, as the Jewish people did not have much loyalty to Rome. Next, we would expect the book to show how loyally and responsibly Christians behaved as Roman citizens. As well, we would expect the author to show how Christians did not burden the Romans with petty problems. Furthermore, we would expect the author to avoid menacing and inconvenient details about Roman rule like persecutions, executions, and brutal carnage.

We might expect some authors to make this case in a subtle way. However, the author of Acts does not attempt to mask the agenda. Indeed, the author has the protagonist, the Apostle Paul, saving Romans from certain death after a shipwreck. As well, the author ends Acts in way that we might expect of an author who wanted to make his case as outrageous as possible. The author wrote about the Roman prisoner, Paul: "For two whole years Paul stayed there [Rome] in his own rented house and welcomed all who came to see him. Boldly and without hindrance he preached the kingdom of God and taught about the Lord Jesus Christ" (Acts 28:30–1 NIV).

My view of Acts differs from Geisler's. I do not consider this an abrupt ending. On the contrary, the ending of Acts neatly wraps up the author's clever fairy tale. How else could it end?

We have little hope for translation if Evangelical Christians remain committed to their culture of exclusion—they simply do not care what *language* others use. I have too much experience with Evangelical Christians to have much hope that any more than a handful will try to put themselves in my shoes—or any other non-Christian's shoes. Few will have even the slightest interest in understanding my position.

We can find many examples of the autistic view of the world among Evangelicals in our culture. For example, many Jewish leaders protested that the movie, *The Passion of the Christ*, portrayed Jewish people in an anti-Semitic way. Evangelical leaders protested right back, claiming that the movie did not stray from the truth as it is outlined in the Bible. Of course, Evangelicals gave no indication that they had any interest in hearing a translation of why these Jewish leaders felt this way. Regardless, it is not hard to find anti-Semitism in Acts or the Gospels. Evangelicals, however, believe their views do *not* cast the Jewish people in an erroneous and negative light. They can remain in this delusion because they simply refuse to listen to the translation of what others tell them. They have their own autistic and self-absorbed universe.

Once again, we have to look at schizophrenia to help understand how this can happen. Julian Jaynes describes one characteristic of schizophrenia that aptly applies to Evangelicals:

> Similarly, the loss of the analog "I" and its mind-space results in the loss of *as-if* behaviors. Because he cannot imagine in the usual conscious way, he cannot play-act, or engage in make-believe actions, or speak of make-believe events. He cannot, for example, pretend to drink water out of a glass if there is no water in it. Or asked what he would do if he were the doctor, he might reply that he is not a doctor.[11]

Of course, I know what most Evangelicals will think if they read this: "I can pretend to drink out of an empty glass." Evangelical readers should think again. Let us try this pretend scenario: the Evangelical plays the role of the person who passionately tries to defend evolution—or a political motive for Acts—or a strong case against inerrancy. Good luck trying to find an Evangelical willing to do this! I have never had an Evangelical Christian switch sides with me in a discussion about Evangelical Christianity. The Evangelical Christians I have met cannot act out a role contrary to their delusional commander's wishes, and most consider it a sin to try.

Evangelical Christians usually make an irrational choice by not switching positions with me. I can defend Evangelical Christianity better than most. I know more than most about the Bible, which I have actually read. I know all the best arguments and when to use them. Mostly, however, I know the secret. If I played the role of Evangelical, I would win at Hooks and Ladders every time because *I would have the power that comes with the indwelling Holy Spirit.*

Appendix A: Paul and Paranoid Schizophrenia

Why Does It Matter?

COMPARING PAUL TO A PARANOID SCHIZOPHRENIC will probably generate more criticism of this book than any other contention. I find this unfortunate, as I do not consider this a central issue that informs my views of Evangelical Christianity. I debated whether to frame my arguments in this way in the book. I considered avoiding any assertion that Paul had many things in common with paranoid schizophrenics because the specific diagnosis had nothing to do with my case against Evangelical Christianity. Indeed, I stumbled across the idea only when I started to write about the absurdity of the "Sinner's Prayer," which I thought would be the last chapter in the book.

How did I stumble onto this? From the start of writing this book, I penned in a notebook ideas that I thought I would need to address in the book to make it complete. As I filled in my notebook, it became clear that I needed to answer one important question, and I knew I did not have the answer. I wrote in my notebook, "Whatever things, thoughts, or feelings make Evangelicals so resistant to change, or resistant even to considering another position—whatever those things may be—that's where the answer is. I need to find out what makes Evangelicals so guarded and tenacious."

Even at the start of this project, I knew that one of the reasons for their resistance came from the complete lack of serious reflection about what a person felt when they recited the "Sinner's Prayer." I considered the average Evangelical's personal thoughts about their conversion and saying the "Sinner's Prayer" to have features similar to schizophrenic thinking. Specifically, paranoid schizophrenics fail to consider how their feelings may affect their conclusions about the world, just as most Evangelicals fail to consider how their feelings may have affected their conclusions about Christianity—and what happens when they say the "Sinner's Prayer." I explain this in detail in the book in the section titled, "Explanation Personal God." With Evangelicals, it seems that basing this one, albeit important, belief on a disordered thought process leads to more disordered thinking.

I also knew that Evangelicals derive their views about salvation almost entirely from Paul's letters. As part of the process of this project, I had planned to review Paul's letters thoroughly. Perhaps because I read Paul's letters in a short time with serious scrutiny, Paul's repetitive reasoning process startled me. It struck me that Evangelicals may have seemingly more unfixable beliefs in comparison to other faith groups—like American Catholics—because they base their doctrines and pattern their thinking after writings that had many features in common with paranoid schizophrenia.

I highlighted parts of Paul's letters that fit a pattern consistent with paranoid schizophrenia with different colors (thank God for computers). Some letters had just about all highlights, while other letters—or parts of letters—had few, if any, highlights. Further research informed me that the letters with few or no highlights—like 2 Thessalonians—are the letters some historians do not believe Paul wrote. I think they are probably correct.

On the other hand, the letters like Philippians and Second Corinthians chapters 7–9 had very little highlighting but nonetheless appear to have been written by Paul. If Paul did write them, he did so at a time when his thinking lacked the schizophrenic features found in his other work. Chapters 7–9 of Second Corinthians, for example, could not be less typical of paranoid schizophrenia reasoning. Since chapters 10–13 are essentially a protracted psychotic rant, it is hard for me to imagine that the same person wrote both. Thus, even if Paul wrote all of Second Corinthians, I believe it is unlikely that he wrote it as one letter within a short period of time.

My task in reviewing Paul's letters had little to do with diagnosing a modern psychiatric problem. I set out simply to analyze Paul's thinking and reasoning skills in an effort to understand Evangelicals and the Evangelical community. After much thought, research, and analysis, I believe it is fair to conclude that Paul's reasoning fits a pattern consistent with that of paranoid schizophrenia. To be sure, I think it is clear that Paul has flawed reasoning regardless of whether it correlates with characteristics of paranoid schizophrenia. But given that most people accept that paranoid schizophrenic delusional thinking poses problems, a comparison of Paul's thoughts to paranoid schizophrenic thinking admittedly helps make the point that adopting his reasoning may cause problems.

Consider this: what was the source of Paul's knowledge of the gospel? One possibility is that Paul merely repeats or summarizes what he learned from other Christians. However, Paul himself rules this out in Galatians:

> I want you to know, brothers, that the gospel I preached is not something that man made up. I did not receive it from any man, nor was I taught it; rather, I received it by revelation from Jesus Christ (Gal 1:11–12 NIV).

With the possibility that Paul received his content from another man eliminated, several possibilities remain. First, we can take Paul at face value when he writes that he received "the gospel I preached ... by revelation from Jesus Christ." But there is another possibility to contemplate. If Paul describes himself in a manner common to those with paranoid schizophrenia, and if he employs patterns of reasoning commonly used by those with paranoid schizophrenia, then the possibility of Paul inventing his gospel in his head deserves consideration. After all, if Paul fabricated his well-formed and complex delusional system in his brain, he would share this characteristic with most people who have the modern diagnosis of paranoid schizophrenia.

Suppose I can make a credible case that Paul's writings exhibit characteristics that suggest he would have had been considered at high risk for a diagnosis of schizophrenia had he lived today and appeared in a clinical setting. If I can do that, this question seems worth addressing: What is more probable?

1. Paul fabricated his gospel in a way that happens commonly in those with paranoid schizophrenia.
2. Paul's gospel came directly from God.[1]

In answering this question, consider this as well: even if someone chooses to believe that God revealed his gospel to Paul, what sort of god picks a man with significant signs of paranoid schizophrenia as his chief messenger?

Diagnosing Paranoid Schizophrenia

Diagnostic Criteria

Suppose Paul showed up in a modern-day psychiatrist's office or hospital. How would a mental health professional assess his mental condition? What questions would the healthcare professional ask? In today's medical community, the *DSM-IV* is the most commonly used standard for formally diagnosing paranoid schizophrenia. The *DSM-IV* describes the symptoms and behaviors exhibited by paranoid schizophrenics and establishes the *criteria* necessary for justifying a *diagnosis* of paranoid schizophrenia.

PROBLEMS WITH DIAGNOSIS

Many problems arise when trying to diagnose a man who lived two thousand years ago. One problem concerns motivation. After all, since Paul is dead we do not have the most compelling reason to make this diagnosis—to treat him and help him function more effectively. This may seem obvious, but it has importance nonetheless. In addition, if Paul were alive today and we wanted to address his mental state, we would find that much of the current research and material available to us deals with biochemistry, neurobiology, and brain function. None of this material has much use when examining patterns of thought in Paul's centuries-old writings.

Another problem concerns our lack of knowledge about Paul and his life. We lack at least two pieces of evidence that would enable us to make a conclusive diagnosis of schizophrenia. First, we do not know the duration of Paul's schizophrenic thinking. Most sources agree that schizophrenic symptoms tend to persist for a significantly longer period than similar symptoms from other disorders. Currently, the *DSM-IV* criteria provide that symptoms must have persisted for a minimum of six months before one can make a diagnosis of paranoid schizophrenia.[2] Although there are no dates in Paul's letters, few people seem to have the impression that he wrote them in fewer than six months. Most seem to agree that he wrote his letters over a period of years, so it is at least possible for us to conclude that Paul's symptoms may have been in existence for more than the minimum period.

The second missing piece of evidence seems hopelessly irretrievable. Did Paul have any medical conditions that could explain his symptoms? We do not know. Nor do we know anything about his diet or any environmental exposure that could have had mind-altering properties. For these reasons, ruling out other medical conditions is impossible and makes any diagnosis of paranoid schizophrenia provisional.

Leaving the possibility of other medical conditions aside for now, can we consider whether Paul meets the other criteria for diagnosing paranoid schizophrenia? The first criterion deals with delusions. Can we say that Paul was deluded? Of course, any analysis of delusions is inherently subjective. Nonetheless, Paul's writings have many elements that could reasonably be described as deluded. Further, certain characteristic features of a delusion recur commonly in paranoid schizophrenia, while these features rarely manifest themselves in other disorders. Indeed, in the *DSM-IV's* criteria for delusions associated with paranoid schizophrenia, if a person's delusion fits the criteria for being bizarre, that feature *alone* would satisfy the criteria that address *thinking* and *reasoning* in support of a diagnosis of paranoid schizophrenia. The *DSM-IV* offers this explanation of bizarre delusions:

> Although bizarre delusions are considered to be especially characteristic of schizophrenia, "bizarreness" may be difficult to judge, especially across different cultures. Delusions are deemed bizarre if they are clearly implausible and not understandable and do not derive from ordinary life experiences ... Delusions that express a loss of control over mind or body are generally considered to be bizarre; these include a person's belief that his or her thoughts have been taken away by some outside force ("thought withdrawal"), that alien thoughts have been put into his or her mind ("thought insertion"), or that his or her body or actions are being acted on or manipulated by some outside force ("delusions of control"). If the delusions are judged to be bizarre, only this single symptom is needed to satisfy Criterion A [*Characteristic symptoms*] for schizophrenia.[3]

Do Paul's letters demonstrate the necessary elements to judge them as containing bizarre delusions? Yes. Many examples provide all the elements for judging them bizarre. Indeed, we could make a credible case for bizarreness simply from this passage in Romans:

> So, my brothers, you also died to the law through the body of Christ, that you might belong to another, to him who was raised from the dead, in order that we might bear fruit to God. For when we were controlled by the sinful nature, the sinful passions aroused by the law were at work in our bodies, so that we bore fruit for death. But now, by dying to what once bound us, we have been released from the law so that we serve in the new way of the Spirit, and not in the old way of the written code.
>
> What shall we say, then? Is the law sin? Certainly not! Indeed I would not have known what sin was except through the law. For I would not have known what coveting really was if the law had not said, "Do not covet." But sin, seizing the opportunity afforded by the

> commandment, produced in me every kind of covetous desire. For apart from law, sin is dead. Once I was alive apart from law; but when the commandment came, sin sprang to life and I died. I found that the very commandment that was intended to bring life actually brought death.
>
> For sin, seizing the opportunity afforded by the commandment, deceived me, and through the commandment put me to death. So then, the law is holy, and the commandment is holy, righteous and good. Did that which is good, then, become death to me? By no means! But in order that sin might be recognized as sin, it produced death in me through what was good, so that through the commandment sin might become utterly sinful.
>
> We know that the law is spiritual; but I am unspiritual, sold as a slave to sin. I do not understand what I do. For what I want to do I do not do, but what I hate I do. And if I do what I do not want to do, I agree that the law is good. As it is, it is no longer I myself who do it, but it is sin living in me. I know that nothing good lives in me, that is, in my sinful nature. For I have the desire to do what is good, but I cannot carry it out. For what I do is not the good I want to do; no, the evil I do not want to do—this I keep on doing. Now if I do what I do not want to do, it is no longer I who do it, but it is sin living in me that does it.
>
> So I find this law at work: When I want to do good, evil is right there with me. For in my inner being I delight in God's law; but I see another law at work in the members of my body, waging war against the law of my mind and making me a prisoner of the law of sin at work within my members.
>
> What a wretched man I am! Who will rescue me from this body of death? Thanks be to God—through Jesus Christ our Lord! (Rom 7:4–25 NIV).

As this book focuses more on the problems with adopting poor reasoning habits, which lead to potentially unethical and harmful actions, I will not rely merely on this one example from Paul. I have included many in chapter 2 of this book and in this appendix.

However, for now, let us put the delusional thinking of Paul aside and examine what criteria remain before we could consider a diagnosis of schizophrenia. The sole remaining criterion (other than the aforementioned issue of other medical conditions) concerns social and occupational functioning. The *DSM-IV* describes this criterion this way:

> For a significant portion of the time since the onset of the disturbance, one or more areas of functioning such as work, interpersonal relations, or self-care are markedly below the level achieved prior to the onset [*of schizophrenic symptoms*].[4]

As this represents an important criterion for paranoid schizophrenia, I am confident that many will refer to the book of Acts as evidence of Paul's high level of function. Long before I began analyzing Paul's letters in detail, I had concluded that Acts was not a credible source of information about Paul or anyone else. I explain some of my reasons for this conclusion in chapter 12. Nonetheless, we have Paul's own witness about himself in his letters. Unless we think he was lying or that someone coerced him or edited what he wrote, we should give far more weight to his own account than we should give to the version written by someone who might never have met Paul.

Paul writes many things that allude to his poor interpersonal relationships and a decrease in his level of function. For example:

> I went in response to a revelation and set before them the gospel that I preach among the Gentiles. But I did this privately to those who seemed to be leaders, for fear that I was running or had run my race in vain (Gal 2:2 NIV).

> I fear for you, that somehow I have wasted my efforts on you.
>
> I plead with you, brothers, become like me, for I became like you. You have done me no wrong. As you know, it was because of an illness that I first preached the gospel to you.
>
> Even though my illness was a trial to you, you did not treat me with contempt or scorn (Gal 4:11–14 NIV).

> Finally, let no one cause me trouble, for I bear on my body the marks of Jesus (Gal 6:17 NIV).

> But, brothers, when we were torn away from you for a short time (in person, not in thought), out of our intense longing we made every effort to see you. For we wanted to come to you—certainly I, Paul, did, again and again—but Satan stopped us (1 Thess 2:17–18 NIV).

> It has always been my ambition to preach the gospel where Christ was not known, so that I would not be building on someone else's foundation. Rather, as it is written:
>
> "Those who were not told about him will see,
> and those who have not heard will understand."

This is why I have often been hindered from coming to you (Rom 15: 20–22 NIV).

When I came to you, brothers, I did not come with eloquence or superior wisdom as I proclaimed to you the testimony about God. For I resolved to know nothing while I was with you except Jesus Christ and him crucified. I came to you in weakness and fear, and with much trembling. My message and my preaching were not with wise and persuasive words, but with a demonstration of the Spirit's power, so that your faith might not rest on men's wisdom, but on God's power (1 Cor 2:1–5 NIV).

We are fools for Christ, but you are so wise in Christ! We are weak, but you are strong! You are honored, we are dishonored! To this very hour we go hungry and thirsty, we are in rags, we are brutally treated, we are homeless. We work hard with our own hands. When we are cursed, we bless; when we are persecuted, we endure it; when we are slandered, we answer kindly. Up to this moment we have become the scum of the earth, the refuse of the world (1 Cor 4:10–13 NIV).

To the weak I became weak, to win the weak. I have become all things to all men so that by all possible means I might save some. I do all this for the sake of the gospel, that I may share in its blessings (1 Cor 9:22–3 NIV).

Because I was confident of this, I planned to visit you first so that you might benefit twice. I planned to visit you on my way to Macedonia and to come back to you from Macedonia, and then to have you send me on my way to Judea. When I planned this, did I do it lightly? Or do I make my plans in a worldly manner so that in the same breath I say, "Yes, yes" and "No, no"?

But as surely as God is faithful, our message to you is not "Yes" and "No." For the Son of God, Jesus Christ, who was preached among you by me and Silas and Timothy, was not "Yes" and "No," but in him it has always been "Yes." For no matter how many promises God has made, they are "Yes" in Christ. And so through him the "Amen" is spoken by us to the glory of God …

I call God as my witness that it was in order to spare you that I did not return to Corinth. Not that we lord it over your faith, but we work with you for your joy, because it is by faith you stand firm …

So I made up my mind that I would not make another painful visit to you. For if I grieve you, who is left to make me glad but you

> whom I have grieved? I wrote as I did so that when I came I should not be distressed by those who ought to make me rejoice. I had confidence in all of you, that you would all share my joy. For I wrote you out of great distress and anguish of heart and with many tears, not to grieve you but to let you know the depth of my love for you (2 Cor 1:15–20, 23–24; 2:1–4 NIV).
>
> By the meekness and gentleness of Christ, I appeal to you—I, Paul, who am "timid" when face to face with you, but "bold" when away! I beg you that when I come I may not have to be as bold as I expect to be toward some people who think that we live by the standards of this world ...
>
> For some say, "His letters are weighty and forceful, but in person he is unimpressive and his speaking amounts to nothing." Such people should realize that what we are in our letters when we are absent, we will be in our actions when we are present (2 Cor 10:1–2, 10–11 NIV).
>
> On my return I will not spare those who sinned earlier or any of the others, since you are demanding proof that Christ is speaking through me. He is not weak in dealing with you, but is powerful among you. For to be sure, he was crucified in weakness, yet he lives by God's power. Likewise, we are weak in him, yet by God's power we will live with him to serve you....
>
> We are glad whenever we are weak but you are strong; and our prayer is for your perfection. This is why I write these things when I am absent, that when I come I may not have to be harsh in my use of authority—the authority the Lord gave me for building you up, not for tearing you down (2 Cor 13:2–4, 9–10 NIV).

These passages present a picture of a man who often failed to show up in places where he had promised to go and who was weak, timid, and unimpressive in his personal encounters. This at least suggests a pattern of diminished functioning. We have enough evidence to suggest that Paul may have exhibited behavior that would satisfy the *DSM-IV* criteria and at least let us consider the possibility that Paul would have fit our current definition of paranoid schizophrenia.

Before moving on, one more issue needs clarification. The *DSM-IV* and similar tools are products of the recent trend toward the establishment of objective criteria for the diagnosis of psychiatric problems. This has led to profound changes in the approach used by mental health professionals in making diagnoses. Specifically, professionals no longer focus on the classic descriptions of schizophrenia that have characterized literature for over a century, and they now deemphasize the characteristics that we call "phenomenology," which is rooted in the concept of phenomena.

For example, in the past psychiatrists and other mental health professionals focused on a person's sense of self and explained schizophrenic behavior as the result of a poor sense of self. They would, for instance, interview family members and find that their now floridly psychotic patient had shown signs of a poor self-image that were present long before the patient was admitted to the mental ward. But the scientific community understandably challenged the mental health profession for justifying its conclusions after the fact. A thorough review of the literature on schizophrenia will reveal that very few well-regarded studies have focused on the behaviors of schizophrenics before they showed signs of schizophrenia. As a result, it seems presumptuous to assume that something like a poor sense of self or a lack of ego boundaries causes schizophrenia even though these characteristics may often be associated with schizophrenia.

Regardless of whether these phenomena have scientific merit for explaining or describing schizophrenia, psychiatrists and psychologists are familiar with them. Many may still think of schizophrenia in these terms even though they may discuss it using the more objective criteria outlined in *DSM-IV*. In other words, the current focus is on behaviors that we can observe now, while the patient is standing in front of us, rather than on things that may have existed before the patient is present for diagnosis or treatment.

Because of this trend, there is little recent medical emphasis on the relationship between the patient's lack of a sense of self and schizophrenia. Nonetheless, the correlation, even if not useful for diagnosis or treatment, can be considered important. Certainly mental health professionals who deal regularly with schizophrenics are aware of it. But regardless, there is, to my knowledge, no research or evidence that shows a positive benefit from a belief in one's own worthlessness. For this reason, I have extracted a number of passages from Paul's letters that describe his lacking sense of self and his belief in his own worthlessness and toxicity. Even if they do not aid in a diagnosis of schizophrenia, these undesirable traits have had a powerful impact on the modern Evangelical community.

To explain why some of these phenomenological traits have fallen into disfavor, let us take a look at one of the classic traits strongly associated with paranoid schizophrenia—ambivalence. In psychiatry, ambivalence refers to the coexistence of opposing feelings, like love and hate.* Many of Paul's expressed beliefs and feelings can reasonably be described as ambivalent.

For example, in first-century Judaism, Jews were permitted to eat only food that satisfied certain rigorous religious standards. Paul wrote the following about an encounter with one of Jesus' disciples, Peter:

> When Peter came to Antioch, I opposed him to his face, because he was clearly in the wrong. Before certain men came from James, he used to eat with the Gentiles. But when they arrived, he began to draw back and separate himself from the Gentiles because he was afraid of those who belonged to the circumcision group. The other Jews joined him in his hypocrisy, so that by their hypocrisy even Barnabas was led astray (Gal. 2:11–13 NIV).

Paul felt strongly about what he described as Peter's hypocrisy—Peter's willingness to eat with Gentiles when only Gentiles were present while simultaneously refusing to eat with Gentiles when observant Jews were around. Most people, including me, interpret Paul's concern about Peter's hypocrisy as focusing on Peter's willingness to ignore Jewish customs of cleanliness when it suited him, while pretending to orthodoxy when his fellow Jews were present. This seems clear until we find that Paul says this also:

> Be careful, however, that the exercise of your freedom does not become a stumbling block to the weak. For if anyone with a weak conscience sees you who have this knowledge eating in an idol's temple, won't he be emboldened to eat what has been sacrificed to idols? So this weak brother, for whom Christ died, is destroyed by your knowledge. When you sin against your brothers in this way and wound their weak conscience, you sin against Christ. Therefore, if what I eat causes my brother to fall into sin, I will never eat meat again, so that I will not cause him to fall (1 Cor 8:9–13 NIV).
>
> "Everything is permissible"—but not everything is beneficial. "Everything is permissible"—but not everything is constructive. Nobody should seek his own good, but the good of others.... If some unbeliever invites you to a meal and you want to go, eat

* Many people confuse ambivalence with indifference. Indifference, however, means "unconcerned" or "uncaring."

> whatever is put before you without raising questions of conscience....
>
> For why should my freedom be judged by another's conscience? If I take part in the meal with thankfulness, why am I denounced because of something I thank God for?
>
> So whether you eat or drink or whatever you do, do it all for the glory of God. Do not cause anyone to stumble, whether Jews, Greeks or the church of God—even as I try to please everybody in every way. For I am not seeking my own good but the good of many, so that they may be saved (1 Cor 10:23–24, 27, 29–33 NIV).

In other words, Paul suggested that it might be a good idea to conform one's behavior to the expectations of one's audience, just as Peter did! Can we call this ambivalence? After all, Paul writes about how he "opposed him [Peter] to his face" shortly after he wrote about how he made a trip to Jerusalem specifically to get Peter's, and other leaders', advice and approval. In the same letter to the Galatians where Paul pointed out Peter's hypocrisy, Paul refers to Peter as an important leader whose opinion about Paul matters. The following quote suggests Paul felt ambivalently about Peter:

> I went up again to Jerusalem ... But I did this privately to those who seemed to be leaders; for fear that I was running or had run my race in vain....
>
> I had been entrusted with the task of preaching the gospel to the Gentiles, just as Peter had been to the Jews ... God ... was at work in the ministry of Peter as an apostle to the Jews ... James, Peter and John ... recognized the grace given to me. They agreed that we [Paul and his entourage] should go to the Gentiles, and they to the Jews. All they asked was that we should continue to remember the poor, the very thing I was eager to do (Gal 2:1–2, 7–10 NIV).

Nevertheless, from Paul's writings it is hard to label his position objectively. I may consider Paul ambivalent because I feel the evidence of Paul's other schizophrenic traits allows me to read into these passages a pattern of ambivalence. An Evangelical, however, might argue that Paul makes perfect sense. While Paul might have been willing to forsake strict observance out of good motives—so that he wouldn't cause his "brother to fall into sin"—Peter might have been acting out of a bad motive, hypocrisy. Taking this a step further, I could claim that Paul's confidence in Peter's motives shows Paul's autistic traits—he thinks he knows what Peter was thinking and he thinks that we can see what he saw. An

Evangelical who wanted to defend Paul could fairly describe this as bias and a guess.

So how can we make an assessment of Paul's or anyone else's mental state with any kind of objectivity? This problem has undergone scrutiny in the last few decades, and this is why psychiatry has focused on the establishment of specific and reproducible ways to describe behavior and thinking processes that recur commonly in schizophrenia, instead of focusing on phenomenology. For example, in chapter 9 we reviewed circumstantiality, tangentiality, and loose associations. These processes show up far more in the thoughts and speech of schizophrenics than they do in those without schizophrenia.

Getting back to our example of Paul and Peter, we may not agree about Paul's ambivalence, but we may arrive at a consensus about his thinking. Based on Paul's reasoning in 1 Corinthians, for example, what conclusions can we make about Paul's views of Peter "drawing back and separating from the Gentiles?" It is unlikely that we will agree on a consistent answer from Paul's writings. This could represent normal disagreement, but it also shows that Paul did not arrive at a coherent answer to this question. After all, Paul placed enormous emphasis on the Law and commandments—especially on things like circumcision and clean and unclean food. As a result, we might have expected to find clear answers to questions about adherence to the Law of God in Paul's writings.

But did Paul ever give a clear answer to the question he tried to answer: "What foods can a Christian eat without sinning?" Paul used circumstantial reasoning when he introduced a "weak brother" who might "stumble" and be "destroyed by your knowledge" into his answer. Thus, attempts to find an answer to the question—based on Paul's letters—become hopelessly subjective. Furthermore, despite his circumstantial reasoning Paul never came around to answering the question. Indeed, Christians could use Paul's letters to justify almost any eating habits or restrictions—and they often do.* More importantly for this discussion, however, Paul never answered this question coherently. His disordered thinking caused his writing to veer off track to such an extent that he

* Evangelicals provide an interesting example. Many will not touch a glass filled with wine to their lips. Yet, this is more than simply disapproval of drunkenness; its basis seems solely related to not being a "stumbling block" to others. The same Evangelical, for example, may have no problem taking medicines like cough syrups that contain alcohol.

never resolved, or accepted as unresolved, questions that he considered very important.

Along with thought processes, we can judge thought content somewhat objectively—sometimes. Paranoid schizophrenics tend to think about few things outside their delusional thoughts. This was true of Paul as well. Paul did not care too much about any details in this world. And though it is obvious that his attention should focus on issues important to the churches to which he writes, this does not tell the whole story. Beyond just remaining focused on Christ and the church, Paul focused on almost nothing except the Law, commandments, and the mechanism of Gentiles' incorporation into God's covenants with the Jewish people. This includes, of course, Paul's grandiose belief that God chose him alone as the messenger to the Gentiles. Nothing else seems to matter. Indeed, Paul tells very few stories that give his writing context. As well, when he does tell a story he makes it clear that his experiences had little impact on his thinking. For example, in Galatians 1 and 2 Paul makes this clear:

> But when God, who set me apart from birth and called me by his grace, was pleased to reveal his Son in me so that I might preach him among the Gentiles, I did not consult any man, nor did I go up to Jerusalem to see those who were apostles before I was (Gal 1:15–17 NIV).
>
> Those men added nothing to my message. On the contrary, they saw that I had been entrusted with the task of preaching the gospel to the Gentiles, just as Peter had been to the Jews (Gal 2:6–7 NIV).

As we have seen before, Paul did not learn about the gospel from other Christians, nor did he regard his life experiences as providing any useful background for his task. Instead, he received his message and his assignment directly from God.

I have added below a general analysis of Romans 1–10 to provide an example of my evaluation of Paul's reasoning and thought processes. I hope this will make my methods clear and show how I came to my conclusions. I also hope readers will be able to view the words of Paul in a different context, without the gloss of two-millennia worth of explanations and interpretation.

Paranoid Schizophrenic Characteristics of the Apostle Paul Found in Romans 1–10

Probably the easiest way to see in Paul's writing the characteristics I have described is to examine a portion of it in some detail. Here I have gone through the first ten chapters of Paul's letter to the Romans, verse by verse. I have identified the paranoid schizophrenic quality of the passage that follows, along with a brief explanation of the reasons I consider the passage to embody the particular characteristic. The verse itself then follows.

ROMANS 1

- *Loose association* (How is the Gospel the power of God?)

I am not ashamed of the gospel, because it is the power of God for the salvation of everyone who believes: first for the Jew, then for the Gentile. For in the gospel a righteousness from God is revealed, a righteousness that is by faith from first to last, just as it is written: "The righteous will live by faith" (Rom 1:16–17 NIV).

See chapter 2 in the section "Paul the Mind Reader" for an analysis of Romans 1:18 through 2:1.

ROMANS 2

- *Illogical and delusional* (Paul knew through revelation the mind of God. Paul contradicted what he said about faith repeatedly. As well, saying "first" twice about Jews contradicted his claim about favoritism.)

But because of your stubbornness and your unrepentant heart, you are storing up wrath against yourself for the day of God's wrath, when his righteous judgment will be revealed. God "will give to each person according to what he has done." To those who by persistence in doing good seek glory, honor and immortality, he will give eternal life. But for those who are self-seeking and who reject the truth and follow evil, there will be wrath and anger. There will be trouble and distress for every human being who does evil: first for the Jew, then for the Gentile; but glory, honor and peace for everyone who does good: first for the Jew, then for the Gentile. For God does not show favoritism (Rom 2:5–11 NIV).

- *Circumstantial* (What was Paul's topic? If it was judgment, as it seems to be from the passage above, then these details do not explain too much. He packed his argument with these sorts of semi-related details that did not lead to a better understanding of his arguments.)

All who sin apart from the law will also perish apart from the law, and all who sin under the law will be judged by the law. For it is not those who hear the law who are righteous in God's sight, but it is those who obey the law who will be declared righteous. (Indeed, when Gentiles, who do not have the law, do by nature things required by the law, they are a law for themselves, even though they do not have the law, since they show that the requirements of the law are written on their hearts, their consciences also bearing witness, and their thoughts now accusing, now even defending them.) This will take place on the day when God will judge men's secrets through Jesus Christ, as my gospel declares (Rom 2:12–16 NIV).

- *Tangential* (Teachers of the Law may or may not obey the Law.)

Now you, if you call yourself a Jew; if you rely on the law and brag about your relationship to God; if you know his will and approve of what is superior because you are instructed by the law; if you are convinced that you are a guide for the blind, a light for those who are in the dark, an instructor of the foolish, a teacher of infants, because you have in the law the embodiment of knowledge and truth—you, then, who teach others, do you not teach yourself? You who preach against stealing, do you steal? You who say that people should not commit adultery, do you commit adultery? You who abhor idols, do you rob temples? You who brag about the law, do you dishonor God by breaking the law? As it is written: "God's name is blasphemed among the Gentiles because of you" (Rom 2:17–24 NIV).

- *Loose association* (If the law said males had to be circumcised and a male chose not to have a circumcision, he was not "keeping the law's requirements." This is a good example of how autistic thinking might lead to loose associations. Here, Paul seems to have already made up his mind that God's laws no longer required circumcision. Thus, he seems to have believed that all his readers clearly believed that as well.)

Circumcision has value if you observe the law, but if you break the law, you have become as though you had not been circumcised. If those who are not circumcised keep the law's requirements, will they not be regarded as though they were circumcised? The one who is not circumcised physically and yet obeys the law will condemn you who, even though you have the written code and circumcision, are a lawbreaker (Rom 2:25–27 NIV).

- *Incoherent* (What is a Jew? Paul rendered the label a meaningless abstraction—much like Evangelicals do with True Christian.)

A man is not a Jew if he is only one outwardly, nor is circumcision merely outward and physical. No, a man is a Jew if he is one inwardly; and circumcision is circumcision of the heart, by the Spirit, not by the written code. Such a man's praise is not from men, but from God (Rom 2:28–29 NIV).

ROMANS 3

- *Tangential* (Don't forget, Paul's topic was judgment and the law as it relates to Jews and Gentiles.)

What advantage, then, is there in being a Jew, or what value is there in circumcision? Much in every way! First of all, they have been entrusted with the very words of God.

What if some did not have faith? Will their lack of faith nullify God's faithfulness? Not at all! Let God be true, and every man a liar. As it is written: "So that you may be proved right when you speak and prevail when you judge" (Rom 3:1–4 NIV).

- *Derailment* (Wasn't he just writing about the benefits of being a Jew two sentences ago?)

But if our unrighteousness brings out God's righteousness more clearly, what shall we say? That God is unjust in bringing his wrath on us? (Rom 3:5 NIV).

- *Circumstantial/autistic* (He used a "human argument"—hmm ... is there another kind?)

(I am using a human argument.) Certainly not! If that were so, how could God judge the world? Someone might argue, "If my falsehood enhances God's truthfulness and so increases his glory, why am I still condemned as a sinner?" Why not say—as we are being slanderously reported as saying and as some claim that we say—" Let us do evil that good may result"? Their condemnation is deserved.

What shall we conclude then? Are we any better? Not at all! We have already made the charge that Jews and Gentiles alike are all under sin. As it is written:

"There is no one righteous, not even one;
there is no one who understands,
no one who seeks God."
"All have turned away,
they have together become worthless;
there is no one who does good,
not even one."
"Their throats are open graves;
their tongues practice deceit."
"The poison of vipers is on their lips."
"Their mouths are full of cursing and bitterness."
"Their feet are swift to shed blood;
ruin and misery mark their ways,
and the way of peace they do not know."
"There is no fear of God before their eyes."

Now we know that whatever the law says, it says to those who are under the law, so that every mouth may be silenced and the whole world held accountable to God. Therefore no one will be declared righteous in his sight by observing the law; rather, through the law we become conscious of sin (Rom 3:5–20 NIV).

- *Loose associations* (Paul did not connect faith, the Law, "sacrifice of atonement," and his topic of judgment whatsoever. Neither can most Evangelicals who have no idea how to answer the question, "How did Christ's death serve as atonement?")

But now a righteousness from God, apart from law, has been made known, to which the Law and the Prophets testify. This righteousness from God comes through faith in Jesus Christ to all who believe. There is no difference, for all have sinned and fall short of the glory of God, and are justified freely by his grace through the redemption that came by Christ Jesus. God presented him as a sacrifice of atonement, through faith in his blood. He did this to demonstrate his justice, because in his forbearance he had left the sins committed beforehand unpunished—he did it to demonstrate his justice at the present time, so as to be just and the one who justifies those who have faith in Jesus (Rom 3:21–26 NIV).

- *Tangential* (Paul may have been right—maybe his readers should never boast about anything. But this topic had nothing substantial to do with the law, judgment, and justification through faith. His off-topic remarks continued into Romans 4.)

Where, then, is boasting? It is excluded. On what principle? On that of observing the law? No, but on that of faith. For we maintain that a man is justified by faith apart from observing the law. Is God the God of Jews only? Is he not the God of Gentiles too? Yes, of Gentiles too, since there is only one God, who will justify the circumcised by faith and the uncircumcised through that same faith. Do we, then, nullify the law by this faith? Not at all! Rather, we uphold the law (Rom 3:27–31 NIV).

ROMANS 4

What then shall we say that Abraham, our forefather, discovered in this matter? If, in fact, Abraham was justified by works, he had something to boast about—but not before God. What does the Scripture say? "Abraham believed God, and it was credited to him as righteousness" (Rom 4:1–3 NIV).

- *Illogical* (Above, Paul said that people of faith "uphold the law" [i.e., do works]. Below, he uses a man's job, "work," as an analogy for a man who does "works" and upholds the law. He said that a man without a job [work] could still have his faith credited as righteousness. Paul's analogy is illogical, because using Paul's own claims; a man who had faith would do works, and would therefore not qualify as unemployed in Paul's employment analogy.)

Now when a man works, his wages are not credited to him as a gift, but as an obligation. However, to the man who does not work but trusts God who justifies the wicked, his faith is credited as righteousness. David says the same thing when he speaks of the blessedness of the man to whom God credits righteousness apart from works.

"Blessed are they
whose transgressions are forgiven,
whose sins are covered.
Blessed is the man
whose sin the Lord will never count against him" (Rom 4:4–8 NIV).

- *Tangential* (This may be related to law/sin/salvation, but not in the context of Paul's discussion.)

Is this blessedness only for the circumcised, or also for the uncircumcised? We have been saying that Abraham's faith was credited to him as righteousness. Under what circumstances was it credited? Was it after he was circumcised, or before? It was not after, but before! And he received the sign of circumcision, a seal of the righteousness that he had by faith while he was still uncircumcised. So then, he is the father of all who believe but have not been circumcised, in order that righteousness might be credited to them. And he is also the father of the circumcised who not only are circumcised but who also walk in the footsteps of the faith that our father Abraham had before he was circumcised.

It was not through law that Abraham and his offspring received the promise that he would be heir of the world, but through the righteousness that comes by faith (Rom 4:9–13 NIV).

- *Loose association* (How does living by the law make faith unnecessary?)

For if those who live by law are heirs, faith has no value and the promise is worthless, because law brings wrath. And where there is no law there is no transgression (Rom 4:14–15 NIV).

- *Loose association* (The promise is God's promise to a man [or group]—how did Paul know God's motive for choosing Abraham? Also, connecting a common faith to genetic ancestry, as in the idea that Christians have become Abraham's offspring through faith, is a classic loose association—it is not based in reality.)

Therefore, the promise comes by faith, so that it may be by grace and may be guaranteed to all Abraham's offspring—not only to those who are of the law but also to those who are of the faith of Abraham (Rom 4:16 NIV).

- *Loose association* (It is certainly possible to be the father of many nations without being the father of all nations—Paul's assertions were flat wrong. For example, no one believes that Abraham is the father of any Native American nations–even though he may be the father of many nations in Africa, Asia, and the Middle East.)

He is the father of us all. As it is written: "I have made you a father of many nations." He is our father in the sight of God, in whom he believed—the God who gives life to the dead and calls things that are not as though they were.

Against all hope, Abraham in hope believed and so became the father of many nations, just as it had been said to him, "So shall your offspring be." Without weakening in his faith, he faced the fact that his body was as good as dead—since he was about a hundred years old—and that Sarah's womb was also dead. Yet he did not waver through unbelief regarding the promise of God, but was strengthened in his faith and gave glory to God, being fully persuaded that God had power to do what he had promised. This is why "it was credited to him as righteousness" (Rom 4:16–22 NIV).

- *Loose association and referential thinking* (This is identity blurring—if "credit to him" was intended to be "credit to all with faith," it would have been written, "it was credited to all with faith." Similarly, schizophrenics will often think the radio or TV is speaking or referring directly to them.)

The words "it was credited to him" were written not for him alone, but also for us, to whom God will credit righteousness—for us who believe in him who raised Jesus our Lord from the dead (Rom 4:23–24 NIV).

- *Illogical* (If "credited as righteousness" by faith through Abraham, why did Jesus have to die?)

He was delivered over to death for our sins and was raised to life for our justification (Rom 4:25 NIV).

ROMANS 5

- *Loose association* (He never connects Abraham to law to Christ.)

Therefore, since we have been justified through faith, we have peace with God through our Lord Jesus Christ, through whom we have gained access by faith into this grace in which we now stand. And we rejoice in the hope of the glory of God (Rom 5:1–2 NIV).

- *Circumstantial and tangential* (What does this have to do with justification through faith?)

Not only so, but we also rejoice in our sufferings, because we know that suffering produces perseverance; perseverance, character; and character, hope (Rom 5:3–4 NIV).

- *Tangential, external control, and bizarre* (What did the following have to do with the previous discussion about law and faith?)

And hope does not disappoint us, because God has poured out his love into our hearts by the Holy Spirit, whom he has given us. You see, at just the right time, when we were still powerless, Christ died for the ungodly. Very rarely will anyone die for a righteous man, though for a good man someone might possibly dare to die (Rom 5:5–7 NIV).

- *Incoherent* (This is one of Evangelicals' most well-known verses. Yet, in what strange world do the inhabitants consider having their sons tortured and killed a demonstration of love?)

But God demonstrates his own love for us in this: While we were still sinners, Christ died for us (Rom 5:8 NIV).

- *Loose association* (When did justification through blood come about—how much "more than" what? Why is God mad? Who were God's enemies? Did God think of humans as enemies? If so, did an unchanging God change his mind about us? How did Paul associate reconciliation through death and salvation through life of Jesus?)

Since we have now been justified by his blood, how much more shall we be saved from God's wrath through him! For if, when we were God's enemies, we were reconciled to him through the death of his Son, how much more, having been reconciled, shall we be saved through his life! Not only is this so, but we also rejoice in God through our Lord Jesus Christ, through whom we have now received reconciliation (Rom 5:9–11 NIV).

- *Tangential* (Introducing sin through Adam was barely related to the topic of Paul's previous thoughts, which in turn was already far removed from justification through faith.)
- *External Control* (Sin "entered the world" through one man.)

Therefore, just as sin entered the world through one man, and death through sin, and in this way death came to all men, because all sinned (Rom 5:12 NIV).

- *Circumstantial* (Whether sin was taken into account with or without the law was an over-inclusion of detail.)
- *Loose association* (Sin in the world = death. Yet [sin – law = zero sin]. In other words, if you sin in a place that is lawless, it doesn't count as sin.)

For before the law was given, sin was in the world. But sin is not taken into account when there is no law. Nevertheless, death reigned from the time of Adam to the time of Moses, even over those who did not sin by breaking a command, as did Adam, who was a pattern of the one to come (Rom 5:13–14 NIV).

- *Illogical/autistic* (Paul asked if one man's sin [Adam's] brought death to many, how much more would Jesus' sacrifice have brought life to the many? It is hard to tell if he was talking about simple math or some sort of quality of life measure. Regardless, Paul did not explain what he meant, and it seems as though he was absorbed in his own world.)

But the gift is not like the trespass. For if the many died by the trespass of the one man, how much more did God's grace and the gift that came by the grace of the one man, Jesus Christ, overflow to the many! Again, the gift of God is not like the result of the one man's sin: The judgment followed one sin and brought condemnation, but the gift followed many trespasses and brought justification. For if, by the trespass of the one man, death reigned through that one man, how much more will those who receive God's abundant provision of grace and of the gift of righteousness reign in life through the one man, Jesus Christ.

Consequently, just as the result of one trespass was condemnation for all men, so also the result of one act of righteousness was justification that brings life for all men. For just as through the disobedience of the one man the many were made sinners, so also through the obedience of the one man the many will be made righteous (Rom 5:15–19 NIV).

- *Bizarre/autistic/irrational* (Evangelicals quote the next two verses commonly, and many find them compelling. Yet, they are certainly bizarre. Using Paul's logic, we should make laws that everyone will break so we can benefit from more grace.)

The law was added so that the trespass might increase. But where sin increased, grace increased all the more, so that, just as sin reigned in death, so also grace might reign through righteousness to bring eternal life through Jesus Christ our Lord (Rom 5:20–21 NIV).

ROMANS 6

- *Loose associations/blurred ideas of reference* (Paul did mean that sin increases grace, as if these were volumetric entities. Did Paul die, die to sin, or die with Christ Jesus? It seems that he thought he did. He gave no indication that this was intended as a metaphor.)

What shall we say, then? Shall we go on sinning so that grace may increase? By no means! We died to sin; how can we live in it any longer? Or don't you know that all of us who were baptized into Christ Jesus were baptized into his death? We were therefore buried with him through baptism into death in order that, just as Christ was raised from the dead through the glory of the Father, we too may live a new life.

If we have been united with him like this in his death, we will certainly also be united with him in his resurrection (Rom 6:1–5 NIV).

- *Worthlessness/lack of identity* (Did Paul mean this metaphorically? He gave his readers no indication that he thought of this metaphorically. He seems to have believed that his old self had actually died.)

For we know that our old self was crucified with him so that the body of sin might be done away with, that we should no longer be slaves to sin—because anyone who has died has been freed from sin. Now if we died with Christ, we believe that we will also live with him (Rom 6:6–8 NIV).

- *Loose associations* (Jesus' death equating to a death to sin that extended to all is a loose association that may have been Paul's own invention.)

For we know that since Christ was raised from the dead, he cannot die again; death no longer has mastery over him. The death he died, he died to sin once for all; but the life he lives, he lives to God (Rom 6:9–10 NIV).

- *Controlled by external entities* (Paul asked his reader to allow an external entity [God] to control the parts of their bodies.)

In the same way, count yourselves dead to sin but alive to God in Christ Jesus. Therefore do not let sin reign in your mortal body so that you obey its evil desires. Do not offer the parts of your body to sin, as instruments of wickedness, but rather offer yourselves to God, as those who have been brought from death to life; and offer the parts of your body to him as instruments of righteousness. For sin shall not be your master, because you are not under law, but under grace.

What then? Shall we sin because we are not under law but under grace? By no means! Don't you know that when you offer yourselves to someone to obey him as slaves, you are slaves to the one whom you obey—whether you are slaves to sin, which leads to death, or to obedience, which leads to righteousness? But thanks be to God that, though you used to be slaves to sin, you wholeheartedly obeyed the form of teaching to which you were entrusted. You have been set free from sin and have become slaves to righteousness (Rom 6:11–18 NIV).

- *Autistic/magical* (What other terms could he have used besides "human terms?")

I put this in human terms because you are weak in your natural selves. Just as you used to offer the parts of your body in slavery to impurity and to ever-increasing wickedness, so now offer them in slavery to righteousness leading to holiness. When you were slaves to sin, you were free from the control of righteousness. What benefit did you reap at that time from the things you are now ashamed of? Those things result in death! But now that you have been set free from sin and have become slaves to God, the benefit you reap leads to holiness, and the result is eternal life. For the wages of sin is death, but the gift of God is eternal life in Christ Jesus our Lord (Rom 6:19–23 NIV).

ROMANS 7

(For analysis of most of Romans 7, see the beginning of this appendix.)

- *Loose association* (The marriage illustration is classic schizophrenic loose association. It also suggests concrete thinking, as Paul seemed to believe he was actually a slave to sin—also, bizarre, autistic, and illogical thinking, as Paul wrote that one had to actually die in order to get out from under contract with the law.)

Do you not know, brothers—for I am speaking to men who know the law—that the law has authority over a man only as long as he lives? For example, by law a married woman is bound to her husband as long as he is alive, but if her husband dies, she is released from the law of marriage. So then, if she marries another man while her husband is still alive, she is called an adulteress. But if her husband dies, she is released from that law and is not an adulteress, even though she marries another man.

So, my brothers, you also died to the law through the body of Christ, that you might belong to another, to him who was raised from the dead, in order that we might bear fruit to God. For when we were controlled by the sinful nature, the sinful passions aroused by the law were at work in our bodies, so that we bore fruit for death. But now, by dying to what once bound us, we have been released from the law so that we serve in the new way of the Spirit, and not in the old way of the written code (Rom 7:1–7 NIV).

- *Classic self-description that fits paranoid schizophrenia* (This is the continuation of Paul's rants from verses 7–23, which were reviewed in the beginning of this appendix.)

What a wretched man I am! Who will rescue me from this body of death? Thanks be to God—through Jesus Christ our Lord!

So then, I myself in my mind am a slave to God's law, but in the sinful nature a slave to the law of sin (Rom 7:24–25 NIV).

Romans 8

- *Magical thinking/autistic* (With unfixable toxic essence, a person's mind: "does not submit to God's law, nor can it do so.")
- *External control* (Mind controlled by the Spirit)

Therefore, there is now no condemnation for those who are in Christ Jesus, because through Christ Jesus the law of the Spirit of life set me free from the law of sin and death. For what the law was powerless to do in that it was weakened by the sinful nature, God did by sending his own Son in the likeness of sinful man to be a sin offering. And so he condemned sin in sinful man, in order that the righteous requirements of the law might be fully met in us, who do not live according to the sinful nature but according to the Spirit.

Those who live according to the sinful nature have their minds set on what that nature desires; but those who live in accordance with the Spirit have their minds set on what the Spirit desires. The mind of sinful man is death, but the mind controlled by the Spirit is life and peace; the sinful mind is hostile to God. It does not submit to God's law, nor can it do so. Those controlled by the sinful nature cannot please God (Rom 8:1–8 NIV).

- *Identity lacking* (Paul described himself and others as dead bodies animated by an external entity, which fits anyone's description of schizophrenia.)

You, however, are controlled not by the sinful nature but by the Spirit, if the Spirit of God lives in you. And if anyone does not have the Spirit of Christ, he does not belong to Christ. But if Christ is in you, your body is dead because of sin, yet your spirit is alive because of righteousness. And if the Spirit of him who raised Jesus from the dead is living in you, he who raised Christ from the dead will also give life to your mortal bodies through his Spirit, who lives in you.

Therefore, brothers, we have an obligation—but it is not to the sinful nature, to live according to it. For if you live according to the sinful nature, you will die; but if by the Spirit you put to death the misdeeds of the body, you will live, because those who are led by the Spirit of God are sons of God. For you did not receive a spirit that makes you a slave again to fear, but you received the Spirit of sonship. And by him we cry, "Abba, Father." The Spirit himself testifies with our spirit that we are God's children. Now if we are children, then we are heirs—heirs of God and co-heirs with Christ, if indeed we share in his sufferings in order that we may also share in his glory (Rom 8:9–17 NIV).

- *Autistic thinking/incoherent* (Paul, absorbed in his own world, wrote the following. We cannot know what he may have meant by this as it is outside normal logic or experience.)

I consider that our present sufferings are not worth comparing with the glory that will be revealed in us. The creation waits in eager expectation for the sons of God to be revealed. For the creation was subjected to frustration, not by its own choice, but by the will of the one who subjected it, in hope that the creation itself will be liberated from its bondage to decay and brought into the glorious freedom of the children of God.

We know that the whole creation has been groaning as in the pains of childbirth right up to the present time. Not only so, but we ourselves, who have the firstfruits of the Spirit, groan inwardly as we wait eagerly for our adoption as sons, the redemption of our bodies. For in this hope we were saved. But hope that is seen is no hope at all. Who hopes for what he already has? But if we hope for what we do not yet have, we wait for it patiently.

In the same way, the Spirit helps us in our weakness. We do not know what we ought to pray for, but the Spirit himself intercedes for us with groans that words cannot express. And he who searches our hearts knows the mind of the Spirit, because the Spirit intercedes for the saints in accordance with God's will (Rom 8:18–27 NIV).

- *Grandeur, magical thinking, and autistic* (Christians will be glorified.)

And we know that in all things God works for the good of those who love him, who have been called according to his purpose. For those God foreknew he also predestined to be conformed to the likeness of his Son, that he might be the firstborn among many brothers. And those he predestined, he also called; those he called, he also justified; those he justified, he also glorified (Rom 8:28–30 NIV).

- *Grandiose—special supernatural powers* (Perhaps the following is the type of belief that makes Evangelical Christian beliefs—like paranoid schizophrenic beliefs—resistant to correction with reason and evidence.)

What, then, shall we say in response to this? If God is for us, who can be against us?

He who did not spare his own Son, but gave him up for us all—how will he not also, along with him, graciously give us all things? (Rom 8:31–32 NIV).

- *Special Powers/autism* (Here we find immunity from the corrections, judgments, or reasoning of others.)

Who will bring any charge against those whom God has chosen? It is God who justifies. Who is he that condemns? Christ Jesus, who died—more than that, who was raised to life—is at the right hand of God and is also interceding for us (Rom 8:33–34 NIV).

- *Thoughts of persecution or danger*

Who shall separate us from the love of Christ? Shall trouble or hardship or persecution or famine or nakedness or danger or sword? As it is written:

"For your sake we face death all day long;

we are considered as sheep to be slaughtered."

No, in all these things we are more than conquerors through him who loved us. For I am convinced that neither death nor life, neither angels nor demons, neither the present nor the future, nor any powers, neither height nor depth, nor anything else in all creation, will be able to separate us from the love of God that is in Christ Jesus our Lord (Rom 8:35–39).

ROMANS 9

- *Autistic* (Why should we care that Paul proclaimed his conscience and confirmed that he was not lying? Did he think this would persuade readers of his honesty, or did he think that somehow readers could know his conscience?)

I speak the truth in Christ—I am not lying, my conscience confirms it in the Holy Spirit—I have great sorrow and unceasing anguish in my heart. For I could wish that I myself were cursed and cut off from Christ for the sake of my brothers, those of my own race, the people of Israel. Theirs is the adoption as sons; theirs the divine glory, the covenants, the receiving of the law, the temple worship and the promises. Theirs are the patriarchs, and from them is traced the human ancestry of Christ, who is God over all, forever praised! Amen.

It is not as though God's word had failed. For not all who are descended from Israel are Israel. Nor because they are his descendants are they all Abraham's children. On the contrary, "It is through Isaac that your offspring will be reckoned." In other words, it is not the natural children who are God's children, but it is the children of the promise who are regarded as Abraham's offspring. For this was how the promise was stated: "At the appointed time I will return, and Sarah will have a son."

Not only that, but Rebekah's children had one and the same father, our father Isaac. Yet, before the twins were born or had done anything good or bad—in order that God's purpose in election might stand: not by works but by him who calls—she was told, "The older will serve the younger." Just as it is written: "Jacob I loved, but Esau I hated" (Rom 9:1–13 NIV).

- *Loose association* (Based on scriptural evidence, Paul asked if God was unjust, as God had acted arbitrarily. Paul said God was just. Paul's argument was essentially, when God acted arbitrarily, he was just because he is God, and God can do whatever he wants to do.)

What then shall we say? Is God unjust? Not at all! For he says to Moses,

"I will have mercy on whom I have mercy,
and I will have compassion on whom I have compassion."

It does not, therefore, depend on man's desire or effort, but on God's mercy. For the Scripture says to Pharaoh: "I raised you up for this very purpose, that I might display my power in you and that my name might be proclaimed in all the earth." Therefore God has mercy on whom he wants to have mercy, and he hardens whom he wants to harden.

One of you will say to me: "Then why does God still blame us? For who resists his will?" But who are you, O man, to talk back to God? "Shall what is formed say to him who formed it, 'Why did you make me like this?'" Does not the potter have the right to make out of the same lump of clay some pottery for noble purposes and some for common use? (Rom 9:14–21 NIV).

- *Tangential* (The following paragraph is not directly related to Paul's free-will/predestination arguments above.)

What if God, choosing to show his wrath and make his power known, bore with great patience the objects of his wrath—prepared for destruction? What if he did this to make the riches of his glory known to the objects of his mercy, whom he prepared in advance for glory—even us, whom he also called, not only from the Jews but also from the Gentiles? As he says in Hosea:

"I will call them 'my people' who are not my people;
and I will call her 'my loved one' who is not my loved one," and,
It will happen that in the very place where it was said to them,
'You are not my people,'
they will be called 'sons of the living God.'"

Isaiah cries out concerning Israel:

"Though the number of the Israelites be like the sand by the sea,
only the remnant will be saved.
For the Lord will carry out
his sentence on earth with speed and finality."

It is just as Isaiah said previously:

"Unless the Lord Almighty
had left us descendants,
we would have become like Sodom,
we would have been like Gomorrah" (Rom 9:22–29 NIV).

- *Loose association* (The Old Testament verses, which Paul quoted in the following, were not topical, nor did Paul establish the legitimacy of his stumbling stone argument, as it pertained to the Jews. His commentary about Jews continued into Romans 10.)

What then shall we say? That the Gentiles, who did not pursue righteousness, have obtained it, a righteousness that is by faith; but Israel, who pursued a law of righteousness, has not attained it. Why not? Because they pursued it not by faith but as if it were by works. They stumbled over the "stumbling stone." As it is written:

"See, I lay in Zion a stone that causes men to stumble
and a rock that makes them fall,
and the one who trusts in him will never be put to shame" (Rom 9:30–33 NIV).

ROMANS 10

Brothers, my heart's desire and prayer to God for the Israelites is that they may be saved. For I can testify about them that they are zealous for God, but their zeal is not based on knowledge. Since they did not know the righteousness that comes from God and sought to establish their own, they did not submit to God's righteousness. Christ is the end of the law so that there may be righteousness for everyone who believes (Rom 10:1–4 NIV).

- *Circumstantial* (Presumably Paul was writing about who was justified and how they were justified. This paragraph is full of details that brought him no closer to the answer. Although, he did clarify what he meant when he used the word, "faith.")

Moses describes in this way the righteousness that is by the law: "The man who does these things will live by them." But the righteousness that is by faith says: "Do not say in your heart, 'Who will ascend into heaven?'" (i.e., to bring Christ down) "or 'Who will descend into the deep?'" (That is, to bring Christ up from the dead). But what does it say?

"The word is near you; it is in your mouth and in your heart," that is, the word of faith we are proclaiming: That if you confess with your mouth, "Jesus is Lord," and believe in your heart that God raised him from the dead, you will be saved. For it is with your heart that you believe and are justified, and it is with your mouth that you confess and are saved. As the Scripture says, "Anyone who trusts in him will never be put to shame." For there is no difference between Jew and Gentile—the same Lord is Lord of all and richly blesses all who call on him, for, "Everyone who calls on the name of the Lord will be saved" (Rom 5:5–13 NIV).

- *Derailed* (Paul was discussing justification through faith, and in a semi-related response he asked, "How can they preach unless sent"—which sent him off on a new topic—preaching.)

How, then, can they call on the one they have not believed in? And how can they believe in the one of whom they have not heard? And how can they hear without someone preaching to them? And how can they preach unless they are sent? As it is written, "How beautiful are the feet of those who bring good news!"

But not all the Israelites accepted the good news. For Isaiah says, "Lord, who has believed our message?" Consequently, faith comes from hearing the message, and the message is heard through the word of Christ (Rom 10:14–17 NIV).

Conclusion

As a child, teenager, and young adult, I sat through hundreds of services, Sunday school classes, youth group meetings, and retreats, where these verses were read aloud. Yet it was not until I undertook this project that I realized how weird they were. Centuries of Christians struggling to make sense of Paul have imposed their own understandings on his words, despite a claim to be reading the text literally.

Another fact of Evangelical worship helps disguise the disjointed thoughts found in these ten chapters. Evangelicals rarely read Paul's letters from beginning to end. They are more likely to focus on a phrase—or even one verse—and at most might take a look at one chapter at a time. Even during a Bible study, a special meeting convened for the express purpose of reading the Bible, the study will usually focus on one or two verses, or one chapter, per meeting. A Bible study group that is reading Romans may cover the entire book, but the study will proceed only a few verses at a time.

Paul's Texts on Worthlessness

I have earlier discussed Paul's lacking sense of self and his concept of worthlessness. This theme, too, stretches across most of his writings. I have highlighted some of the places where this theme comes to the fore.

ROMANS

No one who understands, no one who seeks God ... all ... become worthless.... Their throats are open graves; their tongues practice deceit. The poison of vipers is on their lips ... ruin and misery mark their ways (Rom 3:11–16 NIV).

For all have sinned and fall short of the glory of God (Rom 3:23 NIV).

When we were still powerless (Rom 5:5 NIV).

When we were God's enemies (Rom 5:10 NIV).

Therefore just as sin entered the world through one man, and death through sin, and in this way death came to all men, because all sinned (Rom 5:12 NIV).

For if the many died by the trespass of the one man (Rom 5:15 NIV)

We died to sin ... Know that all of us who were baptized into Christ Jesus were baptized into his death? We were therefore buried with him through baptism into death in order that, just as Christ was raised from the dead through the glory of the Father, we too may live a new life.... Our old self was crucified with him so that the body of sin might be done away with, that we should no longer be slaves to sin—because anyone who has died has been freed from sin. Now if we died with Christ, we believe that we will also live with him.... In the same way, count yourselves dead to sin but alive to God in Christ Jesus.... Therefore do not let sin reign in your mortal body so that you obey its evil desires. Offer yourselves to God, as those who have been brought from death to life (Rom 6:2–4, 6–8, 11–13 NIV).

You have been set free from sin and have become slaves to righteousness. I put this in human terms because you are weak in your natural selves. Those things result in death! When you were slaves to sin, you were free from the control of righteousness. You ... have become slaves to God ... For the wages of sin is death, but the gift of God is eternal life in Christ Jesus our Lord (Rom 6:18–23 NIV).

For what the law was powerless to do in that it was weakened by the sinful nature ... To the sinful nature have their minds set on what that nature desires. The mind of sinful man is death (Rom 8:3, 5–6 NIV).

But if Christ is in you, your body is dead because of sin ... he who raised Christ from the dead will also give life to your mortal bodies through his Spirit, who lives in you.... For if you live according to the sinful nature, you will die; but if by the Spirit you put to death the misdeeds of the body, you will live (Rom 8:10–11, 13 NIV).

GALATIANS

But when God, who set me apart from birth (Gal 1:15 NIV).

I have been crucified with Christ and I no longer live, but Christ lives in me (Gal 2:20 NIV).

Formerly, when you did not know God, you were slaves to those who by nature are not gods. But now that you know God—or rather are known by God—how is it that you are turning back to those weak and miserable principles? Do you wish to be enslaved by them all over again? (Gal 4:8–9 NIV).

So I say, live by the Spirit, and you will not gratify the desires of the sinful nature. For the sinful nature desires what is contrary to the Spirit, and the Spirit what is contrary to the sinful nature. They are in conflict with each other, so that you do not do what you want. But if you are led by the Spirit, you are not under law (Gal 5:16–18 NIV).

Those who belong to Christ Jesus have crucified the sinful nature with its passions and desires (Gal 5:24 NIV).

If anyone thinks he is something when he is nothing, he deceives himself (Gal 6:3 NIV).

The one who sows to please his sinful nature, from that nature will reap destruction; the one who sows to please the Spirit, from the Spirit will reap eternal life (Gal 6:8 NIV).

The world has been crucified to me, and I to the world ... What counts is a new creation.... Finally, let no one cause me trouble, for I bear on my body the marks of Jesus (Gal 6:14–15, 17 NIV).

EPHESIANS

As for you, you were dead in your transgressions and sins.... All of us also lived among them at one time, gratifying the cravings of our sinful nature and following its desires and thoughts. Like the rest, we were by nature objects of wrath (Eph 2:1, 3 NIV).

For this reason I, Paul, the prisoner of Christ Jesus for the sake of you Gentiles (Eph 3:1 NIV).

I am less than the least of all God's people (Eph 3:8 NIV).

Put off your old self, which is being corrupted by its deceitful desires (Eph 4:22 NIV).

For you were once darkness, but now you are light in the Lord.... Have nothing to do with the fruitless deeds of darkness, but rather expose them (Eph 5:8, 11 NIV).

"Wake up, O sleeper,
rise from the dead ...
because the days are evil" (Eph 5:14–15 NIV).

PHILIPPIANS

Christ will be exalted in my body, whether by life or by death. For to me, to live is Christ and to die is gain. If I am to go on living in the body, this will mean fruitful labor for me. Yet what shall I choose? I do not know! I am torn between the two: I desire to depart and be with Christ, which is better by far (Phil 1:20–23 NIV).

We who worship by the Spirit of God, who glory in Christ Jesus, and who put no confidence in the flesh (Phil 3:3 NIV).

But whatever was to my profit I now consider loss for the sake of Christ. What is more, I consider everything a loss compared to the surpassing greatness of knowing Christ Jesus my Lord, for whose sake I have lost all things. I consider them rubbish, that I may gain Christ and be found in him, not having a righteousness of my own (Phil 3:7–9 NIV).

The Lord Jesus Christ ... under his control, will transform our lowly bodies so that they will be like his glorious body (Phil 3:20 NIV).

COLOSSIANS

For he has rescued us from the dominion of darkness (Col 1:13 NIV).

Once you were alienated from God and were enemies in your minds because of your evil behavior (Col 1:21 NIV).

Having been buried with him in baptism ... You were dead in your sins and in the uncircumcision of your sinful nature (Col 2:12–13 NIV).

You died with Christ (Col 2:20 NIV).

Set your minds on things above, not on earthly things. For you died, and your life is now hidden with Christ in God. When Christ, who is your life, appears, then you also will appear with him in glory. Put to death, therefore, whatever belongs to your earthly nature ... since you have taken off your old self with its practices ... and have put on the new self (Col 3:2–5, 10 NIV).

1 CORINTHIANS

God chose the foolish things of the world to shame the wise; God chose the weak things of the world to shame the strong. He chose the lowly things of this world and the despised things—and the things that are not—to nullify the things that are (1 Cor 1:27–28 NIV).

I came to you in weakness and fear, and with much trembling. My message and my preaching were not with wise and persuasive words, but with a demonstration of the Spirit's power, so that your faith might not rest on men's wisdom, but on God's power (1 Cor 2:3–5 NIV).

You are still worldly ... Are you not acting like mere men? (1 Cor 3:3 NIV).

For it seems to me that God has put us apostles on display at the end of the procession, like men condemned to die in the arena. We have been made a spectacle to the whole universe, to angels as well as to men. We are fools for Christ (1 Cor 4:9–10 NIV).

So this weak brother, for whom Christ died, is destroyed by your knowledge (1 Cor 8:11 NIV).

Last of all he appeared to me also, as to one abnormally born [*aborted/miscarried*]. For I am the least of the apostles and do not even deserve to be called an apostle, because I persecuted the church of God. But by the grace of God I am what I am (1 Cor 15:8–10 NIV).

If Christ has not been raised, our preaching is useless and so is your faith (1 Cor 15:14 NIV).

If only for this life we have hope in Christ, we are to be pitied more than all men (1 Cor 15:19 NIV).

I die every day—I mean that, brothers (1 Cor 15:31 NIV).

What you sow does not come to life unless it dies. When you sow, you do not plant the body that will be, but just a seed, perhaps of wheat or of something else. But God gives it a body as he has determined, and to each kind of seed he gives its own body (1 Cor 15:36–38 NIV).

2 Corinthians

The earthly tent we live in … We groan, longing to be clothed with our heavenly dwelling, because when we are clothed, we will not be found naked. For while we are in this tent, we groan and are burdened, because we do not wish to be unclothed but to be clothed with our heavenly dwelling, so that what is mortal may be swallowed up by life.… As long as we are at home in the body, we are away from the Lord.… We … would prefer to be away from the body (2 Cor 5:1–4, 6, 8 NIV).

If we are out of our mind, it is for the sake of God; if we are in our right mind, it is for you. We are convinced that one died for all, and therefore all died.…

We regard no one from a worldly point of view. Though we once regarded Christ in this way, we do so no longer. Therefore, if anyone is in Christ, he is a new creation; the old has gone, the new has come! (2 Cor 5: 13–14, 16–17 NIV).

God made him who had no sin to be sin for us (2 Cor 5:21 NIV).

I appeal to you—I, Paul, who am "timid" when face to face with you, but "bold" when away (2 Cor 10:1 NIV).

For some say, "His letters are weighty and forceful, but in person he is unimpressive and his speaking amounts to nothing" (2 Cor 10:10 NIV).

Appendix B: The Hyperbolic Road

"I will show you the most excellent way."*

HERE IS A BRIEF DESCRIPTION of what I regard as the basic building blocks of a "better way." I call it an "attitude of uncertainty," and it is what enabled me to look at the Hooks and Ladders game board with an outsider's perspective.

SUFFICIENT EVIDENCE

W. K. Clifford tells a fictitious story in his essay, "The Ethics of Belief," about a ship owner who has an old ship that he suspects has structural flaws. The ship owner knows he should investigate whether this ship is sea-worthy, but he suppresses his doubts about his ship. Next, in Clifford's story, the ship sets sail with many families aboard and sinks. Clifford then asks, "Is this man guilty?" Clifford answers, yes, the ship owner is guilty.[1] Later he contends we should find the ship owner guilty whether the ship sinks or not. This line of reasoning led him to suggest in his most famous declaration:

> It is wrong always, everywhere, and for anyone, to believe anything upon insufficient evidence.[2]

He goes on to quote Milton, who wrote:

> A man may be a heretic in the truth; and if he believe things only because his pastor says so, or the assembly so determine, without knowing other reason, though his belief be true, yet the very truth he holds becomes his heresy.[3]

In addition, Clifford quotes Coleridge:

> He who begins by loving Christianity better than Truth, will proceed by loving his own sect or Church better than Christianity, and end loving himself better than all.[4]

---

* (1 Cor 12:31). "Excellent way" in Greek is υπερβολην οδον, which loosely translated (very loosely), can be "hyperbolic road."

What I regard as Clifford's most interesting insight can be found in this provocative statement concerning his view of doctrine:

> Inquiry into the evidence of a doctrine is not to be made once for all, and then taken as finally settled. It is never lawful to stifle a doubt; for either it can be honestly answered by means of the inquiry already made, or else it proves that the inquiry was not complete.
>
> "But," says one, "I am a busy man; I have no time for the long course of study which would be necessary to make me in any degree a competent judge of certain questions, or even able to understand the nature of the arguments."
>
> Then he should have no time to believe.[5]

Still Clifford allows that some things warrant a "practical certainty."[6] Thus, relying on someone who proves competent and trustworthy often makes sense.

It did not take long for critics to challenge Clifford. William James, his most famous critic, wrote in *The Will to Believe*[7] that following Clifford's reasoning would have a crippling effect. He claimed it could lead to "a general informing his soldiers that it is better to keep out of battle forever than risk a single wound."[8] Since Clifford suggests having a practical certainty at times, I believe this criticism to be unfair.

However, James makes a better argument that deals with applying Clifford's ethic to matters of religion. He contends that putting off a decision about God until we have *sufficient evidence* could be catastrophic. He argues that while possibly benefiting from not making a mistake, we also risk losing the good if the belief ends up true. If eternal life weighs in the balance, waiting for sufficient evidence does not make sense. He concludes that an individual should have the right to make this decision for him or herself. We, James contends, should not have to worry what someone like Clifford thinks.[9] This thoughtful argument does seem to undermine Clifford's ethical argument.

In addition, when James defends the choice of believing in God insightfully, he dismisses the notion that people make a safe bet when deciding to believe. In chapter 8, as you may recall, Pascal's Wager suggests that we make a safe bet when we choose to believe in God since we have nothing to lose if unbelief is the correct choice but there is everything to lose if it is not. James, however, scoffs at this and points out that if someone from an obscure religion confronted us with the same wager as Pascal, he or she would find few people willing to place that safe bet and start believing in the obscure religion instead of Christianity. The obscure religion has no resonance for us, James argues. Indeed, he surmises that this wager likely had no part in Pascal's own faith.[10] William James passionately and creatively presents some of the most insightful reasons for belief in God.

James frequently points out in his essays that beliefs promote actions. He appeals for judging actions on their own merits. James, however, also ignores a critical point when refuting Clifford. As Clifford states, a belief based on *insufficient evidence* is wrong "whether it turned out to be true or false."[11] James does not address the ethics of actions that are acceptable despite poor reasoning or insufficient evidence. Even more problematic, James defends religious beliefs only where sufficient evidence remains unavailable. James fails to address beliefs that may have sufficient evidence available to reject them.

James also assumes that actions taken by those who believe in God or a god are good, or at worst harmless. Further, he does not address actions taken by organizations in the name of their god or church. Nor does he address a church member's responsibility for actions taken by his or her church. For example, even a casual study of history shows that religious groups often foster extremist behavior, even though the evidence often indicates that the average believer has less extreme beliefs.

Lastly, James ignores the option of maintaining an attitude of uncertainty while acting on insufficient evidence. Such an attitude has ample benefits and indeed may provide the best, most ethical choice when the evidence remains insufficient.

ATTITUDE OF UNCERTAINTY

Richard Feynman, a Nobel Prize-winning physicist, suggested an ethic for reporting and evaluating scientific evidence. He noted that effective science requires an attitude of uncertainty and that scientists learn to put things on a scale of uncertainty. Everything fits between "almost certainly true" and "almost certainly false." One can never say as a scientist one has absolute certainty about anything.

Feynman argued that before we judge the evidence, we cannot claim to know the answer. To begin, we must have uncertainty about the answer. We do not need to gather any evidence if we already know the answer. He explains:

> After we look for evidence we have to judge the evidence. There are usually rules about the judging of the evidence; it's not right to pick only what you like, if you take all of the evidence, to try to maintain

> some objectivity about the thing—enough to keep the thing going—not to ultimately depend upon authority. Authority may be a hint as to what the truth is, but is not the source of information. As long as it is possible, we should disregard authority whenever the observations disagree with it. And finally, the recording or results should be done in a disinterested way ... Disinterest here means that they are not reported in such a way as to try to influence the reader into an idea that's different than what the evidence indicates.[12]

Feynman also explains the benefit of this approach to problem solving:

> It's a kind of scientific integrity, a principle of scientific thought that corresponds to a kind of utter honesty—a kind of leaning over backward. For example, if you're doing an experiment you should report everything you think might make it invalid—not only what you think is right about it: other causes that could possibly explain your results; and things you thought of that you've eliminated by some other experiment, and how they worked—to make sure the other fellow can tell that they have been eliminated....
>
> Details that could throw doubt on your interpretation must be given, if you know them. You must do the best you can—if you know anything at all wrong, or possibly wrong—to explain it. If you make a theory, for example, and advertise it or put it out, then you must also put down all the facts that disagree with it, as well as those that agree with it ... In summary, the idea is to try to give all of the information to help others to judge the value of your contribution; not just the information that leads to judgment in one particular direction or another.[13]

He further explained:

> I'm talking about a specific type of integrity that is not lying, but bending over backward to show how you may be wrong, that ought to be done when acting as a scientist ... If we only publish results of a certain kind we can make the argument look good. We must publish both kinds of results.[14]

Feynman describes this type of scientific integrity when giving governmental advice. He suggested:

> Supposing a senator asked you for advice about whether drilling a hole should be done in his State; and you decide it would be better in some other state. If you don't publish such a result, it seems to me you're not giving scientific advice. You are being used. If your answer happens to come out in the direction the government or the

> politicians like, they can use it as an argument in their favor; if he comes out the other way, they don't publish it at all. That's not giving scientific advice.[15]

Feynman applied these principles when participating in the group that investigated the crash of the space shuttle Challenger. In that investigation, he placed a piece of a rubber O-ring in a glass of ice water and squeezed the O-ring in a vise grip. He showed that the O-ring did not function well when cold. However, Feynman did not stop there. He detailed problem areas in research, engineering, and management at NASA, but this went beyond what the commission felt was necessary. They felt Feynman's investigation embarrassed NASA. Nevertheless, Feynman applied his principles and published his findings in a famous minority report.

Feynman further characterized evaluating evidence in a moral context:

> I believe that in the judging of evidence, the reporting of evidence and so on, there is that kind of responsibility which the scientist feels toward each other which you can represent as a kind of morality. What's the right way and a wrong way to report results? Disinterestedly, so the other man is free to understand precisely what you are saying, and as nearly as possible not covering it with your desires. That is a useful thing, that this is a thing which helps each of us to understand each other, in fact developed in a way that isn't personally in our own interests, but for the general development of ideas, is a very valuable thing. And so there is, if you will, a kind of scientific morality.[16]

Feynman investigated the space shuttle program and found many flaws. We could investigate Evangelicals with the same approach. If God influenced or inspired the writing of the Bible, then it should stand up to this type of investigation. We might all benefit from a consistent, thoughtful, and thorough investigation. To be sure, new information might require us to reinvestigate something else later, but if a thorough investigation supported Evangelical claims, then new information would likely enhance the weight of Evangelical conclusions.

Some may feel that Evangelical Bible scholars have already taken this approach. However, they have not. They start with the premise that the Bible is infallible, authoritative, and inspired by God and move on from there. Evangelicals automatically discard any theory or interpretation disagreeing with their premises. If evidence arises, say, about the authorship of a New Testament book or the dating of a first-century event, they have to make this fit with their original premise that God inspired the writing of the entire Bible. They can never even consider the possibility that evidence may undermine their premises—or question the validity of those premises.

Bibliography

Alanen, Yrjo O. *Schizophrenia: Its Origins and Need-Adapted Treatment.* Translated by Sirrka-Liisa Leinonen. London: Karnac, 1997.

Albl, Martin. "For Whenever I am Weak, Then I am Strong: Disability in Paul's Epistles." In *This Abled Body,* edited by Gale A. Yee et al. Atlanta: Society of Biblical Literature, 2007.

Allen, Mike, and Michael Calderone. "McClellan Points Finger at Bush, Rove." *Politico.* November 21, 2007 . http://www.politico.com/news/stories/1107/6994.html (accessed November 30, 2007).

Altemeyer, Robert. "The Authoritarians." 2006. http://home.cc.umanitoba.ca/~altemey/ (accessed March 1, 2006).

American Psychiatric Association. *Diagnostic and Statistical Manual of Mental Disorders, 4th edition.* 1994.

———. *Diagnostic and Statistical Manual of Mental Disorders, Text Revision.* Washington DC: American Psychiatric Association, 2000.

Andersen, Svend. "Kant, Kissinger, and Other Lutherans: On Ethics and International Relations." *Studies in Christian Ethics,* 2007: 13–29.

Anderson, Leith. "National Asssociation of Evangelicals." *National Association of Evangelicals.* http://www.nae.net/index.cfm (accessed April 3, 2008).

Arnold, Dean E. "How Do Scientific Views on Human Origins Relate to the Bible?" In *Not Just Science,* edited by Dorothy F. Chappell and E. David Cook, 129–136. Grand Rapids, MI: Zondervan, 2005.

Aurelius, Marcus. *Meditations.* Chicago: Gateway, 1968.

Bacon, Leonard Woolsey. *A History of American Christianity.* New York: The Christian Literature Co., 1897.

Bacote, Vincent E., and Stephen R. Spencer. "What Are the Theological Implications for Natural Science." In *Not Just Science,* edited by Dorothy F. Chappell and E. David Cook, 61–78. Grand Rapids, MI: Zondervan, 2005.

Baumgaertner, Jill Pelaez. "Living with the 'Non' in 'Nondenominational'." *The Cresset,* Easter 2007.

Beecher, Lyman. *Autobiography, Correspondence, Etc. of Lyman Beecher, D.D.* Edited by Charles Beecher. New York: Harper, 1864.

Bernheim, Kayla F., and Richard R. J. Lewine. *Schizophrenia*. New York: W.W. Norton & Co., 1979.

Billy Graham Evangelistic Assoc. "Statement of Faith." 2007. http://www.billygraham.org/StatementOfFaith.asp (accessed December 3, 2007).

Burton, Richard. *On Being Certain*. New York: St. Martin's Press, 2008.

Cannella, Gaile S., and Yvonna S. Lincoln. "Predatory vs. Dialogic Ethics: Constructing an Illusion or Ethical Practice as the Core of Research Methods." *Qualitative Inquiry*, April 2007: 315–335.

Carrier, Richard. "A Fish Did Not Write This Essay." *Freethought Today*, September 1995: 8.

———. *Sense and Goodness Without God*. Bloomington, IN: AuthorHouse, 2005.

———. "The Plausibility of Theft." In *The Empty Tomb: Jesus Beyond the Grave*, edited by Robert M. Price and Jeffrey Jay Lowder, 349–68. Amherst: Prometheus, 2005.

Caruana, Patrick. "Prayer: America's Strength and Shield 2." *Focus on the Family Radio Broadcast*. May 13, 2008.

Chappell, Dorothy F., and E. David Cook. *Not Just Science*. Grand Rapids, MI: Zondervan, 2005.

Chernow, Ron. *Alexander Hamilton*. New York: Penguin, 2004.

Christian, C. W. *Friedrich Schleiermacher*. Peabody, MA: Hendrickson, 1979.

Clifford, William Kingdon. *The Ethics of Belief and Other Essays*. New York: Prometheus, 1999.

Coalition on Revival, The. "A Manifesto for the Christian Church." Edited by Jay Grimstead. Murphys, CA: The Coalition on Revival, 2002, original written and signed 4 July 1986.

Collins, Francis S. *The Language of God*. New York: Free Press, 2006.

Cook, E. David. "How Should the Christian's Foundational Beliefs Shape the Work of Scientists?" In *Not Just Science*, edited by Dorothy F. Chappell and E. David Cook, 289–295. Grand Rapids, MI: Zondervan, 2005.

Craig, William Lane, and Bart D. Ehrman. "Is There Historical Evidence for the Resurrection of Jesus? A Debate between William Lane Craig and Bart D. Ehrman." March 28, 2006.

Dawkins, Richard. *The God Delusion*. New York: Houghton Mifflin, 2006.

Dayton, Donald W. "The Battle for the Bible: Renewing the Inerrancy Debate." *Christian Century*, November 10, 1976: 976–980.

Dean, John W. *Conservatives Without Conscience.* New York: Viking Penguin, 2006.

Dennett, Daniel C. *Breaking the Spell.* New York: Viking, 2006.

Dobson, James. *Dare to Discipline.* Wheaton, IL: Tyndale, 1970.

Dorman, Daniel. *Dante's Cure.* New York: Other Press, 2003.

Earll, Steven. "Five Criteria for Addiction Assessment." *Focus on the Family, Pure Intimacy.* 2004. http://www.pureintimacy.org/gr/intimacy/understanding/a0000132.cfm (accessed October 16, 2006).

Eddington, Stanley. *The Nature of the Physical World.* Cambridge: University Press, 1929.

EE International. "Do You Know?" 2003. http://www.eeinternational.org/DYKFS/DYKFS.htm (accessed January 12, 2007).

———. "Do You Know?" 2003. http://www.eeinternational.org/DYKFS/English/DYK_Eng_15.htm (accessed January 12, 2007).

———. "Here is a Suggested Prayer." *EE International.* http://www.eeinternational.org/DYKFS/English/DYK_Eng_17.htm (accessed December 3, 2007).

———. "Statement of Faith." http://www.eeinternational.org/eeinfo.htm (accessed December 3, 2007).

Ehrman, Bart D. *Misquoting Jesus.* San Francisco: Harper, 2005.

Feynman, Richard P. *The Pleasure of Finding Things Out.* New York: Perseus, 1999.

Foucault, Michel. *The Archeology of Knowledge.* Translated by Sheridan Smith. New York: Pantheon, 1972.

Fraser, Nancy. "Recognition without Ethics?" *Theory, Culture & Society*, 2001: 21–42.

Funck, Larry L. "The Creation of Life: Charting When, Where, and How?" In *Not Just Science*, 209–223. Grand Rapids, MI: Zondervan, 2005.

Gardner, Brian. "personal email correspondence." October 28, 2008.

Geisler, Norman, and Frank Turek. *I Don't Have Enough Faith to Be an Atheist.* Wheaton, IL: Crossway, 2004.

Giroux, Henry A. "The Passion of the Right: Religious Fundamentalism and the Crisis of Democracy." *Cultural Studies <=> Critical Methodologies*, 2005: 309–317.

Gladwell, Malcolm. *Blink.* New York: Little Brown and Co., 2005.

———. *The Tipping Point.* New York: Little Brown and Co., 2002.

Golden, Daniel. "Test of Faith." *Wall Street Journal*, January 3, 2006: 1.

Gore, Al. *The Assault on Reason.* New York: Penguin, 2007.

Graham, Billy. "Steps to Peace." *Billy Graham Evangelistic Association.* 2007. http://www.billygraham.org/SH_StepsToPeace.asp (accessed October 29, 2007).

Grimstead, Jay. "How the International Council on Biblical Inerrancy Began." *Reformation.net.* http://www.reformation.net/cor/ICBIbkgrnd.htm (accessed October 16, 2005).

———, ed. "Articles of Affirmation and Denial on the Kingdom of God: A Summary of the Biblical and Historical View." The Coalition on Revival, Inc., 1989.

Halliday, David, and Robert Resnick. *Fundamentals of Physics.* 2nd ed. New York: John Wiley & Sons, 1981.

Harmon, Michael M. "What, if Anything, Is Teleology? The Ambiguous History of "Purpose" in Organizational Thought." *The American Review of Public Administration.* Vol. 18. 1988. 217–244.

Hatfield, Agnes B., and Harriet Lefley. *Surviving Mental Illness.* New York: Guildford Press, 1993.

Hofmeyr, Brenda. "The Power Not to Be (What We Are): The Politics and Ethics of Self-creation in Foucault." *Journal of Moral Philosophy*, 2006: 215–230.

Hofstader, Douglas R. *Godel, Escher, Bach.* New York : Vintage, 1980.

Holmes, Arthur F. *Ethics.* Downer's Grove, IL: InterVarsity Press, 1984.

Howe, Louis E. "Enchantment, Weak Ontologies, and Administrative Ethics." *Administration & Society*, September 2006: 422–446.

Huffman, Douglas S., and Eric L. Johnson. "God Under Fire." Chap. 1, edited by Douglas S. Huffman and Eric L. Johnson, 11–42. Grand Rapids, MI: Zondervan, 2002.

Ingersoll, Robert Green. "Brooklyn Divines (1883)." *Infidels.org.* http://www.infidels.org/library/historical/robert_ingersoll/brooklyn_divines.html (accessed December 10, 2007).

International Council on Biblical Inerrancy. *The Chicago Statement on Inerrancy.* Chicago: International Council on Biblical Inerrancy, 1978.

"Iranian leader: Holocaust a 'myth'." *CNN.com.* December 15, 2005. http://www.cnn.com/2005/WORLD/meast/12/14/iran.israel/ (accessed July 10, 2007).

Isaacson, Walter. *Einstein.* New York: Simon & Schuster, 2007.

James, William. *The Will to Believe.* New York: Dover, 1956.

Jaynes, Julian. *The Origin of Consciousness in the Breakdown of the Bicameral Mind* . Boston: Houghton Mifflin, 1990.

Jost, John T., Jack Glaser, Arie W. Kruglanski, and Frank J. Sulloway. "Political Conservatism as Motivated Social Cognition." *Psychological Bulletin,* 2003: 339–375.

Kant, Immanuel. *Critique of Pure Reason.* Translated by Norman Kemp Smith. New York: The Modern Library, 1958.

Kaplan, Harold I., and Benjamin J. Sadock. *Concise Textbook of Clinical Psychiatry.* Baltimore: Williams and Wilkins, 1996.

Kuhn, Thomas S. *The Structure of Scientific Revolution.* Chicago: University of Chicago Press, 1996.

Lakewood Church. "Our Beliefs." 2007. http://www.lakewood.cc/site/PageServer?pagename=LCH_ourbeliefs (accessed December 3, 2007).

Lausanne Movement, The. "The Lausanne Covenant." July 25, 1974. http://www.lausanne.org/lausanne-1974/lausanne-covenant.html (accessed January 12, 2007).

Lewis, C. S. *Mere Christianity.* San Fransisco: HaperCollins, 1980.

Liberty University. "Admissions." *liberty.edu.* 2008. http://www.liberty.edu/admissions/ (accessed April 13, 2008).

———. "FacultyApp-0503." Lynchburg, VA: Liberty University, 2003.

———. "Liberty University's Code of Conduct 'The Liberty Way'." January 23, 2008.

Litfin, Duane. "President's Commentary." *Wheaton,* Autumn 2008: 68.

MacArthur, John. *The MacArthur Study Bible.* Nashville: Word, 1997.

———. *What's Wrong with America?* 2007. http://www.gty.org/Resources/Transcripts/80-112 (accessed April 13, 2008).

Mack, Burton. *Who Wrote the New Testament?* San Fransisco: HarperCollins, 1996.

Marty, Martin. *A Short History of Christianity*. Philadelphia: Fortress Press, 1987.

McDowell, Josh. *Evidence That Demands a Verdict*. San Bernardino, CA: Here's Life Publisher, 1979.

———. *The New Evidence That Demands a Verdict*. Nashville: Thomas Nelson, 1999.

McMurtrie, Beth. "Do Professors Lose Academic Freedom by Signing Statements of Faith?" *The Chronicle*. May 24, 2002. http://chronicle.com/weekly/v48/i37/37a01201.htm (accessed May 6, 2008).

Minkowski, Eugene. *La Schizophrenie*. Paris: Payot, 1927 [1997].

Mitchell, Matthew W. "Reexamining the 'Aborted Apostle': An Exploration of Paul's Self-Description in 1 Corinthians 15.8." *Journal for the Study of the New Testament*, 2003: 469–485.

Moore, Carrie. "Are Mormons Christians?" *Deseret News*, November 15, 1997.

Myers, David G. *Intuition*. New Haven: Yale University Press, 2002.

New Life Church. "What We Believe." 1999. http://www.newlifechurch.org/beliefs.jsp (accessed January 12, 2007).

Newton, Tim. "Theorizing Subjectivity in Organizations: The Failure of Foucauldian Studies" *Organization Studies*, 1998: 415–447.

NIV. *Holy Bible, New International Version*. Translated by IBS. International Bible Society. Grand Rapids, MI: Zondervan, 1984.

Noll, Mark. *A History of Christianity in the United States and Canada*. Grand Rapids, MI: Wm. B. Eerdmans, 1992.

———. *Between Faith and Criticism: Evangelical Scholarship, and the Bible in America*. Vancouver: Regent College Publishing, 2004.

———. *The Scandal of the Evangelical Mind*. Grand Rapids, MI: Wm. B. Eerdmans, 1994.

Oakeshott, Michael. *On Human Conduct*. Oxford: Clarendon Press, 1975.

"Open Letter to NAE." March 1, 2007. http://www.cornwallalliance.org/docs/Open_Letter.pdf (accessed October 16, 2007).

Paine, Thomas. *Age of Reason: Being an Investigation of True and Fabulous Theology*. New York and London: G. P. Putnam's Sons, 1896.

Panksepp, Jaak, Patrick Lensing, Marion Leboyer, and Manuel P. Bouvard. "Naltrexone and Other Potential New Pharmacological Treatments of Autism." *Brain Dysfunction* 4 (1991): 281–300.

Pelikan, Jaroslav. *Whose Bible Is It?* New York: Penguin, 2006.

Petrocelli, John V., Zakary L. Tormala, and Derek D. Rucker. "Unpacking Attitude Certainty: Attitude Clarity and Attitude Correctness." *Journal of Personality and Social Psychology*, 2007: 30–41.

Pinker, Steven. *How the Mind Works*. New York: Norton, 1997.

Podoksik, Efraim. "Oakeshott's Theory of Freedom as Recognized Contingency." *European Journal of Political Theory*, 2003: 57–77.

Promise Keepers. "Statement of Faith." http://www.promisekeepers.org/FAQ (accessed January 12, 2007).

———. "Statement of Faith." 2007. http://www.promisekeepers.org/about/statementoffaith (accessed December 3, 2007).

Quinn, Warren. *Morality and Action*. Cambridge: Cambridge University Press, 1993.

Rogers, Juliet. "Unquestionable Freedom in a Psychotic West." *Law, Culture and the Humanities*, 2005: 186–207.

Ross, Hugh. *Beyond the Cosmos*. Colorado Springs: Navpress, 1996.

Saddleback Church. "What We Believe." http://www.saddleback.com/flash/believe2.html (accessed January 12, 2007).

Schaeffer, Francis. *How Should We Then Live?* Wheaton, IL: Crossway, 1976.

———. *The Great Evangelical Disaster*. Wheaton, IL: Crossway, 1984.

Schenck, Rob. "Why I Walked Out on Billy Graham." *MichNews.com*, June 30, 2005.

Schleiermacher, Friedrich. *On Religion: Speeches to its Cultured Despisers*. Translated by John Oman B.D. London: K. Paul, Trench, Trubner & Co., Ltd., 1893.

———. *The Christian Faith*. Vol. I & II. 2 vols. New York: Harper Torchbooks, 1963.

Smidt, Corwin. "Evangelicals and the 1984 Election: Continuity or Change?" *American Politics Research*, October 1987: 419–444.

Son Hing, Leanne S., D. Ramona Bobocel, Mark P Zanna, and Maxine V. McBride. "Authoritarian Dynamics and Unethical Decision Making: High Social Dominance Orientation Leaders and High Right-Wing Authoritarianism Followers." *Journal of Personality and Social Psychology*, 2007: 67–81.

Stolz, Jörg, and Olivier Favre. "The Evangelical Milieu: Defining Criteria and Reproduction across the Generations." *Social Compass*. Vol. 52. 2005. 169–183.

Streeter, Tom. *The Church and Western Culture*. Bloomington, IN: AuthorHouse, 2006.

Strobel, Lee. *The Case for Christ*. Grand Rapids, MI: Zondervan, 1998.

———. *The Case for Faith*. Grand Rapids, MI: Zondervan, 2000.

Swindoll, C. *The Grace Awakening*. Nashville: W Publishing Group, 2003.

Timmermann, Jens. "Simplicity and Authority: Reflections on Theory and Practice in Kant's Moral Philosophy." *Journal of Moral Philosophy*, 2007: 167–182.

Van Alstyne, William W. "The Specific Theory of Academic Freedom and the General Issue of Civil Liberties." *The ANNALS of the American Academy of Political and Social Science*, 1972: 140–156.

Waldman, Steven. "Rick Warren's Controversial Comments on Gay Marriage." *Beliefnet*. December 17, 2008. http://blog.beliefnet.com/stevenwaldman/2008/12/rick-warrens-controversial-com.html (accessed December 29, 2008).

Wallace, Daniel B. "My Take on Inerrancy." *bible.org*. August 10, 2006. http://www.bible.org/page.php?page_id=4200 (accessed March 4, 2007).

Warner, Greg. "Jimmy Carter says he can 'no longer be associated' with the SBC." *Baptist Standard*. October 23, 2000. http://www.baptiststandard.com/2000/10_23/pages/carter.html (accessed November 12, 2007).

Warren, Rick. *The Purpose Driven Life*. Grand Rapids, MI: Zondervan, 2002.

Wheaton College. "About Us Welcome to Wheaton." *Wheaton College.* https://wheaton.edu/welcome/aboutus_mission.html (accessed February 29, 2008).

———. "Application for Admission, 2009." Wheaton, 2008.

———. "Statement of Faith." http://www.wheaton.edu/welcome/mission.htm (accessed May 1, 2007).

Willow Creek Community Church. "What We Believe." http://www.willowcreek.org/what_we_believe.asp (accessed January 12, 2007).

Wittgenstein, Ludwig. *On Certainty.* Translated by Denis Paul and G. E. M. Anscombe. New York: Harper Torchbooks, 1972.

Woods, Leonard. *History of the Andover Theological Seminary.* Boston: James R. Osgood & Co., 1885.

Working, Russell. "Wheaton College professor's divorce costs him his job." *Chicago Tribune Web Edition.* April 29, 2008. http://www.chicagotribune.com/news/local/chi-divorced-prof-29-both-apr29,0,6497533.story (accessed April 30, 2008).

Wright, Robert. *Nonzero.* New York: Vintage, 2001.

Notes

1. Introducing Hooks and Ladders

1. *Christianity Today,* the flagship weekly news magazine anchors a multimedia company by the same name. It is actually not in Wheaton, but in Carol Stream, Illinois, a town next to Wheaton.
2. Rom 6:23 NIV.
3. 1 John 1:9 NIV.
4. Wheaton College, "Statement of Faith," http://www.wheaton.edu/welcome/mission.htm (accessed May 1, 2007).
5. Ibid.
6. Ibid.
7. Francis S. Collins, *The Language of God* (New York: Free Press, 2006), 40.

2. The Rules, Paul, and Paranoid Schizophrenia

1. EE International, "Here is a Suggested Prayer," *EE International.* http://www.eeinternational.org/DYKFS/English/DYK_Eng_17.htm (accessed December 3, 2007).
2. "If anyone thinks he is something when he is nothing, he deceives himself" (Gal 6:3 NIV).
3. "Our old self was crucified with him so that the body of sin might be done away with, that we should no longer be slaves to sin" (Rom 6:6 NIV). "Formerly, when you did not know God, you were slaves to those who by nature are not gods. But now that you know God—or rather are known by God—how is it that you are turning back to those weak and miserable principles? Do you wish to be enslaved by them all over again?" (Gal 4:8–9 NIV).
4. Many more examples of Paul's lack of identity, feeling of worthlessness, and toxicity occur in his letters. I have catalogued a few of them in Appendix A.
5. "So I say, live by the Spirit, and you will not gratify the desires of the sinful nature. For the sinful nature desires what is contrary to the Spirit, and the Spirit what is contrary to the sinful nature. They are in conflict with each other, so that you do not do what you want" (Gal. 5:16–17 NIV).

6. "When you were slaves to sin, you were free from the control of righteousness … [Now] you … have become slaves to God" (Rom 6:21 NIV).
7. "So I say, live by the Spirit, and you will not gratify the desires of the sinful nature" (Gal 5:16 NIV).
8. "Although I am less than the least of all God's people …" (Eph 3:8 NIV). "The Lord Jesus Christ … under his control, will transform our lowly bodies so that they will be like his glorious body" (Phil 3:20 NIV).
9. Also, "Since you died with Christ" (Col 1:20 NIV). "But if Christ is in you, your body is dead because of sin" (Rom 8:10 NIV). "Our old self was crucified with him so that the body of sin might be done away with … anyone who has died has been freed from sin" (Rom 6:6 NIV).
10. Also, "God chose the foolish things of the world to shame the wise; God chose the weak things of the world to shame the strong. He chose the lowly things of this world and the despised things—and the things that are not—to nullify the things that are" (1 Cor 1:27–28 NIV).
11. Kayla F. Bernheim and Richard R. J. Lewine, *Schizophrenia* (New York: W.W. Norton & Co., 1979), 50–51.
12. Ibid., 49, quote from Mary MacLane, *The Story of Mary MacLane* (New York: Stone, 1902).
13. Daniel Dorman, M.D., *Dante's Cure* (New York: Other Press, 2003), 255.
14. Ibid. Also, Julian Jaynes, *The Origin of Consciousness in the Breakdown of the Bicameral Mind* (Boston: Houghton Mifflin, 1990), 418.
15. Dorman 2003, 256; and Jaynes 1990, 423.
16. Kayla F. Bernheim and Richard R. J. Lewine, *Schizophrenia* (New York: W.W. Norton & Co., 1979), 40–41.
17. Harold I. Kaplan and Benjamin J. Sadock, *Concise Textbook of Clinical Psychiatry* (Baltimore: Williams and Wilkins, 1996), 26.
18. Three years after Paul had his vision, he went to Jerusalem and saw Peter for fifteen days and saw no other apostle except James—Jesus' brother (Gal 1:18–9). Then, fourteen years later, in response to a revelation, he went again (Gal 2:1–2). Thus, Paul spent at least seventeen years as a Christian, where he did not have personal contact with anyone who knew Jesus (other then the fifteen days he spent with Peter and James). It could be even longer, since it is not clear if the three years Paul referred to was after his conversion or after his

return to Damascus after his vision—but probably the latter. Regardless, the seventeen years that Paul avoided contact with the earthly leaders of his newly found faith who knew Jesus is a long time for a person with a cosmopolitan reputation—especially since Damascus is quite close to Jerusalem. Damascus is practically on the doorstep of Nazareth. For perspective, the Sea of Galilee is almost exactly in the middle of a straight path from Jerusalem to Damascus, but it is actually *closer* to Damascus than it is to Jerusalem.

19. Kayla F. Bernheim and Richard R. J. Lewine, *Schizophrenia* (New York: W.W. Norton & Co., 1979), 40–41.
20. Ibid.
21. Eugene Minkowski, *La Schizophrenie* (Paris: Payot, 1927 [1997]), 5, 77.

4. Explanation Personal God

1. Hugh Ross, *Beyond the Cosmos* (Colorado Springs: Navpress, 1996), 11–13.
2. Billy Graham, "Steps to Peace," *Billy Graham Evangelistic Association* (2007) http://www.billygraham.org/SH_StepsToPeace.asp (accessed October 29, 2007).
3. E-mail correspondence, February 29, 2008, original source unknown.
4. Josh McDowell, *The New Evidence That Demands a Verdict* (Nashville: Thomas Nelson, 1999), xii.
5. Ironically, Aldous Huxley suffered from a serious eye condition that left him intermittently nearly blind. He describes the precarious and variable nature of the sense of sight in his book, *The Art of Seeing*.
6. Perhaps a more typical example of this mind reading is from Lee Strobel's book, *The Case for Faith*, where Strobel quotes Ravi Zacharias, who is more of a populist than an apologist. Zacharias claims, "A man rejects God neither because of the intellectual demands nor because of the scarcity of evidence. A man rejects God because of a moral resistance that refuses to admit his need for God" (p. 247).
7. Bernheim and Lewine, *Schizophrenia* 1979, 36.

5. Evangelical History and Hooks and Ladders

1. Friedrich Schleiermacher, *On Religion: Speeches to its Cultured Despisers*, Translated by John Oman B.D. (London: K. Paul, Trench, Trubner & Co., Ltd., 1893).

2. Ibid., 11, 15.
3. Thomas Paine, *Age of Reason* (New York and London: G. P. Putnam's Sons, 1896), 29–30.
4. Lyman Beecher, *Autobiography, Correspondence, Etc. of Lyman Beecher, D.D.*, Edited by Charles Beecher (New York: Harper, 1864), 43.
5. Tom Streeter, *The Church and Western Culture* (Bloomington, Indiana: AuthorHouse, 2006), 367.
6. The Lausanne Movement, "The Lausanne Covenant" (July 25, 1974). http://www.lausanne.org/lausanne-1974/lausanne-covenant.html (accessed January 12, 2007).
7. Francis Schaeffer, *The Great Evangelical Disaster* (Wheaton, Illinois: Crossway, 1984), 56–61.
8. Jay Grimstead, "How the International Council on Biblical Inerrancy Began," *Reformation.net*. http://www.reformation.net/cor/ICBI bkgrnd.htm (accessed October 16, 2005).
9. International Council on Biblical Inerrancy, *The Chicago Statement on Inerrancy* (Chicago: International Council on Biblical Inerrancy, 1978), 6–9.
10. Grimstead, "How the International Council on Biblical Inerrancy Began"
11. The "standing army" that we raised at the initial Chicago conferences of the International Council on Biblical Inerrancy (ICBI) included more than sixty inerrancy theologians and Christian leaders. Among them were the following major figures: Dr. Jay Adams, Dr. Greg Bahnsen, Dr. James Boice, Dr. Bill Bright, Dr. Edward Clowney, Dr. W.A. Criswell, Dr. Charles Feinburg, Dr. Norman Geisler, Dr. John Gerstner, Dr. Harold Heohner, Miss Weatheral Johnson, Dr. Kenneth Kantzer, Dr. D. James Kennedy, Dr. George Knight, Dr. Henry Krabbendam, Dr. Harold Lindsell, Dr. John MacArthur, Dr. Josh McDowell, Dr. Roger Nicole, Dr. Harold Ockenga, Dr. Ray Ortlund, Dr. Luis Palau, Dr. J.I. Packer, Dr. Robert Preus, Dr. Paige Patterson, Rev. Moshe Rosen, Dr. Lorne Sanny, Dr. Francis Schaeffer, Dr. R.C. Sproul, Dr. Ray Stedman, Dr. Merrill Tenney, Dr. Larry Walker, Dr. John Walvoord, and Dr. Luder Whitlock. The names were obtained from Jay Grimstead, "How the International Council on Biblical Inerrancy Began," *Reformation.net*. http://www.reformation.net/cor/ICBIbkgrnd.htm (accessed October 16, 2005).
12. International Council on Biblical Inerrancy 1978
13. Schaeffer, *The Great Evangelical Disaster* 1984, 61.

14. Francis Schaeffer, *How Should We Then Live* (Wheaton, Illinois: Crossway, 1976), 223. Italics in original.
15. Schaeffer, *The Great Evangelical Disaster* 1984, 81.
16. Ibid.

6. Evangelical Enforcement

1. EE International, "Do You Know?" (2003) http://www.eeinternational.org/DYKFS/DYKFS.htm (accessed January 12, 2007).
2. EE International, "Do You Know?" (2003) http://www.eeinternational.org/DYKFS/English/DYK_Eng_15.htm (accessed January 12, 2007).
3. EE International, "Do You Know?" (2003) http://www.eeinternational.org/DYKFS/English/DYK_Eng_17.htm (accessed January 12, 2007).
4. EE International, "Statement of Faith," http://www.eeinternational.org/eeinfo.htm (accessed December 3, 2007).
5. Willow Creek Community Church, "What We Believe," http://www.willowcreek.org/what_we_believe.asp (accessed January 12, 2007).
6. New Life Church, "What We Believe," (1999) http://www.newlifechurch.org/beliefs.jsp (accessed January 12, 2007).
7. Saddleback Church, "What We Believe," http://www.saddleback.com/ flash/believe2.html (accessed January 12, 2007).
8. Lakewood Church, "Our Beliefs," (2007) http://www.lakewood.cc/site/PageServer?pagename=LCH_ourbeliefs (accessed December 3, 2007).
9. Billy Graham Evangelistic Assoc., "Statement of Faith," (2007) http://www.billygraham.org/StatementofFaith.asp (accessed December 3, 2007).
10. Wheaton College, "Statement of Faith," http://www.wheaton.edu/welcome/mission.htm (accessed May 1, 2007).
11. Promise Keepers, "Statement of Faith," (2007) http://www.promisekeepers.org/about/statementoffaith (accessed December 3, 2007).
12. Promise Keepers, "Statement of Faith," http://www.promisekeepers.org/FAQ (accessed January 12, 2007).
13. Daniel Golden, "Test of Faith," *Wall Street Journal* (January 3, 2006), 1.

14. Russell Working, "Wheaton College professor's divorce costs him his job," *Chicago Tribune Web Edition* (April 29, 2008) http://www.chicagotribune.com/news/local/chi-divorced-prof-29-both-apr29,0,6497533.story (accessed April 30, 2008).
15. Jill Pelaez Baumgaertner, "Living with the 'Non' in 'Non-denominational'," *The Cresset* (Easter 2007).
16. Liberty University, "Admissions," *liberty.edu* (2008) http://www.liberty.edu/admissions/ (accessed April 13, 2008).
17. Ibid., 4.
18. Ibid., 5. The original source was in an outline form and listed "Professional" as the topic of the heading "B." Under (B.) there were many numbered explanations of professional ethical standards, numbered as 1., 2., 3., etc. The hollow bulleted explanations were numbers 5 and 6 respectively. This was altered for ease of reading and to avoid confusion, as leaving these in seemed to confuse nearly everyone who reviewed the manuscript.
19. Liberty University, "Liberty University's Code of Conduct 'The Liberty Way'," (January 23, 2008) 5.
20. Ibid., 8.
21. Ibid., 8–9.
22. Ibid., 9.
23. Ibid., 11.
24. Ibid., 10.
25. Douglas S. Huffman and Eric L Johnson, "God Under Fire," Chap. 1, edited by Douglas S. Huffman and Eric L Johnson, 11–42 (Grand Rapids, Michigan: Zondervan, 2002).
26. Francis S. Collins, *The Language of God* (New York: Free Press, 2006), 42.

7. Evangelical Loyalty to Authority—The Hooks and Ladders Solution

1. Leith Anderson, "National Asssociation of Evangelicals" (National Association of Evangelicals) http://www.nae.net/index.cfm (accessed April 3, 2008).
2. "Open Letter to NAE," (March 1, 2007) http://www.cornwallalliance.org/docs/Open_Letter.pdf (accessed October 16, 2007). A few prominent names on the original letter are: James Dobson (Focus on the Family); Tony Perkins (Family Research Council); Gary L. Bauer (Coalitions for America); Paul Weyrich (American Values);

Jim Daly (Focus on the Family), Ron Shuping (Programming: The Inspiration Television Networks).

3. Billy Graham said this to Bill Clinton publicly on stage in New York at his Crusade on June 25, 2005.
4. Franklin Graham, e-mail correspondence in response to inquiries about his father's comments, June 30, 2005
5. Rob Schenck, "Why I Walked Out on Billy Graham," *MichNews.com* (June 30, 2005).
6. Evangelicals often deny that they have direct communication with God. They might say, for example, that reading God's messages in the Bible does not constitute "direct communication." But whatever word is used to describe this communication is what I am referring to when I say God communicates *directly* with the believer. Suppose, for example, I receive a phone call from a man from Norway, and have a translator translate Norwegian into English and English into Norwegian. The use of a phone and a translator would not dissuade us from calling this direct communication. The more important point to make to Evangelicals, however, is that the belief in the communication has no basis in reality.
7. Mike Allen and Michael Calderone, "McClellan Points Finger at Bush, Rove," *Politico* (November 21, 2007) http://www.politico.com/news/stories/1107/6994.html (accessed November 30, 2007).
8. Rick Warren, *The Purpose Driven Life* (Grand Rapids, Michigan: Zondervan, 2002), 171–227.
9. Robert Altemeyer, "The Authoritarians," (2006) http://home.cc.umanitoba.ca/~altemey/ (accessed March 1, 2006).

8. Answers, Authorities, and Autism

1. The Bible, in any iteration used by Protestants, was assembled far more recently than two thousand years ago. Even Evangelicals who are fully aware of this will talk as if the Bible was completed two thousand years ago.
2. At the time of this writing, you could find the book here: http://home.cc.umanitoba.ca/~altemey/
3. John W. Dean, *Conservatives Without Conscience* (New York: Viking Penguin, 2006).
4. Rick Warren, *The Purpose Driven Life* (Grand Rapids, Michigan: Zondervan, 2002).
5. Ibid., 9, 17–18, 20–21.

6. American Psychiatric Association, *Diagnostic and Statistical Manual of Mental Disorders, Text Revision* (Washington DC: American Psychiatric Association, 2000), 297.
7. Koch's postulates are:
   - The microorganism must be found in abundance in all organisms suffering from the disease, but not in healthy organisms.
   - The microorganism must be isolated from a diseased organism and grown in pure culture.
   - The cultured microorganism should cause disease when introduced into a healthy organism.
   - The microorganism must be re-isolated from the inoculated, diseased experimental host and identified as being identical to the original specific causative agent.

   The third part of Koch's postulate has no validity, because people can be carriers of a pathogen without exhibiting any symptoms.

9. Lack of Confidence and Disordered Thinking

1. As discussed in Chapter 2, many scholars believe when Paul says Jesus appeared to him as one "untimely born" in 1 Cor 15:8 that this should be translated "aborted" or "miscarried."
2. Patrick Caruana, "Prayer: America's Strength and Shield 2," *Focus on the Family Radio Broadcast* (May 13, 2008).
3. Josh McDowell, *The New Evidence That Demands a Verdict* (Nashville: Thomas Nelson, 1999), xxvii. Actually, this version of Josh's story differs from what he wrote in 1977. The original version did not assign the responsibility for change to an external entity. Here is the original version: "Dad, I let Christ come into my life. I can't explain it completely, but as a result of that relationship I've found the capacity to love and accept not only you but other people just the way they are." Josh McDowell, *Evidence That Demands a Verdict* (San Bernardino: Here's Life Publisher, 1979), 366. McDowell's "He Changed My Life" story, first published in 1977, was reprinted in the 1979 edition of his book ETDAV, as quoted here. Josh gives us a clear example, through the multiple editions of his book, of the capacity of people to bend the truth. He has personal evidence of the possibility of people fabricating the evidence reported in a story.

4. Norman Geisler and Frank Turek, *I Don't Have Enough Faith to be an Atheist* (Wheaton, Illinois: Crossway, 2004), 13.
5. Harold I. Kaplan,, and Benjamin J. Sadock, *Concise Textbook of Clinical Psychiatry* (Baltimore: Williams and Wilkins, 1996), 25.
6. James Dobson, "America's Moral Freefall," *Focus on the Family* (Colorado Springs: January 9, 2006).
7. Kaplan and Sadock (1996), 25.
8. Timothy Masters, e-mail correspondence, *Focus on the Family* (January 8, 2008).
9. When I was an enthusiastic Evangelical idealist, I was *certain* that my Evangelical mentors would swiftly work with me to correct the glaring error that resulted when Evangelicals tried to apply the Second Law of Thermodynamics in arguments against evolution. I was hardly a genius to have figured out this logical flaw. After all, our sun supplies energy to the earth constantly. Therefore, we do not live in a closed energy system, and the Second Law of Thermodynamics does not apply to most processes that take place on earth unless you take the Sun's energy into account. Simply put, whatever minuscule amount of things become *ordered* on earth is more than made up for by the input of the Sun ,which breaks nuclear and chemical bonds and produces *disordered* heat energy. The Sun's increased entropy (which in essence means "increased disorder") simply overwhelms any decreased entropy involved in the evolution of complex life forms.

   I did not receive any kudos for my discovery, however, from my Evangelical mentors. Rather, I had my first sensation of freefalling down a few levels of Hooks and Ladders. Their uniform indifference, however, did expedite my exploration into the trustworthiness of my Evangelical mentors.
10. This often separates them from many fundamentalists who believe that a person should presuppose that the Bible is God's Word. Although many non-Evangelicals use the label "fundamentalist" and "Evangelical" interchangeably, many old-school Evangelicals still agree with the uncharitable stereotypes many "elitists" have of fundamentalists. They often view fundamentalists as ignorant and inbred extremists. I bring this up to alert the unwitting non-Evangelical from making a very common mistake of the last thirty years. Many people, for example, have leveled harsh criticism toward the late fundamentalist minister, Jerry Falwell, who founded Liberty University. They assumed (incorrectly) that most Evangelicals had respect for fundamentalist leaders like Falwell. In general, however,

traditional Evangelicals hold their breath whenever a fundamentalist makes a public statement—they wish their Christian brothers from the wrong side of the tracks would stop talking. Simply put, fundamentalists have served as a decoy for Evangelicals. Most traditional Evangelicals agree with the criticisms directed at fundamentalists. Yet, because fundamentalists say and do "crazy" things, they direct attention away from the "less crazy" Evangelicals. Attacks on Evangelicals that only specify fundamentalist targets will miss their mark completely. But figuring out who is who can present a challenge. Liberty University's promotional literature, for example, heralds Liberty as "the largest Evangelical University in the world."

11. Stanley Eddington, *The Nature of the Physical World* (Cambridge: University Press, 1929), 74. Also, Norman Geisler, and Frank Turek, *I Don't Have Enough Faith to be an Atheist* (Wheaton, Illinois: Crossway, 2004), 78.
12. Josh McDowell, *The New Evidence That Demands a Verdict* (Nashville: Thomas Nelson, 1999), xii.
13. Rick Warren, *The Purpose Driven Life* (Grand Rapids, Michigan: Zondervan, 2002), 5.
14. Norman Geisler, and Frank Turek, *I Don't Have Enough Faith to Be an Atheist* (Wheaton, Illinois: Crossway, 2004), 31.

10. Associating Freedom with Slavery, Censorship, and Surveillance

1. Norman Geisler and Frank Turek, *I Don't Have Enough Faith to Be an Atheist* (Wheaton, Illinois: Crossway, 2004), 31. Quote from C. S. Lewis, *The Screwtape Letters* (Westwood, N.J.: Barbour, 1961), 46.
2. I hope readers will forgive me for calling the structure of Evangelical Christianity a corpse in chapter 5, and calling it a parasite here. But my point in chapter 5 was that it served no useful function, and many parasites have that in common with corpses.

11. The Absence of Something

1. Wheaton College, *Application for Admission, 2009* (Wheaton, Illinois: Wheaton College, 2008).
2. Carrie Moore, "Are Mormons Christians," *Deseret News* (November 15, 1997).

3. Greg Warner, "Jimmy Carter says he can 'no longer be associated' with the SBC," *Baptist Standard* (October 23, 2000) http://www.baptist standard.com/2000/10_23/pages/carter.html (accessed November 12, 2007).
4. Brian Gardner, personal e-mail correspondence (October 28, 2008).
5. Beth McMurtrie, "Do Professors Lose Academic Freedom by Signing Statements of Faith?" *The Chronicle* (May 24, 2002) http://chronicle.com/weekly/v48/i37/37a01201.htm (accessed May 6, 2008).
6. E. David Cook, "How Should the Christian's Foundational Beliefs Shape the Work of Scientists?" in *Not Just Science*, edited by Dorothy F. Chappell and E. David Cook, 289–295 (Grand Rapids, Michigan: Zondervan, 2005), 289.
7. Larry L. Funck, "The Creation of Life: Charting When, Where, and How?" in *Not Just Science*, edited by Dorothy F. Chappell and E. David Cook, 209–223 (Grand Rapids, Michigan: Zondervan, 2005), 219.
8. I cannot think of Wheaton for too long without thinking about Dr. Funck. I have nothing but gratitude and admiration for his excellent teaching. So even though I am picking on him here, I hope he will consider this a sign of respect for his teaching, which contributed to one of his students having the confidence to challenge him.
9. Some readers may want me to better explain what I mean about nonexistent entities. Dr. Funck provided a good example to illustrate what I mean in the chapter he wrote. He gave an example of what intelligent design proponents call "the property of specified complexity." So, I will use that as an example of how difficult it can be trying to decide if something has physical properties, and how lost and confusing one can become by mistakenly assigning physical properties to nonexistent entities. In his chapter, Dr. Funck wrote that randomly arranged letters did not have specified complexity, but letters arranged in a sentence did. So as an example of something with the property of specified complexity, Dr. Funck wrote:

    THIS SENTENCE CONTAINS A MESSAGE

    Despite many people intuitively accepting these letters as *specifically complex*, try to keep track of nonexistent concepts that have physical properties assigned to them when trying to explain why. Dr. Funck wrote, "The information stored in DNA is specifically complex in a manner analogous to the sentence." Does that mean information is stored in the sentence? If so, where is it? For that matter, does the information stored in the sentence have anything to do with the sentence not actually being a sentence? Can a sentence contain information about anything other than itself? Are nonsensical sentences, as the one Dr. Funck provided is, specifically complex in the same way that coherent sentences are. The sentence provided supposedly contains a message. Where is the message? Wherever it is, it is not contained in the sentence, or is it? After all, the sentence does not have a period, so maybe the message is in the part of the sentence that is missing. Does the sentence below have as much specified complexity as the one Dr. Funck provided? If not, why not?

THIS daday SENTENZ jN3:16 CONTAiNz QRU 1 MESSSAGE

10. Vincent E. Bacote and Stephen R. Spencer, "What are the Theological Implications for Natural Science," in *Not Just Science*, edited by Dorothy F. Chappell and E. David Cook, 61–78 (Grand Rapids, Michigan: Zondervan, 2005), 72.
11. Dean E. Arnold, "How Do Scientific Views on Human Origins Relate to the Bible?" in *Not Just Science*, edited by Dorothy F. Chappell and E. David Cook, 129–136 (Grand Rapids, Michigan: Zondervan, 2005), 132.
12. Ibid., 136.
13. Ibid., 136.
14. Beth McMurtrie, "Do Professors Lose Academic Freedom by Signing Statements of Faith?" *The Chronicle* (May 24, 2002) http://chronicle.com/weekly/v48/i37/37a01201.htm (accessed May 6, 2008).
15. Ibid.

12. The End Game

1. Lee Strobel, *The Case for Faith* (Grand Rapids, Michigan: Zondervan, 2000), 118–20.
2. Richard P. Feynman, *The Pleasure of Finding Things Out* (New York: Perseus, 1999), 109.
3. Jaak Panksepp, Patrick Lensing, Marion Leboyer, and Manuel P. Bouvard. "Naltrexone and Other Potential New Pharmacological Treatments of Autism," *Brain Dysfunction* 4 (1991): 281–300.
4. Some readers may find it surprising to find an addiction to nicotine included on this list. As a health care professional, however, I assure

you it is justified. After seeing so many children show up over and over again in the emergency room with serious respiratory infections or asthma attacks, it is hard to imagine having less empathy than a person who continues to smoke around these children. But many smokers continue to smoke in the same house as these children, even after the risks that cigarette smoke poses to these children has been explained to them repeatedly. As well, readers old enough to remember when people smoked everywhere will likely recall, those smokers, with rare exception, did not hesitate to smoke anywhere, without ever asking if the people around them minded if they smoked. As laws increasingly restricted the places where people could smoke, smokers defended their right to smoke, and often dismissed other people's contention that their right to breathe clean air should take precedence over a smoker's right to pollute the air.

5. Steven Waldman, "Rick Warren's Controversial Comments on Gay Marriage," *Beliefnet* (December 17, 2008) http://blog.beliefnet.com/stevenwaldman/2008/12/rick-warrens-controversial-com.html (accessed December 29, 2008).
6. Ibid.
7. Daniel C. Dennett, *Breaking the Spell* (New York: Viking, 2006).
8. Richard Dawkins, *The God Delusion* (New York: Houghton Mifflin, 2006).
9. Norman Geisler, and Frank Turek, *I Don't Have Enough Faith to Be an Atheist* (Wheaton, Illinois: Crossway, 2004), 240.
10. Ibid.
11. Julian Jaynes, *The Origin of Consciousness in the Breakdown of the Bicameral Mind* (Boston: Houghton Mifflin, 1990), 421.

Appendix A: Paul and Paranoid Schizophrenia

1. There are certainly many other possibilities that may have explained Paul's writings, thoughts, and actions. For example, he may have merely written down what he was taught by other Christians. Or perhaps he was taught some things that he wrestled with and tried to make sense out of them with his own ways of making all the pieces he was taught fit together. Still, many Christians and non-Christians alike have a sense that Paul's theology, in large measure, "came out of the blue." Indeed, most Evangelicals I know simply take for granted that much of Paul's theology came directly from God and did not come from Paul learning about Jesus and Christianity from others. So

I have merely taken this common Evangelical starting point and asked, "If Paul did learn his theology from others, and the God he said he communicates with was not there, then we would expect him to exhibit other signs of a person who had fabricated a complex delusional system."

To be sure, this same reasoning wouldn't apply to others who were taught Paul's theology. In that case, a person would be trying to put together what someone has taught him or her and would not have created a new complex delusional system on his or her own. Indeed, Paul gives us a unique opportunity, as he is widely recognized as the first to forward the theology that is now simply regarded as "Christian theology." In essence, my premise was simply this: if Paul did not communicate with a god or with other Christians who taught him a similar theology, then Paul created a remarkably detailed and complex supernatural world in his mind. I felt that a person would have a hard time accepting this possibility as likely if Paul did not exhibit other signs of someone who created complex delusions in their minds. In other words, I would have had to find another way of explaining Paul's writings if he did not show any other evidence of paranoid schizophrenic thoughts and reasoning.

2. American Psychiatric Association, *Diagnostic and Statistical Manual of Mental Disorders, Text Revision* (Washington DC: American Psychiatric Association, 2000), 312.
3. Ibid., 299.
4. Ibid., 312.

Appendix B: The Hyperbolic Road

1. William Kingdon Clifford, *The Ethics of Belief and Other Essays* (New York: Prometheus, 1999), 70–77. *The Ethics of Belief* was originally published in 1877.
2. Ibid., 77.
3. Ibid., 77. Quoted from Milton's *Areopagitica.*
4. Ibid., 78. Quoted from Coleridge's *Aids to Reflections.*
5. Ibid., 78.
6. Ibid., 79.
7. William James, *The Will to Believe* (New York: Dover, 1956). Originally published in 1887
8. Ibid., 19.

9. Ibid., 20–27. Clifford died at age 33 of tuberculosis before James first presented the criticisms of Clifford's essay.
10. Ibid., 6–7.
11. Clifford 1999, 71.
12. Richard P. Feynman, *The Pleasure of Finding Things Out* (New York: Perseus, 1999), 103–4.
13. Ibid., 209–10.
14. Ibid., 212.
15. Ibid., 213.
16. Ibid., 109.